A COMPLETE GCSE
COMPUTER STUDIES

Also available from Stanley Thornes (Publishers) Ltd:

Martin Amor & John Fairhurst   A COMPLETE GCSE COMPUTER
STUDIES Teacher's Guide

Mark Bindley   BBC BASIC PROGRAMMING FOR SCHOOLS AND
COLLEGES

J. Higgo *et al.*   132 SHORT PROGRAMS FOR THE MATHEMATICS
CLASSROOM (Published in co-operation with the
Mathematical Association)

A COMPLETE GCSE COMPUTER STUDIES

Martin Amor BA
John Fairhurst BSc

Stanley Thornes (Publishers) Ltd

First published in 1987 by:
Stanley Thornes (Publishers) Ltd
Old Station Drive
Leckhampton
CHELTENHAM GL53 0DN
England

Reprinted 1988

British Library Cataloguing in Publication Data

Amor, Martin
    A complete GCSE computer studies.
    1. Electronic data processing
    I. Title   II. Fairhurst, J.S.
    004   QA76

    ISBN 0-85950-244-9

Typeset by Blackpool Typesetting Services Ltd, Blackpool
Printed and bound in Great Britain at The Bath Press, Avon.

Contents

PART A: OVERVIEW

PART B: COMMUNICATING WITH THE COMPUTER

PART C: INFORMATION SYSTEMS

PART D: COMPUTERS IN ACTION

Preface

Computer Studies is a challenging subject, both to teach and to learn. Unfortunately, achievement at 16+ has fallen short of expectations. There are several reasons for this.

Firstly, the subject itself has an unusually high factual content, which is surrounded by a wall of apparently impenetrable jargon. This is daunting for *anyone*, especially those new to the subject.

Secondly, there has been a tendency to concentrate on programming (with scant regard for good technique) at the expense of acquiring the ability to define and solve problems—with or without a computer.

Thirdly, many courses have stressed the computer *per se* without examining systems as a whole. It is vital to consider not just the hardware and software, but also the information involved, and the way people use it in their work.

This leads to a fourth problem: the chronic lack of understanding of practical applications of computing. It is here that students' performances have often been weakest. This is hardly surprising, as most students lack knowledge of the world outside. The systems which a large industrial company, a county library service or a small medical practice, might need are far from obvious.

Most available textbooks do little to alleviate these problems and even less to guide students through the computing minefield. The sketchy material presented on applications of computing often reflects a serious lack of first-hand, practical experience.

We hope that this book has avoided these problems. We believe it has benefited from having two authors, combining wide experience of commercial computer systems on the one hand, with hard-won classroom expertise on the other.

We strongly endorse the National Criteria for GCSE Computer Studies,* which stress that understanding how a computer processes information is more important and useful than detailed knowledge of its internal workings. They highlight the need for problem-solving ability and the

*HMSO Publications, 1985

appropriate use of computers as tools to this end. They recognise that excessive emphasis on programming skills can actually impede learning, while students might solve more realistic problems with the aid of pre-written, packaged software. Major emphasis is placed on understanding the range and scope of computer applications.

This book deliberately echoes these views, which we believe are guiding the subject in the right direction. Computer Studies should not be producing 'code junkies', but students who understand, and can demonstrate, how the sensible use of computers can help to solve problems and create opportunities in the real world.

We have written a detailed Teacher's Guide as a companion to the pupil's volume. It contains material expanding on the discussion points which are raised in each chapter, as well as sections on suggested reading, educational software, computer careers, etc.

We are grateful to friends, colleagues and pupils for help and suggestions. In particular we would like to thank Alan Hunter (Chief Examiner, Joint Matriculation Board) for his constructive appraisal.

Martin Amor
John Fairhurst
1987

Acknowledgments

The authors and publishers are grateful to the following for supplying and giving permission to reproduce the photographs:

E. J. Arnold, 'Valiant' turtle, Figure 3.11; Quantel, Figure 5.5; Panasonic, Figure 5.9; Lexisystems Ltd, Figure 5.11; Barclays Bank, Figure 5.17; British Telecom, Figures 5.18, 6.2; Compaq Computers Ltd, Figure 6.3; Grid Computer Systems Ltd, Figure 6.5; Zenith Data Systems Ltd, Figure 6.6; IBM UK Ltd, Figure 6.19; Hewlett Packard, Figure 6.20; NASA, Figure 8.1; Wang (UK) Ltd, Figure 8.2; Toshiba Information Systems (UK) Ltd, Figure 8.3; Cray Research (UK) Ltd, Figure 8.6; Wang (UK) Ltd, Figure 14.2; British Telecom, Figure 14.10; ICL, Figure 15.3; Barclays Bank, Figure 17.2; Siemens Ltd, Figure 17.3; Lloyds Bank, Figure 17.5; Bankers' Automated Clearing Services Ltd, Figure 17.7; Midland Bank, Figure 17.9; Barclays Bank, Figure 17.10; Bank of Scotland, Figure 17.12; Glentop Press Ltd, Figure 18.4; Jessop Microelectronics, Figure 18.6; Iansyst Ltd, Figure 18.7; Rediffusion Simulation Ltd, Figure 18.8; Building Design Partnership, Figure 19.1; Caerleon Museum, Gwent, Figure 19.2; Rediffusion Simulation Ltd, Figure 19.2; The Wellcome Foundation Ltd, Figure 19.3; Prime Computer (UK) Ltd, Figure 19.4; Ford Motor Company, Figures 19.5, 19.6; Istel, Figure 19.14; British Gas, Figure 19.15; St Bartholomew's Hospital, Figure 19.16; Drayton Controls Ltd, Figure 20.3; Lucas Engine Management Systems Ltd, Figure 20.5; London Underground Ltd, Figure 20.9; GEC Electrical Projects Ltd, Figure 20.11; Ford Motor Company, Figure 20.12; Austin Rover, Figure 20.13; Meteorological Office, Figures 21.2, 21.6; Metropolitan Police, New Scotland Yard, Figures 21.10, 21.11, 21.12, 21.14; Scientific Research and Development Branch, Home Office, Figure 21.15; *Computer Weekly*, Figures 21.17, 21.19; UKAEA, Figure 21.20; Ford Motor Company, Figure 22.3; *The Gloucestershire Echo*, also The National Star Centre, Figure 22.4; IBM UK Ltd, Figure 25.1.

The authors and publishers also gratefully acknowledge the permission granted by the following Examination Boards to reproduce questions from past examination papers:

Northern Group: Joint Matriculation Board (JMB); Associated Lancashire Schools Examining Board (ALSEB); North Regional

Examinations Board (NREB); North West Regional Examinations Board (NWREB); Yorkshire and Humberside Regional Examinations Board (YHREB).

Midland Group: University of Cambridge Local Examinations Syndicate (CU): Oxford and Cambridge Schools Examination Board (O & C); Southern Universities Joint Board (SUJB); East Midland Regional Examinations Board (EMREB); West Midlands Examination Board (WMEB).

London and East Anglian Group: University of London Schools Examinations Department (LU); East Anglian Examinations Board (EAEB); London Regional Examinations Board (LREB).

Southern Group: Oxford Delegacy of Local Examinations (Ox); Associated Examining Board (AEB); Southern Regional Examinations Board (SREB); South East Regional Examinations Board (SEREB); South Western Examinations Board (SWEB).

Wales: Welsh Joint Education Committee (WJEC).

The authors are grateful to friends and colleagues for help and suggestions, in particular Mrs Sue Dee and Mr David Woodward of Farnborough Sixth Form College, and to Mr Clive Atty of the Wavell Comprehensive School; to Mr David Addison of National Westminster Bank and Mrs Diana Fairhurst of the Dorset Library service. We would also like to thank Alan Hunter, Chief Examiner in Computer Studies for the Joint Matriculation Board, for his constructive criticisms of the typescript.

PART A: OVERVIEW

1 Introduction

SOMEWHERE IN THE UK

Monday morning again. George groped for the snooze button on the radio alarm and rolled over. Five more minutes. The announcer had been just about to warn him of a lorry shedding its load of timber on the Barchester bypass: the route George took to work.

Linda slipped out of bed and went to pour the coffee. It was the only way to get her husband conscious in the morning. Anyway, she had an interview at the Jobcentre at nine-thirty.

Two cups of coffee and a shower later, George was coming round. He put on a clean shirt and his light suit (the forecast said warm and humid). After his bran flakes he felt almost human, so he kissed his wife and set off for work without even swearing at the brown envelope on the doormat (you could always tell it was a bill by the little window).

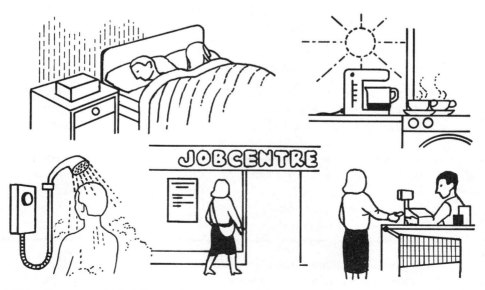

Fig. 1.1(a)   George and Linda's morning

As he joined the traffic on the main road George pushed a button to call his office. There never were messages on a Monday but George felt impressive using his car telephone. There were no messages, and so he put on a compact disc and was settling down to enjoy the drive, when he saw the overhead signs advising 30 m.p.h. "Ridiculous!" thought George, and ignored them. Moments later he slammed on the brakes and just managed to stop before piling into the traffic jam. "It *never* tails back to here . . .", he thought.

Fig. 1.1.(b)

Linda had decided to do some shopping while she was out, and so she drew out some cash on her way to the Jobcentre. The queue was not too bad today, but still there was no suitable work (they knew perfectly well she couldn't operate a Honshu 2000 word processor). "I must bring those books back", she thought as she passed the library on her way to the supermarket.

She only popped in to the supermarket for a few things, but her trolley was surprisingly full when she reached the checkout, so she decided to use her chargecard instead of cash. That always seemed to happen, even when George was with her.

". . . and a lorryload of timber is still completely blocking the Barchester bypass. Avoid it at all costs . . ."

"Now they tell us!" sighed George, crawling four metres further along the Barchester bypass. He pushed a button. "Look at that fuel consumption", he thought, "thank goodness the company's paying! Three more metres, might as well telephone mother . . ."

Q 1.1 *Read the story again carefully. Where might computer technology be involved, directly or indirectly, in this tale? For each example you find, write down exactly how your think computer technology is involved.*

If you did not find any examples, you took the story too literally. If you found ten or so, you have some idea of how far computer technology is intertwined with modern life for many individuals. If you found more than 20 applications, you have a good imagination. You also clearly understand one of the key features of computers: their *versatility*.

Technology Behind the Scenes

Let us look again at George and Linda's morning: how much computer technology lies behind the scenes?

They may or may not have a home computer as such, but the radio alarm almost certainly has a *microprocessor* (i.e. a preprogrammed silicon chip containing microscopic electronic circuits). The coffee was already brewed, so the coffee maker probably has one too. The shower may be electric; many now have a chip to control the temperature and flow. What about George's shirt? One hundred per cent cotton, no silicon there, but it was clean; the washing machine has a microprocessor, possibly also the iron. His suit was made in the modern technological equivalent of the

Fig. 1.2 Examples of computing behind the scenes in George and Linda's life

'sweat-shop'. The fabric was cut under computer control and was made up by a skilled operator using a sewing machine containing another microchip, or microprocessor.

A whole host of computers contributed towards the weather forecast: controlling the satellite, decoding the transmissions, enhancing the images, building models of the atmospheric conditions, plotting isobars etc.

The bran flakes were made and packed under computer control. The bill on the doormat was calculated and printed by computer. Calls from George's car telephone (which has a programmable memory for frequently used numbers) are switched by computerised systems, and a microprocessor controls his compact disc player. The overhead warning signs were under computer control and George probably only managed to stop safely thanks to the chip in his anti-lock braking system.

The banks were not open when Linda drew out her cash and so she probably used a cash dispenser, a type of computer, usually connected to a larger one at the headquarters of the bank or building society. Job-centres have computers for various purposes including word processing, i.e. manipulating words rather than just numbers. The library and the supermarket both control their stock (whether books or groceries) with the help of computers, and when Linda used her chargecard another computer confirmed that it wasn't stolen. Maybe the supermarket's computer was linked to Linda's bank, so that the money was electronically transferred before she had even packed her shopping basket.

George has a trip computer in his company car, keeping track of mileage, fuel consumption and so on. No doubt he has to claim his expenses every week. The company's computer has to process these. There was another company vehicle in the story; the lorry had a 'black-box' microprocessor-controlled journey recorder in the cab. Finally, the timber that blocked the road all morning—it was sawn in a computer-controlled mill.

The Computer Age

George and Linda are not science fiction characters but normal everyday people. Admittedly, George is fond of gadgets, but the story shows that, besides these, there is a vast array of computer technology which we take for granted in everyday life. Much of the technology is hidden from view; no computers were actually mentioned, but dozens were involved. The dawn of the so-called *computer age* was some time ago, and we are now living in the middle of it.

> **Q 1.2** *Make a list of all the microchips (or computers) you think there are in your own home or in the classroom.*

WHAT IS A COMPUTER?

There are many different ways of describing computers. We shall define a computer as a *reprogrammable machine for automatic processing of data*. Such a weighty definition demands some further explanation.

DATA PROCESSING

According to our definition, *data processing* (frequently shortened to DP and sometimes called EDP, for electronic data processing) is what a computer *does*. Literally (from the Latin) *data* means 'things that are

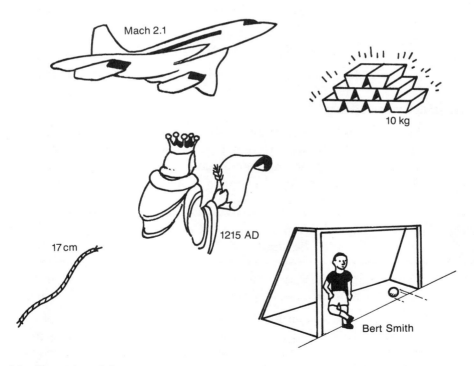

Fig. 1.3 Examples of data

given'; in other words known facts. For example, the length of a piece of string, the speed of an aeroplane, the date the Magna Carta was signed, the weight of a gold bar and the name of Barchester United's reserve goalkeeper are all items of data which can be represented by letters or numbers.

Q 1.3 *List 12 items of data used by computers (or microprocessors) in George and Linda's story above.*

Data and Information

The *structure* and *context* of data must be known before one can tell what it means. For instance, look at the data represented by the following string of symbols:

21 1 1 3 5 ' 2 " 1 0 b l u e 20 / 20

The meaning of this data can only be guessed at. If we know the *structure* of the data, it gets a little clearer:

| 21 | 113 | 5′ 2″ | 10 | blue | 20/20 |

However, one still cannot be sure of the meaning until one is told the *context*, i.e. that all the data relates to Linda, and the data items are:

age	weight	height	clothes	eye	vision
(years)	(lb)	(ft in)	size	colour	
21	113	5′ 2″	10	blue	20/20

Now the data has acquired meaning, and has become *information*.

Automatic Processing

Processing is whatever manipulation must be done to the data in order to obtain the desired results (or output). It may involve addition, averaging, any other mathematical functions, comparison, rounding, checking or conversion. In short it is whatever activity the computer is instructed to perform.

Q 1.4 *Describe four examples of data processing from the story. What data would be input and what processing would be done on it?*

Our computer definition mentioned *automatic* processing of data. How can a machine process data automatically, without human intervention?

It can only do so if it has been programmed, i.e. given a set of explicit instructions to follow. Furthermore, the program must be stored inside the machine so that it can follow the program without a human operator having to feed in the instructions one by one.

This automatic obedience of instructions means that the computer will work away while its human owner is busy elsewhere, but this feature of computing also has a negative side. 'Automatic' can be defined as 'without consciousness, *unthinking*'; and that could not be more accurate than in the case of computers. If by mistake you tell a computer to do something completely idiotic, it cannot stop to consider whether that is a sensible course of action; it will just automatically obey.

Fig. 1.4   Automatic obedience of instructions

This might not matter if you are playing chess, but it could be disastrous if you are controlling a nuclear power station.

Programs and 'Reprogrammability'

A set of instructions, or a *program*, enables a computer to do one specific task. But the power of a computer stems partly from its ability to carry out many tasks; for this to be possible it must be *reprogrammable*. Thus the set of instructions in the computer's memory must be easily changed. In this way, a computer acquires the versatility mentioned earlier. One minute it might be calculating tax liabilities, the next it could be simulating the flight of an aeroplane.

Devices such as the microprocessor in George and Linda's coffee maker, which are *dedicated* to a single task, cannot be described as computers because they cannot be reprogrammed.

?   **Q 1.5**   *Which of these devices using microchips is reprogrammable? Washing machine, hi-fi system, digital alarm clock, home computer.*

COMPUTERS VERSUS HUMAN BEINGS

Speed

Computers, in theory, cannot do anything that a human being could not. The practice is rather different.

Q 1.6 *Someone in the class should be asked to time everyone else for this exercise. Without calculators or computers, add the following numbers together:*

536 475 785, 5 869 797 796, 3 555 546 666, 343 435 111, 13,
46 464 646, 987 654 321, 2 851 040, 33 940 596 821, 3 596 606.

Assuming that you got that sum correct, and could sustain the same speed indefinitely, how many days would it take you to add up one million numbers?

As you can see, some calculations, although they are theoretically within human capabilities, are completely impracticable. Many computers nowadays could add up one million numbers in *far less than one second*.

Storage Capacity

Computers can not only process vast amounts of information, but they can store it as well. *Storing* a million numbers is a modest feat for today's computer systems.

Q 1.7 *Referring again to the story at the beginning of this chapter, identify four types of computation which, because of their speed or sheer volume, would have been impossible for any human.*

Accuracy and Consistency

Most people have heard stories about computers producing gas bills for one million pounds, or suing customers for debts amounting to the grand sum of £0.00. The truth is that computers rarely make errors, and when they do they can usually alert the user to a specific *hardware* or *software* problem.

However computers are quite frequently *incorrectly programmed* or fed with *incorrect data*. Thus although the computer itself is a remarkably reliable machine, the computer system as a whole gets a bad name owing to human error.

When computers are compared with humans for accuracy and consistency in handling information and performing calculations, computers win hands down. They do not get bored, tired, careless or frustrated by dull and repetitive work.

Furthermore, although computers *can* seem temperamental, 'flu, hangovers, love affairs and Monday mornings do not seem to trouble them: they will simply keep on working—accurately and consistently—exactly as instructed by their human operators.

Fig. 1.5 Computers do not get bored

What Computers Cannot Do

Computers cannot *think*. Thousands of scientists around the world are trying to make them do so, but progress is painfully slow. The 'intelligence level' of the most powerful computers has been estimated as a little higher than that of a tapeworm but some way below that of an earwig! So computers cannot exercise judgment or form opinions about major issues, popular music, human beings or fellow computers. They will obey without argument the most ridiculous and illogical instructions that human beings (i.e. *programmers*) can devise. They cannot feel anything and they have absolutely no sense of humour. That may be just as well.

JARGON 1

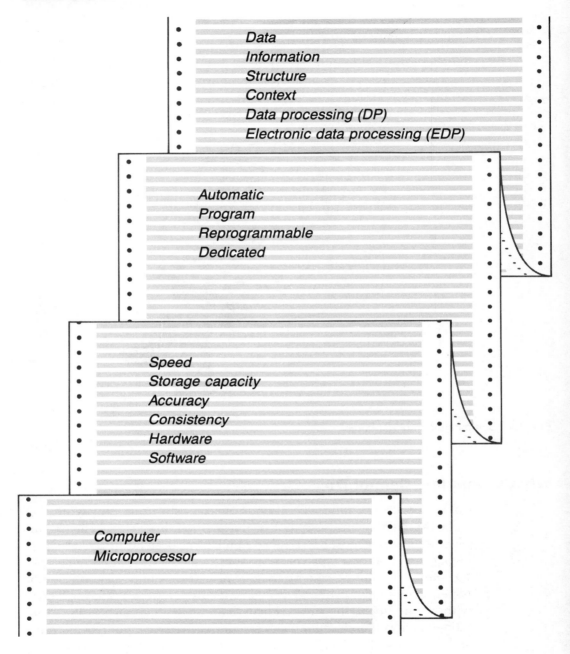

Data
Information
Structure
Context
Data processing (DP)
Electronic data processing (EDP)

Automatic
Program
Reprogrammable
Dedicated

Speed
Storage capacity
Accuracy
Consistency
Hardware
Software

Computer
Microprocessor

2 Computer Systems

You are probably familiar with the typical small computer system. It looks something like this:

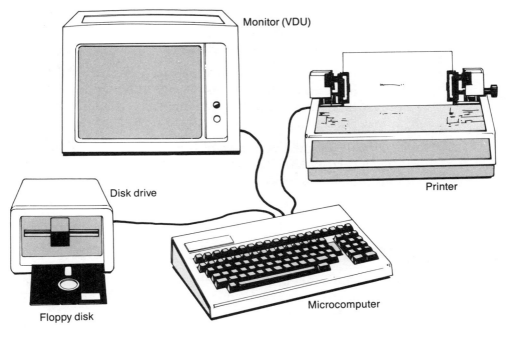

Fig. 2.1 A small computer system

It consists of the computer itself, with a built-in keyboard for putting information into the machine, a screen (or, in computer jargon, a *monitor*) or *visual display unit* (VDU) for getting information out of the machine and a *disk drive* for storing information while the computer works on something else or is switched off. Many home computer enthusiasts are unable to afford a printer, but it is so useful that no serious business system would be without it. Similarly, many home users still use a cheap (but slow) *cassette recorder* instead of a disk drive.

Q 2.1   *Estimate the cost of putting together a system like that shown in Figure 2.1. (If you have no real idea of prices, have a look at some computer magazines in the library.)*

Q 2.2   *In many home computer systems an ordinary television set is used instead of a proper monitor. What is the difference?*

Q 2.3   *What are the pros and cons of buying colour monitors, high-quality printers and disk drives? If you were buying a home computer system would you want any (or all) of these? Would a business?*

HARDWARE AND SOFTWARE

As you are probably aware, there is more to a computer than just the *hardware*—the bits and pieces such as the keyboard and VDU that you can physically pick up (and drop).

The *software*, i.e. the computer's internal programs and the program input by the person using it, is just as important. Poor quality software can cause even the most sophisticated pieces of equipment to turn good data into nonsense.

Of course, even the best software run on the best equipment will not salvage incorrect data. Anyone who has used a computer is well aware of the problem sometimes called the *GIGO principle*; i.e. Garbage In . . . Garbage Out.

MICRO-, MINI- AND MAINFRAME COMPUTERS

Figure 2.1 illustrates a *microcomputer* system that could sit on a table at home or an office desk, and which would normally be used by only one person at a time.

Some businesses have larger *minicomputer* systems, that can serve several independent users at once. And many large concerns have *mainframe* computers that are capable of running a wide variety of programs simultaneously.

These larger systems often allow a number of users to be *on-line* to the computer at one time. Each has his or her own *terminal*, usually consisting of a keyboard and VDU and, perhaps, a printer. Since the terminal is linked to the mainframe or minicomputer, the individual can gain rapid access to the company's central computerised records. This would not be possible if he or she were working a *stand-alone* microcomputer on a desk (although many microcomputers can also communicate with other computers). The terminals linked to the mainframe may be in the same room, in the same building or many miles away and linked by specially provided lines or even via the public telephone network.

Q 2.4   *What problems are there likely to be when many people have access to one central computer and the information stored there?*

Q 2.5   *What problems are likely to arise when computerised information is transmitted some distance over the public telephone network?*

Q 2.6   *Does your school or college have a terminal linked to a mainframe in a university or polytechnic? (Many have.) If it does, find out what you can about it.*

THE THREE STAGES OF DATA PROCESSING

Whatever the size and cost of a computer system, and however complex its software, it still goes through the same three basic stages:

- *input* data
- *process* data
- *output* results.

Fig. 2.2

These three stages apply to manual systems too. For example, many office workers have an 'in' tray, a job to do with the papers that arrive there, and an 'out' tray for finished work.

Think how you would approach a problem, say, in simple arithmetic. First you would read the question (how often have your teachers told you that?); i.e. you *input* the data. Secondly, you would work out what you thought was the right answer; i.e. you *process* the data. And finally you write the answer down or call it out; i.e. you *output* your result.

INFORMATION AND DATA

Data must be processed and/or interpreted before it becomes *information*.

Suppose, for example, you play a game of darts and on your first round you score double 5, 20 and treble 20. These scores represent data; they have yet to be processed or interpreted.

The facts that your total is 90 and that you still have 211 to go before you win and that you have done rather well are all information; this information was deduced from the original data of three individual dart scores.

? **Q 2.7** *What might 07 03 88 signify?*
Explain.

Fig. 2.3 Data must be processed and/or interpreted before it becomes information

THE CENTRAL PROCESSING UNIT (CPU)

Input and output (I/O) devices such as keyboards, monitors and printers, and storage mechanisms, such as disk drives and tape recorders, are not a central part of the computer (even if they are built in). They are known collectively as *peripherals*.

The actual calculations and the manipulation of data take place in the *central processing unit*, the computer's 'brain', usually referred to as the CPU, and sometimes as the *central processor*.

Inside the CPU

There are three main elements of the CPU:

- the *control unit* that co-ordinates everything else

- the *arithmetic and logic unit* (ALU) in which all the calculations take place and all the logical decisions are made

- the *main store*, the computer's *memory* in which the program and data are held.

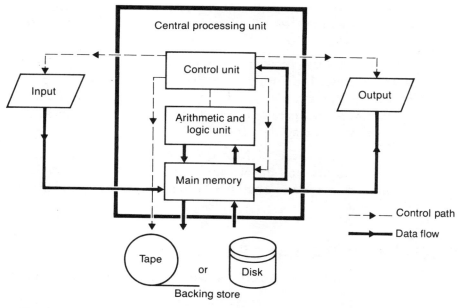

Fig. 2.4 The essential structure of any computer

The main store is also known by a number of other names. Some people call it the *main memory* or *central memory*, others the *internal store* or the *primary store*. Perhaps the most accurate term, best describing its role in the computer, is *immediate access store* (IAS) for it holds the program of instructions and the data to which those instructions apply. Obviously these must be immediately to hand if the computer is to follow the program step by step, continually manipulating the data as instructed, in a few millionths of a second.

The main memory cannot hold large quantities of data permanently. In the first place, there is not usually enough room inside the computer and, in the second place, data written in to the computer is usually lost when the machine is turned off. Thus the internal store has to be supplemented by *backing store*, such as disk or tape drives where the large data *files* can be held and transferred into the main memory as required.

ROM and RAM

Computer hobbyists talk a lot about ROM and RAM and often seem to measure the worth of competing microcomputers in these terms.

Both ROM and RAM are part of the main store. In the ordinary day-to-day use of the computer, ROM or *read-only memory* cannot be interfered with. Hence the description 'read-only'. It contains the computer's resident language (BASIC perhaps) that can be used as soon as the computer is switched on, and the manufacturer's software that controls the operation of the computer so that it responds to keys being pressed, displays characters on the screen, can send or receive messages to or from tapes and disks etc.

RAM or *random access memory*, on the other hand, is freely available to the operator for storing programs and data. Since any part of it can be accessed at any time, the operator is said to have random access. Furthermore the operator can *write* data to RAM, i.e. store information in it, as well as read data from it.

Obviously, the more ROM a computer has, the more extensive and sophisticated its built-in software is likely to be. The more RAM it has the more complex and lengthy the programs it can run and the more data it can hold.

THE HUMAN PARALLEL

Parallels can be drawn between computer systems and human beings.

For example, our eyes and ears are input devices; our voices are output devices, and our hands can be used as a 'printer'.

Our brains are our central processing units; they control all the actions of our bodies and enable us to remember things and work things out.

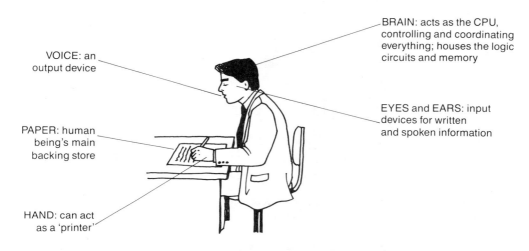

VOICE: an output device

BRAIN: acts as the CPU, controlling and coordinating everything; houses the logic circuits and memory

EYES and EARS: input devices for written and spoken information

PAPER: human being's main backing store

HAND: can act as a 'printer'

Fig. 2.5   Parallels can be drawn between computer systems and human beings

Some sections of the brain are preprogrammed 'read-only memory'. For example we cannot consciously will our hearts to stop beating. There is also plenty of 'random access memory' that we can fill with daily trivia and/or lines from 'Romeo and Juliet' (should we so choose) and use to train (or 'program') ourselves to play chess or bake cakes.

However, the memory capacity inside the brain is limited, and although we cannot clear our minds at will by turning them off like a computer, we still regularly forget things. So we like to make permanent records, usually on paper, our principal 'backing store'.

We should not take the parallel too far, though. We really know little about the workings of the human brain; the more we discover the more complex it seems, especially when compared with a computer which has no intelligence of its own.

ANALOG AND DIGITAL COMPUTERS

In an analog computer a number or code is represented by the varying strength of an electric current. Thus the number 21 might be represented by, say, 2.1 volts and the number 15 by 1.5 volts.

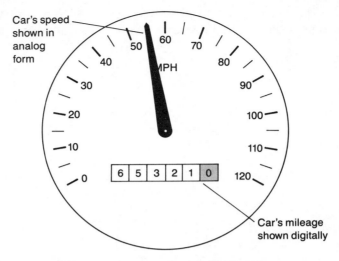

Fig. 2.6 A car speedometer containing both analog and digital elements

There are obvious problems with this. Calculations are not likely to be particularly accurate as small, random fluctuations in voltage could change the result and, in any case, sensitive measurement (say of 0.001 volts) is not easy to achieve.

Today, almost all computers are *digital computers*, i.e. they represent different letters and numbers by different digital codes. Invariably nowadays, computers use the *binary* (base 2) code. The two <u>bi</u>nary <u>dig</u>i<u>ts</u> (or *bits*) 0 and 1 are easily represented in an electric circuit as 'off' and 'on'.

Thus the number 21 has the following binary code equivalent:

00010101

This would then be represented by electric pulses in which the digit 0 is represented by no voltage, and the digit 1 by 5 volts (or thereabouts; small fluctuations in voltage do not matter).

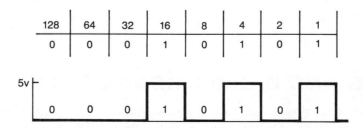

Fig. 2.7 Binary code for the number 21 and the equivalent pulse train

The previous number, 20, is represented by 0 0 1 0 1 0 0. And the next number, 22, is represented by 0 0 0 1 0 1 1 0. In each case there is an exact and clear jump of 1 between the numbers, just like counting on your fingers, and so there is little chance of one number being mistaken for another.

Greater accuracy is readily achieved on digital machines simply by including extra circuitry for the extra digits.

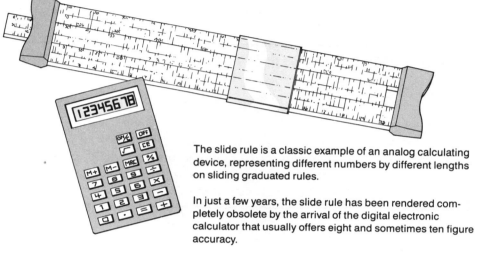

The slide rule is a classic example of an analog calculating device, representing different numbers by different lengths on sliding graduated rules.

In just a few years, the slide rule has been rendered completely obsolete by the arrival of the digital electronic calculator that usually offers eight and sometimes ten figure accuracy.

Fig. 2.8   The analog slide rule and the digital calculator

Although almost all computers are digital (and this book is about digital computers) there are still some physical quantities (temperature, for example) that are normally measured using an analog device (such as an electric thermometer) and input to the computer as analog signals. The computer must then be equipped with an *analog-to-digital* (A/D) *converter* so that it can process the data received.

Q 2.8   *List as many (a) analog devices and (b) digital devices as you can. In each case indicate the physical quantity measured.*

BITS AND BYTES

A *byte* is a string of bits long enough to encode any required individual character (whether a letter, a number, an arithmetic sign such as + or −, or a punctuation mark). Since many of today's computers (from micros to mainframes) use 8-bit codes, like that shown for the number 21 in Figure 2.7, a byte is usually eight bits.

Approximately one thousand bytes make a *kilobyte*, usually denoted by K. Manufacturers often advertise their machines as '128 K' or '512 K'. Thus the Amstrad PC1512 has 512 K, i.e. 512 kilobytes, of memory space; enough room for 512 000 letters or other characters to be stored in the computer.

There are really 1024 bytes in a kilobyte, not 1000. 1024 may seem a rather strange number, but, in fact, it is the power of two closest to 1000 ($2^{10} = 1024$).

Q 2.9 *Why does the number of bytes in a kilobyte have to be a power of 2?*

Q 2.10 *Does it matter that most computers have slightly more memory than their users generally realise?*

Q 2.11 *How many characters do you write on each line in your normal handwriting? How many lines are there on each page of the notepaper you are using? How many pages could you type into the main store of a 128 K computer?*

JARGON 2

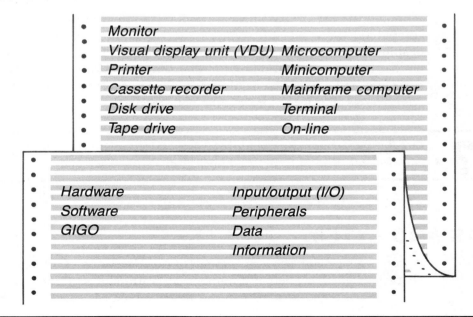

Monitor
Visual display unit (VDU)   Microcomputer
Printer   Minicomputer
Cassette recorder   Mainframe computer
Disk drive   Terminal
Tape drive   On-line

Hardware   Input/output (I/O)
Software   Peripherals
GIGO   Data
                Information

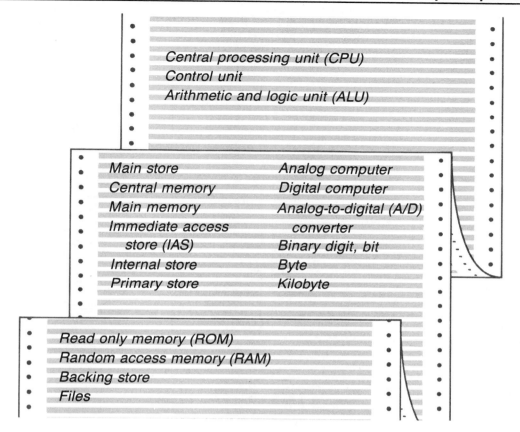

Central processing unit (CPU)
Control unit
Arithmetic and logic unit (ALU)

Main store	Analog computer
Central memory	Digital computer
Main memory	Analog-to-digital (A/D)
Immediate access	converter
store (IAS)	Binary digit, bit
Internal store	Byte
Primary store	Kilobyte

Read only memory (ROM)
Random access memory (RAM)
Backing store
Files

EXERCISES 2

1. Which of the following are hardware and which are software?

   (a) A BASIC program.   (b) Card reader.

   (c) Control unit.   (d) Assembly language.

   (e) Magnetic tape.   (f) Arithmetic and Logic Unit.

2. Write ANALOG or DIGITAL, as appropriate, beside each of the following devices:

   (a) A set of traffic lights.   (b) A gramophone record.

   (c) The data stored on a   (d) A magnetic compass.
       computer's magnetic disk.

(SREB)

3. Below is a diagram of the main parts of a computer system. Using - - - - - for control and ——— for data flow, copy the diagram and draw in all the necessary connections, indicating with arrows the direction of flow.

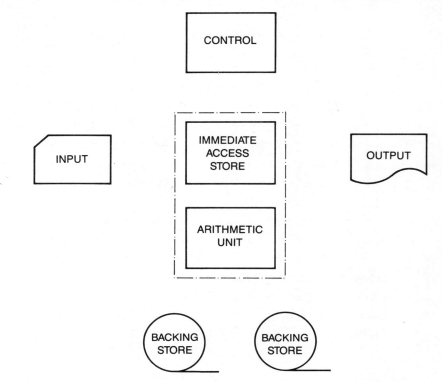

4. (*a*) Describe what you understand by a 'random access store'.

   (*b*) Explain with a reason, whether you consider a magnetic disk unit to be a random access store.

   (EMREB)

5. Name two analog and two digital devices. Why are modern computers digital?

6. (*a*) Explain two functions of the main memory of a computer.

   (*b*) Why do computers need backing store in addition to the main memory?

   (*c*) What is the difference between RAM and ROM?

3 Writing Good Programs

This is a book about computers and their applications. It will not teach you how to program your particular machine in a particular language. However, good programs written in any language share certain features which we shall explore.

By now you will probably have written some simple programs of your own. After an hour or two at the keyboard, most people are able to input something which will solve simple problems, at least.

WHAT MAKES A GOOD PROGRAM?

A program that fails to do the job intended is clearly not up to much. But even a program that does solve the problem in hand can be of poor quality.

There are four fundamental questions that must be asked of any serious program.

- Does it solve the problem it is meant to solve, reliably and efficiently?
- Would someone ignorant of computers find it reasonably easy to use; i.e. is it *user-friendly*?
- Could a moderately competent programmer follow the logic and listing easily enough to make any necessary amendments; i.e. will future *program maintenance* be easy to carry out?
- Is it well *documented*?

If you want to write computer programs to any serious level (which includes any project work that you may do as part of the course) then you must ask yourself these questions continually and make sure that the answer is always emphatically 'yes'. 'Yes, my program is efficient and easy to use. I know because I have tested it carefully.' And, as important, 'Yes, it is clearly laid out and well documented; I know because I have taken the trouble to make it so.'

Hopeless Spaghetti Programs

Novice programmers are often so eager to use the computer that they fail to give a problem adequate thought at the outset. They bash something out on the keyboard, then see if it works; when it does not, they change a line here or there then see if that works; then they add a few lines and try again . . .

A short program intended to solve a fairly trivial problem can be written in this way. But once the problem becomes more complex and the program needs to be lengthier, it cannot.

The resulting program might pass part of the first test; i.e. it might solve the problem; and helpful prompts on the screen may make it user friendly. But it is likely to be a *spaghetti program*, a hopelessly twisted, illogical mess, impossible to follow, to document sensibly, or to maintain.

If all this sounds a shade too familiar, if you are writing spaghetti programs, then *you* are a bad programmer.

THINKING OUT A PROBLEM

Before you can instruct someone (or something, such as a computer) how to perform a particular task, you must be sure how to do it yourself.

This might seem obvious, but the most important reason for spaghetti programming is the programmer's failure to think through exactly what needs to be done.

An Everyday Example

Suppose you were asked (oh horror!) to prepare the meal tonight (but absolutely *no* spaghetti).

It would be sensible to break down the task into three basic sections: first course, main course and pudding, and decide what you want for each.

Then it would be sensible to think through what you need to do for each course. Making the pudding, for example, might break down into two separate activities, say, 'bake the pie' and 'make the custard'.

Then 'bake the pie' breaks down further into 'make the pastry' and 'prepare the filling'. 'Make the pastry' breaks down further, and so on.

What began as a fairly involved task, namely 'prepare the meal', has been broken down into a series of minor tasks each one of which is, on its own, not so hard to do.

We could illustrate the effect of all these subdivisions on a *top down* diagram:

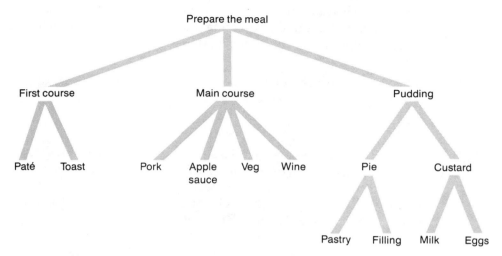

Fig. 3.1   Preparing a meal

?

Q 3.1   *Break down the following tasks into a series of sub-tasks and in each case illustrate your division and subdivision on a top down diagram like Figure 3.1.*

(a) Decorating a room

(b) Going shopping

(c) Gardening

Q 3.2   *Suppose that, in a mathematics lesson, you were asked:* 'Draw the graph of the curve $y = x^2 - 4$, and, using values of x in the range $-4 \leqslant x \leqslant 4$, use your graph to find where the curve cuts the horizontal axis.'

Draw a top down diagram to illustrate how you would go about solving the problem. (You are not asked to do it.)

Q 3.3   *Suppose that, in a geography lesson, you were asked:* 'On the given map find the distance by road between the two points 331 734 and 289 758 if you take the route by way of 301 742.'

Draw a top down diagram to illustrate how you would go about solving the problem. (Again, you are not asked to do it; and anyway you do not have the map.)

STRUCTURED PROGRAMS

Preparing a well written program is similar to this. First, the programmer must be clear about the *program specification*, which describes exactly the required inputs, processing and output. (Often this is not the programmer's decision; see Chapter 9.) Then planning can begin.

Just as it is usual to break down a meal into two, three or even more courses, so it is usual to break long programs down into *modules* or *procedures*.

Each procedure can deal with a smaller, more manageable, section of the problem. It can then be prepared, tested and even documented on its own, by a different programmer if necessary, before it is linked with the others in the main program. (It might of course be suitable for use in other programs too, another advantage of this approach.)

For example a well *structured* program in BBC BASIC could be:

```
10 REM A well structured program
20 PROCinput
30 PROCprocess
40 PROCoutput
50 END
```

PROC is short for *procedure* and is an in-built facility in many versions of BASIC.

Of course, this program will not run until the procedures have been defined; and the procedures might themselves be broken down in a similar fashion. For example, it is usual to check data immediately it is input to the computer. So using the BBC BASIC expression DEFPROC to indicate that a procedure is about to be defined, the program might have additional lines:

```
1000 DEFPROCinput
1010 PROCgetdata
1020 PROCcheckdata
1030 ENDPROC
```

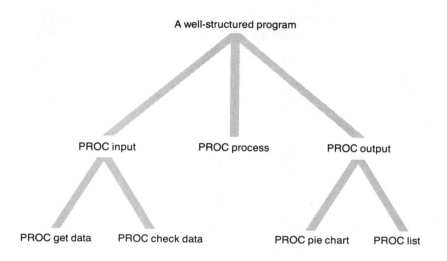

Fig. 3.2 Top down program structure

Computer programmers talk of a *top down structure* for programs laid out this way, so that the problem is split into smaller and smaller parts. They know that the first rule of good programming is:

> Break the program down into manageable parts.

ALGORITHMS

Once the program structure is finalised, the programmer must next decide on how exactly the task assigned to each module will be achieved.

A set of instructions which, taken in order, lead to the solution of a specific problem, is called an *algorithm*.

A computer program is an algorithm. But algorithms do not have to be written in a computer language. On the contrary, algorithms were commonplace, e.g. in cookbooks and do-it-yourself manuals, long before the advent of computers. Furthermore, even in a computing context it is sensible to sort out the algorithm in English before you attack the problem of coding it into a computer language.

FLOWCHARTS

One of the neatest ways of describing an algorithm is to illustrate it as a *flowchart*. The symbols used in a program flowchart are:

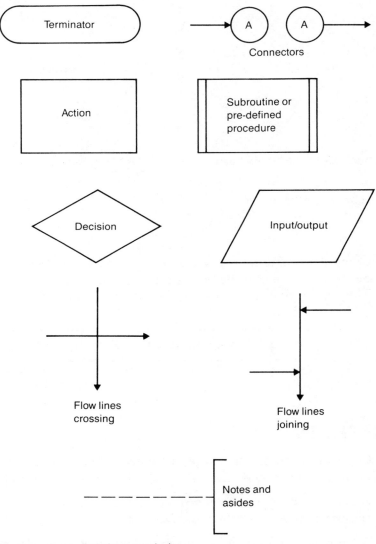

Fig. 3.3 Common program flowchart symbols

Following the flowchart step by careful step (exactly as a computerised robot would) should lead to the last STOP statement with the job done *if* the algorithm is a good one.

Continuing with our kitchen parallel, consider a recipe for making apple sauce. Rather than write a wordy set of instructions, a flowchart should make the process agreeably clear:

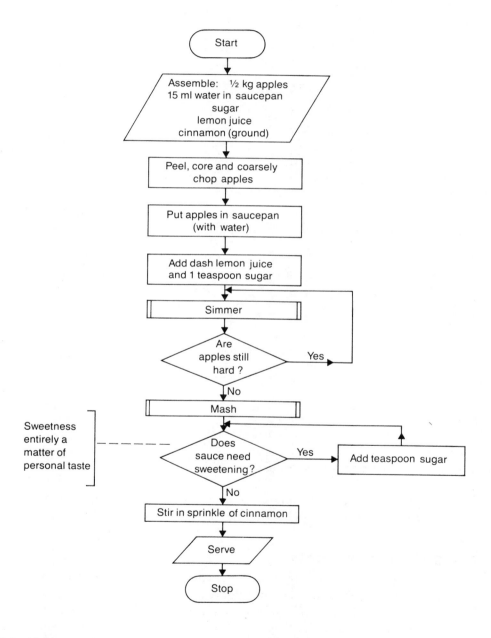

Fig. 3.4 Making apple sauce: an algorithm illustrated by a flowchart

Three Basic Control Structures

In fact any algorithm can be flowcharted (and so any program can be written) using combinations of just three basic *control structures*.

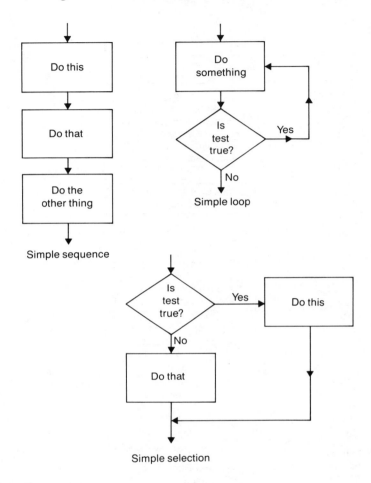

Fig. 3.5   The three basic control structures

Look again at the apple sauce flowchart and you will see that it consists of exactly these three structures arranged one after the other.

Drawing Good Flowcharts

Keep flowcharts simple. Use subroutines and procedures, drawing the special subroutine symbol (Figure 3.3), to keep the structure as clear as possible. Flowchart subroutines separately. Experiment in rough to ensure your eventual layout is clear, and draw your final version with a template and ruler.

Above all else, label your flowcharts *in English* and *not in a computer language*. Spaghetti programmers usually give themselves away when flowcharting an algorithm. Having done things back to front (i.e. having started with the program and then later tried to flowchart it) they rewrite the key statements from their programs and then draw boxes around them.

Q 3.4 *Two procedures—'simmer' and 'mash'—were used in the apple sauce flowchart. Draw simple flowcharts to explain these operations.*

Q 3.5 *The following is an extract from a car owner's workshop manual:*

> *'Unscrew each of the spark-plugs from the four cylinders. It is sensible to label the leads '1, 2, 3, 4' before you remove them from the plugs. Inspect the plugs carefully. If they are pitted and worn replace them with new ones. If you decide not to fit new ones, then clean them by repeatedly brushing the electrodes with sandpaper. When they are clean, replace plugs and refit leads.'*

Redraft the algorithm, putting it into flowchart form.

A Program Flowchart

Suppose we wish to write a program for working out an average of, say, ten different numbers that will be input to the computer when the program is run.

Before we even begin to think of the necessary code, we need to make sure we know *how* to approach the problem. We must decide upon our algorithm.

Imagine *you* are the computer. Worse, you are only allowed to keep the numbers in your head, i.e. your 'main memory'; you are allowed no 'backing store' such as a piece of paper to write things down. How would you do it?

Apart from the mental arithmetic, it is not so hard. You would need to

   (i) be told the numbers one by one
  (ii) add them up as you go, remembering your total so far
 (iii) after the last number, divide the total by ten
 (iv) declare the result.

So, we have the algorithm. Redrafting it as a flowchart makes the control structures—the loops etc.—very obvious.

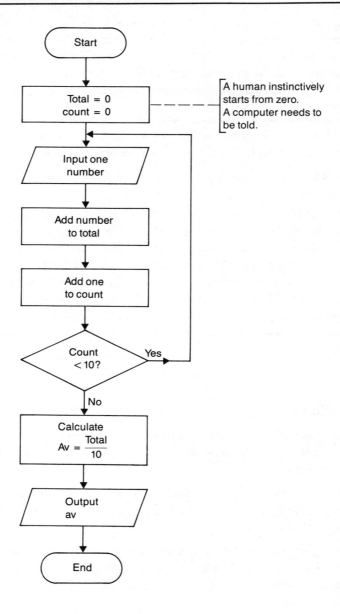

Fig. 3.6 Flowchart for mean average program

Dry Running

Of course, we had better test that it works. Working through a flowchart or program as if you were the computer is usually called *dry running* it. So that you do not lose track, you write down the values of the variables and the decisions you make at each and every stage on a *trace table*.

Q 3.6 *Check that the chart in Figure 3.6 works by dry running it with the following data:*

2   3   6   7   5   13   17   18   12   9

You will need to copy and complete the following trace table:

Step	Data	Count	Count < 10?	Total	Output
1		0		0	
2	2				
3				2	
4		1			
5			Yes		
6	. . .	. . .	. . .	. . .	. . .
7	. . .	. . .	. . .	. . .	. . .

(table continues for as many steps as are needed)

In Q 3.6 you should have traced the chart through and arrived, correctly, at 9.2 as your output. Our algorithm works. So now (and only now) can we begin to start coding it, for the second rule of good programming is

> Do not start coding until you know your algorithm works.

Q 3.7 *Using the flowchart as your starting point, write a computer program to work out the average of ten numbers. Even if you are fairly new to programming you should have found coding the flowchart considerably easier to cope with than if you had been required simply to 'write a program to find the average of ten numbers'.*

Q 3.8 *(a) Write a flowchart to work out values of y from the formula $y = x^2 - 4$ for integer values of x in the region $-4 < x < 4$.*

(b) Write a second flowchart to describe how you would draw a graph from a set of points (x, y) already worked out.

(c) (Harder) using these two charts and the top down diagram you drew in Q 3.2 as your starting points, write a computer program to draw the graph of $y = x^2 - 4$.

Q 3.9 *Trace through the flowchart in Figure 3.7 (overleaf). Use the following data:*

(a) 5, 12, 15, 8, 0   (b) 3, 2.1, 0.3, 5, 7.3, 0

And show your steps on copies of the trace table overleaf.

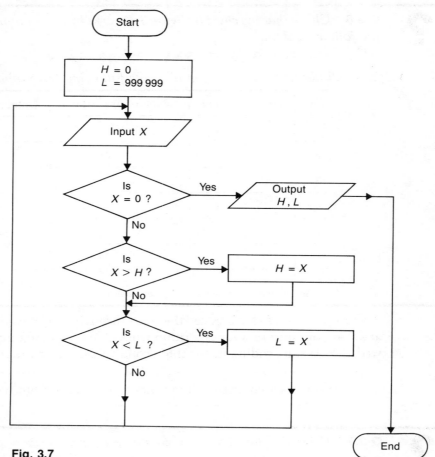

Fig. 3.7

Step	H	L	X	X = 0?	X > H	X < L	Output
1	0	999 999					
2			5				
3				No			
4	. . .	. . .	. . .	. . .	. . .	. . .	. . .

(table continues for as many steps as are needed)

What is the purpose of the algorithm?

Why is 0 of special significance?

Write a program to carry out this same procedure on your computer.

USER-FRIENDLY PROGRAMS

Computers are now commonplace. The people who have to use them as an everyday part of their working lives are often quite *non*-technical.

For this reason, the programmer must ensure that his or her programs are *user-friendly*, i.e. they should guide the user and should not *crash* if he or she pushes the wrong buttons or tries to enter inappropriate data.

There is no criticism in this; business people need to know about business, accountants about accounts; scientists need to know about science; teachers need to know their subjects and their classes etc. Most of them do not want to have to worry about the details of the computer programs they use. Like the car or the telephone, the computer is a tool to serve a particular purpose. Some people enjoy putting such things right when they go wrong, but most people do *not*. Any malfunction is seen for what it is: a confounded nuisance.

Q 3.10 *(a) Could you put the television or telephone right if it went wrong? Should you be able to?*

(b) Should the person using a program be able to fix any errors there may be?

Give reasons for your answers.

Prompts

One important way a programmer can help even the most hesitant and untechnically minded people to use a program successfully is to include plenty of down-to-earth *prompts* that explain, at the appropriate time, what is happening and what action is expected from the user.

For example, a simple line of BASIC might read:

```
20 INPUT A$,B
```

But it would be a bad line. When the program is run it would result in a solitary '?' appearing on the screen, which would fox a lot of people from the outset. And should they strike lucky and push RETURN at some point, there is still a second '?' to come.

Even a user who did understand that the question mark on the screen indicated that the computer was waiting for an *input* of some kind would almost certainly type in the wrong thing, for there is nothing to indicate what is required.

The line should read something like this:

20 INPUT "Your name is " A$ ' "And your age " B

Even better, it might be split into several lines:

15 INPUT "Please type in your name (and then press RETURN)" ' "Your name is " A$ '
20 PRINT "Welcome " A$ " to WRITING GOOD PROGRAMS" ' ' "A demonstration program from Stanley Thornes" ' '
25 INPUT "Now please type in your age (and then press RETURN) " ' "Your age is " B

When this is run by Penelope, aged 8, it should put the following on the VDU screen:

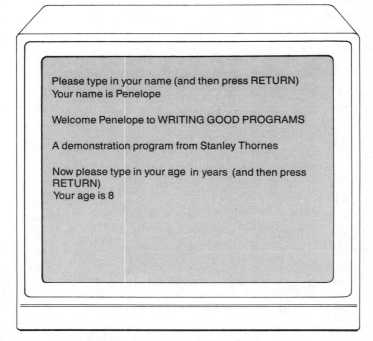

Please type in your name (and then press RETURN)
Your name is Penelope

Welcome Penelope to WRITING GOOD PROGRAMS

A demonstration program from Stanley Thornes

Now please type in your age in years (and then press RETURN)
Your age is 8

Fig. 3.8   Penelope, aged 8, starts to learn to write good programs

The program does not do a lot, but at least it is easy to use; even someone who has never used a computer before should be able to cope.

Error Traps

No matter how good your prompts, people will still push the wrong buttons and try to input wildly erroneous data. After all, even experienced computer buffs can hit the wrong keys.

A program that *crashes* with a 'beep' and some meaningless error message, such as

ERROR 22   LINE 10

whenever something is mistyped, is a bad program.

A program that accepts incorrect data without comment is even worse.

A good program will contain as many *error traps* as necessary to ensure that all inputs are immediately checked (or *validated*) and the user is gently invited to repeat the input if a mistake is made.

?

Q 3.11   *LOAD some commercial software into a computer. Can you cause it to crash? Try pushing all the wrong keys at all the wrong times. (BREAK and ESCAPE are exceptions.) If the program crashes, you have wasted your money.*

Q 3.12   *Write the program code, in a computer language of your choice, that will only accept input of numbers between 11 and 26 inclusive.*

Q 3.13   *The user of the program on the previous page might cause it to crash at line 25. Why?*

Q 3.14 *(more difficult)*   *Some computers have ON ERROR functions or similar. Does yours? Explain its purpose in terms suitable for someone new to programming.*

Q 3.15 *(also more difficult)*   *Write the program code, in a computer language of your choice, that will only accept input of letters from L to Z inclusive.*

All this may seem very elementary. But too often people who work with computers take too much for granted and create programs (and manuals) that are all but impossible to use. No matter how advanced your computing eventually becomes,

Keep your programs *user-friendly*.

MAKING AMENDMENT EASY

Why Bother?

If you have written a few programs of your own, run them for the fun of it and then discarded them, then you almost certainly have given little or no thought to the problem of subsequent amendment. This is fair enough, if all you are trying to do is learn how to program.

However, when your programming skills have matured (if they have not already) you will want to write programs that are of value. You will want to record them on disk or tape; and in the not too distant future, when some new good idea comes to you, you will want to amend them. That is when the trouble begins.

For you can surprisingly easily forget how a program works. Trying to trace it through and work out just what you did can take a lot of time if the program is a substantial one—time largely wasted. If only you had written the original program in such a way that it made sense when you read it again a few months later.

Q 3.16 *Look back on a reasonably large program that you wrote a little while ago. How long does it take you to figure out how it works?*

Show it to some friends. How long does it take them?

Program Maintenance

Commercial programmers are continually rewriting old material. Companies regularly need their established software updated for price changes, new products and new procedures. Frequently, some errors or *bugs* come to light and a program needs correcting. Or maybe the software requirements of a new customer are fairly similar to those of an established one for whom the programmer has already written substantial material. Obviously it is more sensible and faster to adapt the existing software to the new requirements rather than starting from scratch.

It is quite common for a professional program to be rewritten scores or even hundreds of times. Such *program maintenance* is an everyday part of a programmer's life.

The Software Crisis

Surprisingly, the computer business was slow to realise just how important and costly the amendment of existing software would become. Many authors of large programs used on early commercial, military and academic projects gave little or no thought to how their future users might require the programs to be adapted in the light of changing needs.

Very often the original author of a program is not the same person who is subsequently asked to amend it. Programmers regularly work in teams if the job is large. And there are always personnel changes, e.g. when programmers retire, die, or go to work for a competitor.

By the late 1970s and the early 1980s many organisations found themselves spending more on adapting old programs (and correcting the bugs the amendments caused) than on developing new ones.

Not surprisingly, many people in the computing industry began talking of a 'software crisis' and began to look for ways of improving programming methods.

Self-explanatory Programs

If someone else is to amend a program that you have written, they will need to know exactly how it works.

A very short program ought to be fairly clear in any case. But in longer programs the complication is likely to grow well beyond most people's ability to trace it through. Unless of course you, the author, consciously work at making it clear.

Unfortunately some people think it clever to talk and write in terms that no one else can understand. In fact, the reverse is true; clever people make things look so easy when the rest of us find them impossibly hard.

The same goes for computer programmers. The clever programmer is the one who can show the rest of us how it should be done. Someone whose program logic is a dark secret buried behind an incomprehensible listing presumably has something to hide.

Have a look at this one-line program:

```
10 B=0:INPUTA:FORJ=1TOA:INPUTC:B=B+C: NEXT:PRINTB/A:END
```

Q 3.17 *Try to explain the purpose of this program and the functions of the variables A, B and C. Can you make out what the program does? RUN the program, if possible. Can you now make out what it does?*

If you cannot answer Q 3.17, do not worry. The program was not intended to be understood. The author was trying to be 'clever' by writing something that does run on a computer, despite looking like gibberish.

Contrast it with this one:

```
10 REM Mean Averages Program
20 REM
30 REM  = = = = = = = = = = = = = = = = = = = = = = = = = = = = = = = =
40 REM Variables Used
50 REM -----------------------
60 REM number_of_items = number of data items in set
70 REM cumulative_total = cumulative total of data items read in turn
80 REM count = loop counter
90 REM
100 REM  = = = = = = = = = = = = = = = = = = = = = = = = = = = = = = = =
110 REM Initialise variables
120 REM ---------------------------
130 LET cumulative_total = 0
140 LET data_item = 0
150 LET number_of_items = 0
160 REM
170 REM  = = = = = = = = = = = = = = = = = = = = = = = = = = = = = = = =
180 REM Clear screen and give instructions
190 REM ----------------------------------------------------
200 CLS
210 PRINT "This program will work out the mean of a set of data" ' '
220 INPUT "How many numbers are there altogether?" number_of_items
230 REM
240 REM  = = = = = = = = = = = = = = = = = = = = = = = = = = = = = = = =
250 REM Enter values
260 REM --------------------
270 PRINT " ' "Enter each one individually" " 'Press RETURN after each"
280 FOR count = 1 TO number_of_items
290      PRINT "Number"; count
300      INPUT data_item
310      cumulative_total = cumulative_total + data_item
320 NEXT count
330 REM
340 REM  = = = = = = = = = = = = = = = = = = = = = = = = = = = = = = = =
350 REM Output routine
360 REM ---------------------
370 PRINT ' ' ' "The average of the"; number of items " numbers is"; cumulative_
total / number_of_items
380 REM
390 PRINT ' ' '
400 END
```

In fact it is essentially the same program, but the meanings of the variables used and the purposes of all the sections of the program have been made clear. You should have very little difficulty in understanding either the listing or how to respond when you run it.

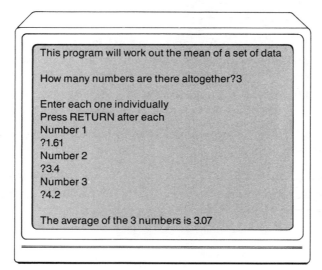

Fig. 3.9 Screen output from Mean Averages program

What Makes a Good BASIC Listing

The various steps that you can take to improve the layout of your program listings depend to some extent on the language you are using, and they should be explained in your programming book (but are so often not).

The Mean Averages program opposite was written in BASIC. It is a good, clear listing exhibiting a number of worthwhile features:

- REM (or *remark*) statements are used extensively to break up and title the program as well as to explain the functions of various lines.

- The variables used are described at the very beginning.

- The variables are given meaningful names.

- There is only one BASIC statement on each line.

- The loop is indented so that its start and end are clear.

Q 3.18 *Clear though this listing is, the program is still not perfect. What happens, for example, if the user enters 0 as the number of items?*

What other user errors would defeat this program?
Have a go at building in all the necessary error traps.

What About Memory Space?

Of course, the Mean Averages program takes up considerably more computer memory than its one-line equivalent. But memory is now a lot cheaper than it once was, and it is no longer such an overriding concern. The first microcomputers for home use, e.g. the Acorn Atom or the Sinclair ZX80, had only 1 or 2 K of user's RAM.

As you become a more experienced programmer you will undoubtedly value this advice:

> Use REMarks extensively so that your programs explain themselves.

?

Q 3.19 *Some books suggest that a program listing should be annotated by hand, perhaps in coloured ink.*
What are the advantages and disadvantages of this?

Q 3.20 *Redraft this listing to make the program both friendly to the user and comprehensible to a fellow programmer:*

10 INPUTN:FORJ=1TO 14:PRINTJ*N;:NEXTJ:END

When RUN, with N given the value 6, this program puts the following on screen: 6 12 18 24 30 36 42 48 54 60 66 72 78 84

Q 3.21 *Redraft this listing to make the program both friendly to the user and comprehensible to a fellow programmer. The output is shown to help you. Actually these are the first ten numbers of the Fibonacci sequence in which after 1 and 1, each subsequent term is the sum of the previous two. Thus 1 + 1 = 2; 1 + 2 = 3; 2 + 3 = 5 and so on.*

```
10 LETA=1:LETB=1:FORJ=1TO5:
PRINTA,B;:A=A+B:B=A+B:NEXT:END
RUN
1  1  2  3  5  8  13  21  34  55
```

Q 3.22 *(more difficult)*   *Repeat question 3.21 for this listing.*

Note that VDU 7 is the BBC BASIC instruction to sound the beeper and that FOR . . . NEXT loops can be used to create pauses.

```
10 LETX=RND(6):FORJ=1TOX:PRINT" # ";:
VDU7:FORK=1TO1000:NEXT:NEXT:
PRINT':FORK=1TO4000:NEXT:GOTO10
```

DEBUGGING YOUR PROGRAM

Once your program is written you will need to *debug* it. There will be errors (bugs); all programmers accept this, no matter how experienced.

There are three types of error:

- syntax errors
- run-time errors
- logic errors.

Syntax Errors

Syntax errors arise when the rules of the program language have been disobeyed, key words have been mistyped or omitted, or punctuation has been misused. For example:

LER X = 6	or IMPUT X	(mistypes)
FOR count = 1	10	(keyword TO missing)
PRINT " Hi!		(incomplete statement)

Possibly they are the easiest to find (although not necessarily to put right) for the computer itself will warn you of their existence. The program will crash and a message such as SYNTAX ERROR AT LINE 230 will appear.

Run-time Errors

Run-time or *execution errors* surface in the course of running the program and are the result of otherwise perfectly correct commands that breach some mathematical or logical rule. For example:

```
10 LET X = 10
20 INPUT N
30 PRINT X/N
40 END
```

is a valid BASIC program. But it contains the seed of a run-time error. For if N is given the value 0 then X/N cannot be calculated, because division by zero is not a permitted mathematical operation.

Logic Errors

Logic errors arise when the program has been poorly designed. Perhaps it branches off in the wrong place, for example. The program may appear to run successfully but in fact is giving incorrect results.

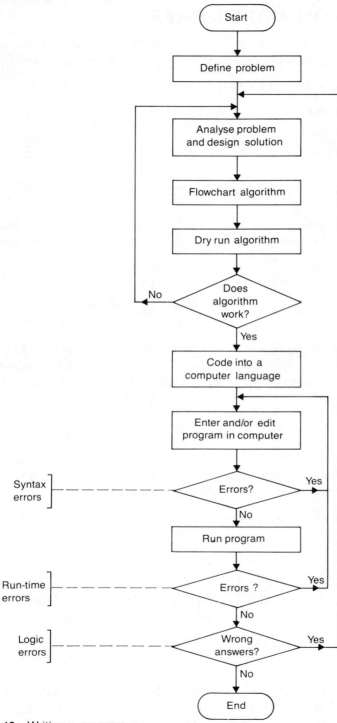

Fig. 3.10 Writing a program

TESTING THE PROGRAM

If you thought carefully about your program before you coded it and thoroughly tested the algorithm, you should not suffer too much from logic errors. If you use the computer frequently, the number of syntax errors you make will significantly diminish as you become more familiar with the keyboard and the language you use. If you are a sympathetic programmer who knows how easily users get things wrong, your in-built error traps ought to prevent run-time errors causing your program to crash. BUT . . .

Any long program inevitably contains those wretched bugs! You must test your program rigorously, deliberately feeding it perverse *test data* that will sort out the effectiveness (or otherwise) of your error traps. You should always work out your *expected results* before testing so that you can compare them with the *actual results* from the computer.

Remember Murphy's law: what can go wrong will go wrong. If there is a way of making your program crash, someone somewhere will find it.

> A good programmer finds out how to make the program crash—and does something to prevent it.

DOCUMENTING THE PROGRAM

To a considerable extent documenting what you think is a successful program is something of a chore. But, like making the bed, if you don't do it, you will later wish you had.

Proper *documentation* is, in any case, part of making your programs easy to use and easy to amend. So do not skip it, but apply our final rule:

> A good program must be properly documented.

That means that it must include at the very least:

- a proper title
- date written and author's name
- specification of the problem and some indication as to how it has been broken down into parts
- input and output specifications
- language-independent flowcharts of algorithms used
- a program listing, with any handwritten comments that may be necessary; although, as we have indicated, it is better to use REM statements that build relevant comments into the program
- test data and sample output
- user instructions.

Documentation is much less of a burden if you do it as you go along. If you leave it until the end, not only will it seem a major task but also you may find yourself forgetting how parts of your own program work.

PROGRAMMING LANGUAGES

Everything we have said so far applies to any program written in any language, although we have used BBC BASIC to illustrate some of the points.

It is really only when the algorithm is charted and tested that a programmer needs to decide which computer language to use to code it.

Of course, the choice may be limited. Perhaps the machine can only run one particular language. Perhaps the programmer only *knows* one.

High- and Low-level Languages

A programmer may choose to use *assembly language* which is a *low-level language* close to the binary codes the computer uses. Some programmers may even write the 0s and 1s which are the *machine code* itself. Both assembly language and machine code are notoriously complex to use (see Chapter 24) although the program, once it works, will run very much more quickly because it will need little or no translation.

High-level languages, such as BASIC, include English-like words and make programming very much easier. However, the programs run a lot more slowly because each high-level language statement must be translated into the equivalent series of machine code instructions that the computer can follow step by step.

Two elementary BASIC program statements:

```
. . . . . .
. . . . . .
1000    LET C = A + B
9999    END
```

have an involved assembly language equivalent:

```
. . . . . .
. . . . . .
LD      HL,(20H)
LD      DE,(30H)
ADD     HL,DE
LD      (50H),HL
HALT
```

and a highly complex machine code equivalent:

```
. . . . . .
. . . . . .
00101010
00100000
00000000
11101101
01011011
00110000
00000000
00011001
00100010
01010000
00000000
01110110
```

BASIC

BASIC (Beginners' All-purpose Symbolic Instruction Code) was designed as a limited version of another high-level language, FORTRAN, specifically to introduce programming at an easy level to those completely new to it.

It is certainly true that most people are able to pick up elementary BASIC very rapidly. For this reason it has become the standard home-computer language. (Manufacturers could then fairly advertise their machines, as Sinclair did in the early 1980s, along the lines of 'Inside a week you will be talking to it like an old friend'.)

However, BASIC encourages people to draft their programs on the computer which, as we have seen, is a bad habit leading to badly thought out, poorly structured programs. Furthermore it is a line-oriented language which allows statements such as

IF . . . THEN GOTO 150 ELSE GOTO 500

which do not exactly help the clarity of the program.

Have a look at this classic 'how you should *never* do it' example:

```
30 REM "COMPUTERS IN SCHOOLS"
40 REM THE JOURNAL OF MUSE
50 GOTO 130
60 GOTO 120
70 N = N + 1
80 END
90 IF N = 18 THEN PRINT "GOTO OR NOT TO GOTO"
100 IF N > 35 THEN GOTO 150
110 GOTO 70
120 PRINT "*** THE GOTO SHOW ***": GOTO 70
130 N = 0: GOTO 60
140 PRINT "GOT TO GOTO GOTO NOW"
150 GOTO 80
160 PRINT "GOTO OR NOT TO GOTO"; GOTO 100
```

 Q 3.23 *Try to trace through the program and work out what would happen if you tried to run it.*

It is fashionable for computer buffs to sneer at BASIC as *the* language of spaghetti programmers. However, it is perfectly *possible* to write good, well-structured programs in BASIC *if* you approach the job in a professional manner.

LOGO

Another language designed specifically for beginners, in fact for children, is LOGO.

In particular, LOGO has very special graphics capabilities, on which its claim to fame largely rests. A so-called *turtle*, actually a transparent plastic pen-plotter on wheels, is controlled by the child with instructions such as FORWARD, BACKWARD or RIGHT 90 (to make a 90 degree turn). Older children work with a 'turtle' on the screen, but the principles are the same.

Fig. 3.11   A LOGO turtle

A few simple commands are sufficient to draw basic shapes, e.g.

```
TO SQUARE
    REPEAT 4
        FORWARD 100
        RIGHT 90
END
```

```
TO TRIANGLE
    REPEAT 3
        FORWARD 100
        LEFT 120
END
```

With a few basic routines established, the child can put them together to make more complex patterns, for example:

```
TO HOUSE
    SQUARE
    TRIANGLE
END
```

Q 3.24 *Pretend you are the turtle and trace through the above LOGO program on a piece of paper (FORWARD 100 you may take to mean 'go forward any convenient length'). Do you get the house as shown in the diagram above?*

Look closely at this program. It has perfect top down structure. What better way to learn programming than to be able to write well structured and interesting programs in primary school?

Pascal

Pascal, named in honour of the French mathematician Blaise Pascal, is now one of the most widely used high-level languages. Although it is harder than BASIC to pick up, it imposes the same top down structure and readability that an experienced BASIC programmer would use.

Look at this Pascal listing. You can probably make out what is happening despite never having seen a line of the language before.

```
PROGRAM average (input, output);
{——program to find the mean of ten numbers——}
VAR
  data: real;
  total: real;
  count: integer;
BEGIN
  total: = 0;
  FOR count: = 1 TO 10 DO
  BEGIN
    read (data);
    total: = total + data;
  END;
  writeln ('The mean of the ten numbers is', total/10);
END.
```

COBOL

COBOL (COmmon Business Orientated Language) was designed to handle business problems such as file manipulation and accounts. Even simple tasks require quite lengthy COBOL programs, but it is easier to produce descriptive reports with COBOL than with, say, BASIC.

FORTRAN

FORTRAN stands for FORmula TRANslation and is the computing language most used by scientists and engineers. It is so well standardised (unlike BASIC which has spawned thousands of different versions) that there are large libraries of subroutines and packages available 'off the peg' for use on any machine that runs the language.

SUMMARY: THE SIX RULES FOR WRITING GOOD PROGRAMS

- Break the program down into manageable parts.
- Don't start coding until you know your algorithm works.
- Keep your programs user-friendly.
- Use REMarks extensively so that your programs explain themselves.
- Find for yourself how to make your program crash—and do something to prevent it.
- Document your program properly.

JARGON 3

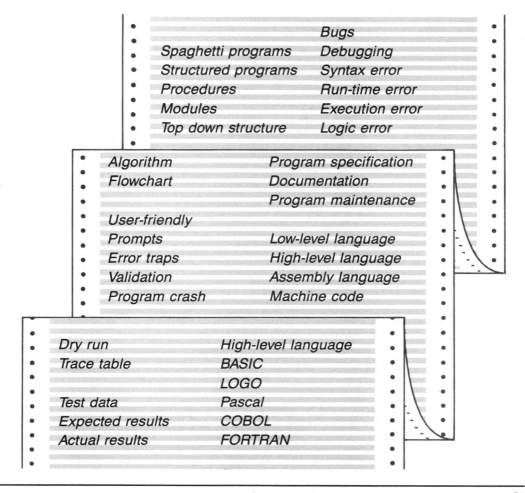

- Spaghetti programs
- Structured programs
- Procedures
- Modules
- Top down structure

- Bugs
- Debugging
- Syntax error
- Run-time error
- Execution error
- Logic error

- Algorithm
- Flowchart

- User-friendly
- Prompts
- Error traps
- Validation
- Program crash

- Program specification
- Documentation
- Program maintenance

- Low-level language
- High-level language
- Assembly language
- Machine code

- Dry run
- Trace table

- Test data
- Expected results
- Actual results

- High-level language
- BASIC
- LOGO
- Pascal
- COBOL
- FORTRAN

EXERCISES 3

1. Study this flowchart carefully and then answer the questions which follow.

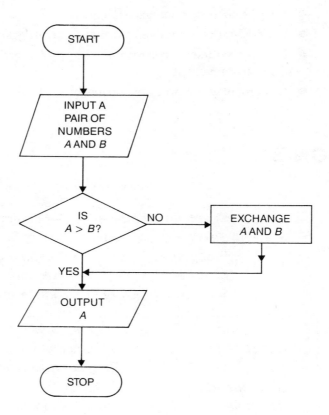

(a) If $A = 1$ and $B = 2$ upon input what would the value of A be on output?

(b) Amend the flowchart so that more than one pair of numbers can be processed.

(c) What test could be used to stop the process, given that the normal values of A and B are never negative, and where would the test box be placed?

(ALSEB)

2. (a) A flowchart and a blank trace table are given below. Complete the trace table by using the following data: 0, 0, 0, 1, 1, 0, 1, 1.

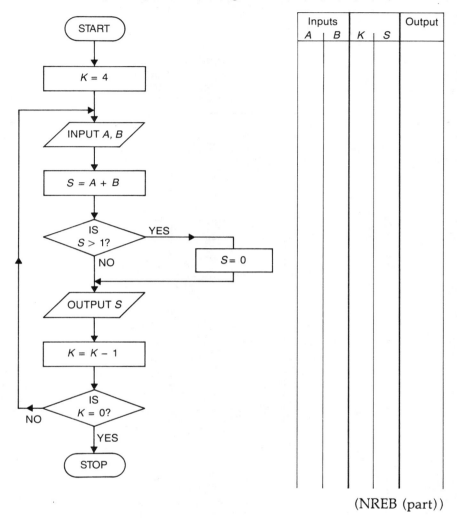

Inputs				Output
A	B	K	S	

(NREB (part))

3. Using only the information given below draw a flowchart to find the cost of making a bus journey.

A passenger aged 60 or over travels free.

The fare is calculated at the rate of 2p per stage.
[a stage is a journey from one bus stop to the next]

There is a minimum fare of 10p for any journey.

A passenger aged under 14 pays half fare, i.e. 1p per stage and a minimum of 5p for any journey.

(SEREB)

4.

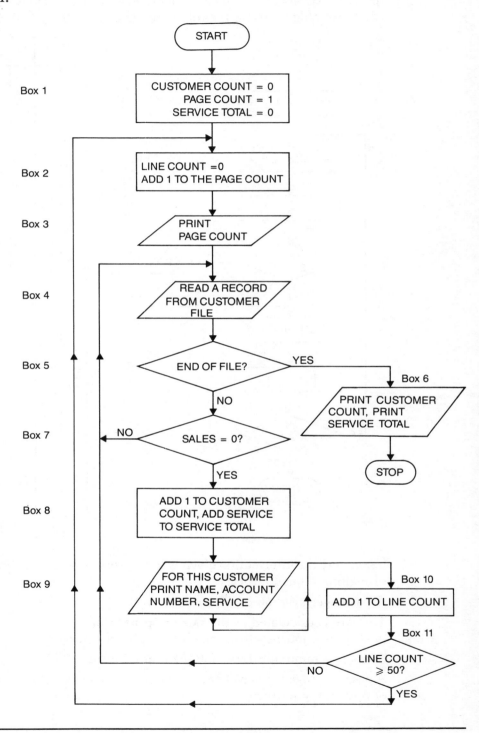

A firm which sells and services washing machines wants to know how much is spent by customers who pay for machines to be serviced but do not buy anything from the firm.

The firm maintains a card file. For each customer, the file has a card which contains:

customer's name,
customer's account number,
customer's sales account giving the total value of purchases,
customer's service account giving the total he has spent on servicing.

The flowchart opposite illustrates a program to print details from this file. Read the flowchart and then answer the following questions. Notice that the flowchart boxes have been numbered.

(a) The page number is printed at the top of each page by the instruction in box 3. What is printed at the top of the first page?

(b) Without changing box 2, how could you alter the flowchart so that the number 1 is printed at the top of the first page?

(c) Excluding the page number, how many lines are there in a full page of output?

(d) When the last card has been processed, what does the value of CUSTOMER COUNT represent?

(e) How would you alter the flowchart so that the total number of customers is printed out after the last card has been read?

(f) How would you alter the flowchart so that the average amount spent by all customers on servicing is printed out after the last card has been read?

(WMEB)

5. A computer is to be used to keep a record of the number of games played and the total number of points scored by teams in a certain sports league. Initially, the computer will start with a list of teams and records of no matches played and no points scored. A team scores 3 points for an away win, 2 points for a home win and 1 point for a draw. A losing team scores no points. The results of each match will be input in the form:

away team, away team score, home team, home team score.

Draw a flow chart which will update the records and at the end give the operator the opportunity to enter further results.

(SUJB)

6. Draw a flowchart to represent an algorithm to process a number of examination results as follows.

   For each candidate the input consists of a candidate code (a 3-digit number) and a mark in the range 0–100.

   For each candidate the required output is the candidate code followed by one of FAIL, PASS, or CREDIT. The pass mark is 40 and the minimum mark for a credit is 65.

   It is also required to output at the end of the results the percentage of candidates processed that are in each classification.

   All marks are recorded as whole numbers and a rogue value of -1 terminates the input.

   Suggest suitable test data for your algorithm.

   (JMB)

7. Describe briefly, firstly, the components you think ought to be part of the documentation that accompanies a large program, and, secondly, what steps can be taken to ensure the code produced for the program is intelligible.

   (O & C)

8. (a) (i) A number of high level programming languages have been standardised. Explain why it has been considered desirable to do this.

   (ii) Account for the fact that there are no similar standards for assembly languages.

   (b) Every program package should be fully documented to help the user and also to enable program updating and maintenance to be carried out.

   (i) Why might updating and maintenance be necessary?

   (ii) Describe, giving examples where appropriate, the documentation which should be provided to enable updating and maintenance to be performed.

   (CU)

9. Compare assembly language and high level language in terms of speed of execution, ease of programming and program portability between machines.

   (AEB 1984)

10. A program written by a student has not worked correctly. The student is told that this is due to *typing errors* and *syntax errors*.

    (a) Explain these two types of errors, and discuss how they might have been avoided.

    (b) After these errors have been eliminated, the program is still unsuccessful. Describe the steps that the student must now take to complete the correction of the program.

    (c) Explain how errors other than those in the program could prevent correct results from being obtained.

    (Ox)

11. Name three different high level languages and for each state their main area of use. For any one of these languages give three reasons why it is considered suitable for its area of use.

    (WMEB (part))

4 Types of Software

THE IMPORTANCE OF SOFTWARE

It should be clear by now that a program is simply a set of instructions to the computer, and *software* is just the collective term for computer programs.

Software is essential to get a computer to do anything at all. The *hardware*, i.e. all the physical devices that can be parts of a computer system, would be completely lifeless without software to drive it. In any case, hardware has become so reliable and relatively cheap that it is no longer of prime importance. By the end of the 20th century, over 90% of computing expenditure will be on software.

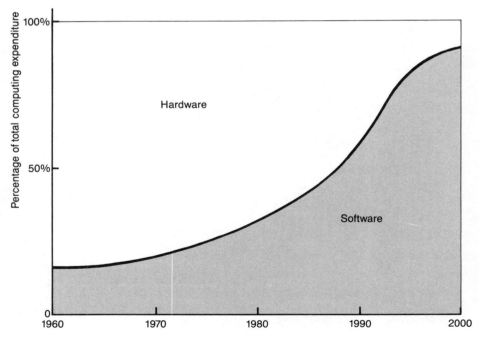

Fig. 4.1 The growing importance of software

Q 4.1 *Why are software costs not falling as fast as hardware costs?*

Anyone automating a system would be well advised to follow three rules:

- Think again. It may well be better to improve the manual system.
- If automation *is* advisable, first find the *software* to do the job.
- *Then* find the best hardware to run it.

Systems Software and Applications Software

Software can be divided into two categories. *Applications software* is directly *applied* to real-life activities, such as printing payslips or playing chess. However, before *any* applications program can be run all computer systems have to be fed with *systems software*, i.e. one or more *systems programs* that govern the operation of the computer.

Q 4.2 *Is a games program, i.e. the sort of thing you can buy in W. H. Smith or Boots, applications or systems software?*

SYSTEMS SOFTWARE

Operating Systems

An *operating system* is basically a program that supervises the running of all the other programs in a computer, which is why it is also called a *supervisor* or a *monitor*.

The simplest kind (such as may be found on many simple microcomputers) permits straightforward loading and running of programs. It acts as a sort of housekeeper, keeping everything (programs, data etc.) in its proper place, and managing the peripherals (cassette deck, disks etc.).

Q 4.3 *List all the peripherals which must be managed by a computer system at your school or college.*

Batch Processing

A more complex operating system controls *batch processing*. Programs are fed through the system like cars on a production line, and the system marshals programs and data for each *job* while keeping them all separate from each other.

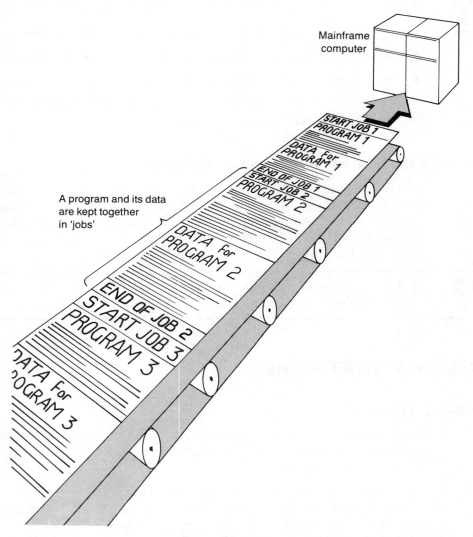

Mainframe computer

START JOB 1
PROGRAM 1

DATA For
PROGRAM 1

END OF JOB 1
START JOB 2
PROGRAM 2

A program and its data
are kept together
in 'jobs'

DATA For
PROGRAM 2

END OF JOB 2
START JOB 3
PROGRAM 3

DATA For
PROGRAM 3

Fig. 4.2 In batch processing, jobs are fed to the computer in a 'stream', like cars on a production line

Multiprogramming

A *multiprogramming* operating system is the next stage in complexity, allowing *several programs* to run at once. Multiprogramming is the norm on mainframes and minicomputers and is increasingly found on more powerful microcomputers.

  Q 4.4   *Can you think of any multiprogramming applications?*

Larger Operating Systems

On large systems many disk or tape drives, screens and printers may be attached at one time. The software must control input and output to and from all these devices. It can even direct the human operators by messages on a screen or printer, e.g. 'Mount disk number PL01 on drive number 5' or 'Load 2-part paper into printer number 1'.

Mainframe operating systems, with strange names like MVS/XA and VME/B, provide many other features too involved to discuss here. But the costs are huge; these are gigantic programs with enormous appetites for storage. Furthermore, *any* large program tends to start its life riddled with bugs, despite intensive testing. One famous operating system was reported to have been released with *five thousand* bugs.

The Portability Problem

Worse still, most mainframe and minicomputer manufacturers have their own peculiar operating system, which prevents *portability*, i.e. the ability to run on one type of machine software which was bought for another. The position is better with microcomputers, with a few operating systems (such as one called MS-DOS) becoming fairly standard.

Q 4.5 *Find out how many different operating systems are used at your school or college. Are they compatible?*

Q 4.6 *Why will games programs bought for say, a Sinclair or an Amstrad machine not run on a different make?*

Programming Language Translators

As it is extremely difficult and laborious to write programs in machine code, *programming languages* (such as BASIC) are used instead. This creates the need for systems programs called *translators*, which translate the code which programmers write (the *source code*) into machine code, the *only* code which the computer can run directly. This translated code is known as *object code*.

If the program is written in *assembly language*, the translator (called an *assembler*) will have a relatively easy task, for assembly language is close to machine code. (See page 46.)

Fig. 4.3 Computers do not understand source code written in a high level language such as BASIC

High-level languages (being closer to English) present more complex translation problems. For instance, the translator software must check, as far as possible, that the programmer has not written such nonsense as:

LET X = Y + 'FRED' or
INPUT 999

Q 4.7 *What is wrong with the two statements above?*

Interpreters

There are two ways of translating high-level source code, *interpreting* and *compiling*. You have almost certainly used an *interpreter* (although you may not have realised it) for it is standard on most home and school microcomputers. The interpreter takes a single line of the source code, translates that line into object code and carries it out immediately. It then takes the next line of source code, translates that, and then carries out the instructions given. The process is repeated line by line until the whole program has been translated and run. If the program loops back to earlier statements, they will be translated afresh each time round.

This means that both the source program and the interpreter must remain in main memory together, which may limit the space available for data. Perhaps the biggest drawback of an interpreter is the time it takes to translate and run a program (given all the repetition which can be involved).

Compilers

When faster execution is needed, a *compiler* will often be used. This program translates the *whole program* before execution. This produces a self-contained *object code program*, which can then be run quite independently (and much faster than it would if interpreted).

Neither the compiler nor the source program needs to be in main storage during running, which frees considerable space for data.

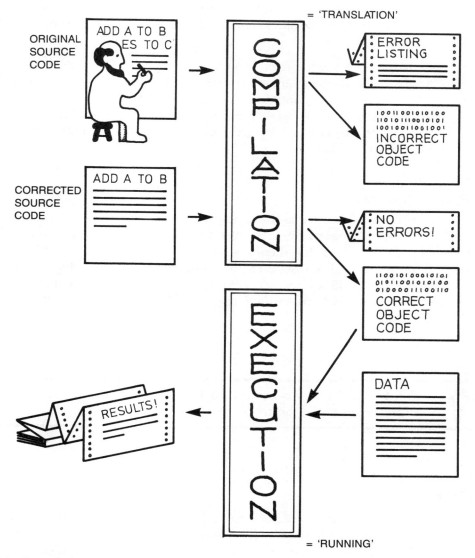

Fig. 4.4 Compilation and execution

Drawbacks of Compilers

As is the case so often with computing, the advantages of compilation are balanced by drawbacks. When an error is detected, during compilation or running, it is not immediately obvious where to find it because all the programmer's sensible names like 'number-of-items' or 'cumulative-total' have been translated into machine code. Therefore the compiler has to be able to show the programmer where (i.e. at which locations or addresses in memory) all the variables are kept. This can be helpful but takes up storage space. The compiler also outputs a list of diagnostic error messages which shows any syntax errors or use of words not allowed in the language. (Compilers cannot, of course, find logic or run-time errors; see Chapter 3).

However, a programmer wishing to correct errors or make any other changes to the program must always go back to the source code, change it, completely re-compile it and finally test the new object program. Changing just a single letter in a program necessitates full re-compilation. It is not surprising that errors often creep into programs during this laborious process.

Language Dialects

High-level languages have many *versions* or *dialects*, developed at different times or by different manufacturers or software houses. It has been estimated that there are over 100 000 versions of COBOL and, as you've probably discovered for yourself, there is a different version of BASIC for almost every machine. Fortunately, there are internationally accepted standards for languages, and most compilers accept standard code.

Q 4.8 *How many versions of BASIC have you come across? What problems does this cause?*

Utilities

Utility programs are used for jobs like sorting, copying, comparing, backing up and restoring files. You may well have run a disk-formatting utility program in order to organise the space on a blank disk before you used it.

APPLICATIONS SOFTWARE

As we have seen, systems software is essential before the computer system can do *anything*; then the *applications* programs actually do the job.

Fig. 4.5 Successive layers of *software* enable *people* to communicate with computer *hardware*

The variety of applications in existence is staggering; one program controls stock in a do-it-yourself store, another transfers a million pounds from a Swiss bank, while a less glamorous program calculates pension contributions for the same company. A fourth is guiding someone through an adventure in a maze of subterranean caverns, while a fifth is rapidly comparing the real terrain beneath a missile with a map stored in its memory. Yet another is teaching a would-be secretary to touch type.

?   **Q 4.9** *Think of six more applications you have encountered.*

Packaged Software

Many applications programs are designed to meet needs which thousands of people share. As a result, software developers may group several programs together (often with a printed manual) in a *package* in order to sell it to these potential users. A *payroll package* is one of the most common examples; others will be found in Chapter 9.

General purpose packages, such as *word processing* programs, are among the most commonly used software in the world. How these programs are used in practice will be examined in detail later.

Packaged versus Custom-built Software

Packages are nearly always cheaper and more reliable than custom-built applications software; the time and expense of designing and building reliable software from scratch by traditional methods is often prohibitive. Computer users therefore often compromise and install a package which may not *exactly* meet all their requirements. There is increasing use of *program generators* in an effort to reduce the cost of applications development yet still enable 'tailor-made' programs. The user (who need not be a skilled programmer) conducts a dialogue with the system about the type of information or processing he or she requires; the package then automatically generates programs to fulfil his or her needs.

Distributing Software

Software is sold in many different forms. A large operating system may be delivered on magnetic tape or disk. The systems software for most home computers is permanently stored in ROM, so that it is always ready to work when the machine is switched on. This is often called *firmware*, as it is software built into the hardware and therefore cannot be changed.

Language interpreters for microcomputers may be built-in as ROM (e.g. BBC BASIC) or supplied on floppy disk (e.g. disk BASIC on the IBM Personal Computer).

Similarly, applications software may be stored on disk, cassette, tape or plug-in ROM, or may be simply written down on paper.

Q 4.10 *Describe two advantages of each of ROM or floppy disk for storing language interpreters.*

Q 4.11 *Do the sample programs printed in a user manual count as software?*

You may have successfully received software from radio or television programmes. Each scrap of code transmitted is racing through space at the speed of light. Faint signals of those first computer software broadcasts should be reaching the nearest stars by now.

JARGON 4

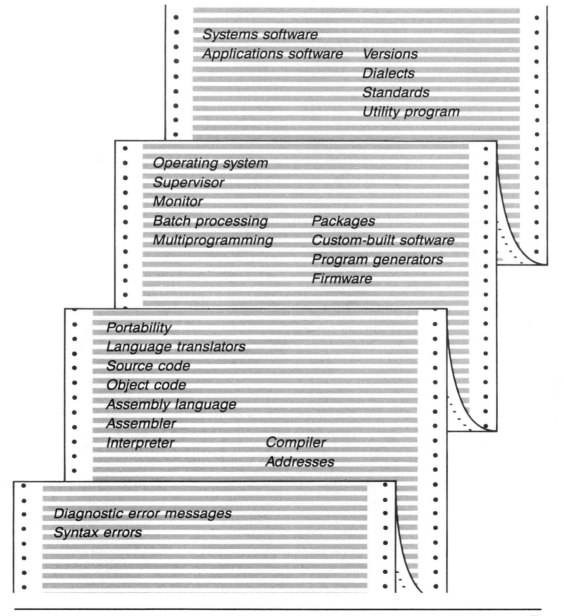

Systems software
Applications software   Versions
                         Dialects
                         Standards
                         Utility program

Operating system
Supervisor
Monitor
Batch processing   Packages
Multiprogramming   Custom-built software
                        Program generators
                        Firmware

Portability
Language translators
Source code
Object code
Assembly language
Assembler
Interpreter   Compiler
                        Addresses

Diagnostic error messages
Syntax errors

EXERCISES 4

1. (a) Explain why a large modern computer is likely to have an operating system.

   (b) Describe the various facilities which you would expect an operating system to provide.

   (CU)

2. (i) Describe the purpose of a compiler.

   (ii) How is it possible for programs written in a high level language such as FORTRAN to be run on a variety of different computers?

   (CU (part))

3. (a) What is a compiler?

   (b) Give two examples of different errors in a program which a compiler would be able to find, and explain why.

   (c) Give one example of an error which a compiler would not be able to find. Explain:

   (i) why this is so;

   (ii) how you would find this error.

   (Ox)

4. (i) Briefly explain the terms Package Program and Compilation.

   (ii) What extra documentation will a package require that would not be relevant for a specially written program?

   (iii) What are the advantages when a package program, containing a variety of alternative options, is made available in the *uncompiled* state?

   (WMEB (part))

5. (a) (i) Briefly describe the tasks carried out by a compiler.
       (ii) Give examples of two program errors which a compiler could be expected to identify, and two program errors which a compiler could *not* be expected to identify.

   (b) (i) Describe the ways in which an interpreter differs from a compiler.
       (ii) Give one advantage and one disadvantage of using an interpreter rather than a compiler.
       (iii) Describe circumstances in which it would be preferable to run a program using an interpreter rather than a compiler.

   (CU)

6. (*a*) Explain the terms
      (i) source code,
      (ii) object code and
      (iii) diagnostic error message.

   (*b*) Compare the use of an interpreter and a compiler for
      (i) the development and
      (ii) the regular running of high level language programs.

   (*c*) State one advantage and one disadvantage of using a language which allows the use of long variable names.

   (*d*) State one reason why the source code might need to be processed more than once during the translation process.

   (LU)

7. (*a*) What name is given to the piece of software which converts, say, a COBOL program into machine code?

   (*b*) (i) Give one example of a program error which such a piece of software would be able to find.
      (ii) Explain why it would be able to find it.

   (*c*) (i) Give one example of a program error which such a piece of software would not be able to find.
      (ii) Explain why it would not be able to find it.
      (iii) Explain how such an error could be found.

   (*d*) Why would such a piece of software written for one machine be unlikely to work on a different make of machine?

   (*e*) A small computer has a main store but no backing store and its only peripherals are a tape reader and a printer.

   A program is to be run on this computer and the following tapes will be used:

      The source program tape.
      The tape containing the software mentioned in (*a*).
      The data tape.

      (i) In which order will the tapes be used?
      (ii) At which stages during processing might an error report be printed?
      (iii) How might the process of running the program have been different if the computer had a backing store?

   (WMEB)

5 Input

ON-LINE AND OFF-LINE

Anyone who has used a home computer will recognise the enormous value of having a keyboard built into the computer and a VDU connected to it. Most business machines are built in a similar way; the keyboard and monitor are either an integral part of the microcomputer or are wired directly to it. Whatever the arrangement, the keyboard and other peripheral devices are said to be *on-line* if they are in direct communication with the computer.

Q 5.1 *Some of the more sophisticated office machines now use an infra-red keyboard-to-computer link that works rather like a TV remote control.*

Is such a link on-line or not? Why is it preferable to a cable?

Larger, mainframe computers will handle data collected from a variety of sources. Some mainframe users will have on-line terminals and so will benefit from the same ease of communication enjoyed by the lone user of a microcomputer. Indeed, for some commercial and industrial jobs (such as ticket sales or controlling fluid flow in a chemical process) an on-line connection would be essential.

Often it is either too expensive or simply not possible to establish a permanent link with the computer. Special arrangements are then made for *off-line* use of the computing facilities. Data *captured* (i.e. collected) off-line must be stored locally in some way and later transmitted over a telephone line or physically transported to the computer centre to be input as a job lot.

Q 5.2 *What uses of a computer (a) must be on-line (b) could be off-line?*

KEYBOARDS

Most data that is fed to a computer arrives there through a *keyboard* either directly (if there is an on-line link) or via tapes and disks (if the keyboard is off-line). Usually, the keyboard is the QWERTY type (so called because of the lay-out of the first six keys in the top row of letters) established as the standard for mechanical typewriters in the late 19th century.

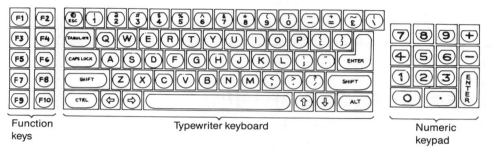

```
Function          Typewriter keyboard          Numeric
keys                                            keypad
```

Fig. 5.1   A typical computer keyboard

Q 5.3   *Is the layout of keys on the QWERTY keyboard efficient? Why has it not been replaced by something better?*

Verification and Validation

In the course of a working day the men and women involved in *data preparation* (i.e. keying the data into the computer) are bound to make mistakes somewhere. Indeed, the excuse 'computer error' is more often than not a cover for the mistakes made by the human operators. Remember: garbage in . . . garbage out.

But, as in other walks of life, human error is inevitable. Even the most highly competent keyboard operator *transcribing* (copying) data from a *source document* will mistype two or three characters in every thousand. This is far too high an error rate for computer work. In any serious application, data input through a keyboard must be checked or *verified*. This usually involves someone else retyping the same data a second time so that the first and second versions may be compared by the machine. The discrepancies will be brought to the attention of the operator (perhaps by an audible 'beep'), who will decide which version is correct.

Note the difference between *data verification*—a clerical procedure to double check that data is correctly typed into the computer—and *data validation*. The latter is a software routine built in to a program to ensure that, once the data is entered, it is, for example, within a given range or of the correct type (e.g. not a letter instead of a number).

Q 5.4 *Why is it better for a second keyboard operator to carry out the verification of a set of data?*

Q 5.5 *When inputting a set of numbers, a keyboard operator mistakenly types the letter O instead of the number zero. The computer automatically rejects the error. Is this verification or validation?*

OTHER METHODS OF INPUT

The keyboard is not the only means of communicating with a microcomputer, although it is the most important one. However, accurate typing is a considerable skill that takes a lot of time and effort to acquire; as microcomputers are becoming ever more widespread, so more and more non-typists are using them, both at home and at work, and interest in alternatives is growing rapidly.

Common Input Options

Most home users regularly input pre-recorded programs from tape or floppy disk, because of the popularity of computer games; *joysticks* and *track-balls* have become widespread, too. Many businesses use a *hard disk* system, and some incorporate specialist software by adding extra ROM to their machines, either by inserting extra microchips into the circuitry inside the computer or by plugging special ROM *cartridges* into the back.

Engineers who use computers to aid their designs have, for some time, used special *light pens* to 'draw' lines on to the VDU screen or select particular program options.

Q 5.6 *Microchips are very cheap, but plug-in ROM cartridges tend to be expensive. Why?*

Q 5.7 *Some producers of commercial software that could be sold wholly on a tape or disk instead ensure that the program only works if an expensive cartridge, known colloquially as a* dongle, *is plugged into the computer. Why?*

The *mouse* is used to move the cursor around the screen and select options from a given menu. It is an alternative to a touch sensitive screen. Both are becoming popular with business users.

Light pens are the basis of many library and supermarket systems. They are also important in computer-aided design.

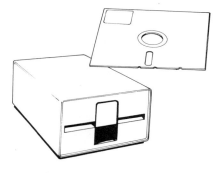

Disk systems have become commonplace in business; they are much faster than tape but more expensive.

Track-balls, like joysticks, have been adapted from their original use in aviation to control movement in computer games.

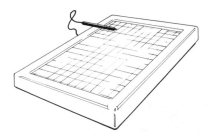

Graphics tablets are used to transmit hand-drawn designs directly to the computer. The designs can then be stored in digital form on tape or disk.

Fig. 5.2   Various input methods

Cassette tapes are a standard companion to the home computer. The slow rate of input to the computer is not crucial to a noncommercial user.

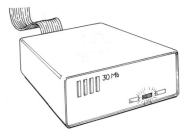

Winchester sealed *hard disk drives* are now common for business microcomputer systems

Joysticks, used to control aircraft, have been adapted to control movement on the screen in computer games. The extra speed and ease of use have made them a popular addition to the home computer.

ROM cartridges and *chips* are sometimes called *firmware*, as they contain nonerasable software and, once plugged in, become part of the hardware.

Their main advantage is that the software they enclose becomes part of the computing system and does not have to be specially loaded.

A cartridge that plugs into the computer through an outside port is often referred to as a *dongle*.

Fig. 5.2 (continued)

The Mouse

Other ways around the keyboard are popular in business computing. One of these is familiarly known as the *mouse*. It is simply a mobile switch that controls the movement of a pointer (called the *cursor*) around the VDU screen. A ball-bearing underneath the mouse transmits the directions of any movement to the computer which manoeuvres the cursor accordingly. So you place the mouse anywhere on the desk top and when you move it to the left the cursor moves left; move the mouse towards you and the cursor moves down the screen, and so on.

The cursor, under mouse control, is used to pin-point one of the various options displayed on the screen. This option can then be selected by pressing a button on the mouse.

The user moves the cursor (arrow) around the screen by moving the mouse on the desk top. When the cursor points to the required option, the user presses the button on the mouse.

Fig. 5.3   The mouse

Touch Sensitive Screens

On some machines, a criss-cross of light beams is arranged around the front of the VDU. These will detect the position of a finger pointing at the VDU and so give the impression of a *touch sensitive screen*.

Like the mouse, the touch sensitive screen allows the operator to choose from the *menu* of options displayed.

As the hardware is more elaborate, it is likely that a touch sensitive screen will be more expensive than a mouse; but, obviously, it is extremely easy to operate and, unlike the mouse, does not require empty desk space.

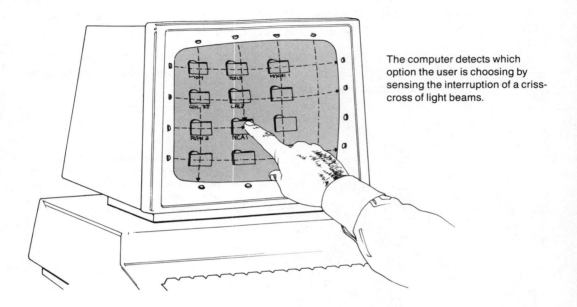

The computer detects which option the user is choosing by sensing the interruption of a crisscross of light beams.

Fig. 5.4 A touch sensitive screen

Graphics Tablets

Graphics tablets—sort of electronic drawing boards—allow pen drawn lines and shapes to appear directly on screen. The user simply draws a diagram on to the horizontal surface of the tablet using the special pen provided. A ruler, compasses and other geometric instruments can be used just as in drawing onto paper.

Such tablets are invaluable in *computer-aided design* (CAD). Normal programming methods (for example, using MOVE, DRAW and PLOT commands) are impossibly time-consuming and tedious for commercial graphics or engineering design purposes. Of course, it is possible to use a light pen to 'draw' on the VDU screen; however a tablet is often preferable since the surface is horizontal and the artist or draughtsman can draw onto it almost as if it were an ordinary piece of paper.

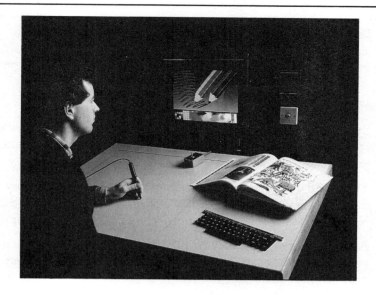

Fig. 5.5   Artist using a graphics tablet with the 'Paintbox' system

Touch Tablets

Tablets can also be used to diplay a *menu* of possible options that the user can pick by pressing on the pad at the appropriate position. Such a pad has all the advantages of a touch sensitive screen but avoids the expense. It also avoids the rather fiddly nature of the mouse.

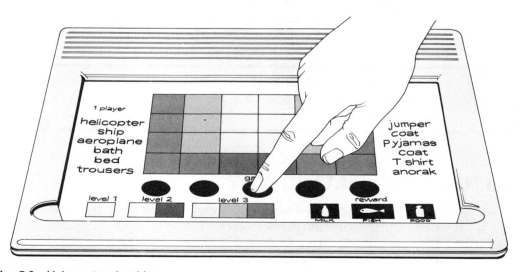

Fig. 5.6   Using a touch tablet

Q 5.8 *Is it likely that such developments as the mouse, the touch sensitive screen, and the touch tablet will replace the keyboard altogether?*

Voice Data Entry

Synthesised voice and music *output* is now fairly well established. But spoken input or *voice data entry* (VDE) is still in its infancy, although, when it reaches maturity, VDE will transform data entry.

There will be enormous advantages to computers that obey spoken commands. The user will be free to do other things, besides use the computer. Keyboard skills will not be needed and input will be rapid.

And, as everyone's 'voice-print' is different, the machine might be protected by an automatic security device that could recognise and respond only to its owner.

There are still considerable technical problems to be overcome. But the first 'voice typewriters' have already been produced and a new generation of computers is emerging.

The computer's vocabulary

At the moment, a computer can only recognise a very limited vocabulary which it 'learns' when the operator, prompted by the VDU, speaks the given words into a microphone attached to the machine. Even this much is useful in any situation where a few command words are likely to be used over and over again. Prototypes have been attached to motorised invalid chairs, for example, and the disabled occupant can order his chair to 'go right', 'stop' etc. without necessarily having much co-ordination of his own.

Q 5.9 *Would computerisation and VDE enable a disabled person to control a motorised wheelchair if the disability interfered with his or her speech?*

AUTOMATED DATA ENTRY

Whenever a human being and a computer *interact*, i.e. they pass instructions and information between each other and respond immediately as if in conversation, then a keyboard, a mouse, or a touch sensitive screen is essential. However, much routine information can be input to the computer with the minimum of human involvement. The computer operators need know nothing of computing nor of the significance of the information being processed. The operator just follows preset procedures such as passing a light pen across a bar code or stacking cheques into an automatic reader. Not only are these procedures very fast, they also eliminate the need to transcribe and verify data, so that the chance of error is very considerably reduced.

Bar Codes

Bar codes have become commonplace. Most grocery items, from cans of coke to soap packets, are now coded in this way. So too are many other retail items that are sold in appropriate packages. Increasingly, books are carrying bar-coded versions of their International Standard Book Numbers (ISBN) on the back covers, and many libraries have adopted their own bar code systems for controlling their stocks.

This bar code is taken from a packet of breakfast cereal (*courtesy* Kelloggs). The digits represented by the bar code are printed underneath. This number is the *European Article Number* or EAN. There are thirteen digits in the number broken up as follows. The first two digits (50) represent the country of origin (in this case the UK). The next five digits (00127) represent the manufacturer (Kelloggs) and the next five are used by the manufacturer to identify the product (06209—Bran Flakes). The last digit is a check digit.

Fig. 5.7   A bar code

Bar codes can be printed in any dark colour using normal printing methods and inks. So, once the code is established, it costs nothing to include it as part of ordinary packaging or on the back of a book.

The codes are read with a special *laser scanner* or with a *light pen* (also called a *wand*). These are sensitive to the amount of light reflected from the dark and light parts of the code (white reflects most of the light that falls on it and black almost none). The presence or absence of reflected light is translated by the scanner into electrical pulses of high or low voltage corresponding to the binary digits 1 and 0.

Every bar code carries a *check digit* at the end (see Chapter 11) as well as a 'start' and 'stop' section. The computer can therefore indicate to the operator, with an audible tone or warning light, whether or not the code has been properly read.

Using bar codes

Bar codes are ideal for coding simple product and stock numbers. Suppose a member of a library is taking out a book. The librarian simply scans the bar code on the borrower's ticket and then the code on the book.

The library's records (of the borrower currently holding each book, the date when return is due etc.) are then automatically adjusted by the computer. The librarian still date stamps the book, although this is only for the borrower's convenience. The library's own administration is complete once the bar codes have been read.

The operator is normally assured that the code has been properly read by an audible *beep*.

If the first attempt at reading the code is unsuccessful, the operator merely passes the pen over the bar code a second time.

Fig. 5.8   Using a light pen to read a bar code

Point of sale terminals

Shops using this system usually link the scanner to a computerised till (or build it in). The till will automatically look up the price of the item in the computer files and display it as if the till had been 'rung up' in the usual way; it will then print details of the purchase on the customer's bill and calculate the total spent. The advantages, in improved speed and accuracy, are considerable, both to the shop and to the customers, and despite the high cost of these *point of sale* (POS) *terminals*, many retailers have invested in them.

Q 5.10   *Look closely at the bar codes on the grocery packets in your larder at home. Can you identify some that are not British?*

What are the 'start' and 'stop' codes?

Q 5.11   *What sort of retail items would it not be appropriate to bar-code?*

Optical Character Recognition (OCR)

The advantages of holding data in a form that can be read by both man and machine are obviously considerable. Virtually all formal documents are already typewritten or printed so that they may be read more easily by the human beings, e.g. customer, employee or accountant, to whom

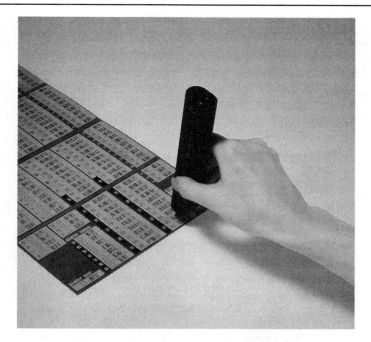

Fig. 5.9 This sheet of bar codes enables the user of a video recorder to program the machine with ease

they are relevant. If these documents could be fed to the computer without retyping them, then a lot of secretarial time would be saved and a potential source of error would be eliminated.

Originally, *optical character recognition* or OCR was possible only with a small number of specially designed typefaces, like that shown in Figure 5.10. However, OCR has such important potential that much money and research time has been spent developing systems that can recognise different letters typed on ordinary typewriters and printers with conventional but clear, high-quality typefaces.

ABCDEFGHIJKLM

OPQRSTUVWXYZ

0123456789

Fig. 5.10 An early OCR typeface

A typical OCR scanner might read 15 complete documents per second, but reading speeds vary considerably, depending on the document size and the number of characters and different typefaces the machine is expected to recognise.

OCR document readers are also expensive. However, OCR scanners are appearing on the market at prices that will make them a feasible option for smaller businesses.

Fig. 5.11 An OCR scanner reading a typewritten page

Turnaround documents

Many organisations use OCR as part of their computerised billing systems. For example, both the Gas and Electricity Boards prepare and address their bills by computer. The customer receives the bill and, in due course, sends it back with a cheque. This may be done directly at the local gas or electricity showroom, by post, or through the banking system. Whichever way is chosen, the original bill, as printed by the Board's computer, is returned to the people who sent it. The bill is said to be a *turnaround document*.

The bill is then read by the OCR scanner, so that the computer may register payment and clear the customer's account.

Notice that, once the meter has been read, human involvement in the billing procedure is minimal. Above all, there is no typing and retyping of figures and so there is no question of random typing errors 'bugging' the system and upsetting customers.

Insurance companies, the Giro Bank and many other commercial organisations use OCR in much the same way. OCR has become one of the most important and widespread methods of data input.

For this reason there has been a great deal of research and development in OCR technology in the past decade. Now it is possible to machine-read not only the special OCR characters but also a variety of standard typefaces. Some machines can even read neat handwritten lettering.

Q 5.12 *What major use would the Post Office have for OCR devices that could read handwriting?*

Q 5.13 *Write out ten times in your usual handwriting "Cheltenham GL53 0DN". Look closely at the various versions and circle the differences between them. (Be honest.) Now compare your versions with a friend's.*

What are the implications of all this for OCR?

Optical Mark Recognition (OMR)

Although the variation of handwriting styles is so enormous (too enormous for machines to read, at least in the immediate future), it is a relatively simple matter for hand-made *marks* to be read automatically.

The examination candidate's answers—A C B E B B D E—to the eight questions are indicated by the pencil marks, as shown. These marks are read by the OMR scanner so that the computer can compare them with the correct mark pattern and award a score.

Qn \ Ans	A	B	C	D	E
1.	(■)	( )	( )	( )	( )
2.	( )	( )	(■)	( )	( )
3.	( )	(■)	( )	( )	( )
4.	( )	( )	( )	( )	(■)
5.	( )	(■)	( )	( )	( )
6.	( )	(■)	( )	( )	( )
7.	( )	( )	( )	(■)	( )
8.	( )	( )	( )	( )	(■)

Fig. 5.12   A multiple choice answer sheet: an example of optical mark recognition (OMR)

Mark sense cards

The marks are made in predetermined positions on a specially designed *mark sense card*. The card can then be read automatically on an *optical mark reader*, a scanning device similar to an OCR scanner but simpler, since it has to recognise only the positions of the marks and not recognise a large number of characters.

Ink marks are acceptable to most scanners if the marks are firmly made and dark enough. Soft pencil marks are usual, however, as these are not likely to be missed by the machine. Some older machines will *only* accept pencil marks, since they do not work optically but depend on the conductivity of graphite pencil marks instead. The card itself is usually printed in a light coloured ink, often pink or blue, called the *drop out ink* because it is not visible to the automatic reader.

Using OMR

OMR is ideal for processing large quantities of simple, repetitive data such as students' answers to a multiple-choice examination, electricity or gas meter readings, orders taken over a range of stock, or answers to market research questionnaires. In all these applications, retyping the information in order to put it into the computer would be a lengthy, tedious and inaccurate process. As with other automatic methods the main advantage of OMR is that it eliminates altogether the need to transcribe data.

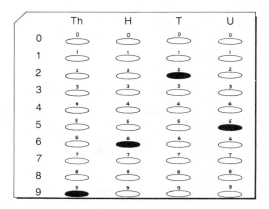

Fig. 5.13   A meter reader's record card

Furthermore, OMR documents can be easily and quickly filled in by almost anyone, although completed documents, covered in soft pencil marks, must be treated with care because smudged or dirty documents will be rejected by the automatic reader.

As the OM scanner must read a whole document at a time, the processing of mark sense cards can be rather slow by computing standards—typically three or four A4 documents per second. For this reason, data is often transferred to tape or disk first and only then input to the computer.

> **?** **Q 5.14** *Would you object if someone retyped your answers (and those of thousands of others) to an important multiple-choice examination before they were marked?*

Magnetic Ink Character Recognition (MICR)

The main clearing banks of the United Kingdom have been processing cheques automatically for some years. In 1966 they agreed to a common system by which each cheque would be coded for identification in magnetic ink, and would be sorted using machines capable of *magnetic ink character recognition* (MICR).

Along the bottom of any cheque there are three codes: the cheque number, the bank's number and the customer's number. These numbers are written in a highly distinctive style that can be read by a machine.

Fig. 5.14   E13B: the MICR character set used by the banks in the UK and the USA

Once the cheque has been used and then presented back to the bank a fourth code, representing the amount to be paid, is added using a special keyboard machine. Once this is done, the details of the cheque can be input to the computer.

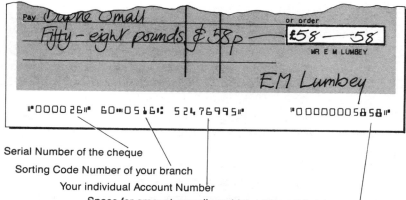

Serial Number of the cheque

Sorting Code Number of your branch

Your individual Account Number

Space for amount encoding which will be added when the cheque is paid in

Fig. 5.15   MICR coding on a bank cheque

The document reader

An MICR document reader can process some 40 cheques per second. Besides this great speed, MICR is also important to a bank in that magnetic characters on a cheque can be read despite being written over (whether by an innocent, flowery signature or in an attempt at fraud). Furthermore, a cheque could well be folded for posting, it might change hands several times and receive all sorts of rough treatment that would upset an optical reader but not a magnetic one.

Fig. 5.16 CMC7: the MICR character set used by Continental banks and by the British Post Office on its postal orders includes letters as well as numbers

MICR is expensive. The printing on the cheques must be of the highest possible quality, even higher than that required for optical character recognition. The readers, too, are very costly.

However, MICR has been an outstanding success. Without it the banks would simply not be able to handle as many cheques and transactions as they do and their customers would have to check their accounts carefully and regularly for the inevitable clerical errors.

 Q 5.15 *Why is the use of MICR almost entirely confined to the banks?*

Magnetic Strip Codes

Banks also make widespread use of *magnetic strip codes*. These magnetically read bar codes are embedded into the plastic of every cash card and credit card. When a customer wishes to use one of the banks' 24-hour automatic service tills, he or she feeds his card into the machine, which recognises the account number from the magnetic strips. To prove he is the legitimate card holder, the customer keys in his *personal identification number* (PIN), known only to him and the bank, and then uses the till.

Some retailers have experimented with magnetic bar codes rather than optically read ones. However, as the available technology has improved, so it has become clear that optical systems are cheaper and perfectly reliable for shop-keeping purposes. Optically read codes, though, could

The front of the bank card has embossed lettering that is readable by human beings and which allows details to be carbon copied rapidly using a simple mechanical device.

The reverse side of the card carries a magnetic strip code embedded in the plastic, as part of the black strips at the top. This makes the card machine-readable in a way that is not easily tampered with.

Fig. 5.17 Coding on a bank cash card

be altered or copied too easily for use on bank cards and obviously banks must do all they can to ensure that their systems are secure.

Magnetic strip codes are becoming immensely important. More and more retail transactions are credit-based, and stores are becoming equipped to read credit cards in much the same way as bank service tills do now.

Automatic Payment

In the near future, the magnetic card will form the basis for many day-to-day transactions which will be paid for automatically without the need for any human involvement other than, of course, the purchaser himself. For example, it is already possible to buy petrol late at night at some unattended petrol stations using an ordinary credit card and a specially automated pump.

Fig. 5.18 Using a British Telecom Phonecard

It is also possible to buy rail tickets in much the same way at main railway stations.

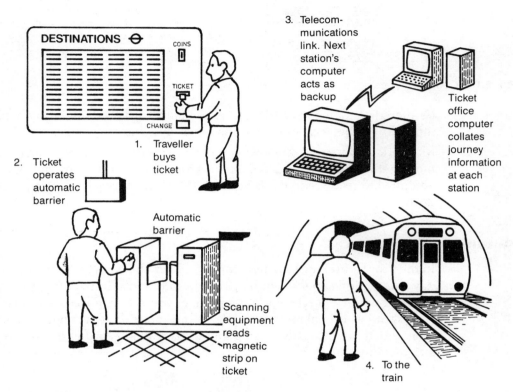

Fig. 5.19 Magnetic card input on the London Underground

Cardphones

British Telecom has operated a number of *Cardphones* since 1982. Credit card holders can pay for their calls from these specially adapted public telephones in much the same way as they can pay at the 'PINpoint' petrol pump. They first insert their card and then type in the PIN number and make the call; the cost is automatically charged to the credit card account.

However, another alternative method of payment is of some significance. British Telecom also sell special *Phonecards* (Fig. 5.18) that can be used in the *Cardphone* instead of a credit card. These plastic cards can be bought at most Post Offices for £1, £2, £4, £10 or £20 and are magnetically encoded with the appropriate number of telephone charge units. A special display on the *Cardphone* indicates the number of units left on the card when it is first inserted and progressively deducts them as the caller's telephone charges accumulate. When the call is finished, the card is automatically ejected so that the remaining unused units may be used at a later date.

Q 5.16 *(a) What information is encoded on the Phonecard?*

(b) As the card is inserted, what information is relayed to the Cardphone?

(c) Why does the user of the Phonecard not need to type in his PIN as he would if he were using a cash-dispenser?

(d) What happens to the card before it is returned?

Q 5.17 *What are the advantages of the Cardphone system*

(a) to British Telecom
(b) to the customer?

Q 5.18 *What other day-to-day transactions might be paid for by magnetically encoded prepayment cards like the Phonecard introduced by British Telecom?*

Identity Documents

Because it is difficult to tamper with, magnetic encoding is certain to become an important feature of identity documents. For example, a magnetic strip is included on the new European Community passports and some football clubs have been considering the use of magnetic-card based identity systems to exclude undesirables from matches. In 1983, the UK government began issuing National Insurance numbers on machine-readable plastic cards (you may well have just been issued with yours) although, at the moment, there is no network of machines with which to read them.

Q 5.19 *When the government introduced machine-readable National Insurance cards it provoked a considerable controversy.*

What do you think was the main fear of the critics?

Q 5.20 *What practical difficulties have faced those football clubs that have tried to introduce a computerised, magnetic card identity system?*

Why have they issued their own cards and not tried to base their identity systems on the new National Insurance card?

Q 5.21 *What advantages will a magnetic strip code on European passports give to the police and immigration authorities?*

OFF-LINE INPUT

Punched Cards

In the early days of computing, punched cards and tapes were of much greater significance than they are now. Even so, card systems are still not uncommon since the original investment was necessarily large and many of the systems continue to work effectively.

The standard card (called the Hollerith card after Herman Hollerith, founder of IBM, whose initial success centred on the punched card) is divided into 12 rows and 80 columns. Each card represents up to 80 characters of input and each column carries the code, according to the holes punched, for just one character.

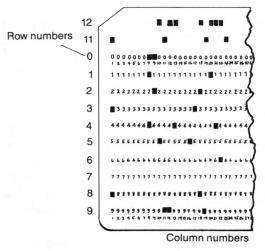

Rows 11 and 12, at the *top*, are (with row 0 sometimes included) called the *zone punch*. Holes punched here tell the computer to expect a letter or some other character.

Rows 0 to 9 are called the *numeric punch*. Holes punched here either represent the numbers themselves or form part of the code of a letter or other character.

In the card shown, the symbol £ (column 1) is represented by holes punched in rows 11, 3 and 8, the letter U (column 8) by holes in rows 0 and 4, and the number 5 (column 16) by a hole in row 5 only.

Notice the trimmed top left-hand corner that provides an at-a-glance check that the cards are all the same way up.

Fig. 5.20 An 80-column punched card

The key punch

The holes are punched on a special machine, a *key punch*, which is used rather like a typewriter. Usually, the key punch types the characters on the top of the card as well as punching the appropriate combination of holes.

The cards are then verified, either by passing them through the same machine switched to verification mode, or by passing through a second machine. Either way, the same data is retyped so that the machine can compare the second version with the first. Once checked, the cards are placed in a *card reader* which converts the punched holes into the equivalent electrical codes that the computer uses. Most card readers work photo-electrically. Light is shone on to the card, passes through wherever a hole has been punched and is detected by a light-sensitive cell on the other side which generates a small electric pulse. On each reading the cards are examined twice in this way and the input is accepted only if the two readings match.

Advantages and disadvantages

Clearly, these procedures are cumbersome and slow. Even though the cards can be read reasonably speedily, as many as 30 per second, punching and verifying is very time-consuming. Moreover, computer cards are bulky to store and sensitive to the environment (damp cards will stick together and cause problems in the card reader). They cannot be repunched with new information, although the greater part of the card will not have been utilised. The same card can be read over and over again, though, but it will eventually wear out.

On the other hand, cards are fairly cheap; they can be inserted, resorted or removed easily, so small errors are simply corrected; but, if you should drop a pack of computer cards . . .

Kimball Tags

The use of punched cards has dramatically declined in the recent past, but they remain important in one or two specialist areas. In particular, some retailers, especially clothes shops, have developed a semi-automatic system using small punched cards or tags, usually known as *Kimball tags*.

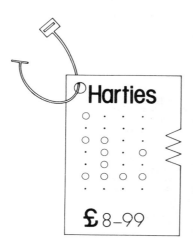

The holes encode a limited amount of information, the garment code and possibly the branch or the department of sale.

Fig. 5.21 A Kimball tag

The tags, necessarily made of stiff card since they are likely to be handled by the public, are punched at the computer centre with the garment's stock number. The price is also printed on each card, but this is only for the customer's convenience.

The tag is then physically attached to the garment (a shirt perhaps) which is then sent to the appropriate store as part of a consignment of new stock, all items of which have been tagged in the same way.

When the store sells the shirt, the assistant removes the tag and keeps it with all the others taken from the other items sold that day. At the end of the day's trading, the tags are sent, as one large batch, back to the computer centre where they are machine read. (Alternatively, the tags can be read by in-store terminals.) In this way, the head office can computerise stock records and trading receipts from a number of branches without investing in a great deal of hardware.

Q 5.22 *Punched cards are things of the past. Do you agree?*

Q 5.23 *Next time you buy something from Marks and Spencer or another large clothing chain, keep the customer's half of the Kimball tag for your computer studies file.*

In what other ways is the store using computing technology?

Paper Tape

In principle, the punching and reading of paper tape is exactly like punching and reading cards. However, paper tape is continuous (perhaps a hundred metres long or more and this offers a number of advantages.

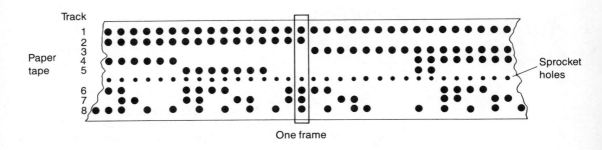

Fig. 5.22 Punched paper tape

Data items cannot be inadvertently placed out of sequence. On the other hand, any change requires a completely new tape and is not simply a matter of replacing one or two cards.

Magnetic Tape

Magnetic tape has almost completely replaced paper tape as an input method. Tapes are inexpensive, clean, readily transportable, reuseable and able to hold a great deal of information.

Of course, the tape itself must be handled carefully, as heat, dust or magnets could corrupt the recording. However, the advantages by far outweigh these objections.

Large installations use, as standard, half-inch tapes on reel-to-reel drives. The capacity of these tapes is huge. Each spool of tape may be 800 metres long and hold 40 or 50 million characters.

Information collected from other automated sources (for example, from a batch of mark sense cards) may be put on tape before it is input to the computer at great speeds.

Key-to-tape

Alternatively, data may be keyed to tape through a *magnetic tape encoder*. Verification of this *key-to-tape* input is essential and can be completed on the same machine switched to 'verification mode'. Once a mistake is detected, it is a simple matter for the encoder to substitute the correct version by simply *overwriting* i.e. by recording the new characters over the old.

Some *validation* of data is also possible at this stage, for the encoder includes a small microprocessor that will not accept, for example, a number in the middle of a list of names.

Disks

Plastic based *floppy disks* are a widespread method of data entry and storage on microcomputers. Larger, metal based *hard disks*, also called *Winchester disks*, are used with all minicomputers and mainframes as well as a growing proportion of microcomputers. Hard disks are even faster than reel-to-reel tape units, although floppies are slower. Information collected from a number of floppy disks may be transferred to reel-to-reel tape before input to the computer.

Apart from speed, there are other advantages of disk systems and many organisations use off-line *key-to-disk* as the primary method of data preparation. Several keyboards can write data to a single disk unit (each tape encoder can only write to its own tape). Also verification procedures are further simplified, since there is no tape to rewind.

Direct Sensors

Computers are also used extensively in the control of scientific and industrial processes. None of the *file-handling* input methods so far discussed is appropriate to such *process control*, as the computer must collect a rather different type of data, e.g. temperature, pressure, rate of flow of fluids etc., using an appropriate electrical *sensor*.

Such sensors are usually analog devices and their output must be translated into digital form by an *analog-to-digital* (A/D) *converter* before input to the computer.

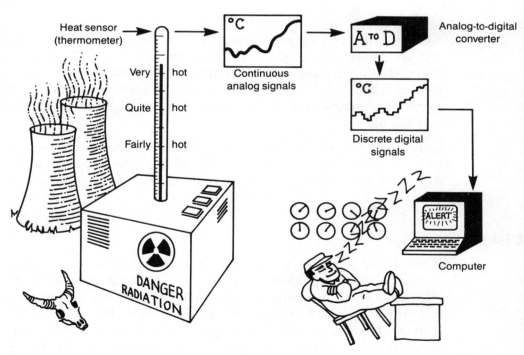

Fig. 5.23 Direct sensor input

For example, the temperature at the centre of a nuclear power generator must be carefully controlled; an electrical thermometer generates an electric current which rises and falls in strength according to the temperature. This current is converted to digital form and then input to the computer which can react almost instantaneously to any change.

JARGON 5

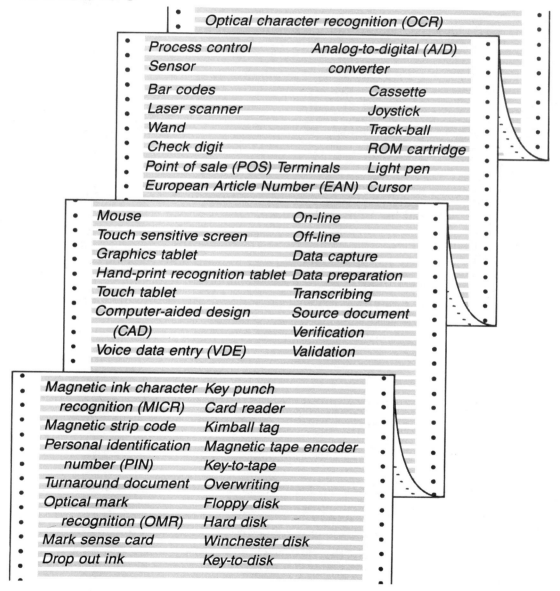

Optical character recognition (OCR)

Process control
Sensor

Analog-to-digital (A/D)
converter

Bar codes
Laser scanner
Wand
Check digit
Point of sale (POS) Terminals
European Article Number (EAN)

Cassette
Joystick
Track-ball
ROM cartridge
Light pen
Cursor

Mouse
Touch sensitive screen
Graphics tablet
Hand-print recognition tablet
Touch tablet
Computer-aided design
    (CAD)
Voice data entry (VDE)

On-line
Off-line
Data capture
Data preparation
Transcribing
Source document
Verification
Validation

Magnetic ink character
    recognition (MICR)
Magnetic strip code
Personal identification
    number (PIN)
Turnaround document
Optical mark
    recognition (OMR)
Mark sense card
Drop out ink

Key punch
Card reader
Kimball tag
Magnetic tape encoder
Key-to-tape
Overwriting
Floppy disk
Hard disk
Winchester disk
Key-to-disk

EXERCISES 5

1. Write down *four different* methods of inputting data into a computer. In *each* case state an application which would be suitable for the given method of input.

    (WJEC)

2. Describe the use and the advantages of
    (*a*) a mouse.
    (*b*) a joystick.
    (*c*) a touch sensitive screen.
    (*d*) a light pen.
    (*e*) a graphics tablet.
    (*f*) a track-ball.

3. What applications of voice data entry are in use today? What is the potential for VDE in the future?

4. Data may be input to a computer on card and paper tape.
    (*a*) Name three other methods of inputting data.
    (*b*) (i) Write two sentences describing one of the methods you have chosen.
    (ii) Give one reason for the development of this method.

    (SEREB)

5. (*a*) Verification is an expensive process. Why is it done?
    (*b*) Explain how verification is carried out when using punched cards.

    (LREB)

6. Explain the difference between *validation* and *verification* of data.

7. (*a*) What are magnetic ink characters?
    (*b*) Where might they be used?

    (EMREB)

8. MICR and OCR are methods of data input.

   (a) Give one advantage of using MICR rather than OCR.

   (b) Give one advantage of using OCR rather than MICR.

   (c) Give one disadvantage of *both* these methods of input.

   (d) State one application that uses MICR. Why is MICR used in this application?

   (e) State one application that uses OCR. Why is OCR used in this application?

   (LREB)

9. The examples below are all used to input data directly into a computer. Give an example of where each could be found.

(a)   (b)   (c)

   (SEREB)

10. (a) State one advantage and one disadvantage of OMR.

    (b) What is *drop-out ink*?

11. The figure below shows the bottom part of an ordinary cheque. What do the three code numbers mean?

    What fourth number will the bank later add to the cheque? Why is it necessary for them to do this?

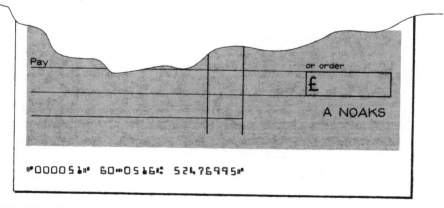

12. What is a *Kimball tag*? Who might have use of one? How is it used?

13. Data is input from the following media: *floppy disk, Winchester disk, reel-to-reel tape, cassette tape.* Place them in order of increasing speed.

14. (*a*) Explain what is meant by a turnaround document and describe the advantages of using such a document.
    (*b*) Describe a data processing system which uses turnaround documents. Pay particular attention to:
       (i) the data which appear on the turnaround documents, and the sources of the various data items;
       (ii) other data which are used or produced by the system;
       (iii) the hardware which is used for the output and input of the data on the turnaround documents.

    (CU)

15. The Government keeps National Insurance records on every adult in the UK. Individuals are identified by a unique National Insurance number, which is stored on a magnetic strip embedded in a plastic card.
    (*a*) How is the magnetic strip used?
    (*b*) What are the advantages to the Government?
    (*c*) Are there any dangers in storing this information in this way?

16. A large office block with a security problem has decided to invest in a computer controlled security system.

    Each entrance to an office will be fitted with an electronic door lock linked to the computer and at the side there will be an electronic card-reader with a numeric key pad (0–9). Every person entitled to use the building will be issued with a card similar to a bank 'cash point' card with a number encoded in it.
    (*a*)   (i) In what form is the number stored on the card?
          (ii) Explain why a numerical key pad is also required.
          (iii) What is the main function of the computer?
          (iv) Draw a block diagram to show the inter-connections between the computer and one door.
    (*b*) Explain how the system would work as an employee tried to use a door.

(c)   (i) If the computer is used to control many doors, how would a particular door be identified?

     (ii) Some of the employees will require access through many doors whilst the others' access will be limited to certain doors at certain times.

        Briefly describe how the computer could achieve this and indicate any additional information that it would require.

(WMEB)

6 Output

VISUAL DISPLAY UNIT

Some input devices, e.g. tapes, disks and cards, double up as output devices. They are known as *input/output* (I/O) devices. The most common I/O device, without which most computer systems could not properly function, is the *visual display unit* (VDU).

Although it is strictly an output device, the VDU has an important input role, for everything a user types into the computer appears on the screen. Without this immediate visual *echo* most people would find their input hopelessly full of errors.

Q 6.1 *Next time you use the computer turn off the monitor for a few lines of input. Then turn the monitor back on. How many typing mistakes did you make?*

Interactive Computing

Fast *interactive computing*, with the user and computer in instant communication with each other, is taken for granted today. It is only possible because of improvements in both hardware (so that immediately effective input and output is possible) and software (to control fast running programs).

Successful interactive home computing invariably depends on a good quality VDU. If the VDU is of poor quality, say a black and white, second-hand TV set, then the lack of quality will considerably detract from some of the uses to which the system might be put. This is most obvious in computer games where good graphics are usually essential. See Figure 6.1.

Professional microcomputer systems (and a good few home systems too) use a *monitor* rather than a television set. Monitors are slightly more expensive than TVs, but the image on the screen is a lot sharper. The computer output is directed to the VDU screen without passing through the aerial socket and system of the TV set.

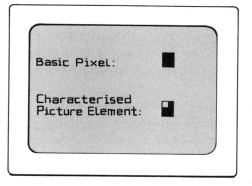

A computer builds up pictures on the screen by colouring in small rectangular *picture elements* or *pixels*.

The computer reserves an area of main memory for the screen display and so the more pixels that are involved, the more memory is used.

In *low resolution graphics* a small number of large pixels are used to give a rather poor picture. For example, a diagonal line across the screen looks more like a staircase. Low resolution graphics were common on the earlier home computers which had little RAM to spare.

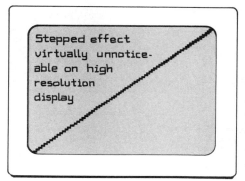

High resolution graphics, using a large number of small pixels to give a good picture, are possible only on machines with enough memory to cope both with the user's RAM requirement and the screen display.

Many machines (for example, the BBC) work in several different user-chosen *modes* which enable the programmer to decide the proportion of memory space the screen display can be allowed to absorb.

Fig. 6.1 High and low resolution graphics

Q 6.2 *Why is the sharper image of a monitor important to a professional computer system?*

Viewdata

Often a monitor screen is linked to the computer some distance away through ordinary telephone lines. (Old, slow and cumbersome *teletype* machines in which the computer output was literally typed out character by character are no longer used.)

Viewdata services, such as British Telecom's *Prestel* service, work in this way. Thus output from the same mainframe Prestel computer may appear simultaneously on screens up and down the UK.

The information conveyed may be of various kinds. It may be general information such as railway timetables or the cricket score, or information relevant only to an individual user who is perhaps arranging to book an airline or theatre ticket or is checking on his bank balance.

People who use it may have a special Prestel keypad that plugs into a socket on the telephone or an adaptor, which itself plugs into the telephone network to link their computer with the Prestel computer.

Fig. 6.2 Prestel

(Note: Do not confuse interactive viewdata systems like *Prestel* that involve computers with one-way broadcast Teletext services such as the BBC's *Ceefax* and ITV's *Oracle* that are only extensions of the TV network.)

PORTABLE SCREENS

VDUs (and printers) tend to be the bulkiest part of a computer system, making it difficult to move them from site to site. To some users this is of no consequence; it is possibly an advantage, for a heavy machine is less vulnerable to casual theft. However, many people such as sales-people, building surveyors etc. would benefit from a small lightweight portable microcomputer that could literally be carried in a briefcase.

?   **Q 6.3**   *Write down a list of three or four types of microcomputer user (a) for whom the bulk of the computer system (so long as it can sit on a desk or trolley) is of little importance and (b) for whom a lightweight readily transported machine would be of enormous value.*

Devising small printers that can be built into such portable machines was not such a problem to computer manufacturers but developing compact screens proved to be more difficult. As a consequence, the first computer systems advertised as miniaturised and transportable either lacked adequate screen displays or were rather too large to carry comfortably.

Fig 6.3   This portable microcomputer has as much processing power as some early mainframe computers

TV sets and monitors alike depend on the cathode ray tube for producing an image. Unfortunately the cathode ray tube is bulky. It can be scaled down, but only by reducing the size of the image and, obviously, there comes a point at which the detail on the screen, in particular the lettering, is too small to read comfortably.

?   **Q 6.4** *Why is a colour tube necessarily considerably bulkier than a black-and-white one?*

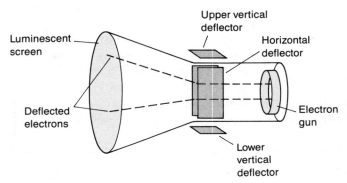

Upper vertical deflector

Luminescent screen

Horizontal deflector

Deflected electrons

Electron gun

Lower vertical deflector

The picture is formed by deflecting a stream of electrons up and down and left and right as they make their run-up to the screen.

    This requires substantial hardware behind the screen, giving the cathode ray tube its length and the VDU its depth.

Fig. 6.4   The cathode ray tube

LCD versus LEDs

Some manufacturers circumvented the problem by using a one-line *liquid crystal display* (LCD) or an arrangement of *light emitting diodes* (LEDs) to produce a microcomputer display rather like that on a calculator. The crystals that make up an LCD reflect light when a low-voltage current is applied to them; they are cheap and reliable but need a good light source to be read clearly. Light emitting diodes are rather like tiny light-bulbs; they take more current than LCDs but are their own light source. The red indicator light on a disk drive, for example, is usually an LED.

?   **Q 6.5** *Can you read your calculator and/or digital watch in the dark? Is the display an LCD or LED?*

     Q 6.6 *Why do the on/off lights and digital displays of mains-driven equipment (such as TV sets, hi-fi channel indicators and video recorder displays) tend to be LED whereas those of portable equipment (calculators, watches) tend to be LCDs?*

Flat Screens

One-line LCD or LED displays may be perfectly adequate for straightforward numerical problems of the type solved on a calculator; they are more than acceptable, too, on simple devices such as Texas Instruments' 'Speak 'n' Spell' (an educational toy) and help to keep the price down. However, they are not satisfactory for someone wishing to input a complex problem or review more than just a few lines of text.

For this reason much research and development has gone into the production of a *flat screen*, i.e. of the same length and breadth as an ordinary TV screen but, unlike the cathode ray tube, no more than a centimetre or two deep.

Fig. 6.5 This highly portable microcomputer incorporates disk drives and a plasma screen

Plasma screens that work on similar principles to fluorescent neon display signs are one solution. Large LCD or LED screens capable of displaying pages of text and graphs are another.

Fig. 6.6 Zenith portable microcomputer with full size, back lit LCD screen

Flat screens were an expensive option until the mid-1980s but now the main technnological and cost problems have been solved. Inexpensive, flat TV screens will soon be commonplace. Not only will the world of microcomputing benefit, but also the ordinary TV viewer, who will be able to hang the television set on the wall and use the sideboard space that it used to take for something else.

PRINTERS

Despite the advances of technology and the talk of 'the paperless office', human beings still seem to prefer to deal with much of their information on paper—*hard copy*—that they can read and write on, to sign and, if need be, to present to a court of law.

Although there are many advantages in storing information electronically, it seems that no computer system is complete without a printer to produce output on paper.

Q 6.7 *What are the advantages of preparing and storing information electronically? What are the disadvantages and why do people so often prefer to work on paper?*

Q 6.8 *List three documents of different types that need to be in a hard copy form. Give your reasons.*

Q 6.9 *What sort of information might be kept on a computer without ever being printed out?*

Interfacing Printer and Computer

The control unit (CU) of the computer directs the peripherals as well as its internal workings. If a particular peripheral is to run on a particular computer then it needs the correct *interface,* i.e. the appropriate hardware (sockets or *ports,* plugs, leads etc.) and operating software to compensate for the difference in the speed and codes of the computer and the peripheral device.

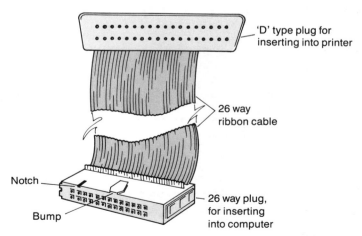

'D' type plug for inserting into printer

26 way ribbon cable

Notch

Bump

26 way plug, for inserting into computer

Fig. 6.7 Elaborate plugs and sockets, specially shaped to prevent them being plugged in upside down, back to front, or into a non-compatible system, link the computer to its printer

Printers are an important example of this, for there are several major printer standards all quite different from each other, e.g. Centronics parallel, RS232 serial, etc. and a number of minor ones peculiar to particular computer manufacturers. As a consequence, you cannot simply plug any printer into any computer, as you might the VDU.

It is possible to buy interfaces to enable a computer to communicate with a peripheral not built for it. For example, some manufacturers of electronic typewriters now market *interfaces* as in between devices that enable their typewriters to be driven by a computer as an inexpensive substitute for a printer.

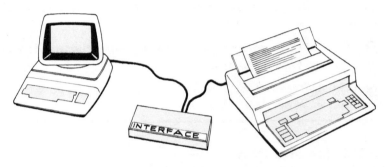

Fig. 6.8 Many computer hobbyists buy special interfaces which link an electronic typewriter to their computer as an alternative to buying a printer

Q 6.10 *The cost of an electronic typewriter with computer interface is similar to that of a printer. Why might someone prefer this arrangement to a proper printer?*

Q 6.11 *Why would an electronic typewriter linked to a computer not be adequate for professional use?*

Q 6.12 *Look in the manual of the computer you use (whether at home or at school or college) and find out which printer interface(s) it has.*

Why could you not plug in the lead for a different interface?

Four Problems

Because hard copy is so important a lot of attention has been given to the problem of producing computer output in printed form. Four basic but conflicting factors are involved:

- speed
- printing quality
- noise
- cost

Speed

Computers work at enormous speed and dramatically faster than most printers—even the good ones. So, during printing, a computer is idle for much of the time, simply waiting for the printer to catch up with it.

Because of the difference in the working speeds of the computer and the printer, output is usually stored, temporarily, in a *buffer*, a section of memory either in the CPU or in the printer, which the computer can fill in a fraction of a second and the printer can empty in its own good time.

While the buffer is being emptied, the computer can do little but wait, although as soon as there is room, it will send the next section of text, so refilling the buffer and so on until there is no text left. Better printers have their own control mechanisms and a buffer large enough to store whole documents, so that the computer is quickly freed to begin its next job.

Since computer printers work so quickly, *continuous* or *fanfold* paper is used much of the time.

The sprocket holes on the side are used to drive the paper through the *tractor feed* mechanism of the printer. Usually the paper is perforated so that the sprocket holes may be detached from the print-out and individual sheets separated from each other.

On some printers, the paper is driven through the machine between two rollers that press tightly against it—exactly like the system used on an ordinary typewriter. Such a *friction feed* is necessary to print into single sheets of ordinary paper.

Many printers offer both tractor and friction feed options.

Fig. 6.9 Continuous fanfold paper

Q 6.13 *Is it possible to pass fanfold paper through a friction-feed printer? What are the advantages of tractor feed?*

Q 6.14 *When might it be preferable to use single sheets of paper rather than continuous stationery?*

Printer speeds are usually measured in *characters per second*, abbreviated to cps, i.e. the number of characters, including spaces, punctuation marks and so on, printed in each second. Human typists' speeds are usually measured in words per minute; very fast printer speeds are sometimes given in *lines per minute* (lpm) or even in pages per minute.

?

Q 6.15 *If an average English word (including a space at the end) is five characters long, how fast, in characters per second, is a typing speed of 40 words per minute?*

Q 6.16 *How fast do you type? Time yourself next time you use a computer and work out your speed in characters per second.*

If there are 1600 characters on this page how long would it take you to type it all out?

How long would it take a computer-driven printer working at 100 cps?

Printing quality

Then there is the question of printing quality. A business using its computer as a word processor (see chapter 13) to assist it in preparing letters and reports to its customers requires print-out of *letter quality* i.e. output that looks as if it had been typed on an electric typewriter. Of course, someone using a printer at home or school for less formal purposes can make do with much lower standards.

Noise

Noise is also a problem. Human typists working at perhaps thirty or forty words per minute can make an office sound busy. Computer driven machines banging away at ten or twenty times that speed can make so much noise that to conduct other business, such as talking on the telephone, becomes impossible.

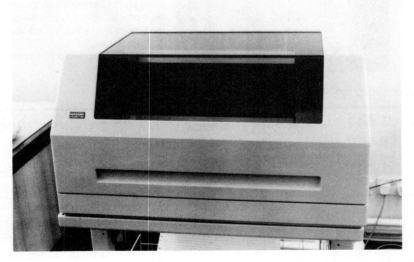

Fig. 6.10 An acoustic hood. In some offices the printer is enclosed in its own special housing to reduce noise

The problem is a real one and many offices place their printers in special cabinets to reduce the noise, although that makes using the printer just that little bit less convenient, especially if the machine is printing out single sheets which a secretary has to feed to it one at a time.

Cost

And then, as always, there is the problem of cost. Good printers are not cheap. A printer that works rapidly, yet quietly and produces good quality output could easily double the cost of a computer system.

? **Q 6.17** *Try to find out the price of the cheapest computer-printer on the market. Why is it so cheap? What are its disadvantages?*

What sort of printers might you buy for

(a) under £300   (b) under £500   (c) under £1000?

IMPACT PRINTERS

It is convenient to divide printers into two broad categories. *Impact printers* print on to a page by striking an inked ribbon and so form an impression on the paper behind it. An ordinary typewriter works in exactly this way.

Non-impact printers (as the name implies) form an impression on the paper in some other way. A photocopier, for example, is a non-impact device.

Dot-matrix Printers

Almost certainly your school or college will have a *dot-matrix printer*. Characters are formed by striking the ribbon not with fully formed characters, as on a typewriter, but with a rectangular array of dots.

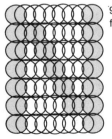

9 x 7 half-space matrix
forming the letter N

The output from a dot-matrix printer, whether a letter or a more elaborate picture, is formed from a series of small dots.
For many purposes this is adequate, but often a letter quality print-out is required.

Fig. 6.11 Dot-matrix output

Dot-matrix printers are relatively cheap and fairly fast, printing out (according to the machine) between 50 to 400 cps. But they can be rather noisy and the print-out is not of letter quality.

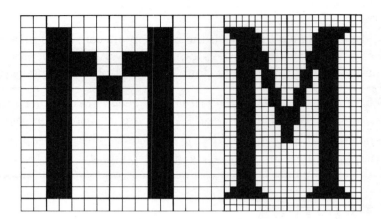

Fig. 6.12 20×28 dot-matrix resolution gives much better quality than a 5×7 grid

The quality of output from a dot-matrix printer is obviously much improved if the number of dots that make up each character is increased. The earliest machines used a vertical row of seven pin heads which printed five times for each character. Thus each character was formed from a 7 × 5 array of dots; the latest use 18 × 24 and even 24 × 24 arrays, and in some cases pass over the same line twice, adding in still more dots, in order to produce what is called *near letter quality* (NLQ) print-out.

Fig. 6.13 Dot-matrix graphics output

There is a trade-off between the speed of a dot-matrix printer and the quality of output. Producing near letter quality output is a slow process and usually matrix printers with an NLQ facility can be switched between slow NLQ and fast 'draft' modes.

```
Near Letter Quality output is possible
on some dot matrix printers. It looks
like this...
The letters are printed twice which
improves the quality but reduces the
printing speed.
```

Fig. 6.14   Dot-matrix near letter quality output

Daisy-wheel Printers

A *daisy-wheel* printer operates much like a typewriter, although the typeface is mounted on a so-called *daisy-wheel* rather than on individual hammers.

Fig. 6.15   A daisy-wheel has 100 spokes, each carrying one character

The wheel is mounted just in front of the ribbon and is free to rotate rapidly from character to character. When correctly positioned, so that the required letter is uppermost, the wheel is struck from behind by a hammer, so forming an image on the paper in exactly the same way that a typewriter would. In fact most electronic typewriters now use the daisy wheel.

Speeds vary considerably, from as few as 12 or 14 cps for older, cheaper machines to as much as 90 cps for the fastest.

> A DAISYWHEEL PRINTER (or typewriter) produces
> real letter quality printout. As this example shows,
> the results are almost as good as the printing used
> for a book such as this. High quality printing is
> essential for marketing and presentation purposes.

Fig. 6.16   Output from a daisy-wheel printer

In general, daisy-wheel printers cost rather more than dot-matrix printers. However, the price of daisy-wheel printers is falling, so that now the more expensive dot-matrix printers cost as much as basic daisy-wheel printers, or more. Daisy-wheel printers are also rather noisy and are restricted to printing only the character set on the daisy wheel (although letter styles can be changed easily enough, simply by changing the daisy wheel). Dot-matrix printers can print anything, including graphs. On the other hand daisy-wheel output is of genuine letter quality and most businesses use this type of printer for their word-processing requirements.

Impact Line Printers

Both dot-matrix and daisy-wheel printers are *serial* printers, producing one character at a time in order.

Line printers, as the name implies, can produce a whole line at a time, which obviously speeds up the printing process very considerably. Powerful mainframe computers have used line printers since the 1950s.

Some impact line printers provide a complete character set at each printing position, usually in the form of embossed characters on the surface of a cylinder, hence the term *barrel* (or *drum*) *printer*.

Letters are not printed one at a time, as they would be with a serial printer, instead the hammers (one for each printing position, mounted on the other side of the paper from the drum) strike the instant the required letter reaches the appropriate position: thus all the 'A's in the line are printed together, then the 'B's, then the 'C's and so on.

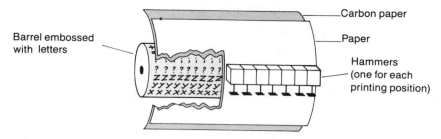

Fig. 6.17 A barrel printer

> **?** **Q 6.18** *How many times must the drum rotate to complete one line?*

Chain printers work in a similar fashion, except that the printing head is a continuous steel band; again the characters are printed the moment they arrive in the correct position.

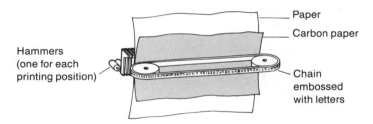

Fig. 6.18 A chain printer

Even the slowest line printers print several lines per second, equivalent to about 200 cps. The fastest print as many as 1200 lines per minute, or about 1500 cps for a line of 75 characters.

NON-IMPACT PRINTERS

Non-impact methods of printing avoid the noisy process of hammering a type-head against a ribbon and paper. They can also offer the prospect of extremely rapid printing, even whole pages at a time.

Thermal Printers

Thermal printers use electrically heated pins to create an image (of the dot-matrix type) on specially treated paper. The paper is either aluminised or treated with other chemicals so that it colours when subjected to heat.

Some of the cheapest printers are of this type.

The heat-sensitive papers are often produced in narrow rolls, 5 cm or 7.5 cm wide, and are designed to be used in the tiny printers built in to some calculators.

The need for special paper is a major disadvantage, for the paper is generally expensive and (if aluminised) can be unattractive. However, thermal printers are virtually noiseless (and that can be of great importance in some circumstances, e.g. in a hospital) and do not require a great deal of power, so they can run off batteries.

Ink-jet Printers

Ink-jet printers are capable of extremely fast speeds (45 000 lines per minute, for the fastest versions); with suitable inks, they can print onto almost any surfaces, not just paper. For example, they are used for marking the 'best-before' dates on the bottom of most metal cans of drink. The printing is silent and can be of very high quality; they can print in colour and are not restricted to a basic character set, and so they can print charts and diagrams.

Although the high-speed, high-quality versions are very expensive, there are cheap ink-jet printers well within the price range of the ambitious hobbyist or of the business needing a printer that can produce coloured graphics as well as text.

Fig. 6.19 Loading envelopes into an ink-jet printer

The printer works by squirting very fine jets of quick-drying ink through a set of tiny nozzles. In some systems, the ink is electrically charged, so that it can be directed electrostatically. This gives a better quality print than in other systems that build up characters as a series of dots as in a dot-matrix printer.

Q 6.19   *Find out what you can about print speeds, colours, cost etc. for several 'cheap' (say under £1500) ink-jet printers.*

Q 6.20   *If a cheap ink-jet printer builds up characters as a series of dots, what advantages does it have over a conventional dot-matrix printer?*

Q 6.21   *What do you think are likely to be the most common running problems associated with an ink-jet printer?*

Laser Printers

Laser printers work on principles borrowed from photocopiers. An image is written onto a photosensitive drum by a laser light beam controlled by the computer. The drum is then brushed with a supply of dry ink (like the 'toner' that has to be put inside a photocopier) which sticks only to the laser-charged part of the drum. The inky image on the drum is then 'fixed' onto paper by a combination of pressure and heat.

Laser printing is generally quiet and of good quality; it can also be extremely fast (200 pages per minute). The first (very expensive) machines of this type to be used commercially in the UK were installed by the banks, who print out from their large computer systems several hundred thousand bank statements every day (see Chapter 18). They have to have the dramatic speed that laser printing can give and, for them, the large investment required was money well spent.

As is so often the case, costs have plummeted since the first machines were installed, and the ideas have been adapted to more modest machines that can print out 12 or so pages per minute and which are realistically priced for medium-sized office systems using one high-quality printer to serve a network of several computers.

Q 6.22   *Try to find the price of the cheapest laser printer on the market. How fast can it print?*

Magnetographic Printers

It is also possible to magnetise a drum rather than to laser charge it. Research into such *magnetographic* techniques suggests that a magnetographic printer would be as fast as a laser printer, but, since it would have fewer moving parts, it would be less prone to breakdown.

The lead in developing these machines has been taken by French and Japanese companies, who launched their first machines for commercial use in 1985.

OTHER OUTPUT METHODS

Plotters

In many engineering and scientific applications, precise (and often coloured) drawings are essential. A black and white, dot-matrix print-out would fall a long way short of the quality required. In almost any job involving *computer-aided design*, from architecture to map-making, a *plotter* like the one shown in Figure 6.20 would be used. The drawing arm is free to move sideways with any one of the fourteen available pens in its clasp; the paper is positioned by friction wheels so that the arm can reach any point on it. If required, each pen could hold ink of a different colour.

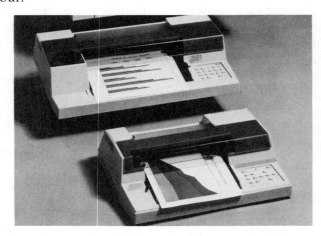

Fig. 6.20   Pen plotters producing graphs and bar charts in full colour

On some *flat-bed* plotters, the paper is supported horizontally and the pen, under computer control, moves across it. Industrial cutting torches, which cut steel plate to specific shapes, work on similar principles.

FAX

Facsimile (FAX) *machines* can convert hard-copy input, e.g. a page of print or a drawing, into digital form for transmission to another FAX machine somewhere else. The machine at the receiving end converts the digital signals back into hard copy.

Computer output, whether text or graphics, can also be transmitted in digital form over telephone links to work a printer or plotter many miles away.

Thus whether or not he is using a computer, an architect in Glasgow, say, can send a copy of his drawings to a colleague in Hong Kong in a few seconds. Traditional post would take about a week.

Computer Output on Microfilm (COM)

Paper is not the only possible hard-copy medium. Large quantities of computer output, e.g. library catalogues (see Chapter 16), might be better stored on long reels of *microfilm* or single sheets of film (called *microfiche*).

Microfilm can only be read with a special reading device and cannot be altered; however it is ideal for storing records and catalogues which will only be referred to occasionally. Information that would otherwise take up three thousand A4 sheets of paper can be stored on one standard size 16 mm roll of microfilm.

Q 6.23   *Many paper records and old newspapers originally published on paper have been transferred (photographically—no computer needed to be involved) to microfilm. Why?*

Q 6.24   *Next time you visit your town's main library, ask for their catalogue. Are they using microfiche?*

Rather than print out a computer record on paper and then photograph it, the record can be transferred directly from the computer to the micro-film at speeds of up to 120 000 cps (that is about 60 frames, each carrying information equivalent to a typed A4 page, each second). This *computer output on microfilm* (COM) can then be stored for easy reference when required.

Voice and Music Synthesis

Computer synthesised voice and music output is now well established. Several 'up-market' makes of car include voice synthesised seat-belt and other warnings. And Texas Instruments' 'Speak 'n' Spell' speaks out each letter as the child presses the keys and concludes "Yes, that is correct" or "No, that is incorrect. Try again". Even home microcomputers offer voice synthesis add-ons and many microcomputers drive music synthesisers in much the same way.

Q 6.25 *Is voice output just a gimmick? Why might spoken warnings be more useful than warning lights? Can you think of other useful applications of spoken output?*

It is important to note the difference between recorded and synthesised speech. Early 'speaking' machines, such as a 'speak your weight machine', simply played back previously recorded snippets of an ordinary tape recording. Today, the telephone 'speaking clock' still works that way.

Computerised voice synthesis is more flexible than that, allowing the computer to 'speak' with words that it makes up from the sounds stored within it as digital codes. Storing words in this way absorbs a lot of memory, and so at the moment the vocabulary of any voice output device tends to be fairly limited. However, as computer memory falls in price, so voice output is likely to increase in importance.

JARGON 6

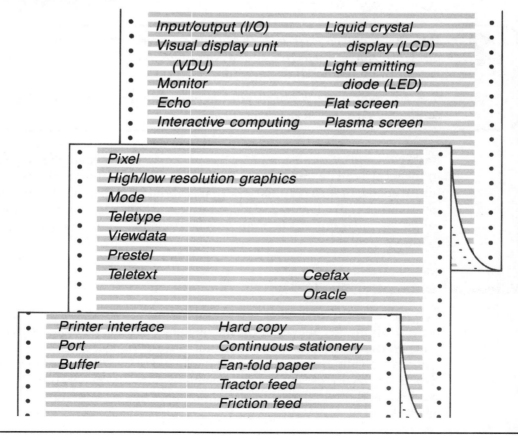

Input/output (I/O)
Visual display unit (VDU)
Monitor
Echo
Interactive computing

Liquid crystal display (LCD)
Light emitting diode (LED)
Flat screen
Plasma screen

Pixel
High/low resolution graphics
Mode
Teletype
Viewdata
Prestel
Teletext

Ceefax
Oracle

Printer interface
Port
Buffer

Hard copy
Continuous stationery
Fan-fold paper
Tractor feed
Friction feed

Characters per second (cps)	Serial printer
Lines per minute (lpm)	Line printer
Letter quality print-out	Barrel printer
Near letter quality (NLQ)	Drum printer
Word processor	Chain printer

Computer-aided design (CAD)	Impact printer
Plotter	Dot-matrix printer
Facsimile (FAX)	Daisy-wheel printer
Microfilm	
Microfiche	Non-impact printer
Computer output on microfilm (COM)	Thermal printer
	Ink-jet printer
Voice synthesis	Laser printer

EXERCISES 6

1. Explain the difference between viewdata systems like *Prestel* and teletext services such as *Ceefax* and *Oracle*. Who uses teletext? What are the possible uses of Prestel?

2. Explain how a cheap flat screen will make an important difference to many computer users.

3. What are meant by the terms interface and buffer? Why does the link between a computer and a peripheral usually depend on both?

4. Various output devices are listed below:

   dot-matrix printer; magnetic tape; microfilm; teletype; line printer; graph plotter; magnetic disk.

   (*a*) Name *two* devices from the list which are backing stores as well as output devices.

   (*b*) Give one major application of:

       (i) microfilm;   (ii) graph plotter.

   (*c*) Give one advantage and one disadvantage of each of the following compared to a dot matrix printer.

       (i) microfilm.   (ii) graph plotter.

       (iii) line printer.   (iv) teletype.

   (SWEB)

5. A great many printers are now available, ranging from small, slow devices to large, versatile, fast printers. Describe various types of printer which are now in use, giving an indication of their operating speeds and paying particular attention to

 (i) the different facilities which they provide,

 (ii) typical applications for which they are appropriate.

(CU)

6. (*a*) Name two devices that can be used to produce graphs.

 (*b*) Briefly explain the particular advantage of each of these devices.

 (*c*) Indicate at which stages these devices would be used in an architects' office.

(WMEB)

7. List the advantages and disadvantages of the following output devices:
Laser printer; teletype; drum line-printer; microfilm output.

8. Old teletype mechanisms have now largely been replaced by FAX devices. What is a FAX device? What disadvantages of teletype has FAX overcome?

9. What is the difference between microfilm and microfiche? Computer output on microfilm or microfiche (COM) has a number of advantages and disadvantages compared with paper output. Explain why with reference to a common application of COM.

10. Synthesised voice output is now well established in several fields. Briefly outline three different applications of voice output, explaining why it has proved so useful.

7 Storage

MAIN STORE

The *main store* or *main memory* of the computer is part of the *central processing unit* (CPU). It stores the program that the computer is currently running together with all the relevant data. Obviously if it is to complete its calculations quickly and accurately, the computer needs to keep handy the data and the instructions telling it what to do; for this reason, the main memory is sometimes called the *immediate access store* (IAS).

RAM and ROM

RAM or *random access memory* is that part of memory where users put their programs and data which they can change at will.

The contents of RAM are lost as soon as the computer is switched off, that is the memory is *volatile*.

Part of the main store is unavailable for storing the user's programs because it contains the computer's operating system and (if there is one) its resident high-level language (such as BASIC). This is the computer's *read-only memory* (ROM), so called because the computer operator can read the contents but not change them in any way.

In fact, the contents of ROM are stored there permanently—fixed by the original manufacturer of the chip itself. The user cannot change the contents of ROM and cannot lose them by turning off the machine.

PROM

The contents of *programmable ROM* or PROM are also permanently fixed, but the contents are arranged (once and once only) after the chip is manufactured. Programming a PROM is a specialist job that usually involves destroying unwanted circuits and connections electrically.

EPROM

Erasable PROM is a little more flexible in that, by using a special ultra-violet light machine, the (specialist) user can erase the chip and, in due course, reprogram it electrically. But while plugged into the computer the EPROM behaves like simple ROM; the operator can neither change the contents nor lose them by turning off the computer.

> **?**
>
> **Q 7.1**   *Why must every computer contain ROM?*
>
> **Q 7.2**   *What are the advantages and disadvantages of PROM and EPROM?*
>
> **Q 7.3**   *Many computers are now equipped with rechargeable batteries that power the memory circuits when the mains supply to the computer is switched off. In this way the contents of RAM are preserved. What are the advantages and disadvantages of this?*

BACKING STORE

Main memory is expensive and always limited in size. Often a complete *file* is larger than a microcomputer's main memory, and so it would not be possible, in any case, to store it inside the computer all at one time. And, of course, the computer operator must have somewhere to keep his or her programs and data while the computer is switched off.

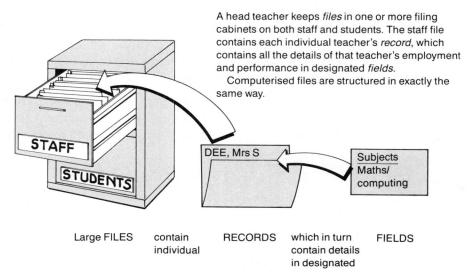

A head teacher keeps *files* in one or more filing cabinets on both staff and students. The staff file contains each individual teacher's *record*, which contains all the details of that teacher's employment and performance in designated *fields*.
Computerised files are structured in exactly the same way.

| Large FILES | contain individual | RECORDS | which in turn contain details in designated | FIELDS |

Fig. 7.1   Notice the difference between files, records and fields

Some form of semi-permanent *backing store* or *secondary store*, external to the CPU, is therefore essential to any computer system. Even the least ambitious owners of the cheapest home computers quickly come to realise the very limited use they can make of their machines unless they also buy a cassette recorder to go with them.

Q 7.4 *List the advantages and disadvantages of storing, for example, all the names and addresses and personal details of all the students at your school or college in the main memory of a computer.*

Q 7.5 *If you had a computer at home but no backing store of any kind (no plug-in cartridges, cassette tapes or disks) what might you use it for?*

Possible *storage media* that have been used extensively in the past include punched cards, paper tape and magnetic drums. Today, most computer systems depend on magnetic tapes or magnetic disks.

Magnetic Tape

Recording programs and data on tape is a common practice. Tape is cheap and reasonably compact and so is readily stored and transported. It can be used over and over again and copied easily.

Fig. 7.2 Cartridges are a neat and useful way of organising small lengths of magnetic tape. There are several different standard sizes of cartridge, of which the home tape cassette size is just one. These *data cartridges* can store as little as 100 kilobytes or as much as 70 megabytes

Industrial *reel-to-reel* tape is longer and stronger than domestic tape and normally twice the width ($\frac{1}{2}$ inch rather than $\frac{1}{4}$ inch) but works on the same principles.

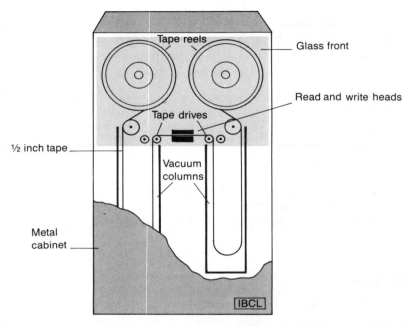

Fig. 7.3 A typical magnetic tape unit is about 1.5 m (5 ft) tall. The tape is sucked into the vacuum columns to help to keep it clean and cool and to make it form large loops; these help the smooth running through the machine and prevent the tape from breaking

A reel of standard tape might be as much as 2400 feet long (about 730 metres) and might possibly store as many as 125 megabytes, that is 125 million characters.

Fig. 7.4 Just as tape cartridges come in several sizes, so do reel-to-reel tapes. Usually tapes are 600, 1200, 2400 or 3600 ft long and are wound on reels of 7, 8½ or 10½ inches diameter

Each character is usually coded on nine tracks. The ninth track carries a *parity bit* by which the computer checks that it has correctly read the other eight. (See Figure 7.5 and Chapter 11.) There is a read/write head for each of the nine tracks.

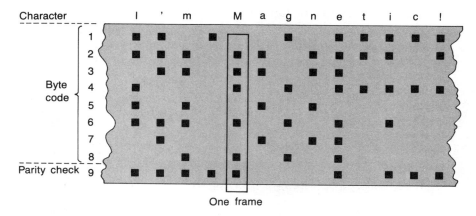

A magnetised spot denotes the binary digit 1 and a blank denotes 0. Thus an eight-bit byte can be coded in a single *frame* spanning eight parallel tracks.

The ninth track carries a *parity bit* by which the computer can check whether or not it has correctly read the other eight. The parity bit is set so that every frame of nine bits contains an even number of 1s. If the computer finds an odd number of spots in one frame, it knows it has misread the code.

The frame illustrated in the figure is a possible binary code for the letter M, namely 0 1 1 1 0 1 0 1. As there are five 1s in this byte, the parity bit is also 1, making six 1s altogether. Thus the nine-bit frame reads 0 1 1 1 0 1 0 1 1 and contains an even number of spots.

Fig. 7.5   A nine-track magnetic tape

Q 7.6   *In Figure 7.5, is the parity bit correctly set for the other 12 bytes illustrated on this section of tape?*

Q 7.7   *This check is known as* even parity. *How would* odd *parity work?*

Q 7.8   *This method of checking the correct reading of the tape is* not *fool-proof. Explain.*

Just as you can play a music cassette over and over again or record over the top of it, so you can with magnetic computer tape. Reading the tape does not destroy the track (thus it can be read time and time again) but old data can be recorded over or *overwritten* with new.

It is usual to space out the data held on the tape. On some tapes each *block* of data is of a fixed length; on others the block corresponds to the combined lengths of a number of records. Data is read a whole block at a time in order to speed up the reading process (which varies, according to the machine used and the number of bytes packed into each inch of tape, from 30 000 to 300 000 characters per second). The *inter-block gap* is a blank section of tape that allows the *tape drive* to stop and then accelerate up to the exactly correct speed before reading the next block. (The stop/start rhythm of a large computer tape drive is very different from the continuous running of a domestic tape recorder.)

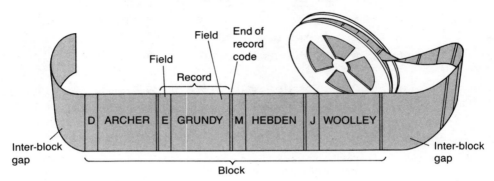

Fig. 7.6   Layout of data on magnetic tape

Blocking data in this way also allows the computer to process a file piece by piece. This is crucial if the file is too large to fit into main memory all at one time.

Floppy Disks

Floppy disks are made of flexible plastic (hence the term 'floppy') and are coated with the same magnetic material that covers magnetic tape. Data is recorded on them in exactly the same way, a blank representing 0 and a magnetised spot representing 1.

If the 'write protect' notch is blocked, say by a piece of gummed paper, then the disk drive cannot record new data on the disk. The data already on the disk is therefore secure from loss.

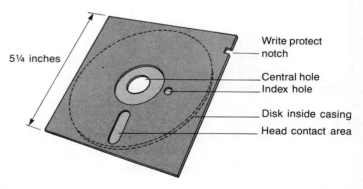

Fig. 7.7   The 5¼ in floppy disk

Like so much else in the computing world, disk technology has improved rapidly in the last few years and no doubt will continue to do so. Not only have storage capacities steadily increased but also the physical size of floppies has been reduced.

The original standard floppy disk had a diameter of 8 inches; those old disks now look cumbersome against today's standards of $5\frac{1}{4}$ and $3\frac{1}{2}$ inches.

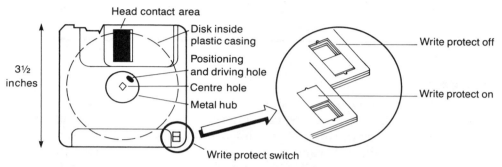

Fig. 7.8   The design of the 3½ inch disk is rather different from that of the 5¼ inch disk. The case is of stronger plastic and more elaborately shaped. The write protect mechanism is built in and the central hub is made of metal

A basic $5\frac{1}{4}$ inch disk suitable for the least expensive drives might carry 40 magnetic tracks on just one side of the disk and be able to store 100 kilobytes. Slightly more sophisticated systems might carry 80 or more tracks on each side of the disk. The best of the $5\frac{1}{4}$ inch floppy disk systems are able to store as much as 3 or 4 megabytes.

The smaller $3\frac{1}{2}$ inch disks also come in *single-* or *double-sided* versions, and, typically, store 1 megabyte—room for 1 million characters.

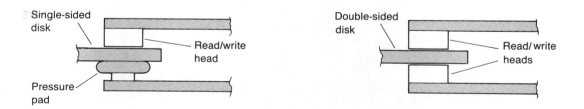

As the name suggests, single-sided disks can be read only on the one magnetically treated side. The floppy disk is supported on the underside by a pressure pad that moves in unison with the read/write head. A double-sided disk can be read on either side by one of the two read/write heads. It is not necessary to turn the disk over manually.

Fig. 7.9   Single- and double-sided disks

?

Q 7.9 *Is the disk system at school or college 40 or 80 track? Are the disks $5\frac{1}{4}$ or $3\frac{1}{2}$ inch and are they single or double sided? What is the storage capacity of each disk?*

Q 7.10 *Why is a dual disk drive preferable to a single drive?*

Q 7.11 *Why is it not possible to write to the reverse side of a double-sided disk in a single-sided disk drive by turning over the disk?*

Q 7.12 *Why are tape and disk sizes always given in feet and inches and not in metric units?*

Hard Disks

Large computer systems use *hard disks* which are made of aluminium rather than plastic (hence the term 'hard'), but coated with the same magnetic material, and which work in the same way. Not only are the disks double sided and able to carry a much larger number of tracks than is possible on floppies (800 on each side of a typical 14 inch hard disk) but they also come in *disk packs* in which a number of disks are mounted together on a single spindle, each with its own read/write head. Such a pack may hold several hundred megabytes.

Fig. 7.10   Loading a disk pack

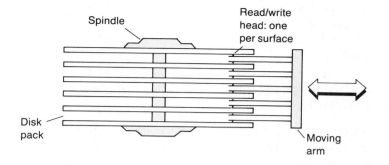

On many drives, the disk pack is served by a moving arm with just one read/write head for each surface, as on a floppy disk drive.

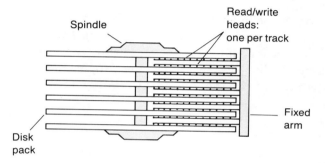

On a *fixed-head disk drive* there is a read/write head for *every* track. This arrangement costs rather more, but access time is reduced.

Fig. 7.11   Reading from, and writing on, hard disks

Winchester Disks

Some disk packs are permanently mounted within a sealed disk drive unit. Because the unit is sealed the disks should remain perfectly clean and dust free, and so the need for maintenance is reduced.

Such sealed units are generally referred to as *Winchester disks*. They are made in various sizes, from 14 inches downwards. 5 and 3 inch Winchester disks, storing as much as 50 megabytes, are now common and are highly suitable for use with microcomputers.

The Disk Operating System (DOS)

Floppies and hard disks are organised in similar ways. The tracks on the disk are concentric circles; they do not spiral inwards like the groove on a gramophone record. Each track is divided into *sectors* so that a particular file can be accessed rapidly from an appropriate *address*, usually coded by three numbers: surface/track/sector. For example, information for a student named Woodward, stored on a pack of six double-sided disks, might be recorded on the upper side of the third disk, probably numbered surface 5; the information on one student would cover only a small part of the disk surface, say, track 10, sector 3. When the record called 'Woodward' was originally stored, the operating system not only recorded the file but also automatically added to the disk index 'Woodward: 5/10/3'. If the file is a long one, it may well be split up and stored in several different places on the disk, although the user is not normally aware of that fact.

When the user next instructs the computer to LOAD 'Woodward' the operating system checks the index for the address (5/10/3) and moves the reading-arm to the required position for track 10. Sector 3 will be found in a matter of moments and the record will be read by the reading head on surface 5.

The precise organisation of the index and of the tracks and sectors on a disk, known as its *format*, depends on the *disk operating system* (DOS), which varies from machine to machine. It is possible to buy preformatted disks for the most common disk systems, but many people simply run a special disk formatter program on the computer to format a new blank disk before they use it.

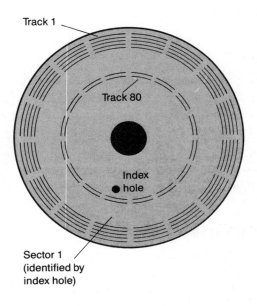

Track 1

Track 80

Index
hole

Sector 1
(identified by
index hole)

Fig. 7.12 The layout of a disk surface

Sequential versus Direct Access

An important drawback to tape storage is the difficulty of accessing information held in the body of the tape. To read the one-thousandth record it is necessary to read (or at least wind through) the other nine hundred and ninety-nine records that precede it. It could take several minutes to find the right section of tape carrying the required record. This *serial* or *sequential access* can slow down a computer operation considerably.

Disk systems allow *direct* or *random access*; i.e. the record can be located from some in-built code or from an index and so retrieved without the need to read through other stored data first.

The difference between sequential and direct access should be well understood by anyone interested in recorded music. If you like a particular track halfway through an album, it is much harder and slower to find on a cassette tape (because you only have sequential access) than it would be on an LP record (where you have direct access).

In some applications, sequential access is a suitable method to use. For example, preparing payslips for all the employees on a company's payroll would be a problem best approached sequentially (e.g. in alphabetical order). Often tape is used for rapid input of data collected by some slower mechanism such as a key-to-tape device or on mark sense cards which the OMR reader transfers to tape (see Chapter 5). Again, it is sensible to input the data in sequence, so the tape's inability to do otherwise is not a handicap.

In other applications the delays that sequential access would cause make tape-based backing store unacceptable. For example, if a bank's central computer had to wind through long stretches of tape in order to check the account of every customer using the many cash-dispensing machines up and down the country, the three or four minutes waiting time for each customer would accumulate into long delays that would make the cash machines virtually unusable.

Tape systems are generally less expensive to instal and run than disks, but the advantages of direct access are such that disk systems are becoming ever more widespread.

Q 7.13 *List three or four computer applications in which two or three minutes' delay in accessing data from backing store would be unacceptable.*

Q 7.14 *What is the (approximate) cost of a basic cassette deck and of a cassette tape suitable for use with a home microcomputer? What is the cost of the cheapest disk drive and of a disk to use with it?*

Optical Disks

Improvements in recording techniques have meant, over the years, a steady increase in the storage capacity of magnetic disks. However, *optical disks* (also called *laser disks*), which use a completely different technology, have enabled a dramatic leap in storage possibilities, from megabytes (millions of characters) to *gigabytes* (thousands of millions of characters).

The optical disk consists of a metallic alloy sandwiched between layers of glass or transparent plastic. A high-powered laser beam 'burns' dark patches on the recording medium so that light and dark patches correspond to the 0s and 1s of binary code. The disk is read by illuminating it with a low-powered laser beam and detecting the dark patches by the reduced amount of light they reflect.

A hi-fi compact disc player works on exactly the same principle.

The read-only problem

Until recently it was impossible to change the contents of an optical disk. Once the data had been burnt onto the disk it was there forever.

This may be acceptable in many applications, especially for education and reference purposes and for home entertainments. For example, the entire contents of a multi-volume encyclopaedia can be held on just one compact optical disk. Or a single disk might carry a set of highly sophisticated home computer games.

However, for day-to-day data processing, even on a home computer system, it is important to be able to record data onto the disk, to edit it and re-record it. Some companies have succeeded in developing the technology, and erasable *read/write* optical disks now exist. In time, they will become commonplace.

Q 7.15 *Why have video tape recorders proven so much more popular than video disc players? Why have laser-based compact audio discs nonetheless succeeded?*

Q 7.16 *What computer applications can you think of in which read-only backing store would not prove a problem?*

Bubble Memory

Bubble memory is another magnetic technique. The 'bubbles' are actually small areas magnetised with the opposite polarity (i.e. magnetic north instead of south, or vice versa) to the thin film of magnetic crystalline material that contains them. A bubble in a given location indicates 1; no bubble indicates 0.

A magnetic field moves the bubbles around the chip; but the bubbles are microscopic and stay within the magnetic film; there are no moving parts in the conventional sense.

Bubble memory is *non-volatile*, and so data is not lost when the power is turned off. Storage capacities are high; a cartridge of bubble memory might store as much as 32 megabytes. It is also very robust; its performance is unaffected by dirt, dust, humidity and wide fluctuations in temperature; it has a high level of immunity to radio and electromagnetic interference and to nuclear radiation; and, as there are no moving parts, bubble memory is resistant to vibration and shock. However, bubble memory is expensive and not a challenge to disk-based backing store in the home or office. But, in military and space applications and also in some industrial contexts, the ruggedness of bubble memory is essential.

Fig. 7.13 Applications of bubble memory

JARGON 7

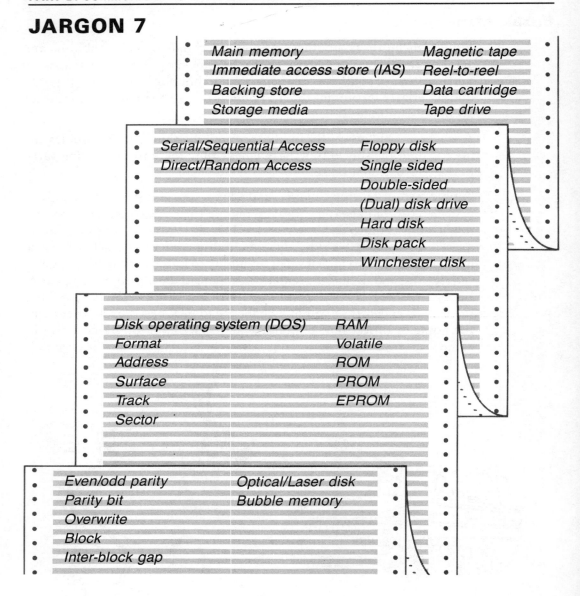

Main memory

Immediate access store (IAS)

Backing store

Storage media

Magnetic tape

Reel-to-reel

Data cartridge

Tape drive

Serial/Sequential Access

Direct/Random Access

Floppy disk

Single sided

Double-sided

(Dual) disk drive

Hard disk

Disk pack

Winchester disk

Disk operating system (DOS)

Format

Address

Surface

Track

Sector

RAM

Volatile

ROM

PROM

EPROM

Even/odd parity

Parity bit

Overwrite

Block

Inter-block gap

Optical/Laser disk

Bubble memory

EXERCISES 7

1. Explain the terms:

   (a) byte (b) kilobyte, K

   (c) megabyte (d) gigabyte

2. Why must a computer have sufficient main memory to hold the program of instructions and relevant data? Why is backing store so important?

3. A famous microcomputer manufacturer includes in advertisements for his computer further adverts for a set of games programs available on standard tape cartridge, a complex educational program available on floppy disk and a word-processing system available on ROM.

   Explain the terms: *cartridge, floppy disk* and *ROM*. Has the manufacturer chosen the storage medium most appropriate for each item of software?

4. Explain the terms *direct access* and *sequential access*; describe an application suitable for each.

5. The figure below shows part of a school's pupil file held on magnetic tape. Copy the diagram. Write in the empty circles the correct letters to show each of the following: A—a block; B—a record; C—a field. What does the circle labelled D show?

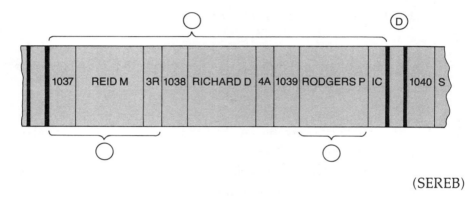

(SEREB)

6. What is the purpose of the inter-block gap between records on a long piece of magnetic tape?

7. One frame on the tape encodes one byte of data with an extra track for the parity bit. Explain.

8. What are the advantages of reel-to-reel tape over cartridges? What are the disadvantages?

9. Compare magnetic tape storage with magnetic disk storage.

   In your answer discuss methods of data access, speed of data retrieval, the amount of data stored and a typical application implemented on each storage medium with reference to the suitability of the chosen storage medium for each application. (WJEC part)

10. Magnetic disks and magnetic tapes are two common methods of storing a lot of data.

    (*a*) Explain, with the aid of diagrams if necessary, how data is actually stored on disks and on tapes, referring to tracks, blocks and sectors where appropriate.

    (*b*) Describe the type of access possible with both magnetic disk and magnetic tape.

    (*c*) State a typical application for each of the following bearing in mind the type of access possible as answered in (*b*).

    (i) magnetic disk   (ii) magnetic tape

    (EMREB)

11. What are the advantages and disadvantages of a *Winchester hard disk* system over a *dual floppy disk* system?

12. What three items of information are needed by a computer for it to find data stored on a disk pack?

13. How might a computer operator ensure that data held on a floppy disk is not accidentally lost?

14. It is possible to store large quantities of data in RAM, either by ensuring a battery powers the RAM when the computer is switched off or by using non-volatile bubble memory.

    Explain the terms *RAM, non-volatile* and *bubble memory.*

    When might it be appropriate to use

    (i) battery driven RAM?

    (ii) bubble memory?

15. Non-magnetic disks are likely to become of prime importance in the next few years. Explain recent developments in optical disk technology and the main advantages and disadvantages of storing information on optical disks.

8 Types of System

MAINFRAME, MINI- AND MICROCOMPUTERS

Computers began to be used commercially in the 1950s. They were big machines, and each one would fill a whole room. Physically large *mainframe* computers are still widely used.

Fig. 8.1 The launch control at NASA's Kennedy Space Centre, Florida, is packed with mainframe computers

Because they are sensitive to dust and temperature changes, mainframes may need specially built rooms with air-conditioning. Special power supplies are installed with cabling under the floor and emergency power supplies are provided in case of power cuts. Some mainframe computers get so hot that they need to be cooled by water or gas.

Minicomputers appeared in the late 1960s. These smaller machines can normally operate in an ordinary office, but still take up a considerable amount of room.

Fig. 8.2 A minicomputer system

Microcomputers were not available until 1977, but within a few years they outnumbered mainframes and minicomputers together. Early machines such as the Apple and the PET were aimed at the small business or professional user. Soon after, companies like Sinclair and Acorn were selling powerful, low-priced machines for the home. Most microcomputers will fit on a desk top but some are compact enough to be carried in a briefcase or even held in the hand. The extraordinary rate of development of microprocessors means that a modern microcomputer can have the same power that a mainframe would have had ten years ago.

Fig. 8.3 A portable microcomputer

SIZE AND POWER

Sheer size is not always a guide to the power of a computer. There are no clear dividing lines between mainframes, mini- and microcomputers.

Power is usually indicated by the speed of the main processor, measured in *millions of instructions per second* (MIPS).

Microprocessors vary in the amount of data that they can handle in a single instruction. Some cope with eight bits at a time, some with 16 and others with 32. Each step up in capacity increases the overall speed of processing data.

Another advantage of larger bit capacities is that the processor can directly address a great number of different storage locations. Compare this with postal addresses. If an address were restricted to ten characters, it would be much harder for every household in the country to have a unique address. So with computers; the more bits in the address, the more unique locations to which data can be 'posted'.

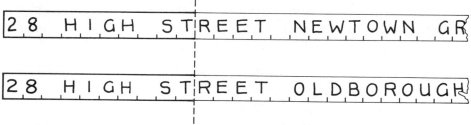

Fig. 8.4 Many postal addresses would be indistinguishable if only the first ten characters were used

Memory Capacity

Memory sizes vary a great deal from computer to computer. They are measured in *kilobytes* (one kilobyte can store approximately one thousand characters) or in *megabytes* (approximately one million characters). The figures below give an idea of relative sizes. Notice how much overlap there is:

- microcomputers: 1 kilobyte to 16 megabytes
- minicomputers: 64 kilobytes to 64 megabytes
- mainframe computers: 500 kilobytes to 2048 megabytes.

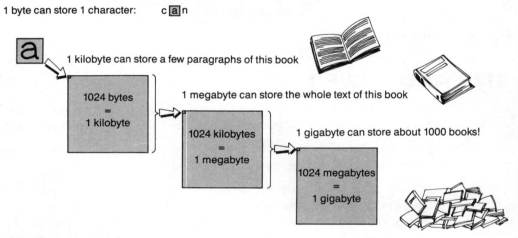

1 byte can store 1 character: c [a] n

1 kilobyte can store a few paragraphs of this book

1024 bytes = 1 kilobyte

1 megabyte can store the whole text of this book

1024 kilobytes = 1 megabyte

1 gigabyte can store about 1000 books!

1024 megabytes = 1 gigabyte

Fig. 8.5 Storage capacity

> **Q 8.1** *How much user-addressable memory (i.e. RAM) is there on the microcomputer you use?*
>
> *If there are 2000 letters and other characters on each full page of this book, how many pages could be input to your computer?*
>
> *There are 480 pages in the whole book. How many copies of it could be input to a 64 megabyte mainframe computer?*
>
> **Q 8.2** *List as many advantages and disadvantages as you can think of for someone using*
>
> *(a) a 'stand alone' microcomputer*
> *(b) a terminal with telephone link to a mainframe computer.*

Peripheral Storage Capacity

The volume of *backing store* available often determines the effective power of a system. On-line disk storage (under the control of the CPU) for a mainframe system is often measured in *gigabytes* (1024 million, i.e. over one billion bytes).

Minicomputers commonly have several megabytes on-line. Microcomputers, again, vary enormously. Many home microcomputers have no on-line storage at all but desk-top machines can have from 100 kilobytes to 100 megabytes of disk space.

Is Bigger Better?

Despite the difference in size, speed and capacity, mainframes, mini- and microcomputers still work in the same way.

Small machines obviously score on size, cost and staffing requirements, but there are a number of jobs that they simply cannot do. Some applications require such vast quantities of on-line storage that only a mainframe could cope. The Driver and Vehicle Licensing Centre at Swansea, for example, must have mainframes to cope with the sheer volume of its vehicle records held on every driver and vehicle in the country.

Fig. 8.6 The main processor of the Cray 2 'supercomputer'. It is about 2.5 m high. The supercomputer is used for weather forecasting, seismic analysis for the oil industry etc.

Advanced graphics, such as those required by the more complex computer-aided design (CAD) systems are confined to larger machines. So, too, are the most sophisticated forecasting systems.

Q 8.3 *Suggest some computing jobs that are too large to be handled by a desk-top microcomputer.*

Q 8.4 *Some microcomputers have overtaken minicomputers in processing power. Are minicomputers likely to survive?*

TRANSACTION AND BATCH PROCESSING SYSTEMS

Systems must respond to thousands of daily events, or *transactions*. For example: a businessman books a flight to New York, or a production worker puts in two hours' overtime, or a space craft deviates one degree from its course, or a cricket enthusiast checks the test match score via *Prestel*.

This *transaction processing* must take place whether or not a computer is involved. An employer would probably not process the worker's overtime immediately; at the end of the week all the transactions for that worker's overtime (and normal working hours), along with those for other employees, would be collected into a *batch* and processed together.

A clerk could add up all the hours worked by each person and calculate the wages. Alternatively, all the transactions could be handled by generating a record on a computer file for each one and then processing the file as a single unit. This *batch processing* may be carried out on any size of computer.

Remote Job Entry (RJE)

There is no need for a computer to be in the factory or even in the wages office for the wages to be automatically calculated. Perhaps the factory is in Birmingham but the company has a large computer in Bristol. The week's wages data is sent in a batch via a *remote terminal*, i.e. a terminal some distance from, but linked to, the computer. This is called *remote job entry* (RJE). Once the wages are calculated, the output is sent back from the mainframe to the remote terminal, where wage slips are printed out.

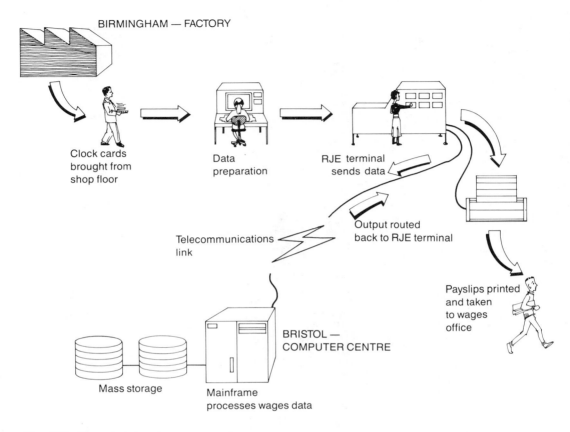

BIRMINGHAM — FACTORY

Clock cards
brought from
shop floor

Data
preparation

RJE terminal
sends data

Telecommunications
link

Output routed
back to RJE terminal

Payslips printed
and taken
to wages
office

BRISTOL —
COMPUTER CENTRE

Mass storage

Mainframe
processes wages data

Fig. 8.7 Remote job entry

ON-LINE AND REAL-TIME SYSTEMS

In the wages example, the terminal (whether local or remote) must be *on-line*, i.e. it must be connected to the main computer and under its control. But it only needs to be on-line for a few moments to transmit and receive data. It can be *off-line*, or disconnected, while the actual processing takes place. It follows that the output is a day or two out of date, but this does not matter if the wages can be paid at the end of the week.

The cricket enthusiast, on the other hand, whose terminal might be a television set or home computer with viewdata facilities, needs to be on-line to the Prestel computer continuously in order to keep up to date with the score. This ability to find out the current situation at any time is a major advantage of on-line systems.

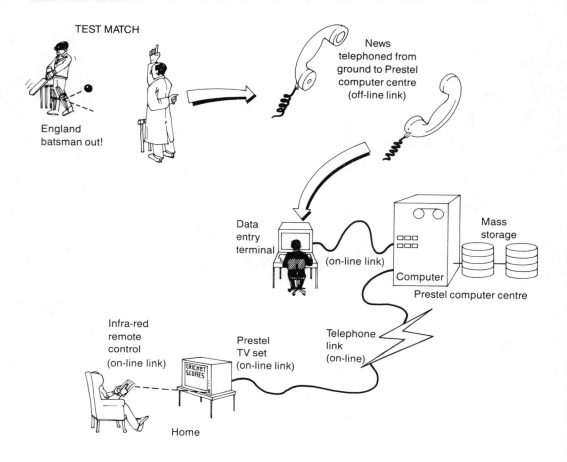

Fig. 8.8 On-line and off-line links

Interaction

Many applications of computers demand immediate *interaction* between the user and the machine, which means that both input and output must be rapid. Interactive computing at a popular price is something that we now take for granted, but it is a relatively recent development (dating from the late 1970s).

Without this interaction home computing would never have been possible. Imagine a beginner trying to learn to program on a system that took two hours to respond to even the most minor of errors. It would not be possible to run many effective educational programs for children. Electronic games of the 'space invader' type would be quite impossible, for the whole point is to test the user's skill and reaction speed at the controls.

Q 8.5 *List the ways you could use a home computer. Now cross out those which would* not *be possible without very rapid response from the computer.*

Interaction also enables the user to hold a 'conversation' with the computer. *Direct data entry* (DDE), whereby data is input for immediate processing, depends upon this conversational mode which allows results to be rapidly displayed and invalid data to be put right there and then.

Real-time

Commercial systems of this sort usually provide rapid results with response times of no more than a few seconds. But when a spacecraft veers off course it is crucial to respond instantly. Astronauts' lives are at stake: a delay of even a second could be fatal. The data that represents the course deviation must be processed so rapidly that the course correction can be made instantaneously. This is a *real-time* system: one able to respond fast enough to affect the process or activity which it supports.

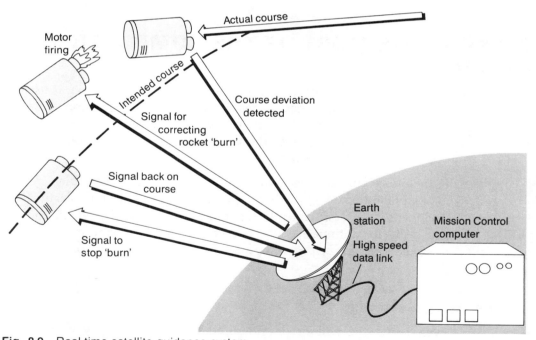

Fig. 8.9 Real-time satellite guidance system

Q 8.6 *Think of some other uses of a computer for which a delay of a second or two would be too long.*

Airlines also use real-time systems for booking passengers. The business-man in London booking his flight to New York must not be sold a seat which was reserved in Manchester by someone else two minutes pre-viously. The computer system handling the bookings must therefore maintain a completely up-to-date picture of the actual seat availability at any time. Batch processing of bookings would cause chaos.

? ■

Q 8.7 *What distinguishes on-line and real-time systems?*

Q 8.8 *Explain why the following are on-line, real-time, both or neither:*

(a) *an automatic sprinker system activated by a fire in the office*

(b) *a computer-controlled alarm that automatically calls the fire brigade with a pre-recorded message as soon as it senses a fire in the office*

(c) *the night watchman who telephones the fire brigade as soon as he is aware of the fire.*

MAKING THE MOST OF THE COMPUTER'S SPEED

When a program is run on a computer, the actual processing is usually very rapid, but input and output of data take up far more time. In particular, printers are very slow compared with the CPU. In the time it takes to print out one line, the CPU could perform several thousand operations if it did not have to wait for the printer.

If the processor can deal with only one device, this problem is un-avoidable and the CPU will be idle for much of the time. Fortunately peripherals can sometimes be operated independently, which enables processing to continue even though some of the peripherals in use are still busy. This allows the processor to 'get ahead' of the printer or disk drive.

Time-sharing Systems

Even so, the CPU will still be underused if it can process only one program at a time. The peripherals will not be used at all if that program does not involve them. *Multiprogramming* is a time-sharing technique that enables two or more programs to be in the main memory at once. The processor keeps each program with its associated data quite separate from the others. A fraction of a second (a so-called *time slice*) is spent on each program in turn. One program can be printing, another inputting data from tape and a third calculating, all apparently at the same time. Clearly the system's resources are better used in this way.

Multi-user Systems

Many organisations have a number of terminals linked to a central mainframe. These may be *dumb terminals*, i.e. without their own processing ability, but it is more common to find *intelligent terminals* or *local processors* bearing some of the processing load. This is generally faster and more convenient, and eases the pressure on the main computer.

But even with local intelligence, time sharing *between users* is necessary to enable them all to send, process and receive data at the same time. Without this *multi-access* they would have to follow a very strict timetable. Often there would simply not be enough hours in the day for everyone's processing if every job had to wait until the previous one had finished before it could start. For this reason, time-sharing methods are the norm on large computers, common on minicomputers and used increasingly on microcomputers.

Multiprogramming and Multi-access

Notice the difference between multiprogramming and multi-access. A bank's cashcard system is a multi-access system that enables hundreds of customers to do similar things simultaneously while the central computer is running only *one* program. Contrast this with, for example, a university computer centre where 20 students are running different programs of their own at different terminals but using the one mainframe. This is multi-access with multiprogramming. Thirdly, a businessman using a small but powerful 'stand-alone' microcomputer might input his sales data while the machine is printing his entire stock master file. He is a single user benefiting from multiprogramming.

Q 8.9 *Do the following systems make use of (a) time sharing, (b) multi-access, (c) multiprogramming?*

   (i) a programmable calculator

  (ii) Prestel

 (iii) a computerised airline booking system

 (iv) a computerised supermarket checkout system

  (v) the on-board computer in the space shuttle.

LOCAL AREA NETWORKS (LANs)

It often makes sense for two or more computers in one office to share resources such as disk drives and a printer. Not only is this cheaper, it also allows several people to call up the same information. This is an important advantage, e.g. for two typists who will frequently want to use the same standard document layout, or for the several doctors of one group practice who need to look up computerised patient files, etc.

Local area networks (LANs) make this possible. There may already be one in your school or college. The computers and peripherals are cabled together so that the students can load and run the same programs and share expensive printing and disk drive facilities.

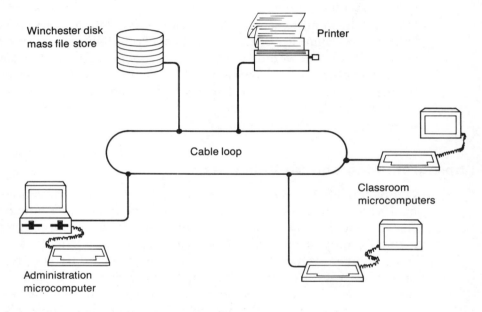

Fig. 8.10 A school's local area network (LAN)

?

Q 8.10 *How many microcomputers are there in your school or college? How much would it cost to provide each one with its own dual disk drive and printer?*

Q 8.11 *If the computer you use is part of a network, then you could load* other peoples' *programs and they could load* yours. *Is this a good idea?*

Q 8.12 *Why might the school's head teacher not want to link the administrative computer to the network?*

Special network software is necessary to sort out *who* is transmitting *what* data to *which* location. The problem of controlling this 'data traffic' obviously grows with the size of the network.

Telecommunications

What if the shared data is not stored locally? Telecommunications links are essential if data is to be transmitted over any distance, as in several of the examples given. Special hardware devices called *modems* and *acoustic couplers* can link a computer to the telephone network.

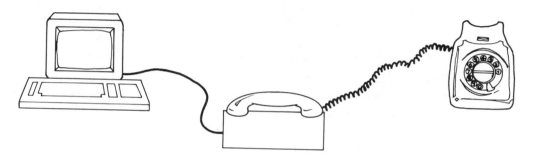

Fig. 8.11   An acoustic coupler with a telephone handset inserted. The acoustic coupler converts the computer output to sound which is broadcast into the telephone mouthpiece in the ordinary way

Digital data is converted to an analog form (which is how telephone conversations are normally transmitted) suitable for sending along telephone lines. A second modem or coupler is needed at the other end to convert the signals back to digital form.

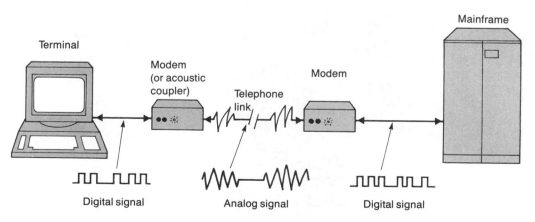

Fig. 8.12   Modems linking a remote terminal to a mainframe computer. A modem is 'wired in' so that electronic impulses are fed directly to the telephone lines

Electronic Mail

Because of the rising costs of conventional labour-intensive mail services, a huge variety of other information is also being transmitted electronically. Organisations with several offices send not only routine data for batch processing, but also other items of *electronic mail*, such as memos, letters, reports, sales inquiries, copies of drawings and photographs, voice messages and so on.

All this has been added to existing telephone and telex usage. Not surprisingly the land based telephone network, which still includes mechanical elements and copper wires, often proves too unreliable to cope with this data transmission, for which, of course, it was never designed. Increasing use is therefore being made of microwave, optical fibre cable and satellite communications. All these technologies are tumbling in cost as research advances and demand grows.

Companies are gradually bringing together this wide range of communication into *integrated networks* that combine the capabilities of carrying data, text, images and voice.

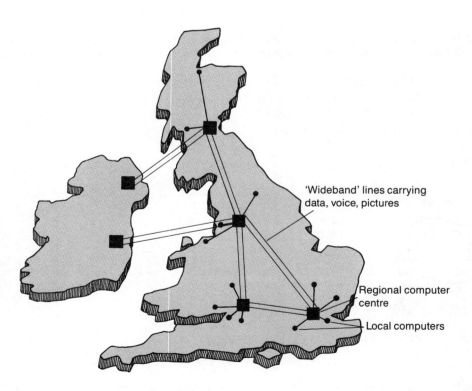

Fig. 8.13 An integrated telecommunications network

Computer Bureaux

A *computer bureau* is a company that sells computer time to organisations who do not have sufficient computing facilities of their own. As computer bureaux have many customers, often requiring on-line facilities, they depend heavily on telecommunications and have to use efficient time-sharing methods to cope with the volume of processing.

Bureaux also provide many other services, such as data preparation, supply of standard or tailor-made software, consultancy, training and so on.

SYSTEMS APPLICATIONS

Data Processing (DP)

All computer systems process data, but the term *data processing* (DP) is often used to describe batch systems dealing with *historical* data, i.e. about events that happened last week or last year. Such systems are chiefly used for *accounting* applications (see Chapter 12).

Information Retrieval

Many on-line systems are used to retrieve information from files or *databases*. The cricket enthusiast checking the Test Match score is, in fact, accessing a *database* of information stored on the Prestel computer.

There are thousands of applications for information retrieval; some examples will be studied in detail later.

Word Processing (WP)

The written word is one type of information used by almost everyone. You are using it now. *Word processing* systems allow text to be stored, corrected, changed and retrieved at will.

Many organisations send out standard letters by storing the body of the text on disk and reprinting the letter with just the different names and addresses of the various recipients inserted (see Chapter 13).

Process Control

Increasingly, computers are used to control the operation of physical processes, such as factory production or air-conditioning. Real-time systems are usually essential for these *process control* applications.

For example, a modern biscuit factory uses a computer to weigh ingredients to a precise recipe while the production line is running at full speed. Sugar, for example, may be added through a computer-controlled valve that closes the moment a sensor indicates the weight is precisely correct.

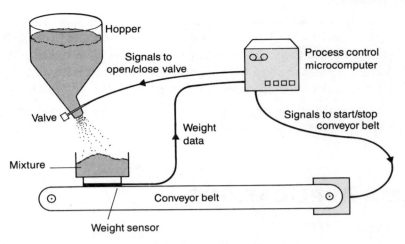

Fig. 8.14 Process control; weighing materials in a production process

Similarly a thermostat indicates to a computer-controlled air-conditioning system in a luxury hotel that a particular room is too hot or too cold.

Other control applications are discussed in Chapter 20.

Simulation

Computers can be used in *simulations*; i.e. for *modelling* the real world. Applications can range from a model of a small company's finances to one of the whole economy, or from a model of a simple laboratory experiment to one of a vast chemical factory. If the model properly mimics the real-life situation it can be used to predict the consequences of, for example, a 10% drop in a company's sales, or a rise in atmospheric pressure on tomorrow's weather.

Engineering Design and Manufacture

Engineers, architects, industrial designers and production manufacturers find computers increasingly vital to their work.

Drawings can be speedily produced and altered with *computer-aided design* (CAD) and other *graphics packages* linked to special plotters.

The behaviour of materials and components can be estimated and predicted with remarkable accuracy.

Bottlenecks and other problems in the manufacturing process itself can be forecast and avoided with special *computer-aided manufacturing* (CAM) software.

JARGON 8

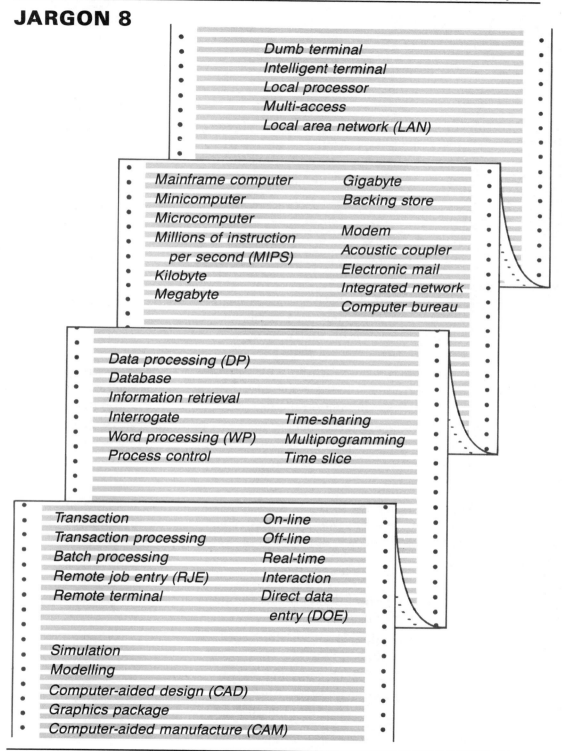

Dumb terminal
Intelligent terminal
Local processor
Multi-access
Local area network (LAN)

Mainframe computer
Minicomputer
Microcomputer
Millions of instruction
    per second (MIPS)
Kilobyte
Megabyte

Gigabyte
Backing store

Modem
Acoustic coupler
Electronic mail
Integrated network
Computer bureau

Data processing (DP)
Database
Information retrieval
Interrogate
Word processing (WP)
Process control

Time-sharing
Multiprogramming
Time slice

Transaction
Transaction processing
Batch processing
Remote job entry (RJE)
Remote terminal

On-line
Off-line
Real-time
Interaction
Direct data
    entry (DOE)

Simulation
Modelling
Computer-aided design (CAD)
Graphics package
Computer-aided manufacture (CAM)

EXERCISES 8

1. (a) How is the *power* of a computer usually measured?

   (b) State two other factors influencing the effective power of a computer system.

2. (a) What are the main differences between a typical home computer and one used by a small business? Discuss the power, storage capacity, peripheral devices and applications.

   (b) How have these differences changed in recent years?

3. (a) State three advantages of microcomputers over mainframe computers.

   (b) State three advantages of mainframes over microcomputers.

4. 'Because of their cheapness and versatility, microprocessors and micro-computers are being used in an increasing number and variety of applications. It is likely that by the end of the 1980s the large mainframe computer will have become extinct.'

   (a) Describe four ways in which microprocessors/microcomputers are being used. Indicate the effect, if any, which each of these applications is having on the use of large mainframe computers.

   (b) Comment on the suggestion, made in the quotation above, that by the end of the 1980s no large mainframe computers will be in use.

   (CU)

5. State clearly the distinction between on-line and real-time processing. Illustrate your answer by briefly describing one application of on-line processing and one application of real-time processing.

   (LU)

6. Explain which of the following computer applications are on-line, real-time or off-line:

   (a) a warehouse stock system, linked to the head office in London by a terminal

   (b) a bank's branch computer system

   (c) a fire warning system

   (d) a shop system using kimball tags.

7. Explain the terms:
   (*a*) interactive computing   (*b*) batch processing
   (*c*) remote job entry (RJE)   (*d*) direct data entry (DDE).

8. Explain the terms:
   (*a*) time sharing   (*b*) multiprogramming
   (*c*) time slice   (*d*) multi-access.

9. What is a local area network? Who may have use for one, and why?

10. What is a computer bureau? Who may have use for one and why?

11. The following are specific examples of situations using computers
    (*a*) fully automated power station,
    (*b*) on-line literature search,
    (*c*) producing mailing lists,
    (*d*) automatic railway signalling.

    Specify in each case whether the example is an application of process control, information retrieval or word processing.

    (AEB 1984)

9 Developing Systems

A system can be defined as a set of things connected or associated so as to form a complex whole. Some systems occur naturally, e.g. the solar system, or the human central nervous system.

Other systems are man-made. They can be physical, such as a national railway network or a hi-fi system. Some are procedural, such as the jury system or the electoral system. There are systems of government (democracy, communism), social systems (tribes, castes, classes) and many others.

> **Q 9.1** *Think of five man-made systems. They need not involve computers.*

When we talk of designing systems, we usually mean *information systems*. These are designed to collect, store, process and manage the flow of information within an organisation.

Some information systems do not feature computers. And even in those that do, the computer is not necessarily the most important part. The information itself, the way it is collected or distributed and above all the people who use the information in their work (accountants, salespeople, production managers, buyers, administrators or anyone else in the organisations) are all just as vital.

> **Q 9.2** *Many* manual *information systems are so simple and effective that the expense of computerisation is not justified. Can you think of some examples (a) at home; and (b) at school or college.*

THE PHASES OF SYSTEMS DEVELOPMENT

The entire process of developing a computerised system can be broken down into nine phases as follows:

- Systems analysis
- Defining objectives
- Feasibility study
- System design
- Program design
- Coding
- Testing
- Documenting the system
- Implementing the system

SYSTEMS ANALYSIS

The first job for the *systems analyst* is to understand clearly the *terms of reference* for any investigation which may be requested. These will set the main goals and limits for the study. For example, the management of a large mail-order company decided to look at ways of improving their response to telephone inquiries and orders. An analyst was asked to examine this area to see whether better or faster replies could be achieved. *Written* orders, inquiries and complaints were not to be studied, nor was the dispatch of goods.

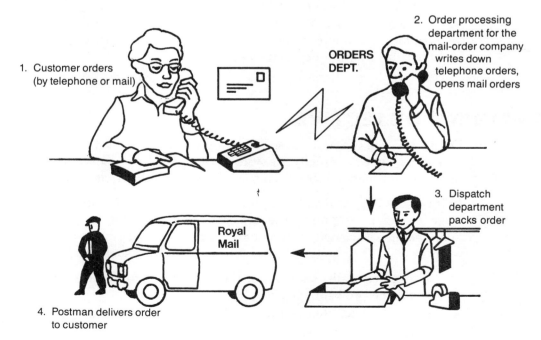

1. Customer orders
   (by telephone or mail)

2. Order processing department for the mail-order company writes down telephone orders, opens mail orders

ORDERS DEPT.

3. Dispatch department packs order

4. Postman delivers order to customer

Royal Mail

Fig. 9.1 A mail-order company

The investigation should first answer the question: what exactly is going on now? The analyst examines the activities of all those involved with the system, by observing people at work, by interviewing them, by studying forms and other documents used, by inspecting records and files, or by any method which will throw light on the existing system.

? Q 9.3 *What problems might a systems analyst encounter while carrying out the above tasks?*

Such investigations can take weeks or even months. People are often poor at describing their work, and may unintentionally mislead the analyst. Staff may feel threatened by a stranger entering their workplace with a lot of questions. Unless they feel at ease with the systems analyst, they may describe their roles 'by the book' recounting the way the instruction manual (or the boss) says the job *should* be done, not how they *actually* do it.

? Q 9.4 *Do you do a part-time job? Try describing concisely and accurately what you do.*

A good systems analyst must therefore be skilled at dealing with people, at understanding their problems and concerns. Many analysts are now called *business analysts*, reflecting the importance of business awareness. The system may actually be designed by another, more technical, analyst, but what is most important is that the people who use the system and their information needs are well understood.

DEFINING OBJECTIVES

Before a system can be designed, the people concerned must agree on the objectives, i.e. what exactly the system is intended to do. This may sound obvious, but many poor systems are designed without clear goals.

In the mail-order company mentioned above, the systems analyst spent three weeks investigating the system. After the findings had been analysed and discussed with managers and staff, the system objectives were agreed. They included performance objectives such as:

- No telephone caller should hear the ringing tone for more than thirty seconds before being answered.
- Staff should be able to find out within 15 seconds if a particular catalogue item is in stock.
- All complaints must be dealt with within 24 hours.

Fig. 9.2 A telephone complaint

 Q 9.5 *How far could a computer help in achieving each of these objectives?*

FEASIBILITY STUDY

A *feasibility study* is often carried out to see whether it is at all possible (given the limits on such factors as cost and time) to produce a system which meets the objectives.

 Q 9.6 *Why bother with a feasibility study?*

SYSTEM DESIGN

Once the objectives are agreed, and if the results of any feasibility study are favourable, work can begin on designing the system. Decisions must now be made about what software and hardware (if any) will be required. Remember that a *complete* system is being designed; all aspects must be considered. Sometimes hardware choices are limited—some expensive machinery may have been previously installed.

Manual procedures must be rethought. Who is responsible for doing what, and when? The analyst may need to design new *forms*, to permit the capture, storage or passing on of information with a minimum of error.

The overall design must be clear on ten key points:

- Outputs required
- Inputs required
- Data sources
- Methods of data capture
- Storage methods
- File structures
- Processing required
- Screen dialogues
- Normal procedures and timing
- Emergency procedures.

All the above aspects of a system design must be written down in a *system specification*. This will also include system flowcharts and the plans for system testing and implementation.

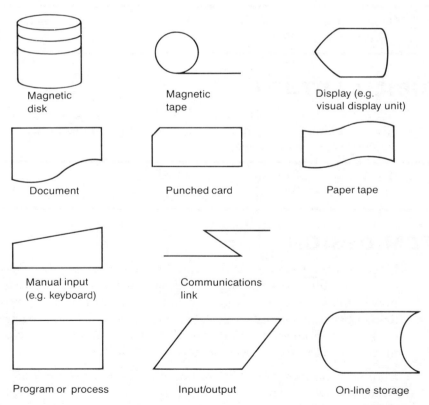

Fig. 9.3 Systems flowchart symbols commonly used in addition to the programming flowchart symbols given in Chapter 3

Outputs

The *outputs* from the system are often considered first; people are keen to know what information they can expect to obtain. The analyst must know who needs the output and in what form it should be presented, e.g. visual display or printout, how many copies of the printout are required, who will receive them, and whether pre-printed stationery (e.g. payslips or invoices) will be needed.

Thought must be given to how often output is required; e.g. every few minutes, daily, once a month etc. If large volumes of information are consulted only occasionally, perhaps microfilm would be an acceptable alternative to reams of printout.

Inputs

Deciding on the outputs will help the analyst to define the required *inputs* (what data must be put into the system), the *sources* of data (where will all the data come from) and the methods of *data capture* (how to get this data into the system).

Data Sources

Some data will come from *external* sources, and some from *internal* sources. For example, if a customer telephones the mail-order company to enquire about a sweater, the customer's name, the style, size and colour

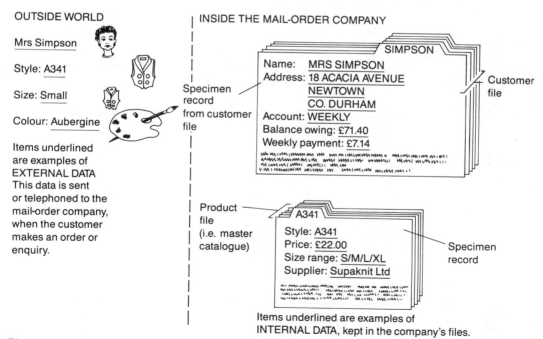

Fig. 9.4 Internal and external data

of the sweater are all external data items; i.e. they come in from outside the system. But the customer's name is also stored internally on the company's files, along with the account details. Other internal data would include the current price of the sweater, which is printed in the mail-order catalogue.

Q 9.7 *What information would the customer's account details contain?*

Q 9.8 *Think of two other internal data items and two other external data items which the company might need.*

Data Capture

Data capture and entry can be the most time-consuming part of a system. The data needed may be scattered in various departments in the organisation. It is also likely to have been recorded in different ways, for some people like to write down every detail, others prefer to record a bare minimum and some keep it all in their heads.

Telephone inquiries to the mail-order company all came into the sales department. However, the analyst discovered that some of the data was not being captured at all, and so there was no way for the management to tell how many inquiries (or indeed complaints) were being satisfied. The system proposed by the analyst included a procedure for recording all inquiries; this was helped by a carefully designed, standard form on which inquiries and/or orders could be written.

Q 9.9 *Try designing a suitable form for this mail-order company.*

Storage Methods

Quite often a form, or rather the paper used, is the first *storage medium* selected by an analyst. Magnetic media are not the only ways of storing information.

However, once the forms are filled in, they are often used as *source documents* for data entry. The analyst in the mail-order company concluded that automation of stock records was essential to meet the objective of providing very rapid stock information.

Q 9.10 *Can you think of examples where stock information can be rapidly obtained without a computer?*

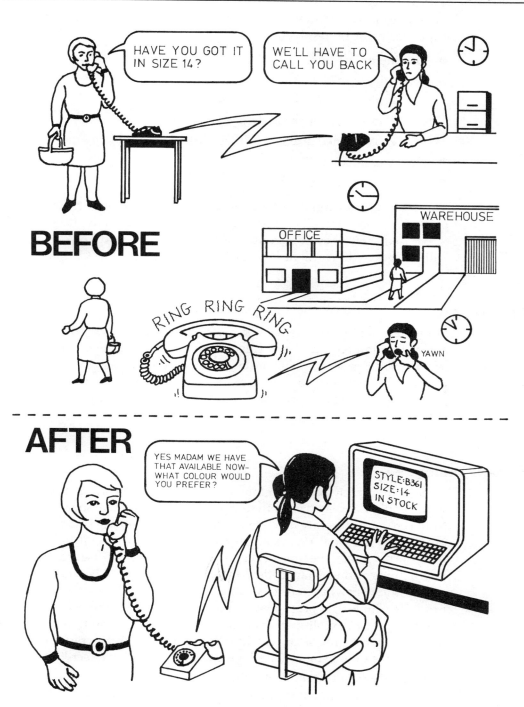

Fig. 9.5 A mail-order company before and after automation of its stock records

Having decided that some peripheral storage will be needed, the following issues must be resolved:

- On-line or off-line?
- What medium?
  - disk: floppy, hard, optical
  - tape: half-inch, cartridge, cassette
  - other media: e.g. EPROM cartridge, bubble memory
- How much storage?
- How fast must access be to the information?

These questions cannot be answered without working out the appropriate *file structures*. This in turn involves exact definition of the *records* to be used, how they are grouped together in files, and how those files will be accessed. We shall look at this in more detail in Chapter 10.

Processing

Some data will of course need *processing* before it is stored or output; e.g. validation, comparison, calculation of totals, adjustment of stock levels. All the processing (including input/output processes) must be split up into the necessary programs. For each program, the files used and processing required are set out in a document called a *program specification*.

Screen Dialogues

Most computer systems developed and installed nowadays are on-line, with people using screens both to aid input and to receive speedy output. Much effort is therefore made to ensure the quality of the *screen dialogue design*, i.e. the way the system requests and accepts input, and how it presents output on the screen. A successful dialogue will use plain English instructions rather than codes or jargon. There will be standardised *screen layouts*, which are clear and uncluttered. The system will give *prompts* (think of a prompter in the theatre) to help the user to decide what to key in next. It may also include a *help* feature so that by typing in 'help' or pressing a certain key the user can ask for more detailed instructions or assistance with a given task. As we have seen in Chapter 3, *user-friendly* procedures are of extreme importance.

The clumsy and unhelpful dialogue in Figure 9.6 is from a system still in use. The instructions entered via the keyboard are shown in bold type and the computer responses are in ordinary type.

```
/09:30:86 08:16:27.49 UCSW TS4000 SYS.,TRM=0420,ACV=0018,SYC=NML
/LOGON
/SALLY
/09:30:86 08:16:56.23 NOT FOUND ZW00395.QRY. MSG 0004
/LOGON
/DAVIES
/09:30:86 08:17:33.80 NOT FOUND ZW00398.QRY. MSG 0004
/LOGON
/J DAVIES
/09:30:86 08:17:59.44 LOGON P.700 ZW00400.QRY. MSG0009
/PWD
/SALLY
/09:30:86 08:18:39.03 LOGON P.717 ZW00412.QRY. USR#3576 MSG0011
/OK
/LOAD RESMOD07,5,,6000,T=5.0
/09:30:86 08:19:19.22 SYSLG UPE ERROR USR#3576 MSG0126
/LD RESMOD07,5,,6000,T=5.0
/09:30:86 08:19:55.10 SYSLG UPE ERROR USR#3576 MSG0126
/LD "RESMOD07",5,,6000,T=5.0
/09:30:86 08:26:30.47 SYSLG SKG USPROG. USR#3576 MSG0201
/09:30:86 08:27:55.51 SYSLG LDG USPROG. USR#3576 MSG0207
/09:30:86 08:28:03.23 SYSLG FRSP=6K,TALLC=3000CRU. USR#3576 MSG0278
/OK
/
```

Fig. 9.6 This obsolescent computer dialogue gives the user no guidance at all, and yet it demands very accurate input. After the lengthy rigmarole above, the system has merely loaded a program

?   **Q 9.11** *How might the dialogue in Figure 9.6 be improved?*

The most sophisticated dialogues attempt to accept instructions in ordinary English. This ambitious task demands storage of a large vocabulary and detailed processing on the user's actual words to try to 'understand' the request. No system can yet fully cope with the complexity, or the vagueness, of everyday English, but Figure 9.7 (overleaf) shows how close a system can get. The 'human' part of the dialogue is again in bold type.

The details of the dialogues, including screen layouts, must be included in the program specifications.

?   **Q 9.12** *Select a simple program of your own (pick one involving considerable input and output). Write instructions to a new user on how the screen dialogue works.*

Normal Procedures and Timing

The systems analyst must specify how and when each program should be run; i.e. daily, weekly, as required etc. Some programs may depend on others, e.g. a print program listing details of a master file may produce an out-of-date report unless an updated program is run first. Once again,

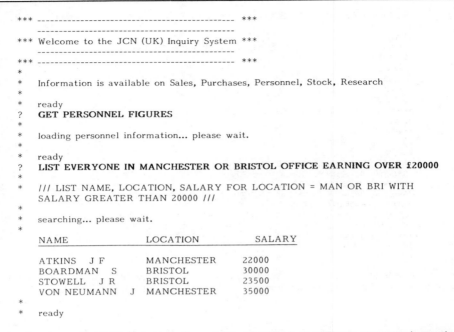

```
*** ------------------------------------------------ ***
    ------------------------------------------------
*** Welcome to the JCN (UK) Inquiry System ***
    ------------------------------------------------
*** ------------------------------------------------ ***
*
*   Information is available on Sales, Purchases, Personnel, Stock, Research
*
*   ready
?   GET PERSONNEL FIGURES
*
*   loading personnel information... please wait.
*
*   ready
?   LIST EVERYONE IN MANCHESTER OR BRISTOL OFFICE EARNING OVER £20000
*
*   /// LIST NAME, LOCATION, SALARY FOR LOCATION = MAN OR BRI WITH
    SALARY GREATER THAN 20000 ///
*
*   searching... please wait.
*
    NAME                LOCATION        SALARY

    ATKINS   J F        MANCHESTER      22000
    BOARDMAN   S        BRISTOL         30000
    STOWELL   J R       BRISTOL         23500
    VON NEUMANN   J     MANCHESTER      35000
*
*   ready
```

Fig. 9.7 This 'near-English' dialogue allows a very flexible input. The system analyses the user's requests (in bold type) and translates them into its own codes. It can cope with a wide variety of English phrases, e.g. 'Tell me who', or 'How many' or 'What is the highest'. Translations of all these have been built into the software

it is the analyst's job to work out the normal routines of running the system, including, where necessary, the timing and frequency of runs. Procedures for making security, or *backup*, copies of files must be part of the normal routine.

Emergency Procedures

An equally vital part of the design effort is directed towards planning the actions to take if the system breaks down. These include:

- determining the nature of the problem (software, hardware)
- switching to an alternative system, either by
    - (*a*) reverting to a manual system
    or (*b*) using another computer

Q 9.13 *Companies with similar systems can make a mutual 'standby' agreement for emergency processing. What are the likely problems with this?*

PROGRAM DESIGN, CODING AND TESTING

The programmer(s) then design the programs, taking care to ensure that each program will work exactly as specified. If the program specifications are not completely clear or if they contain possible errors, they must be tidied up with the analyst's help, *before* too much programming work has been done.

Sometimes the same person specifies, designs and codes the program. In this case, it is a good idea for someone else in the team to check the work, or glaring errors may be missed.

We have discussed at length (in Chapter 3) the art of designing, coding, testing and documenting *good* programs. Re-read Chapter 3 and then answer Q 9.14.

? **Q 9.14** *What makes a good program?*

DOCUMENTING THE SYSTEM

Just as each program must be carefully documented, so must the entire system. Systems documentation must include *systems flowcharts* (such as that in Figure 9.8 overleaf) for each part of the system and *file specifications* showing the layout of each file, the expected maximum and minimum file sizes and the media used.

? **Q 9.15** *Look at the systems flowchart in Figure 9.8 which illustrates an on-line system for processing orders received by a mail order company.*

(a) Which are input files and which are output files?

(b) Explain why some arrows are one-way and others are two-way.

(c) Why does the system need to be on-line?

(d) What storage medium should the mail-order company use?

(e) What use would the company make of the following files?
(i) Sales details file   (ii) Outstanding orders file
(iii) Warehouse lists

The timing and sequence of running different parts of a system must be clearly written down—otherwise a new operator might try to run, say, the 'month end' program before the final week's data had been input!

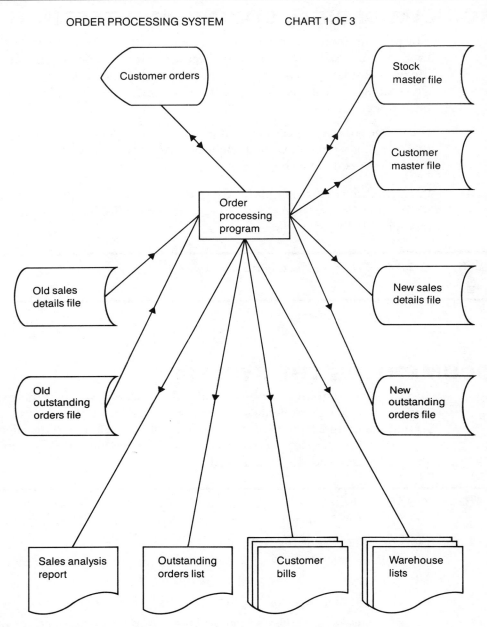

ORDER PROCESSING SYSTEM   CHART 1 OF 3

Fig. 9.8   Part of the on-line order processing system for a mail-order company

Instructions for using the system are often contained in a *user manual*. These days, many systems provide user instructions on the screen. This can be helpful as it allows selective presentation of just the relevant information at any given stage—see Figure 9.9.

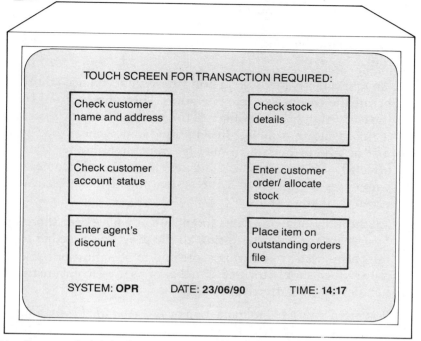

Fig. 9.9   It is often more helpful to have the users' instructions clearly laid out on-screen, rather than rely on their reading the manual

IMPLEMENTING THE SYSTEM

Having spent a good deal of time and money on developing a system, a manager might be forgiven for thinking that the job was finished. Surely after all that effort the system can just be 'switched on'? It is because of this assumption that even well designed systems sometimes fail.

In fact, *implementation*, i.e. the job of getting the system up and running smoothly, can be as challenging and painstaking as systems analysis and design. The following seven steps are usually involved:

- Ordering
- File setup
- Staff training
- System testing
- Parallel running
- Live running
- Post-implementation review

Any hardware and software must obviously be ordered, but so must the *consumables*, i.e. disks, tapes, continuous stationery, printed forms, ribbons, daisy-wheels etc.

All necessary *files* must be created and *loaded* with the relevant data. It is easy to underestimate the time needed for this task. Some of the files may be new, but others can sometimes be created by converting existing files.

Anyone directly involved in using the system will need thorough training before the system goes into operation. This training should not take place too early, though, or people will forget how to use the system by the time it finally starts running. In addition, some general background information about the system may be valuable for other staff not directly affected. There may be staff resistance to overcome, especially if employees are afraid that the system might make them redundant or downgrade their skills.

All the individual programs should already have been thoroughly tested. *System testing* involves testing all the programs together to ensure that the entire system performs according to specifications. Exhaustive test data, which should include actual data, is used to ensure that the system handles errors correctly.

It is often advisable to make one or more *parallel runs* running the new system side by side with the existing system to prove that the results agree. Bugs are often found at this stage, and it is obviously safer to remove them now before everyone is relying on the new system.

Now at last the system is ready for *live running*. The old system may be retained, if only to fall back on in case of breakdown of the new one. A *post-implementation review* is often held, after a few weeks or months. The analyst(s), the people using the system and (quite often) the suppliers of software or hardware meet to examine whether the system is living up to expectations and agree on any necessary corrections or improvements.

PACKAGED SYSTEMS

Designing systems from scratch is obviously time-consuming; it typically takes several months or even years to complete a system. This means that the sheer cost of custom-designed software is often prohibitive. Even large organisations often cannot afford the luxury.

Fortunately, thousands of 'off-the-shelf' software packages are now available. Hundreds of different companies may use the same standard accounting packages. They are able to do this because the way companies keep their accounts can be surprisingly similar, although their products or services may be very different.

Accounting Packages

One accounting area which is frequently managed with the help of packaged software is the *payroll system*. Without automation, calculating all the bits and pieces that make up each individual employee's pay can take many hours. Only the smallest companies nowadays run a manual payroll system. A packaged payroll system is examined in Chapter 13.

Sales ledger systems are probably the other most common accounting packages. Again, nearly every company sells something, and must keep up-to-date records of *how much* they have sold, of *what*, *when* it was sold, and *to whom*.

Q 9.16 *What other vital piece of information must the company keep about their sales?*

Some companies (like Universal Record Distribution, see Chapter 12) decide that their requirements simply cannot be met by any software package on the market, and have their own system designed. However, this is an unusual and risky step to take. An off-the-shelf package will always be cheaper and should be more reliable than a custom-built system.

Q 9.17 *Why should a package be more reliable than custom-built software? When might it not be?*

General-purpose Packages

There are three very common ways of dealing with information, each of which can often be dramatically assisted by a standard software package:

(a) Documents: letters, reports, memos, circulars, manuals, books. A *word processing* package may help in producing, storing, changing and reproducing documents.

(b) Numbers: often in tabular form, e.g. budgets, forecasts, accounts. A *spreadsheet* package can speed up otherwise laborious figure work.

(c) Complex information: about customers, about products, about employees etc. A *database* package can help to organise, store and retrieve information rapidly.

Specialist Packages

As well as these general-purpose packages, many are designed to cater for one particular profession or industry. So doctors or surveyors or interior designers or solicitors can buy a package specially created for them—or so the software supplier may claim! Equally, there are packages aimed at every industry and occupation, from art galleries to video clubs, from freight forwarders to fish farmers.

A good example of the benefits of packaged software is provided by local authorities. Councils all over the country are major users of computer systems. They have many complex jobs to fulfil, such as maintaining roads and property, or administering a wide variety of benefits and grants. But for years councils up and down the country spent huge sums on 're-inventing the wheel'; i.e. on designing systems which had already been designed in similar form by some other authority. All councils collect rates and rubbish, manage fleets of vehicles, run libraries and schools, pay staff and so on. Fortunately there is now a growing range of flexible software packages which one council can buy from another.

What Packaged Software Cannot Do

A software package, however well designed and executed, cannot do away with the need for proper systems analysis. The analyst must always find out how the existing systems work and spend enough time determining the real information needs of the individual or the organisation. Having done that, however, a good systems analyst will often conclude that a packaged software solution offers the most cost-effective way of meeting those needs.

Once a package has been chosen, there is a temptation to think that implementation will take care of itself. It will not. Getting a package installed and working smoothly is often just as complex and challenging a task as with a custom-built system. If corners are cut when implementing a software package, it can fail spectacularly.

JARGON 9

Manual procedures *Internal and external*
Forms *data sources*
Outputs *Data capture*
Inputs

Information system *Systems analyst*
Business analyst
Terms of reference
Feasibility study
Systems specification

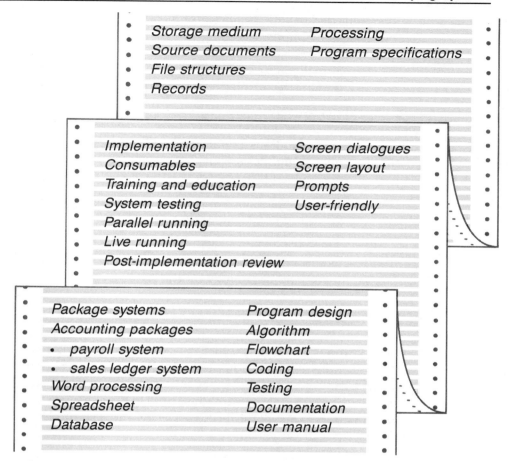

Storage medium   Processing
Source documents   Program specifications
File structures
Records

Implementation   Screen dialogues
Consumables   Screen layout
Training and education   Prompts
System testing   User-friendly
Parallel running
Live running
Post-implementation review

Package systems   Program design
Accounting packages   Algorithm
   payroll system   Flowchart
   sales ledger system   Coding
Word processing   Testing
Spreadsheet   Documentation
Database   User manual

EXERCISES 9

1. Before a computer system is installed a systems analyst would be called in to ensure that the requirements of the customer would be met. The following is a list of the stages that the analysis covers. Put these stages into the correct order and briefly summarise the work involved at each stage.

> Project approval
> Training
> Feasibility study
> Detailed system design
> Monitoring the 'live system'
> Implementation
> Problem identification

(ALSEB)

2. A computerised-record-system for pupils at a school has been devised to produce lists of pupils according to age, sex, form (class), and alphabetical order for use by the school secretary. The computer system consists of a small microcomputer system complete with VDU screen and keyboard, a character printer and a floppy-disk storage-system.

As chief systems-analyst, you are aware that the school secretary has no knowledge of programming and will not be required to learn programming. Furthermore, the secretary has had no previous experience with using this microcomputer system.

(a) Specify the outline documentation which will be required in order:

   (i) to make use of the program package, and to enter into a data file details of new arrivals in the school;

   (ii) to make use of the system hardware.

(b) What would you wish to have built into the programs in order to minimise invalid data entry by the secretary?

(Ox)

3. Home-Warm is a company which specialises in installing central heating systems in houses. The various items which are used in the central heating systems (radiators, boilers, pipes etc.) are bought from suppliers and stored in the Home-Warm warehouse until they are needed. Home-Warm employs fitters to install the heating systems and also employs office staff to carry out clerical work.

Home-Warm is considering using a computer to assist in the management and operation of the company. Identify and describe four tasks for which the computer could be used.

For two of these tasks, describe and give examples of the data which would be input to, and output from, the computer. Also indicate suitable methods of collecting the data.

(CU)

4. When a new computerised system is first suggested, a *systems analyst* is usually employed to carry out a feasibility study and to prepare a report for management.

Assuming that it is decided to continue with the computerisation, state and describe the other steps involved on the part of the systems analyst in the successful computerisation of a previously manual system.

(JMB)

10 Files

Most of us are familiar with paper *files*. You probably use a notebook, a ring binder or a folder to keep together your notes on a particular subject. Many householders keep files containing all their bills, and all schools and colleges keep files about their students. Files are simply *collections of data*, usually connected in some way, e.g. all notes on English Literature, all student records for Form 5D etc.

Computer files are exactly the same in principle; only the *storage medium* is different.

> **?** **Q 10.1** *Write down two examples of paper files which you or your family use. What does the data have in common in each case?*
>
> **Q 10.2** *Write down two examples of computer files which you have come across. Say what the data has in common and what storage medium is used for each file.*

Stored information is useless unless it can be found again when required. Files are usually *structured* in some way to make it easier to extract information from them. Many offices keep a file containing a copy of every letter written by anyone in the office. This file soon grows so large that nothing could be found if copies were just thrown in anyhow, and so care is taken to file copies in strict sequence, according to the date they were written. Other files are more structured; a customer file, for instance, might be kept in alphabetical order, but *within* that structure all correspondence to and from each customer is in order of date.

When files are being designed, for manual or computer systems, close attention must be paid to the organisation and layout of the data which they will contain.

FIELDS AND RECORDS

Each item of data in a file, e.g. the *student's name* in a class file, is called a *field*.

Knowing just a student's name on its own (e.g. 'Noaks A') is obviously useless, unless other data about Noaks can be found at the same time. So all the fields connected with Noaks (e.g. his address, date of birth, parents' or guardians' name(s), telephone number etc.) are grouped together to form a *record*. In this example there would be one record for each student in the class.

? **Q 10.3** *Can a single character be a field? Can a single field form a record?*

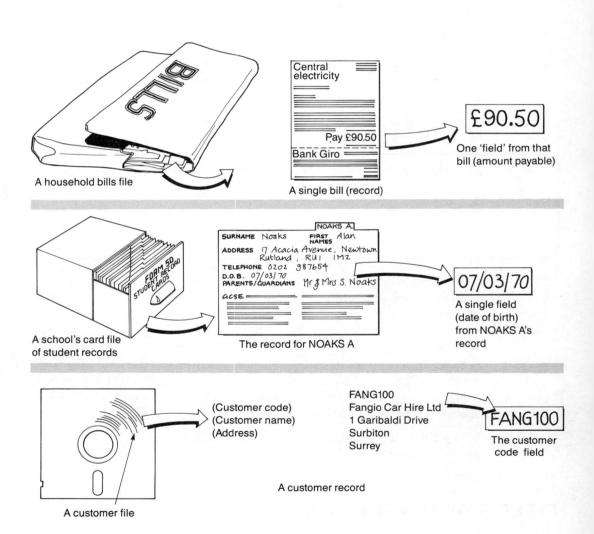

A household bills file

A single bill (record)

One 'field' from that bill (amount payable)

£90.50

A school's card file of student records

The record for NOAKS A

A single field (date of birth) from NOAKS A's record

07/03/70

A customer file

(Customer code)
(Customer name)
(Address)

A customer record

FANG100
Fangio Car Hire Ltd
1 Garibaldi Drive
Surbiton
Surrey

FANG100

The customer code field

Fig. 10.1 The relationship between files, records and fields is the same for manual and computer files

So a file is a collection of related records, while a record is simply a sensible grouping of related fields.

Level of storage

Example data

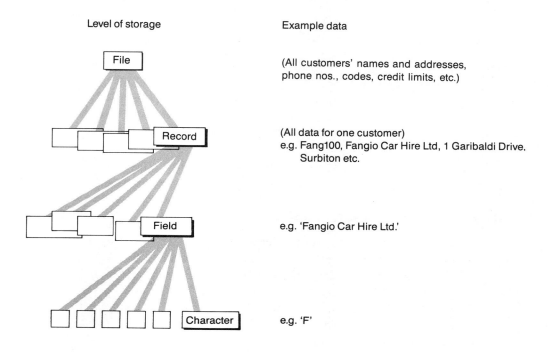

(All customers' names and addresses, phone nos., codes, credit limits, etc.)

(All data for one customer)
e.g. Fang100, Fangio Car Hire Ltd, 1 Garibaldi Drive, Surbiton etc.

e.g. 'Fangio Car Hire Ltd.'

e.g. 'F'

Fig. 10.2   The hierarchy of data

It should be fairly obvious why organisations (and individuals) need to keep files. People simply cannot *reliably* keep enough information in their heads; they need permanent records as aids to memory.

The same is true for a computer. Although its main memory is normally more reliable than that of a human being, its capacity is small compared with the volume of information which needs to be stored. Remember too that main storage is *volatile*; i.e. stored data is lost when the power is switched off. So computer systems also need to store data in permanent files on disk or tape.

?   **Q 10.4**   *A typical telephone directory contains 800 pages each containing 300 telephone numbers. Assuming that a single name, address and telephone number takes up 64 characters, how many 256 K computers would you need to store this data in main memory?*

SETTING UP A FILE

Suppose that you want to create a file of information on endangered species. The *record structure*, i.e. the fields required, might be as follows:

Field no.	Field name
1	Reference number
2	Name of animal
3	Main habitat
4	Estimated population (minimum)
5	Estimated population (maximum)

It is important to distinguish between the *field name*, e.g. Main habitat, and the *data* which will be stored in it, e.g. Ethiopia.

Fixed- and Variable-length Fields

For each field the maximum length in characters (i.e. the *field size*) must be decided. For example, the names stored in most files will comfortably fit into a 30-character field. However, some species at risk have very long names, and so a *fixed-length* field of 40 characters will be allowed. This means that *every* name, including short ones, takes up a full 40 characters. So the name 'red wolf', which needs only eight characters (remember the space between 'red' and 'wolf'), wastes 32 characters (usually filled in with spaces) in the name field.

Ref. No.   Name   Main
                                                                                                 Location

| 0 0 0 9 0 | N O R T H E R N   S Q U A R E - L I P P E D   R H I N O C E R O S | U G A N D |

| 0 0 1 1 0 | R E D   W O L F | T E X A S |

Fig. 10.3 Fixed-length fields. Shaded areas indicate the space wasted by having a fixed length for the 'NAME' field. This wastage is usually acceptable because of the convenience of fixed length records

This wasted space is often unimportant; storage is cheap nowadays. But if the file is too big to manage, or space is scarce for some reason, it may be better to choose *variable-length* fields. This can save a lot of space, but the system must have some way of knowing when one field ends and another starts. This is usually achieved by some kind of marker between fields.

The advantage of fixed-length fields is that it is always clear exactly where each one begins and ends, no matter what the data may be.

Q 10.5 *Why is it important to know where fields start and finish?*

It is easy to see what type of *field contents* there will be in the endangered species file. The name and habitat(s), for instance, will be *alphabetic fields* containing words, whereas the population fields and the reference number will be *numeric fields*, containing only numbers.

Field no.	Field name	Alphabetic or Numeric	Length in characters
1	Reference number	N	5
2	Name of animal	A	40
3	Main habitat	A	20
4	Estimated population (minimum)	N	5
5	Estimated population (maximum)	N	5
		Total	75

Fixed and Variable Data

The data in fields 1–2 is unlikely to change and can be regarded as fixed data. The habitat and population estimates (fields 3–5) may vary and will require periodic updating.

Key Fields

How can a particular record be located in a file? A paper file, such as a telephone directory, is simply searched until the required name is found. In computer jargon, we would say the file is searched until a *match* is found between the name we were seeking (e.g. J. Davies) and the name contained in a particular record (i.e. directory entry). But what happens if we find 11 people called 'J. Davies' in the directory? We should need to know the correct address as well as the name before we could be sure of finding the right one.

This type of difficulty in finding records can be avoided if every record in a file contains a field called a *key field* which has a different value for every record on file. In this way the key field *uniquely* identifies the record. A surname on its own is evidently *not* an adequate record key for searching a telephone directory, and even when initials are added there can still be 'duplicates'.

Q 10.6 *Why should key fields be reasonably short?*

Q 10.7 *How many different species could be stored in this file?*

For our endangered species file, we could have used the 'name of animal' as the key field, but a 40-character key is perhaps too long. Each species on the file will therefore be given a unique 5-digit reference number, which will be used as the key for locating records. Note that we could have more than one key field, so that we could locate a species either by its reference number, or by its full name.

Q 10.8 *What would be a suitable key field for:*

(a) a student record in a class file?

(b) a customer record in a sales file (contains details of a company's sales to its customers)?

Having designed the records, the *file size* (in characters or bytes) can be estimated very simply:

length of one record = length of field 1 + length of field 2

+ length of field 3 + ... etc.

file size = length of one record × number of records

It is sensible to allow plenty of extra room for files. There are three reasons why more space is often required than the original estimate:

- The number of records is often *underestimated* in the first place; we might want to store more than planned.

- As time goes by, the volume of data frequently *increases*; in our example the number of endangered species is, unhappily, growing all the time. Room must be allowed for the file to grow accordingly.

- When we need to *change* data stored on file (e.g. after a new survey of population size) we may have to create a completely new version of the file. Allowing space for the old *and* new versions would *double* the storage requirement.

File size often helps to decide the most suitable *storage medium*; a file might simply not fit on a floppy disk, or might be *made* to fit because the data needs to be quickly available and direct access to records is essential.

ENDANGERED SPECIES MASTER FILE

REF NUMBER	NAME OF ANIMAL	MAIN LOCATION	POPULATION MIN	POPULATION MAX
00010	BLUE WHALE	ANTARCTIC REGION	0070000	0020000
00020	BRANDERS SWAMP DEER	MADHYA PREDESH, INDIA	0005000	0000090
00030	CARIBBEAN MONK SEAL	CARIBBEAN ISLANDS	0000000	0000050
00040	GOLDEN LION MARMOSET	SOUTH EAST BRAZIL	0040000	0000600
00050	JAVAN RHINOCEROS	JAVA	0001000	0000060
00060	MEDITERRANEAN MONK SEAL	MEDITERRANEAN	0030000	0000600
00070	MEXICAN GRIZZLY BEAR	SIERRA MADRE, MEXICO	0000300	0000100
00080	NORTHERN KIT FOX	SASKATCHEWAN, CANADA	0000000	0000050
00090	NORTHERN SQUARE-LIPPED RHINOCEROS	UGANDA	0002500	0000100
00100	NOVAYA ZEMLYA REINDEER	NOVAYA ZEMLYA, USSR	0002000	0000075
00110	RED WOLF	TEXAS, USA	0000000	0000040
00120	SAN JOAQUIN FOX	NEW MEXICO, USA	0015000	0000600
00130	SOMALI WILD ASS	ETHIOPIA	0040000	0000800
00140	SUMATRAN RHINOCEROS	SUMATRA	0010000	0000175
00150	WOOLLY SPIDER MONKEY	SOUTH EAST BRAZIL	0000000	0000100

Fig. 10.4 15 records on the endangered species file

FILE ORGANISATION

Sequential, Indexed or Direct?

We must also decide on the *file organisation method*, i.e. how the records are physically arranged on the chosen medium.

The simplest way is to use a *sequential file*, where records are just written in sequence, one after another. Often the records are sorted into a particular order (e.g. alphabetical order) when the file is set up. This is called the *key sequence*. The main drawback of this type of file is obvious. When you want to *access* (i.e. 'get at', to read or write) a particular record, you may have to read all the records from the beginning of the file until you find the one you want.

This problem can be avoided by using an *indexed file*, which has two separate parts, one containing the *index*, the other containing the data itself. The index file stores the *addresses* of the data records, i.e. exactly where each record can be found. For each record *key* there is an entry in the index *pointing* to the physical location of the record itself (see Figure 10.6).

Direct files (also called *random files*) are also organised so that you can go directly to the record you want, by specifying the key. The system calculates the physical location of the record by applying a formula to the key. Direct files are much less commonly used than sequential and indexed files.

File Design

In summary, anyone setting up a file must consider eight factors:

- *Record structure*: which fields must be stored and in what order?
- *Field sizes*: length of each field in characters
- Whether *fixed-* or *variable-length* records are to be used
- *Field contents*: whether words or numbers, and which data is constant, and which is changeable
- *Key fields*
- *File size*: i.e. how many records will there be?
- *Storage medium*
- *File organisation method*

ACCESS METHODS

The method of file organisation may depend upon how it is stored. For example, magnetic tape only allows *sequential access* (sometimes called *serial access*). A file held on tape can only be read record by record until the correct one is found.

Fig. 10.5 Sequential access can cause serious delay

Suppose a golf club has a system which uses a sequential file to store members' details, arranged in alphabetical order of name, and the club secretary wants to check the membership number of, say, Mr. Z. Zuckermann. He (or the program he was using) would have to scan all the way through the file starting from, say, Mrs. A. Aaronson.

Indexed access on the other hand enables almost immediate access to the required record. The system takes the key of the record—ZUCKERMAN Z—and 'looks it up' in the index to find the physical location of the record. It can then go straight to that point to read the whole record from the data file. This is possible only with a storage medium such as magnetic disk that enables any record to be read almost immediately by accurate positioning of the read/write head.

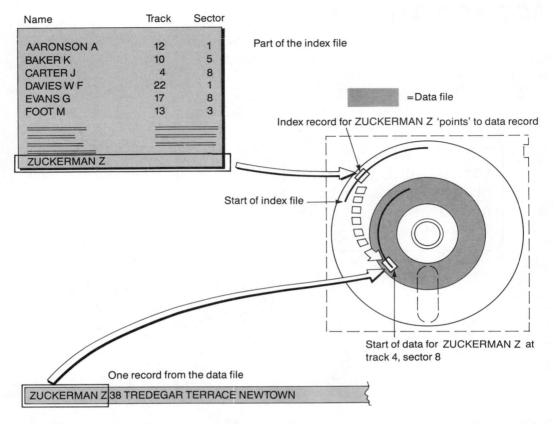

Name	Track	Sector
AARONSON A	12	1
BAKER K	10	5
CARTER J	4	8
DAVIES W F	22	1
EVANS G	17	8
FOOT M	13	3
ZUCKERMAN Z		

Part of the index file

= Data file

Index record for ZUCKERMAN Z 'points' to data record

Start of index file

Start of data for ZUCKERMAN Z at track 4, sector 8

One record from the data file

ZUCKERMAN Z 38 TREDEGAR TERRACE NEWTOWN

Fig. 10.6 An indexed file. Note that the index file is separate from the main data. An index record contains only the keyfield (e.g. ZUCKERMAN Z) and the corresponding data record location (e.g. track 4, sector 8)

For true *direct access*, the system uses the key field to *calculate* (rather than look up in an index) the physical location where it will find the required record. For example, a simple spare-parts file could be organised so that the record for part number 14 (i.e. key = 14) is located at track 1, sector 4 of a magnetic disk (Figure 7.12 will remind you what tracks and sectors are). Part number 73 would be found at track 7, sector 3, and so on. More complex formulae are often used to convert the key into the record location, but the end result is the same.

You can use a form of indexed access on a gramophone record to select a particular track:

- First, to find the track you want, read the printed notes (i.e. the index) on the sleeve, which tell you that it is, say, track number 3.
- Then lower the stylus directly onto track 3.

Q 10.9 *Design a simple record format for a file of addresses and telephone numbers to be used on a home computer system (use Figure 10.4 to help you).*

What assumptions have you made in organising this file?

If the file is to hold up to 200 records, estimate its likely size (in kilobytes).

MASTER FILES AND TRANSACTION FILES

Files that contain mostly *fixed* data (e.g. names, addresses, telephone numbers, account numbers, credit limits etc.) are called *master files*. A customer file, a student file and our file of endangered species are all master files. A system may contain more than one master file, e.g. a school record-keeping system may have a pupils master file, a teachers master file and a subjects master file.

Some of the data in a master file will become out of date as a result of events (or *transactions*) taking place and the master file needs *updating* periodically, say daily or weekly or monthly.

Whenever a company sells something to a new customer its customer file needs altering. This is done by *inserting* a new record for this customer. Should a student leave school, the pupils master file must be updated by *deleting* the appropriate record. If an expedition to Sumatra finds very few rhinoceros surviving, the population figures in our file must be *amended*.

These examples illustrate the three *transaction types*:

- *insertion*: creating a new record
- *deletion*: removing an existing record
- *amendment*: altering an existing record

Changes such as these are often gathered together into a *transaction file*, and this file is used to make all the adjustments to the master file at one time.

Q 10.10 *What data might be contained in transaction files to update these master files:*

    (a) a customer accounts file?

    (b) a student records file?

    (c) a stock master file?

Processing Files

When the master file is updated with the new information held in a transaction file, each record on the transaction file must be *matched* with the equivalent master record. Clearly, for this to succeed, both records must use the same key field.

If the master file is an ordinary sequential file, the transaction file must also be *sorted* into *key sequence* because the master file can only be read straight through from beginning to end; you cannot 'go back a few records'.

If the transactions file contains a change for a record that is out of sequence, then the computer will be unable to match it with any of the remaining records on the master file. It will continue searching, in vain, until it reaches the end of the master tape, and the updating program will have failed.

FIELD NAMES
(Update program must be
designed to recognise these)

NEW VALUES
(To amend data on
master file)

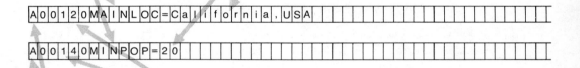

TRANSACTION CODES
A = AMENDMENT
D = DELETION of record
I = INSERTION of new record

TRANSACTION KEYS
(Reference numbers to match
with master records)

Fig. 10.7 A transaction file to update the endangered species master file. Note that this file contains two amendment transactions only. Transaction files are often much larger and typically contain a mixture of transaction types (amendments, insertions and deletions)

Q 10.11 *Turn back to the endangered species master file on page 183 and explain what would happen if it were updated with the following transactions file.*

Transaction code	Key	Transaction	Details	
A	00120	MAIN-LOC	=	California, USA
A	00140	MIN-POP	=	20
D	00150			
A	00020	MAX-POP	=	180

Why are no transaction details given for the adjustment to record 00150?

Q 10.12 *If the endangered species master file was held on tape so that only sequential access was possible, why would the transactions file in Q 10.11 require adjustment before the updating procedure began?*

Q 10.13 *Must a transaction file be sorted into key sequence before updating an indexed master file? Give a reason for your answer.*

Q 10.14 *What would happen if you tried to:*

(a) amend or delete a record which was not on file?

(b) insert a record which was already on file?

How would you cope with the problem in each case?

Q 10.15 *Would it be possible to insert a record between the Red Wolf and the San Joaquin Fox in the file shown in Figure 10.4?*

Where have you encountered a similar problem before?

ANCESTRAL FILE SYSTEMS

Notice that, on successful completion of a sequential update, we have a new version *and* an old version of the master file. The old version could be deleted, but what if the changes turned out to be incorrect, or the new version was lost altogether? We should be glad to have a previous version to fall back on; the new file could then be reconstructed by running the update program again on the old file.

It is therefore common practice, and a sensible precaution, to keep at least two versions of master files. They are often called successive *generations* of the file; our new endangered species file is referred to as the *son* and the old one as the *father*.

When a further update is carried out, the new file is a new son, the previous son becomes the father, and the file which was father becomes *grandfather*. It is common for organisations using such *ancestral file systems* to keep as many as six generations of a given master file!

The Choice of File Organisation

Computer systems, like programs, should be kept as simple as possible. Usually that means using sequential files. However, the choice also depends on the size of the file and how it will be used.

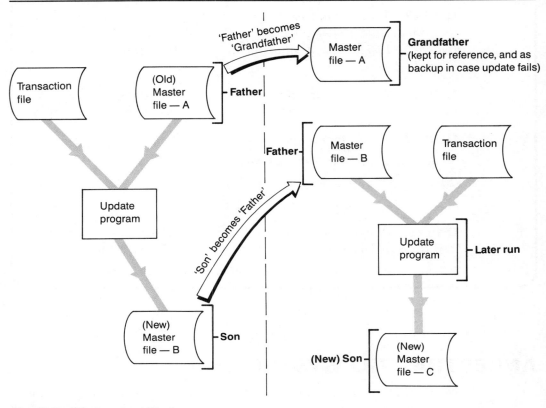

Fig. 10.8 The Ancestral File System

What if we want to be able to read a *particular* record on the endangered species file in order to check populations? This is sometimes called *file interrogation*. Finding the red wolf should only take a few moments with the file as it is, but what if there were 10 000 species stored? It could take several minutes with a sequential file, and so we should have to consider indexed (or possibly direct) organisation.

Another factor is the proportion of the records on file that are typically accessed at any given time. If you normally update most, or all, the records on file, e.g. a weekly payroll file, then sequential organisation will do fine. But if you frequently wish to change just one or two records, e.g. in a name and address file, indexed or direct access is more convenient. Note that for this type of update you do not need to create a completely new master file; because each record can be exactly located via its key. Performing an *update in place* on the master file is a common technique.

Method of organisation	Sequential	Indexed	Direct
ADVANTAGES	Simple to set up Simple to use Ideal when most or all records must be accessed by a program May require less programming skill Efficient use of storage space Suitable for tape storage	Speed of access very good (especially for large files) Allows speedy file interrogation (e.g. to answer telephone inquiries) Updates can be done in place without increasing space needed Suitable when updates often affect only a few records	Speed of access excellent Updates can be done in place without increasing space needed Suitable when updates affect only a few records Allows speedy file interrogation (e.g. to answer telephone inquiries)
DISADVANTAGES	Poor access speed unless file is fairly small On-line queries usually impossible (unless file is small) Any update requires creation of a whole new file	Two separate files usually needed (index file and data file) Can become disorganised when many records are added—so needs periodic reorganisation May require more programming skill Needs more space than sequential equivalent	Maximum likely size of file must be decided and all the space allocated when creating file Can be difficult to devise the algorithm which converts a record key to a physical location May require more programming skill Can be very wasteful of space

Fig. 10.9 Advantages and disadvantages of different file organisation methods

File Maintenance

Occasional changes to a master file, e.g. to correct a figure or the spelling of a name, are called *file maintenance*. Maintenance ensures that recorded data is accurate. It can be distinguished from regular updating, which might be done, for example, to add each month's sales figures into the cumulative total.

Q 10.16 *What file organisation method would you suggest for the following? Explain your choice.*

(a) *a manufacturer's customer account file, updated monthly and used to print monthly statements for all customers*

(b) *a bank's customer account file, used as above but also to answer telephone inquiries*

(c) *a travel agent's file of available holidays*

(d) *the income tax records of every adult in the country.*

DATABASES

A collection of related data files is known as a *database*. More and more organisations are bringing together all their data into this type of 'pooled' information structure. This is easier said than done, but when it is successful the database approach has major advantages. Firstly, it avoids duplication: the data is captured once only, where ordinary file-based systems might have collected it several times.

For example, when an engineering company sells a machine tool, the accounts department captures the data to produce the invoice and to chase up the payment, the production department records it in a separate system, so as to plan production, and the stores department needs the data to control the stocks of components.

If, on the other hand, the company had a well-designed database system, the sale would be entered once only, and each department could access the data when required.

Secondly, it makes it easier to use the data in new ways that were not originally foreseen when the system was installed. The sales department might need to *forecast* future sales on the basis of the actual sales over the last three years. With the database system, all the past sales data is readily available.

To gain these benefits, special software is needed to manage all the files, to simplify updating and to make it easy for users to access the data in the most flexible way. Such software (usually a set of programs) is called a *database management system* (DBMS). Some DBMSs require highly skilled programmers to learn special, complex languages before they can even begin to handle information, which seems to defeat the object. The better ones are much friendlier.

Q 10.17 *Does your school/college have DBMS software? Find out what you can about it, e.g. how easy is it to:*

(a) set up a data structure?

(b) enter data into it?

(c) modify it?

(d) get information from it?

(e) read and understand the user manual?

A *relational* database management system is the type most commonly available on microcomputers (and increasingly on larger machines). It is so named because the contents of files can easily be related, by having a common name for a field, as in Figure 10.10. All the data can be represented by tables of information, as shown.

STOCK FILE

Description	Partno	Price	Qty: on hand
Widget, small	64374	00.15	300
Grommet, 1 cm	23231	00.50	24
Gadget, medium	66550	25.75	5
Thingummy	33987	4.00	18
Widget, large	64377	00.80	112
Sink, kitchen	93002	60.50	1
....			
....			

ORDERS FILE:

Customer	Partno	Order Qty
Acorn Computers Ltd.	33987	12
Burroughs Machines Ltd.	66550	6
Cray Research (UK) Ltd.	93002	50
Digital Equipment Co. Ltd.	23231	1000
....		

Fig. 10.10 Two database files linked by a common field name, 'Partno'. Data from these two files might be combined when producing dispatch notes or invoices

'Intelligent' File Storage Systems

When really vast databases are being searched, even the most powerful computers seem slow. A reporter, for example, might want to search a newspaper database for every reference to electoral reform in the last 20 years. This job could tie up a mainframe for quite some time.

File storage systems that are *intelligent* can accelerate these searches. The computer can ask the storage system to search for any article containing the words 'electoral reform'. The computer then carries on with another job while special hardware in the *storage device* conducts the search and retrieves all the relevant references.

JARGON 10

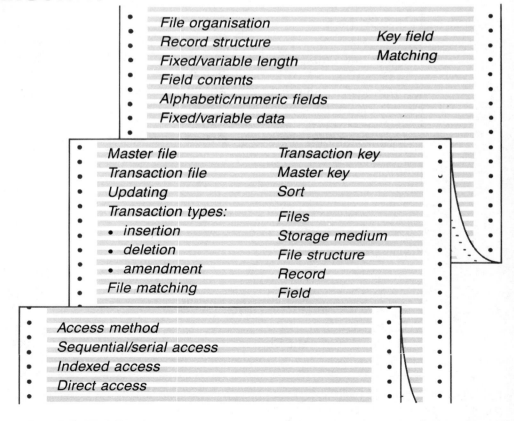

File organisation
Record structure
Fixed/variable length
Field contents
Alphabetic/numeric fields
Fixed/variable data

Key field
Matching

Master file
Transaction file
Updating
Transaction types:
• insertion
• deletion
• amendment
File matching

Transaction key
Master key
Sort
Files
Storage medium
File structure
Record
Field

Access method
Sequential/serial access
Indexed access
Direct access

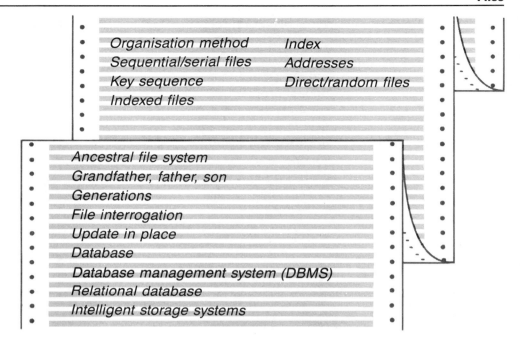

- Organisation method
- Sequential/serial files
- Key sequence
- Indexed files
- Index
- Addresses
- Direct/random files

- Ancestral file system
- Grandfather, father, son
- Generations
- File interrogation
- Update in place
- Database
- Database management system (DBMS)
- Relational database
- Intelligent storage systems

EXERCISES 10

1. What is a 'database'?

2. Explain the meaning of, and the connections between, the following terms:

   (*a*) file, record and field;

   (*b*) master, duplicate and transaction files.

   Describe how a serial access file is updated.

   How does this process differ if the file is a direct access one?

   (SUJB)

3. A company is considering placing its personnel records on magnetic disks. There will be frequent changes to these records as well as routine processing. What would be the advantages and disadvantages of organising the records (i) sequentially, (ii) randomly, on these disks?

   (O & C)

4. Explain how an indexed-sequential file could be set up to store and process customer records. Your file should be able to handle the needs of customers of either a mail order firm or a bank.

   (O & C)

5. By selecting seven labels from the list, copy and complete the diagram below so that it shows a general method of updating a serial access file.

   List of labels: errors;
   old master file;
   update program;
   sorted transactions;
   new master file;
   unsorted transactions;
   sort program;
   central processing unit.

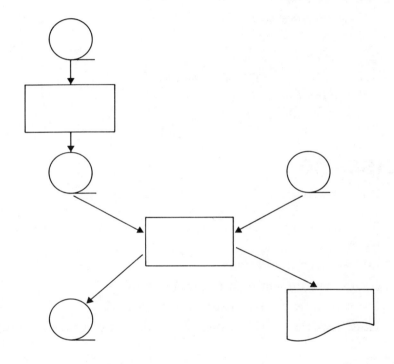

(Southern Group CEE)

6. (a) (i) What is the meaning of the term file updating?

   (ii) Why do file records need to be matched before processing/ updating?

   (iii) Why are master serial file records normally kept in sequence?

   (iv) Why is processing easier if the updating file is sorted into the same sequence?

   (v) How many files are normally involved in a serial file update; explain the purpose of each one.

(b) Give the meaning of the terms *addition, modification* and *deletion* in the context of *file amendment*.

Copy and complete the following table using Yes and No to show the necessary action for each type of amendment:

Type of amendment record / Action to be taken	Locate record in master file	Alter details in master record	Create new master record	Write record to master file
Addition				
Modification				
Deletion				

(c) Why does serial file processing involve two versions of the master file? What is the security technique used when serial file processing?

(WMEB)

7. The outline system flowchart below shows some typical commercial data processing. New data on the transaction file is being used together with data on the master file to produce printed results and an updated version of the master file. Magnetic tape is used for holding both versions of the master file.

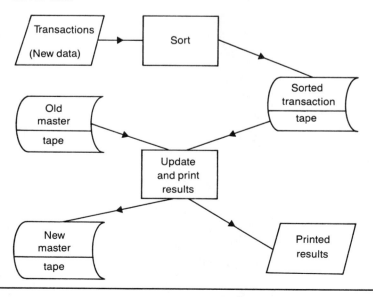

(*a* (i) Into what order must the transaction records be sorted by the sort process?

(ii) Why must this order be used?

(iii) What does updated mean in this situation?

(*b*) Choose one computer application which could be described by this flowchart and then answer the following questions:

(i) What is the application you have chosen?

(ii) State two items of information which are input as 'transaction' data in your chosen application.

(iii) State three items of information which are held on the master file in your chosen application.

(iv) State three items of information which are printed out in your application.

(NREB)

11 Reliability and Security

ACCURACY AND RELIABILITY

An elderly lady once received a computer-printed letter, threatening court action for recovery of a debt. The amount claimed was £0.00. Many people might simply blame 'the computer' and tear up the letter, but this lady had no knowledge of computers and was very distressed by the incident. In due course, an apology arrived from those responsible, but the damage had already been done.

It was reported recently how a US Army supply clerk, needing a spare part, punched the number 4772 into a computerised ordering system. Eventually a seven-ton ship's anchor was delivered to the base at Fort Carson, Colorado: 1000 miles inland. The clerk thought he had ordered a headlight, which had the part number 4972.

Fig. 11.1 One tiny mistake can cause a big problem

Fortunately, cases like these are rare nowadays, but they still occur. Too often, the computer is the scapegoat, but the *people* who design, program, install or control the system are really guilty.

Q 11.1 *How could the two cases above have arisen? What safeguards would you suggest in each case to prevent similar problems in future?*

DEPENDABLE SYSTEMS

Organisations depend more and more on computer systems for their very survival. These systems must provide accurate information which can be relied on, and so appropriate checks and safeguards must be built in at the design stage. People who operate a system must be adequately trained so that they understand their role and are less likely to make mistakes.

ENSURING THE ACCURACY OF DATA

We met GIGO (garbage in—garbage out) in Chapter 2. How can we prevent 'garbage' (incorrect data) from getting into systems?

Encouraging users or operators to check data carefully will help; people usually have quite a lot of common sense, but you cannot *rely* on it. No one thought of checking why a land-locked military base should need an anchor.

When *batches* of data are being input, *verification* is essential. A second person re-enters all the data, which the system compares with the version entered by the first, so that the machine can alert the operator to any differences found. Verification is not effective if the same person enters the data twice, because he or she may repeat the same mistakes.

Validation

Data entry is often carried out by staff who are quite unaware of what the data represents. So even when data has been entered accurately, it may still be *invalid* if a source document contains nonsense. For this reason input data is frequently fed into a *validation program*, which rejects invalid data with an appropriate message to help the user to correct it. Validation cannot ensure that the data is actually *correct*, but can check that it is sensible and possible.

Perhaps the simplest form of validation is a check on *data type*, usually to see whether data is numeric or alphabetic. For example, a sum of money might be entered as £26.7B when it should have been £26.78; a validation program would reject the item as non-numeric. If no validation is done, a human being would probably assume the 'B' should have been an '8'; however, the computer, lacking any common sense, would fail to complete the addition in process.

Another common validation technique is *range checking*. A billing system might be programmed to reject amounts billed if they were less than £1 (hardly worth sending out a bill; the odd pence could be stored and added to a subsequent bill) or more than £10 000 (perhaps no customer should ever owe this much). This type of check will easily prevent the erroneous issue of bills for £0.00.

Batch Totals and Hash Totals

Batches of data are often passed from one department to another, one city to another, or even transmitted across the world. It is important to ensure that data is not lost or distorted en route.

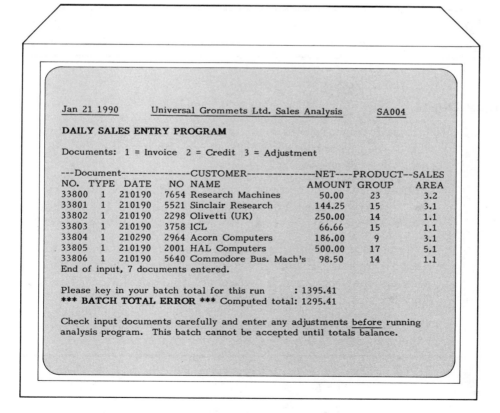

Fig. 11.2   Manually and automatically calculated batch totals

Larger computer sites employ *data control* clerks to carry out these checks and make sure that the right data gets into the right system at the right time. They often work out (with calculators) *batch totals* to test that all the data has been correctly entered.

For example, a company might enter a daily batch of invoices to a sales analysis system (Figure 11.2). The batch total (the total value of all seven invoices in this case) is manually calculated and keyed into the computer after all invoices have been entered.

The computer total is then displayed and compared with the manual total. In this example there is an error of £100, which the operator must find and rectify before the program will continue.

As a further check, the same program could keep a running total of, say, telephone numbers or customer account numbers. Such a *hash total* is not meaningful as a total (adding up telephone numbers is pointless in itself) but the *computer's* total can again be compared with a manually calculated total to ensure that all the numbers have been correctly entered.

Q 11.2 *Calculate a hash total of account numbers for the batch of invoices in Figure 11.2. How could this total be used by the system?*

Check Digits

Automatic checking of some data items can be helped by adding a *check digit* at the end of the field itself. A common type is called a *modulo 11* check digit, which works as follows.

Suppose a five-digit account number is 47856. Dividing it by 11 gives 4350 with a remainder of 6. Tacking 6 onto the end of the account number (giving 478566) gives a six-digit number exactly divisible by 11.

If an operator misread this number on a source document and keyed in 418566 by mistake, the system would reject the account number as invalid (provided the program included a check digit calculation). This is because 418566 is *not* exactly divisible by 11.

Note that if the remainder is 0, the check digit 0 is still tacked on the end. If the remainder is 10, then the Roman numeral X is used.

Q 11.3 *The following numbers carry a modulo 11 check digit at the end. Which have been misprinted?*

(a) 82313   (b) 90128   (c) 193160   (d) 35331X

This method is not perfect. Suppose two digits, say 6 and 8, had been accidentally swopped, and the same number (478566) was entered as 476586. This is called a *transposition error*. The wrong number, 476586, is also exactly divisible by 11, and so our checking routine would be fooled, and the error would slip through the validation process.

Q 11.4 *Work out a modulo 11 check digit for your date of birth (written as a number in the format DDMMYY). See if the check can be fooled by swopping pairs of digits in your final (7-digit) number.*

Weighted Modulo 11 Check

This weakness is avoided with the *weighted modulo 11 check*, which gives a *weighting* to each digit, as follows:

- The five-digit account number is 47856.
- Rearrange the number vertically.
- Starting from the *bottom*, multiply the first digit by 2, the second by 3, and so on.
- Add the products:

$$
\begin{aligned}
4 \times 6 &= 24 \\
7 \times 5 &= 35 \\
8 \times 4 &= 32 \\
5 \times 3 &= 15 \\
6 \times 2 &= 12 \\
\hline
\text{Total} &\quad 118
\end{aligned}
$$

- 118 divided by 11 gives 10 remainder 8.
- $11 - 8 = 3$.
- This time 3 is tacked on the end to make the final six-digit number 478563.

When an account number is checked, the same calculation is performed with the check digit itself having a weighting of 1. If the remainder is 0, the data is accepted as valid.

$$
\begin{aligned}
4 \times 6 &= 24 \\
7 \times 5 &= 35 \\
8 \times 4 &= 32 \\
5 \times 3 &= 15 \\
6 \times 2 &= 12 \\
3 \times 1 &= 3 \\
\hline
\text{Total} &\quad 121
\end{aligned}
$$

121 divided by 11 gives *remainder 0*, and so the account number is valid.

This method may seem longwinded, but it is virtually foolproof and the computer can of course perform the check in a split second.

Q 11.5 *The following numbers carry a weighted modulo 11 check digit at the end. Which have been misprinted?*

(a) 82317   *(b) 90123*   *(c) 32410*   *(d) 6033X*

Q 11.6 *(a) Calculate a weighted modulo 11 check digit for a spare part, number 4972. Can you see how this would have avoided the clerk's problem with the anchor on page 199? (Try the weighted modulo 11 check with the incorrect part number 4772 but your correct check digit attached).*

(b) Check the ISBN (International Standard Book Number) printed on the back of this book. Is the final digit a modulo 11 check, a weighted modulo 11 check, or neither?

Parity Bits

Even individual characters can be automatically checked for accuracy, using *parity bits* (these were explained in Figure 7.5). Parity checking is particularly useful when sending data along a communications line; even over a short distance data can become garbled, and so continuous parity checks are performed while transmitting. If a parity check fails, the data in question can be retransmitted.

Q 11.7 *The following characters were at the end of a message received by a microcomputer:*

$$10101100$$
$$01000010$$
$$11011001$$
$$11000101$$
$$00100001$$

Even parity was used. Which parity bit is incorrect?

Use the table of ASCII character codes in your computer manual to decipher the message.

All these checks can help to reduce 'garbage in', but we may still get 'garbage out' if the computer program itself goes wrong. The need for thorough testing of all programs cannot be overstressed.

SECURITY

Systems must also be made *secure*; i.e. data must be protected from unauthorised disclosure, modification or destruction (whether accidental or intentional). Security is threatened in various ways; some threats are physical, others involve misuse of the computer. They can be grouped into five danger areas:

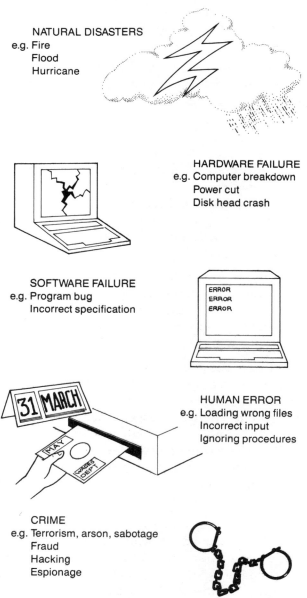

NATURAL DISASTERS
e.g. Fire
    Flood
    Hurricane

HARDWARE FAILURE
e.g. Computer breakdown
    Power cut
    Disk head crash

SOFTWARE FAILURE
e.g. Program bug
    Incorrect specification

HUMAN ERROR
e.g. Loading wrong files
    Incorrect input
    Ignoring procedures

CRIME
e.g. Terrorism, arson, sabotage
    Fraud
    Hacking
    Espionage

Fig. 11.3 The five danger areas for system security

Natural disasters include fire, floods, hurricanes and so on.

Computers, like any other machines, occasionally break down. Among the most common *hardware failures* are printer breakdowns, trouble with disk or tape drives (the media themselves can wear out, of course) and problems with power supplies, e.g. sudden voltage changes and power cuts.

Software failure is quite common. Bugs seem to survive even after stringent testing and lead to incorrect results and damaged (or even destroyed) files.

Other forms of *human error* include using the wrong program or data files, and failing to follow procedures (including such safety precautions as taking back-up copies).

Crime

As the use of computers has grown enormously in recent years, so has computer-related crime. Overt attacks on computer installations, e.g. terrorist bombs, arson and sabotage, sometimes hit the headlines. But these are only the tip of the iceberg; an alarming amount of computer crime goes unreported, much of it committed by employees with access to the vulnerable systems.

Many organisations (especially banks) have covered up cases where they have lost large sums of money by computer fraud, fearing that the publicity might harm confidence in their business. In the UK there is no law compelling them to report such crimes to the police; until there is, computer crime will continue to grow.

Many employees in computer installations regard processing time as 'free' and use it for private purposes. Other thieves steal money directly. They may try to set up dummy accounts into which cash is diverted by entering false invoices into a purchase ledger system which will then print a cheque to pay the bill. Another method, used in one famous case, involved rounding down everyone's pay cheque to the nearest ten pence and paying all the odd pennies into a dummy account controlled by the thief. Frauds like these can go unnoticed for some time because financial losses are not immediately obvious to the company concerned.

Disgruntled employees may carry out covert sabotage. One computer operator was found guilty of deliberately causing system failures so that he could go home early. Other cases involve *logic bombs*, which consist of illegal code lying dormant in the system until 'triggered' on a preset date (usually after the employee has left). The code then corrupts or wrecks the system.

Outsiders can sometimes gain remote access to computer systems which use communications links, by finding out the telephone numbers, passwords and *logging-on* procedures. Illegal attempts to break into systems in this way are called *hacking*. All *hackers* are guilty of stealing processing time (which is common theft even if they claim that it was 'just for fun'); some have more sinister motives such as fraud, industrial espionage or theft of data to be used for bribery or extortion.

Security Strategy

There are three main objectives of a *security strategy* for computer systems:

- minimise the chance of a breach of security
- minimise the harm done if a breach does occur (sometimes called *damage limitation*)
- enable the organisation to recover quickly after a security breach.

Security Controls

Physical controls

Access to computer installations must be restricted, whether by barbed wire, armed guards and dogs (as at a military installation) or by a simple lock on the computer room (as in many schools and colleges). Means of *identification* of authorised staff include identity cards (which often enable access by operating security doors), handprints and voiceprints.

Communications systems are particularly vulnerable to illegal access, as the criminal does not need to break into any buildings, but has only to *tap* into the cables, which may be ordinary telephone lines. Increasingly, such systems may use light travelling along *optical fibres* (which are harder to tap) rather than conventional cabling.

Duplication of hardware has become a common security precaution. The Concorde aircraft uses three intercommunicating computers for navigation so that even if two fail the third can still manage. Similarly, many banks have installed *fault-tolerant computers*, with *dual processors* (complete failure of one processor leaves its twin to carry on as if nothing had happened, while engineers locate the problem).

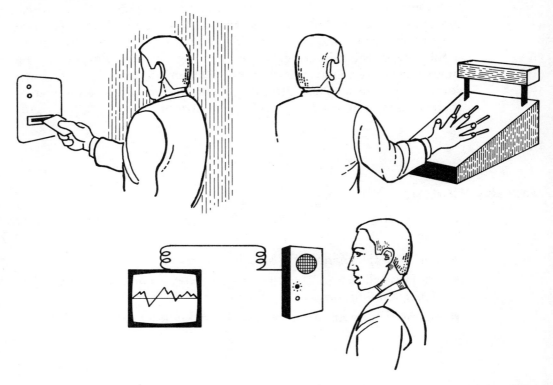

Fig. 11.4 Identity cards, handprints and voiceprints are among the methods of identifying authorised personnel and preventing unauthorised persons gaining access to the computer

Simple security measures for *every* computer user include taking great care of *storage media*. Floppy disks, for example, are prone to many risks such as fingerprints, spilt coffee, heat, dust, smoke, pressure (particularly writing on labels *after* they are stuck on), bending etc. (see Figure 11.5).

All media, and of course the whole installation, must be protected against fire, e.g. by smoking restrictions. Damage can be limited by automatic sprinkler systems and storing media in fireproof safes.

Hard disks may contain sensitive or secret data which cannot be stored in a safe (unless the disk drive is of the removable cartridge type). As a result many hard disk microcomputers feature a simple lock on the front, which looks rather like a car ignition lock. The user must turn a key in the lock before the computer can be used.

Logical controls

Controls which are built into the system design are called *logical controls*. Among the simplest is use of *passwords* which must be keyed in by the user before data can be accessed. Individual files or even records can be

Fig. 11.5   Floppy disks are prone to many risks

password-protected. However, passwords must be carefully chosen; e.g. avoid using obvious words such as your name, or a character string which could easily be stumbled upon. A hacker once got into Prince Philip's private files on Prestel, partly because the password was '2222222222'.

Many hackers can be foiled by a 'dial-back' system. On receiving the password from a remote user, the system automatically disconnects and then dials the telephone number which has been allocated that password, in order to reconnect the terminal. This means that the system cannot be accessed from an unauthorised location, in most cases forcing the criminal to trespass in order to use an unauthorised telephone.

The use of ancestral file systems (see Chapter 10) is common to guard against accidental data loss or corruption. This can be built into normal system operation: several file 'generations' can be kept automatically, without relying on those operating the system to create them.

Administrative controls

Administrative aids to security include regular back-up procedures (*back-up copies* are often called *security copies*). It is important to keep originals and back-up copies in different places; the authors have seen cases where back-up floppy disks were in the same box as the masters; if the box had been stolen or left on a hot radiator everything would have been lost.

Another valuable security principle for sensitive systems is *separation of responsibility*. A single programmer designing all the programs for, say, a bank's cashcard system, is obviously in a better position to defraud the bank than one who contributes only a single program. The situation could be even more dangerous in defence systems, where the defection of a single programmer to a potential enemy could perhaps jeopardise an entire early warning system.

Large companies check all their computer systems regularly to ensure that they are working reliably, as well as to uncover irregularities or frauds. This process is known as *computer systems auditing*.

For most computer installations, a combination of physical, logical and administrative controls is used to form a complete security system. Even small computer users, e.g. businesses, schools and colleges, must ensure the security and accuracy of their data, especially data that concerns individuals. *Privacy* and *data protection* are discussed in Chapter 22.

?

Q 11.8 *Think of two examples of security controls which might be used in:*

(a) a bank's cashtill system

(b) a student records system

(c) a company's weekly wages system.

Q 11.9 *What security precautions should you take when writing a complex computer program at school or college?*

RECOVERY

Even with the tightest possible security measures, breaches of security still occur, and organisations must plan how they would cope with the worst. *Disaster planning* involves working out what to do in the event of all conceivable security failures. These *recovery procedures* range from simple action to restore corrupted files to major schemes which provide for processing of all systems at another site if, say, fire devastates the installation.

Anyone designing a system is well advised always to bear in mind Murphy's Law: what *can* go wrong, *will* go wrong.

JARGON 11

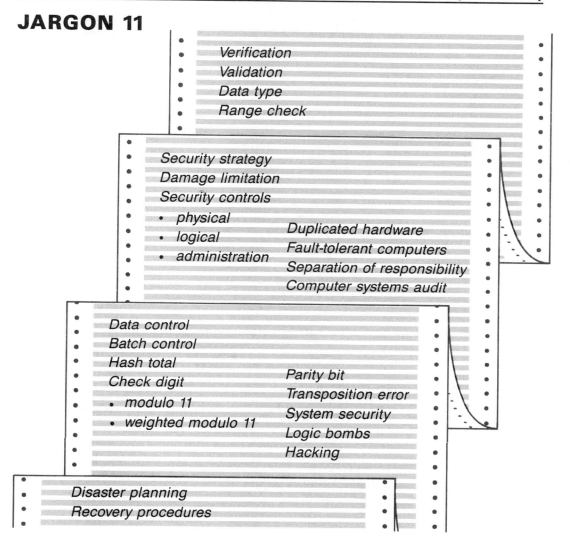

Verification
Validation
Data type
Range check

Security strategy
Damage limitation
Security controls
• physical
• logical   Duplicated hardware
• administration Fault-tolerant computers
                Separation of responsibility
                Computer systems audit

Data control
Batch control
Hash total
Check digit   Parity bit
• modulo 11   Transposition error
• weighted modulo 11 System security
                    Logic bombs
                    Hacking

Disaster planning
Recovery procedures

EXERCISES 11

1. Name a computer application for which security of the files is important. Explain why this is so and how security might be ensured.

(Oxford)

2. (a) What is a check digit and why is it used?
   (b) Using a weighted modulo 11 system, calculate a check digit, showing how it is derived, for the account number 798.

(AEB 1984)

3. The diagram below shows part of a 'grandfather-father-son' system for updating a magnetic tape file. This method is used in order to make sure that information can be replaced in case of accident.

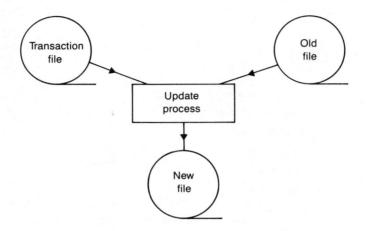

Which file is

(a) the 'son'?   (b) the 'father'?   (c) the 'grandfather'?

(YREB, 1982)

4. (a) What is a parity digit?
   (b) Give two examples of where a parity digit might be used.

(WMEB)

5. (a) What is the difference between hash and control totals?
   (b) Give three computing examples where they are used to help maintain the accuracy of the data.

(WMEB)

6. What is a weighted modulo 11 check digit?

7. 'In recent years there have been many more computer crimes.'
   (i) Explain what is meant by 'computer crimes'.
   (ii) Give two specific examples of computer fraud.
   (iii) Give two reasons why computer fraud is difficult to detect.

(AEB (part) 1984)

PART D: COMPUTERS IN ACTION

12 Case Study: Universal Record Distribution Ltd.

A COMPANY IN DIFFICULTIES

Universal Record Distribution Ltd. (URD for short) is a small company in the music business. The firm buys records and tapes from production companies and sells them to about 200 retail shops throughout the country. URD tries to cater for all tastes and stock a wide variety of music, ranging from classical works to the latest hits.

URD's management feels that sizeable stocks must be kept so that orders can be met rapidly. If customers (record shops) are kept waiting for deliveries they may go elsewhere for their supplies. However, it is getting harder and harder to keep a comprehensive stock as more and more records are released. This has pushed up URD's costs, especially as all new records are also available on cassette and many on compact disc. Although business is good, URD is running short of cash and faces the choice of either reducing stocks (with possible loss of orders) or finding another way of improving *cash flow* (i.e. simply, cash coming in minus cash going out).

? **Q 12.1** *How can URD be short of cash if business is good? Do you think a computer could help?*

URD holds an emergency board meeting. The managing director points out how much money is tied up in stock, and how much customers owe the company. His concern is shared by the finance director, who complains that accounts staff are too busy dealing with paperwork to spend time chasing customers for payment. The obvious way out, she says, is to reduce stocks. But the sales director insists that cutting stocks would be suicidal. It was eventually decided to hire a consultant to investigate the situation and to advise on the best course of action to improve cash flow.

? **Q 12.2** *Before reading on, write down the main areas of expenditure and income for any business.*

The consultant concentrated on how money was spent (cash flowing out of the company) and how it was received (cash flowing into the company). After investigating these areas, the consultant's conclusions were as follows.

Expenditure

The two major items of expenditure at URD were salaries and stock purchases. No significant savings could be made on salaries as all staff were working hard and salary levels were about average for the industry. Stock, however, was a different matter: many titles were in stock which had not sold a copy for over a year, and yet these slow-selling records were still being ordered. URD had no effective system for adjusting stock levels to customer demand.

Income

The only source of income was from sales of records and tapes. The consultant found that sales were healthy, but the average order was worth only £50. There was no incentive (such as a discount) for the shops to make bigger orders. As a result several shops had more than 50 orders in the pipeline at once. This in turn put pressure on the URD clerks who kept the *sales ledger* (an accounts book which records all sales to customers and payments received from them). The customer sometimes received the bill several weeks after the goods themselves.

To make matters worse, some customers took up to three months to pay: URD staff were too busy to send reminders or telephone to chase up payment. This, the consultant concluded, was the major cause of cash flow difficulty.

Recommendations

The consultant's recommendations were:

1. Encourage customers to increase their average order by immediate introduction of quantity discounts.
2. Computerise the sales ledger, in order to:
   (*a*) ease the pressure on the sales ledger clerks
   (*b*) speed up billing
   (*c*) tighten control over customers' credit, by sending regular statements and reminders, thereby improving cash flow.

3. Stop supplying any customer who fails to pay outstanding bills within a set time (e.g. 30 days).

4. Modify the system for purchasing stock to take greater account of customer demand. Stop ordering any item which has not sold for 12 months; reduce re-order quantities of records declining in popularity.

5. When these changes have been successfully implemented, consider computerisation of stock control.

The consultant thought it would be unwise to try to change everything at once. Steps 1–3 should be carried out first, as they would have the greatest impact on the cash flow problem (even allowing for the computer costs, which were carefully estimated). Notice that recommendations 1, 3 and 4 are alterations to the *manual* systems; the consultant did *not* think that a computer could solve all the company's problems.

The recommended automation of the sales ledger was based on careful study of the *volumes* of data being handled by the clerks, and the changes which might occur. Care was also taken to recommend hardware and software which would allow for expansion, and computerisation of other functions, such as stock control, payroll etc.

URD management agreed with all the recommendations, and introduced discounts to encourage larger orders and began computerising the sales ledger.

SALES LEDGER COMPUTERISATION

A meeting was held to explain the computerisation plans to all employees who would be affected, and to reassure them that no redundancies were planned.

Software and Hardware

The automated sales ledger would involve a standard software package, which would be installed on a local area network (LAN) system. To begin with, two microcomputers would be attached to this network; the applications software would allow both to be working on the sales ledger at once. Up to 16 machines could eventually be attached to the network to cater for growing demand and/or installation of other systems.

Sales ledger systems are not all identical. There are hundreds of different packages on the market, but they all have major features in common, and the package chosen for URD was quite typical.

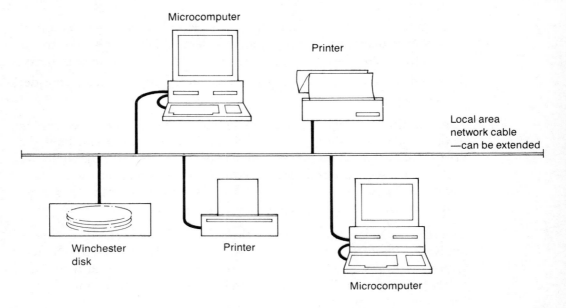

Fig. 12.1   Universal Record Distribution Ltd: hardware configuration

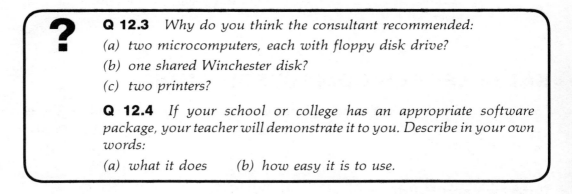

Q 12.3   *Why do you think the consultant recommended:*

(a) two microcomputers, each with floppy disk drive?

(b) one shared Winchester disk?

(c) two printers?

Q 12.4   *If your school or college has an appropriate software package, your teacher will demonstrate it to you. Describe in your own words:*

(a) what it does   (b) how easy it is to use.

Purpose of a Sales Ledger

The purpose of a sales ledger is to keep track of how much is owed to the company, and by whom. This is usually achieved by keeping a separate record, or *account*, for each customer. Each sale to that customer results in the issue of a bill or *invoice* which is recorded in that account. The same goes for *receipts*, i.e. cheques or cash from the customer are also entered in the account. A handwritten sales ledger account from the previous URD system is shown in Figure 12.2.

SALES LEDGER		ACCOUNT: MEGASTAR RECORDS PAGE: 1		
Date	Details		Debit	Credit
Oct 4	GOODS (INVOICE 18762)		20.00	
7	GOODS (18791)		17.50	
11	GOODS (18830)		12.84	
13	GOODS (18847)		11.25	
18	GOODS (19101)		68.00	
20	CASH (CHQ 2378)			20.00
22	GOODS (19164)		9.50	
22	GOODS (19166)		35.21	
22	GOODS (19205)		16.77	
24	GOODS (19313)		103.20	
25	CASH (CHQ 2390)			30.34
26	CASH (CHQ 2386)			68.00
28	GOODS (19558)		19.00	

Fig. 12.2 Sales ledger account from the manual system

The Main Files

In order to instal the new system, each URD customer was given a unique account number by which they could be identified. Two computer files had to be set up: the *customer master file* and a file of outstanding transactions called the *open-item file*. The customer master file (the record format is shown in Figure 12.3) holds the fixed customer data (address, credit limit, etc.) as well as the variable details (how much the customer has bought this month, this year, etc.).

The open-item file (record format as in Figure 12.4) contains a separate entry for each outstanding transaction for every customer. These could be invoices that have not been paid, or (more rarely) cash or cheques that are not yet matched to particular invoices.

```
System        :   SALES LEDGER
File          :   CUSTOMER MASTER
Organisation  :   INDEXED, KEY IS CUSTOMER ACCOUNT NUMBER
No. of Records :  MIN. 150   MAX. 500

                  RECORD LAYOUT


Field Description                      Type and Length

CUSTOMER ACCOUNT NUMBER                     9(6)
NAME                                        X(30)
ADDRESS (for invoices)                   4 x X(25)
DELIVERY ADDRESS                         4 x X(25)
TELEPHONE NUMBER                            9(10)
CUSTOMER CODE                               X(1)
SALESMAN CODE                               9(3)
SALES MONTH-TO-DATE                         9(8)
COST OF SALES MONTH-TO-DATE                 9(8)
SALES YEAR-TO-DATE                          9(8)
COST OF SALES YEAR-TO-DATE                  9(8)
CREDIT LIMIT                                9(5)
Record Size                                 287      characters


Note: 'X' means alphanumeric,  '9' means numeric
```

Fig. 12.3   Customer master file record layout

```
System         :   SALES LEDGER
File           :   OPEN-ITEM
Organisation   :   INDEXED, KEY IS CUSTOMER ACCOUNT NUMBER
No. of Records :   MIN. 100,   MAX. 2000

                   RECORD LAYOUT


Field Description                       Type and Length

CUSTOMER ACCOUNT NUMBER                      9(6)
TRANSACTION CODE                             9(1)
(1 = INVOICE, 2 = CREDIT NOTE,
 3 = CASH/CHEQUE, 4 = ADJUSTMENT)
TRANSACTION DATE (DDMMYY)                    9(6)
TRANSACTION NUMBER                           9(6)
ALLOCATION                                   9(6)
NET AMOUNT                                   9(6)
VAT AMOUNT                                   9(5)
Record Size                                  36      characters
```

Fig. 12.4   Open-item file record layout

An On-line System

Some sales ledger systems update both the customer master file and the open-item file with a single transactions file containing all the necessary amendments for a longish period (perhaps a week, or even a month). Such *batch processing* is always necessary with off-line systems.

The URD system, however, is on-line: the operator enters *individual* transactions which are processed immediately to update the files. The customer master file and the open-item file are both *indexed* files, and so they can be *updated in place*. This means that any amended record can be written in exactly the same place in the file as the original record, thus neatly obliterating the old data.

This makes it particularly important to take regular back-up copies of the main files; some companies do this several times each day.

Transaction Types

Although transactions are processed immediately, URD staff always input cash or cheques separately after all invoices, credit notes and adjustments have been entered. This makes it much easier to trace any mistakes. The system generates a hash total of customer numbers as well as a money total for each session (Figures 12.5 and 12.6); URD clerks calculate these totals manually beforehand as a safeguard to ensure accurate entry.

Nov 13 1990   Universal Record Distribution: Sales Ledger   SL03

TRANSACTION ENTRY PROGRAM

NO.	NAME	DATE	TYPE	NO.	ALLOC.	NET AMOUNT	VAT AMOUNT	TOTAL AMOUNT
22055	Nova Records Ltd.	131190	1	20013	–	65.00	9.75	74.75
12342	Comet Sounds	131190	1	20014	–	22.45	3.37	25.82
58333	Planet Breakers	131190	2	01877	19990	12.50	1.87	14.37
14146	Galactic Noise Co.	131190	1	20015	–	105.00	15.75	120.75
23848	Black Hole Records	131190	1	____				

130724 = Hash Total of Cust. Nos.

TOTAL: 206.95

Key in customer account number: 23848
Press the number of the transaction you want:
  1 = Invoice   2 = Credit Note   3 = Adjustment   4 = Cash/cheque   1

Fig. 12.5 Entering invoices and credit notes on the microcomputer screen

Dec 20 1990   Universal Record Distribution: Sales Ledger   SL03

TRANSACTION ENTRY PROGRAM

-CUSTOMER-		-TRANSACTION-			-NET-	-VAT-	-TOTAL-
NO.	NAME	DATE	TYPE	NO.	AMOUNT	AMOUNT	AMOUNT
14146	Galactic Noise Co.	201290	4	105	105.00	15.75	120.75
22055	Nova Records Ltd.	201290	4		65.00	9.75	74.75
18282	Megastar Records Ltd.	201290	4	2417	103.20	15.48	118.68
12342	Comet Sounds	201290	4	911	22.45	3.37	25.82
30030	Inner Space Music	201290	4	____			

96855 = Hash Total of Cust. Nos.   TOTAL: 340.00

Key in customer account number: 30030
Press the number of the transaction you want:
   1 = Invoice   2 = Credit Note   3 = Adjustment   4 = Cash/cheque   4

Fig. 12.6   Entering cash and cheques on the microcomputer screen

?

Q 12.5   *When does the company issue (a) an invoice, and (b) a credit note?*

Q 12.6   *Why are adjustment transactions sometimes needed?*

Each invoice entered increases the customer's current month balance and total outstanding balance on the master file. The invoice is also stored on the open-item file (as it is an outstanding transaction). The same applies to credit notes, except that they *reduce* the relevant balances.

When cash or a cheque received from a customer is input to the ledger, the system shows the operator all outstanding items for that customer, so that the operator can match or *allocate* the payment to a particular invoice. It may not be obvious which invoice the customer means to pay, and some customers help by quoting the invoice number(s) with their payment. This allocation is shown in Figure 12.6 and stored on the open-item file. Some payments may not be for the full invoice value but will reduce the balance owing.

Month-end Procedures

At the end of each month, a special program is run to clear out the open-item file by deleting invoices that have been paid. When an invoice has been only partly paid, it stays on file but with the amount reduced.

When this process is complete, only unpaid (or partly-paid) invoices should remain on the open-item file.

Q 12.7 *What do you think would happen if a customer pays too much cash? How would the system cope?*

Reports

The system provides a variety of printed reports which include monthly summaries of sales and of cash receipts. Two other vital documents produced are the *customer statement* and the *aged debtors report*. They are simpler than they sound.

The statement (Figure 12.7) shows a summary of the customer's account, i.e. what they have been invoiced and what they have paid, and con-

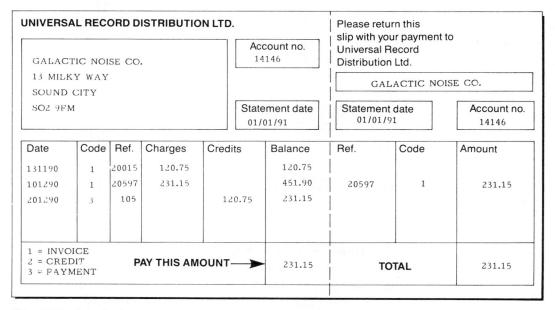

Fig. 12.7 A typical customer statement

sequently how much they still owe. URD could produce statements (for all or selected customers) at any time, but URD finds it convenient to send all customers a statement early each month. The statement has a tear-off slip which the customer is encouraged to return with payment to help to ensure that the payment is correctly credited to their account.

The aged debtors report (Figure 12.8) shows which customers are in debt (i.e. owe money) to URD. It also shows *how long* each debt has been owed—one, two, three months or more—that is why it is called 'aged' debt. This report helps URD to 'chase' payment from customers; it is easy to see the biggest and the longest standing debts.

Jan 4 1990   Universal Record Distribution: Sales Ledger   Page 1

AGED DEBTORS SUMMARY REPORT - AREA CODE 4 - CENTRAL

CUSTOMER NO.	NAME	TOTAL DUE	CREDIT LIMIT	CURRENT	31-60 DAYS	61-90 DAYS	90+ DAYS	OVER CREDIT LIMIT
23848	Black Hole Records	345.75	1000	145.20	-	200.55	-	
12342	Comet Sounds	1225.00	1000	90.33	-	-	1134.67	***
14146	Galactic Noise Co.	862.40	2500	862.40	-	-	-	
30030	Inner Space Music	1345.00	1000	211.60	-	322.44	810.96	***
18282	Megastar Records Ltd.	1865.89	1000	54.66	1719.50	91.73	-	***
58333	Planet Breakers	2245.88	2500	-	-	-	2245.88	
	GRAND TOTALS FOR AREA 4 :	7889.92		1364.19	1719.50	614.72	4194.51	

Fig. 12.8 An aged debtors report

RESULTS OF COMPUTERISING THE SALES LEDGER

The effects of computerisation at URD were dramatic. Despite slight teething troubles (like the half-day delay because no one had ordered spare printer ribbons) the company's cash flow showed a marked upturn within three months of the computer system going live. URD managers believed that there were four reasons for this improvement:

- Some customers were so surprised (or shocked) at receiving detailed statements that they actually sent a cheque off to URD *without* being bullied.
- When it came to chasing up the bad payers, it was far easier to identify them; URD staff were able to concentrate on collecting the oldest and the biggest debts.
- The sales ledger clerks had more time, so that the invoices themselves were sent out at the same time as the goods: not two or three weeks later.
- Finally the company found that, although the *number* of orders was about the same, the average *size* of each order was bigger. This last benefit was not a result of computerisation, but of introducing quantity discounts to encourage larger orders.

The company had *not* tried to computerise everything at once, but had concentrated on the most urgent problem. Moreover, the project had been carefully planned and executed, and so the result was a highly successful computer system.

JARGON 12

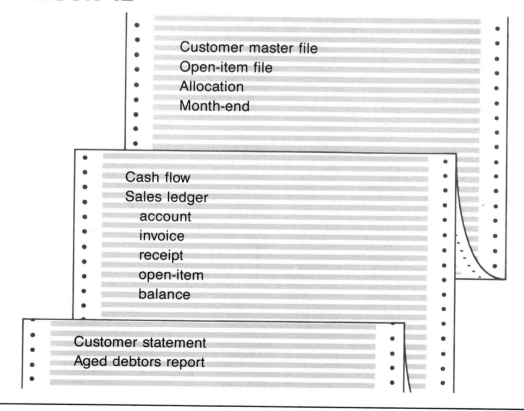

Customer master file
Open-item file
Allocation
Month-end

Cash flow
Sales ledger
    account
    invoice
    receipt
    open-item
    balance

Customer statement
Aged debtors report

EXERCISES 12

1. Selecting from the captions given, copy and complete these three systems flowcharts (which represent the Universal Record Distribution sales ledger system).

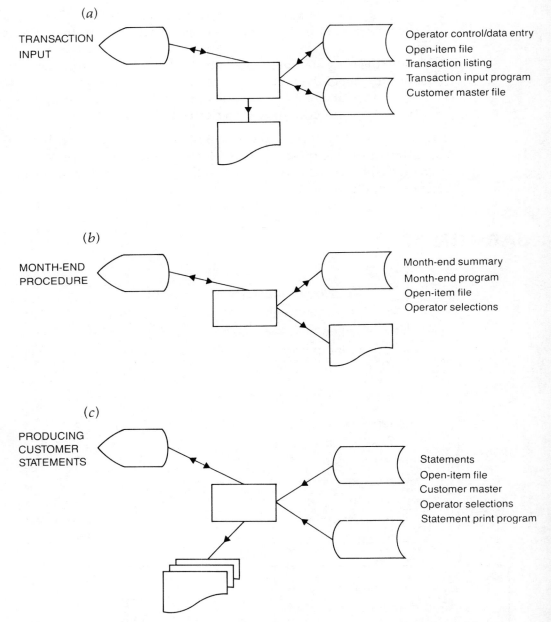

(a)

TRANSACTION
INPUT

Operator control/data entry
Open-item file
Transaction listing
Transaction input program
Customer master file

(b)

MONTH-END
PROCEDURE

Month-end summary
Month-end program
Open-item file
Operator selections

(c)

PRODUCING
CUSTOMER
STATEMENTS

Statements
Open-item file
Customer master
Operator selections
Statement print program

Why are the arrows (except one) one-way in flowchart (c)?

2. A newspaper boy has been given a microprocessor and wants to write a program to process the customers' accounts from his newspaper round.

   For each customer, he inputs

   1. daily cost of morning papers (delivered Monday to Saturday)
   2. daily cost of evening papers (delivered Monday to Saturday)
   3. cost of Sunday papers.

      (*a*) Draw a flow chart to input the data for *one* customer and output that customer's weekly bill.

      (*b*) The customers are charged for delivery as follows:—
         1. 5p per week for morning papers
         2. 5p per week for evening papers
         3. 2p for Sunday papers.

   If the boy has 40 customers, draw a flow chart to *input* the cost of papers and *output* the weekly bill for *each customer in turn*.

   (Notes—(1) There must be three inputs for every customer—if he does not buy a particular *type* of paper, the cost of that paper is input as zero. (2) Your flow chart will have to test whether or not to charge delivery for each type of paper.)

   (SWEB)

3. Every year the Post Office produces a series of special issues of stamps depicting different topics. The Post Office announces at the beginning of the year the particular date from which each issue will be available. A certain collector wishes to purchase each of the special issues on the first day it is available and keep a detailed record about these stamp issues.

      (*a*) How could he keep a manual record to ensure that he does not miss the first day of issue?

      (*b*) Give two different items of data about each stamp which could be recorded.

      (*c*) Give a manual method of recording this data.

      (*d*) What information could be retrieved from the recording of this data?

      (*e*) How could a computer be used to help with the handling of this data?

   (AEB 1984)

13 Case Study: Office Computing

Eurotraining Ltd is a private business school providing a wide range of courses in European languages, management skills, Common Market law and so on. The company has about 200 customers throughout Europe and offices in Paris, Brussels and Bonn as well as in Oxford Street, London.

The courses vary from one-day business seminars to full-time language courses lasting several weeks. Some of the shorter courses are run as often as 20 times a year.

In addition to full- and part-time teachers, the company employs ten administrative staff at its London office. Until recently, they were working without computers but now three microcomputers have been installed, each with its own disk storage but sharing one high-quality printer. There were four main purposes for the investment in the computer systems: filing and information retrieval, word processing, mailing customers and automating the payroll.

FILING AND INFORMATION RETRIEVAL

The sales manager, whose job it is to secure as many course bookings as possible, needs rapid answers to questions such as:

- Which customers have sent students on course code RDB in the last two years?
- Which customers spent more than £5000 with us in the last year?
- Which courses were so heavily subscribed that we had to put students on the waiting list?
- Which customers have previously expressed interest in course code ESM?

Answering any of these queries using the old manual system was time-consuming and inefficient. The correspondence to and from customers had filled two 'large filing cabinets. Course index cards, salespeople's reports, and other documents filled two more. The secretaries were searching for hours to answer even simple enquiries, and the company was losing possible sales when information about likely customers was missed.

As is often the case with manual filing systems, the information held by Eurotraining was too haphazard in content and too unsystematically arranged to fit easily into a computerised system. So, as a first step, the company had to tidy up the customer files. All the information was gathered together into one central filing system. Simple forms were used to record the important facts about each customer in a standard format.

? **Q 13.1** *Eurotraining has decided to centralise all the customer information from several separate manual files. What are the advantages and disadvantages of this?*

This exercise alone revealed many weaknesses of the old system. For example, it was found that the head of administration, the sales manager's secretary and the sales force were all keeping their own customer files. This meant that a lot of information was duplicated, and worse still each person held some useful customer details that were unknown to the other members of the team.

The reorganisation improved the ease of access to the information and paved the way for computerising the customer records. The company decided to reduce the design and programming effort and costs by using a *database software* package (see Chapter 10). This standard package was supplied 'off the shelf' by the computer dealer. Buying standard software in this way dramatically increases the speed of implementing a computerised system. The alternative, developing 'custom-built' software, is a lengthy and expensive process. Eurotraining would have had to employ specialists to design a completely new system, write special programs and test the operation in detail. Since the company's applications were standard, they had no need to go to such lengths.

With the database package, Eurotraining was able to create a computerised customer file very rapidly with a record structure as shown in Figure 13.1.

Customer Number	Customer Name	Address Line 1	Address Line 2	Address Line 3	Address Line 4	Telephone Number			COMPANY
Main Language	Second Language	Third Language							LANGUAGES SPOKEN
Enquiry Date	Course Code	Response	Enquiry Date	Course Code	Response				ENQUIRIES (up to 20)
Course Code	Fee Paid	Date	Location	Course Code	Fee Paid	Date	Location		COURSES ATTENDED (up to 50)
Main Contact	Position Held	Telephone Extension	Second Contact	Position Held	Telephone Extension				CONTACTS (up to 5)

Fig. 13.1 Eurotraining's customer record layout

Q 13.2 *(a) Estimate the approximate storage space taken up by the customer record shown in Figure 13.1 (Assume maximum use of variable fields.)*

(b) From the answer to (a) estimate the space needed for the whole file (Eurotraining has about 200 customers).

From this main file, subsidiary files or listings are extracted by simple commands typed in at the microcomputer keyboard, giving quick answers to the sales manager's questions. For example, it takes two minutes to create a file containing just the records of those customers who have sent students to course code RDB in the last two years. The same file could have taken several days to produce using the old manual system.

Q 13.3 *Eurotraining decides to create an additional file to store information about each of its courses. What items of data would it be advisable to store in this file?*

(a) Design a suitable record structure. Illustrate your solution with a diagram.

(b) Explain the purpose of each item of information you include.

Note that the database software package was as important as the computers themselves in transforming Eurotraining's file handling. Without such 'off the peg' software, the company would have had to develop its own (at much increased cost and delay).

> **?**
>
> **Q 13.4**   *Find out what you can about the available database software packages for a microcomputer known to you (whether your own computer at home or one you use at school or college). You may be able to find a review in a computing magazine or talk to a local computer dealer.*
>
> *Write an account of your chosen package explaining*
>
> *(a) what it does   (b) what it costs*
>
> *(c) what peripherals are needed to support it and what they cost.*
>
> **Q 13.5**   *Will Eurotraining's customer information be more secure, after computerisation, from:*
>
> *(a) accidental loss of information   (b) theft by competitors?*

WORD PROCESSING

Anyone who has ever written essays, reports, or even letters has experienced the same problem: what happens when mistakes are noticed—words misspelt, ideas in the wrong order, paragraphs omitted or badly worded? If the mistakes are few, it may be possible to correct them by crossing out a few words and squeezing in revisions. But the result looks untidy, and the only way to make big changes is to rewrite the whole thing.

The same applies to documents which are typewritten. Small errors may be rectified with correction fluid and careful repositioning. Some electronic typewriters allow correction of a few individual characters. But any substantial changes in text will mean the typist must start again.

Eurotraining's secretaries have always been involved in a lot of routine typing. The company frequently writes very similar letters to large numbers of its previous customers advertising forthcoming courses. And course manuals, which are part of every course and often run to hundreds of pages, need continual revision to keep the contents up to date.

Word processing (WP) provides a much faster way of editing and revising documents. The text is typed at a keyboard, but instead of printing out each character as the key is struck the computer stores it in memory and displays it, together with as much as a page of text, on a screen.

The word processing software then enables the operator to correct spelling mistakes, delete or insert text, and change the sequence of sentences or paragraphs. All this takes place before a single word is printed. When the operator is satisfied with the work it can be printed out by keying in a simple command.

As the document is *stored*, usually on disk, further revisions can be made with ease and the minimum of typing. Any number of perfect copies can be printed, a useful facility when the same letter is to be sent to several different companies.

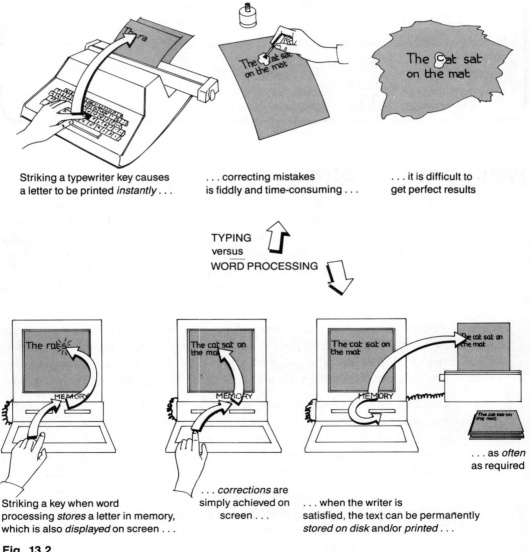

Striking a typewriter key causes a letter to be printed *instantly* . . .

. . . correcting mistakes is fiddly and time-consuming . . .

. . . it is difficult to get perfect results

TYPING versus WORD PROCESSING

Striking a key when word processing *stores* a letter in memory, which is also *displayed* on screen . . .

. . . *corrections* are simply achieved on screen . . .

. . . when the writer is satisfied, the text can be permanently *stored on disk* and/or *printed* . . .

. . . as *often* as required

Fig. 13.2

Q 13.6 *Outline three specific limitations of a typewriter that word processors overcome.*

Q 13.7 *Find out what you can about the available word processing packages for a microcomputer known to you.*

Write a short account of your chosen package explaining

(a) what it does   (b) what it costs

(c) the peripherals necessary to support it and what they cost.

Q 13.8 *If you have word processing software available to you, use it to produce your own personal profile (or curriculum vitae). The suggested layout in Figure 13.3 may be helpful, but feel free to modify it as you see fit.*

<u>PERSONAL PROFILE</u>

NAME   : Lesley BROWN

DATE OF BRITH   : July 4, 1971

NATIONALITY   : British

ADDRESS   : 44 Kingsway, BARCHESTER, Newshire, BA61 2NW

EDUCATION   : Green Park County First School (1976-82)
                          Barchester Comprehensive School (1982 to date)

SUBJECTS STUDIED   : English, French, History, Mathematics, Computer Studies
                          Biology, Music, Art & Design, Business Studies

QUALIFICATIONS   : Passed Oboe examination (at Grade 4)
                          Awaiting GCSE results in all above subjects

INTERESTS   : History of Music, Computer-synthesised Music, Oil Painting,
                          Travel, Swimming

ACHIEVEMENTS   : Represented Barchester Comprehensive School in the orchestra
                          (oboe) and the swimming team (1st prize, 1987 Newshire Schools
                          Championships). Climbed Mont Blanc with school team on an
                          exchange visit, August 1986. Taught myself touch typing
                          (30 words/min.).

WORK EXPERIENCE   : Saturday job at Iceberg Freezer Centre, Barchester (work
                          has included stocktaking, restocking freezers, operating
                          checkout, handling customer enquiries and complaints).

VOLUNATARY WORK   : Regular visitor to Green Park Hospice

REFERENCES   : The Headmaster, Barchester Comprehensive School,
                          West Way, Barchester, BA13 7OQ

                          Mr J White, Manager, Iceberg Freezer Centre,
                          Queens Parade, Barchester, BA16 1DD

Fig. 13.3 A suggested layout for a personal profile (see Q 13.8)

Other features of a word processing package allow a document to be *searched* for a particular word or phrase, which is then replaced or amended as necessary. Large blocks of text can be moved from one document to another. Headings can be automatically positioned at the centre of the page and so on. Some systems will even highlight spelling mistakes.

Dedicated word processors, although simple to use, are not capable of processing other information in the way that a computer can. Eurotraining opted to use a word processing software package on the company's microcomputers (bought at the same time as the database package). This enables Eurotraining to use the same machine for updating customer records in the morning, say, and revising course manuals in the afternoon.

Mailing

Eurotraining made sure that the word processing software and the database package were *compatible* so that information could be transferred between them.

For example, the sales manager sometimes sends a letter to all the customers who have sent students on a particular course in the past. This involves three stages.

Firstly, using the database package, a file of all appropriate customers is extracted from the customer database (Figure 13.4). It takes only a minute or two to create such a file.

COMPANY	ADDRESS	CONTACT Title/Initial/Surname			POSITION	COURSE CODE
Ace Engines Ltd	Unit 4, The Industrial Estate, Newtown NTW 13P	Miss	A	Spanner	General Manager	EM 8/9/86
Gigabyte (UK) Corporation	Gigabyte House, Gigabyte Road, Gigabyte GBY 1OB	Mr	G	Byte	Personnel Director	EM 17/11/86
Societé Pour L'Avenir Doré	Maison d'Ordinnateurs Rue du Temple, Toulouse France	M	J	Audubert	Directeur	EM 8/9/86

Fig. 13.4 Extracted customer file

Secondly, a standard letter is written and keyed into the microcomputer with special characters to show where variable information, such as names and addresses, is to be inserted (Figure 13.5).

EUROTRAINING Ltd

987 Oxford Street, London W1 (tel: 01-010-9911)

```
#Title/Initial/Surname#
#Position#
#Company#
#Address line 1#
#Address line 2#
#Address line 3#
#Address line 4#                    January 5,1987


Dear #Title/Surname#

We see from our records that you have sent students
to our courses in Effective Management in the past.

You might like to know that we shall be running this
course again this year (March 23-25) at our Brussels
centre.  Places are still available,and I am enclosing
the revised details.

I hope we may look forward to welcoming delegates
from your organisation.


Yours sincerely



I. Sellam
Sales Manager
```

Fig. 13.5 Standard letter with special codes for merging in address details

Thirdly, using a mailing program, the extracted customer data (Figure 13.4) is *merged* with the standard letter to print out an individual letter for each of the past customers (Figure 13.6). In this way, several hours' work of data extraction and typing is avoided. Such *mailshots* are frequently used by companies as part of their marketing efforts.

EUROTRAINING Ltd

987 Oxford Street, London W1 (tel: 01-010-9911)

```
Miss A Spanner,
General Manager,
Ace Engines Ltd,
Unit 4,
The Industrial Estate,
Newtown,
NTW 13P

                                    January 5,1987


Dear Miss Spanner

We see from our records that you have sent students
to our courses in Effective Management in the past.

You might like to know that we shall be running this
course a      this year (Mar          our Br   sels
cen
```

Fig. 13.6 The personalised letter now includes the customer's details

Q 13.9 *Eurotraining is planning an international conference to which it intends to invite all Members of the European Parliament. Letters of invitation have been drafted in four relevant languages: English, French, German and Italian.*

Describe all the stages involved in producing a mailshot so that each MEP will receive a personalised letter in the appropriate language.

Q 13.10 *Write a letter (using word processing software) for, say, a job application. Base it on Figure 13.7 if you wish, but use your own name, address etc. The letter should make use of the following features of the package:*

  (i) setting margins
 (ii) setting a tab stop (for your address)
(iii) right justification (to obtain a tidy right-hand margin)
 (iv) underlining, or bold type if preferred, for the heading.

Q 13.11 *Could your letter be adapted for use in a mailshot to several companies? If you think it could, explain one advantage and one disadvantage of such an approach.*

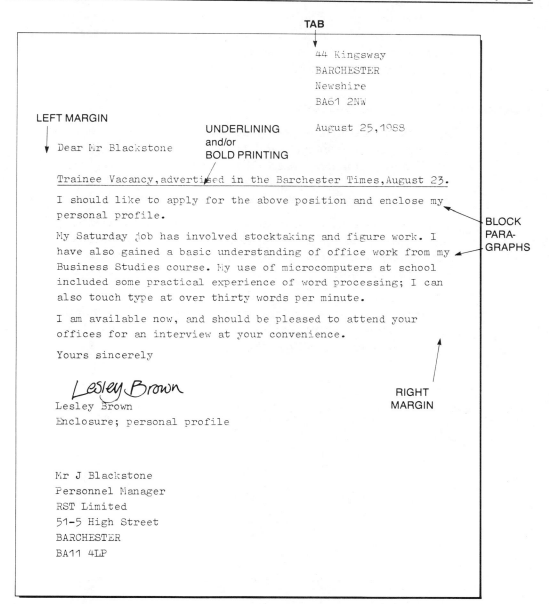

TAB

44 Kingsway
BARCHESTER
Newshire
BA61 2NW

LEFT MARGIN

UNDERLINING
and/or
BOLD PRINTING

August 25,1988

Dear Mr Blackstone

Trainee Vacancy,advertised in the Barchester Times,August 23.

I should like to apply for the above position and enclose my
personal profile.

BLOCK
PARA-
GRAPHS

My Saturday job has involved stocktaking and figure work. I
have also gained a basic understanding of office work from my
Business Studies course. My use of microcomputers at school
included some practical experience of word processing; I can
also touch type at over thirty words per minute.

I am available now, and should be pleased to attend your
offices for an interview at your convenience.

Yours sincerely

Lesley Brown
Lesley Brown
Enclosure; personal profile

RIGHT
MARGIN

Mr J Blackstone
Personnel Manager
RST Limited
51-5 High Street
BARCHESTER
BA11 4LP

Fig. 13.7 A typical job application letter (see Q 13.10)

PAYROLL

When purchasing hardware, Eurotraining had ensured that there would
be sufficient capacity for administrative systems. Therefore as soon as
word processing and the sales and marketing systems were running
smoothly, the company set about implementing a payroll package.

Eurotraining employs only about 80 people (including part-timers) at the UK head office but it still takes the junior accountant nearly two days every month to process the salaries manually. If automation could cut this to one day, the costs could easily be justified.

Purposes of a Payroll System

Employees, of course, expect to be paid on time. In addition, however, an employer must calculate and deduct *income tax (pay-as-you-earn,* or PAYE) and *National Insurance* (NI) contributions from each person's pay. These deductions must be paid to the Government. All payroll systems must, by law, maintain accurate records of all pay and deductions.

When you see a job advertised at a salary of, say, £10 000 per year, this means *gross pay,* i.e. before any deductions. Tax and National Insurance may not be the only deductions; employees may, for example, contribute to a *pension fund.*

All the deductions are subtracted from the gross pay to calculate *net pay,* i.e. what the employee actually receives at the end of the month or week. Each employee is entitled to a written or printed *payslip* showing gross pay, deductions and net pay (Figure 13.8).

Pay Advice	Name M. T. GREY	Location OXFORD ST.	Ref. No 0017	N.I. No YZ1234156A	Period 03	Pay Date 31/03/85	Payroll H. Q. SALARIES		
PAY BASIC 666.66	BONUS 100.00								**GROSS PAY** 766.66
	N.I. Cat.	Pension (Vol.)	Pension (Ord.)	N.I. Contrib.	Tax	Tax Code	Basis		**TOTAL DEDUCTIONS**
DEDUCTIONS	CAT.(0)	30.00	38.33	69.00	174.80	220L			312.13
					R denotes Refund				
	Pension Fund & Ref. No.		Pension to Date	N.I. to Date	Tax to Date	Taxable Pay to Date	NET PAY		
	GEN. 5.0%		734.17	727.50	1820.01	8083.33	454.53		

Fig. 13.8 A monthly payslip printed by the Eurotraining payroll system

 Q 13.12 *There are often additions to pay as well as deductions. Can you think of at least two ways such additions might arise?*

The Payroll Package

The package chosen by Eurotraining uses (like many payroll systems) two important files.

The *employee master file* contains a record for each employee (Figure 13.9) which holds permanent details, e.g. name, address and salary, as well as current data such as this month's figures.

FIELD DESCRIPTIONS		DATA
Employee Number	:	0017
Employee Name	:	M. T. GREY
		321 OCKENDON ROAD
		LONDON
		N1 7ZZ
Pay Location	:	OXFORD ST.
Start Date	:	020287
Termination Date	:	
Payment Method	:	Bank dep.
Weekly/Monthly	:	M
Payroll	:	H. Q. SALARIES
N.I.Number	:	YZ123456A
Basic Salary	:	8000.00
Overtime Rate	:	
Productivity Bonus	:	Y
Pension Ref. Number	:	MG001
Contribution Rate (%)	:	5.0
Voluntary Contr. (£)	:	30.00
Current Period:		
Basic	:	666.66
Overtime	:	
Bonus	:	100.00
Sick Pay	:	
Pension	:	68.33
N.I. (employee)	:	69.00
N.I. (employer)	:	80.12
Tax	:	174.80
Net Pay	:	454.53
Year-to-date:		
Basic	:	7333.33
Overtime	:	
Bonus	:	750.00
Sick Pay	:	
Pension	:	734.17
N.I. (employee)	:	727.50
N.I. (employer)	:	844.71
Tax	:	1820.01
Net Pay	:	4801.65

Fig. 13.9 One record from Eurotraining's employee master file

The *payroll parameter file* contains details such as the different income tax rates for different pay levels, rates for NI contributions and sick pay entitlement.

Running the Payroll

As Eurotraining's staff are all paid monthly, most of the salaries can be automatically calculated: gross pay = annual salary/12. But several employees (including the secretaries) are paid for any overtime worked, and so the numbers of hours of overtime must be recorded on timesheets for input to the system.

?

Q 13.13 *A manufacturing company runs a weekly payroll paying staff by the hour. 'Time-and-a-half' (i.e. $1\frac{1}{2}$ times the standard rate) is paid for overtime during the week, 'double time' (i.e. twice the standard rate) for weekend work.*

(a) What data items would be needed on the employee record in addition to those shown in Figure 13.9?

(b) What data items would have to be collected each week and input into the payroll system?

The payroll system is very simple to operate. The operator selects 'run salaries' from a menu on screen. The program asks the operator to load the special payslip stationery into the printer, then works right through the employee master file.

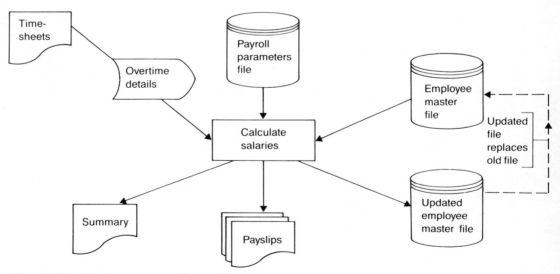

Fig. 13.10 Employee master file updating

For each person on file all deductions and additions are calculated using the individual's details (salary, tax code etc.) together with the parameters (tax rates, NI rates etc.) stored in the parameter file. The program prompts the operator to input the number of hours of overtime for eligible staff. The results are printed on individual payslips for each employee and are used to update the employee master file.

Q 13.14   *The chart in Figure 13.10 assumes that the employee master file and the payroll parameter file are both up to date.*

What details are likely to change in these files?

Draw a systems flowchart to illustrate the process of updating these files before the payroll program is run.

Q 13.15   *Can you think of other programs which a payroll system needs, besides the actual 'doing the payroll' program described?*

The whole process of running the monthly salaries for Eurotraining (*including* taking back-up copies of the files) now takes about one hour, instead of nearly two days! As an added bonus the system automatically produces summary reports for Eurotraining's manager to use and which the Government also requires.

STAFF REACTIONS

Secretaries and other staff at Eurotraining were initially hostile to the computerisation plans. Not only were they required to learn new, more complex, skills, but the changeover itself involved them in considerable extra work (in fact, the company had to take on extra temporary staff for two months while the old manual files were reorganised). More importantly, secretaries knew that the management was hoping to reduce staff once the systems were working. Some people felt sure they would lose their jobs.

In the event things did not work out that way. Once the new systems were established, Eurotraining's managers began to realise the potential they offered for marketing the company's services in ways that had previously been impossible. So although typing was completed much more rapidly, new work arose (mailshots, maintaining customer files etc.) to fill the secretaries' time.

This work, combined with increasing sales, kept all the staff so busy that redundancies were unthinkable. Now everyone agrees that the micro-computer systems have benefited company and staff alike.

Q 13.16   *Find out from someone (relative, friend, school/college secretary etc.) who works in an office about any computer systems they use and how they react to them.*

JARGON 13

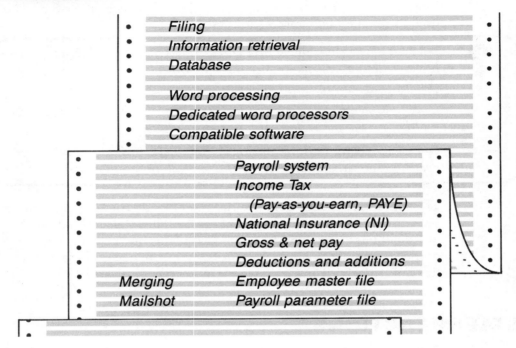

- Filing
- Information retrieval
- Database

- Word processing
- Dedicated word processors
- Compatible software

- Payroll system
- Income Tax
  - (Pay-as-you-earn, PAYE)
- National Insurance (NI)
- Gross & net pay
- Deductions and additions
- Merging   Employee master file
- Mailshot   Payroll parameter file

EXERCISES 13

1. (*a*) Word processing is the application of computer technology to typewriting.

   (i) Where is the text stored as it is typed?

   (ii) Where is the text stored afterwards?

   (iii) Give three examples of the types of commands that are available to the operator.

   (iv) What will be shown on the screen in addition to a selection of the available commands?

   (v) In what form is the final copy of the text produced?

   (vi) Give two advantages to be gained from the use of a word processor.

   (*b*) What are the component devices essential in a word processing installation?

   (*c*) The minutes of a meeting have been typed on a word processor and stored on a disk. The draft copy shows one mistake, in the middle of a long paragraph the word 'the' has been typed in twice.

   Briefly describe how the operator would correct the minutes.

   (WMEB)

2. (a) Describe two ways in which word processing machines can be used to help improve the working life of an office typist or secretary.

   (b) Why is it likely that an office manager would welcome the introduction of a word processing machine?

   (c) Why might some typists be worried by the introduction of a word processing machine?

   (CU)

3. (a) Explain what is meant by word processing.

   (b) Choose three different jobs where word processing might be used.

      (i) State the job and explain how word processing might be used.
      (ii) For each job give a different benefit of using word processing.

   (AEB 1984)

4. Eurotraining decides to create a new file to hold information on the teaching staff (some of whom are part-time) and their contacts with various experts *not* on the payroll but who lecture occasionally at specialists' seminars.

   (a) What information should be held on such a file and why?

   (b) Design appropriate record formats.

   (c) Some information on the file (such as the quality of a teacher's performance) may be confidential. How might it be protected?

   (d) Once the file is established how might Eurotraining create a subsidiary file listing those lecturers who might help at a weekend conference entitled 'New business opportunities in South America'?

   How would Eurotraining use its computer to invite the chosen speakers to take part?

5. An employee works 20 days per month and uses a computer to calculate how much money he has earned. He feeds into the computer the number of hours he has worked each day during the month. He is paid at the rate of £5.67 per hour for the first 150 hours worked and then at the rate of £7.50 per hour for any additional time.

The output is of the form

TOTAL WAGES EARNED = £880.50
NUMBER OF HOURS WORKED = 154

Draw a flowchart and write a program in a suitable high-level language (e.g. BASIC) which will include a loop to:

(a) read in the number of hours worked each day for 20 days

(b) check if the total number of hours is greater than 150

(c) calculate the amount of money earned at the appropriate rates

(d) output the total wages earned and the total number of hours worked.

Include a DATA line in your program which contains the hours worked for five days.

(YHREB 1983)

6. Repeat question 5 with the following modification:

Tax is chargeable at *tax rate* % on income earned over the employee's tax allowance of £ *allowance* per month.

tax rate and *allowance* are to be input at the beginning of the program.

7. (a) A small company which pays all its employees in cash every Friday uses a bureau to process its employees' wages.
Give *two* advantages for the company in using a bureau rather than buying its own computer.
Give *two* reasons why the company may, at a later date, decide to buy its own computer.

(b) At the end of each week every employee completes a mark sense form. (A completed form is shown in Figure 13.11.) The form shows the hours he or she has worked that week. The company sends the form to the bureau. Nearly all employees have two rates of pay:

Rate 1—An employee's basic rate of pay
Rate 2—The overtime rate.

The rates for each employee are held on the employee master file, and are shown as R1 and R2 on the mark sense form. Use the information marked on the form to complete these sentences:

(i) The employee's number is . . .
(ii) The number of hours overtime worked on Wednesday is . . .
(iii) The week number is . . .
(iv) The employee worked on . . . days this week.

(c) Give *two* benefits gained from using these mark sense documents to input the data.

Name: *John Richards*

| Employee Number | Mon hrs at R1 R2 | Tue hrs at R1 R2 | Wed hrs at R1 R2 | Thu hrs at R1 R2 | Fri hrs at R1 R2 | Sat hrs at R1 R2 | Sun hrs at R1 R2 | Week Number |

Fig. 13.11

(*d*) There is a different form, called a 'Rate 3' form, for any hours which an employee works at special rates.

    (i) Use the following expressions to complete the systems flowchart in Figure 13.12 showing the first stage in processing the wages (the validation or data vet stage):
validated data; Rate 1 and 2 pay claims; validation program; Rate 3 pay claims; error report.

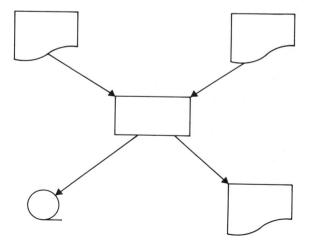

Fig. 13.12

      (ii) Give *two* reasons why an employee's data might cause an error report to be printed.

      (iii) Explain what you would expect to happen to any rejected pay claims to ensure that the employee gets paid.

(e) When the details of hours worked have eventually been validated, the wages can be processed. Use the following expressions to complete the systems flowchart showing this run in Figure 13.13: pay slips; sort program; transactions (unsorted); master file; updated master file; list of notes and coins required; wages program; transactions (sorted).

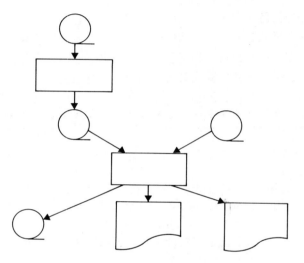

Fig. 13.13

(f) Give one other computer run, apart from the validation and wages runs, which is essential each week if the wages are to be paid correctly.

(g) Suggest a way in which the company could protect itself against employees who claim for more hours than they have actually worked.

                                                  (LREB)

14 Case Study: The Electronic Office

TEETHING TROUBLES

Although the people at Eurotraining (Chapter 13) were eventually happy with their computer systems there were quite a few teething troubles in the early months.

It had taken weeks to get all the microcomputers connected to the printer, and it took a further week to obtain a daisy-wheel which would print a '£' sign instead of '$'.

All the secretaries went on a two-day training course to learn how to use the word processing package, but it was some months before they were really skilled enough to work at full speed. In the meantime producing important documents sometimes seemed to take *longer* than before. This caused some bottlenecks; people were wasting time waiting until a micro-computer was free. Eventually a rota system for using the machines was devised; this was quite effective, but there was often a queue to use the daisy-wheel printer.

HARDWARE AND SOFTWARE CHANGES

Everyone at Eurotraining had thought the computer systems would last for many years. In the event, three years after installing the first micro-computer, nearly all the hardware and software had been replaced.

The first addition was a high-speed dot-matrix printer, which reduced the queue for the printer. The daisy-wheel printer was kept for printing important documents. But the demand for quality printing continued to grow, and so the company had to install a desk-top laser printer.

?   **Q 14.1** *Explain the terms daisy-wheel, dot-matrix and laser printer.*

The microcomputers have been replaced with powerful 32-bit models with built-in telephone handsets and *auto-dial modems*.

They share, on their *local area network* (LAN), high-capacity disk drives, with fast tape drives attached for regular backing up. The computers can now be linked, not only locally to each other, but also via a *wide area network* (WAN) to many other computers, in the UK and elsewhere.

?

Q 14.2 *Would these powerful new microcomputers still need floppy disk drives? Explain.*

Q 14.3 *Explain the function of a modem.*

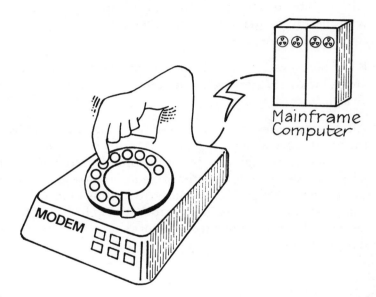

Fig. 14.1 Auto-dial modems will 'dial' and connect the user to a central computer using a previously stored telephone number

Perhaps the most significant change of all is the appearance of micro-computers on the desks of all the *managers*. No longer is computing or word processing regarded as menial work suitable only for secretaries and junior administrative staff.

THE ELECTRONIC OFFICE

Anyone walking into the Eurotraining headquarters could not fail to notice the major investment in computing technology. But how does such a small company justify its expensive *electronic office*?

Fig. 14.2 Using word processing, electronic mail and on-line telephone directories in an 'electronic office'

All the 'everyday systems' are now running smoothly. Staff take their computerised payslip for granted, and fewer customers owe the company money now that the invoicing and sales ledger systems are in full operation. Perhaps most important, the sales and marketing database, which has been gradually improved, is providing vital up-to-date information about existing and prospective customers. As a result the company has expanded very quickly.

ELECTRONIC MAIL

One of the critical changes in working methods has been the adoption of *electronic mail*. As many as three out of four business telephone calls are unsuccessful at the first attempt because the line is engaged or the person called is in a meeting or out of the office. Conventional mail was usually far too slow. Eurotraining decided to send its messages and documents electronically.

Q 14.4 *Why did the company not test out electronic mail with just one 'pilot' location?*

Voice Messaging

The most useful form of electronic mail, according to Eurotraining staff, is the facility for sending and receiving *voice messages*. The caller 'dials' (by selecting a name from a telephone directory on screen) a colleague who might be sitting next door or in another country. If the call succeeds they have a normal telephone conversation. If it fails the caller leaves a spoken message in an *electronic mailbox*, a storage area reserved for that individual on a computer system. This computer is not one of Eurotraining's computers, but a mainframe computer in Northampton (it could be located anywhere) which is kept running 24 hours a day. Eurotraining pay a fee to the electronic mail company for the use of the software and the mailbox storage facilities.

The person to whom the message is addressed returns to his or her workplace and switches on the microcomputer (or other terminal). Entering the personal password causes automatic dial-up and connection to the mailbox computer giving access to the individual mailbox and the waiting messages.

Fig. 14.3

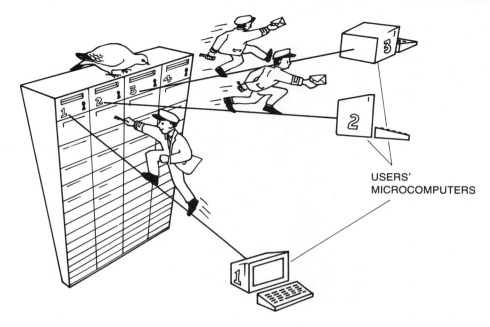

Fig. 14.4 An electronic mailbox can be thought of as a kind of computerised pigeonhole

> **?** **Q 14.5** *Find out what you can about a commercial electronic mail service (e.g. the British Telecom Gold Service, linked with Prestel). How are individual mailboxes protected from unauthorised access?*

Documents

While voice messaging is being introduced by many companies the bulk of electronic mail continues to be text, i.e. written notes, memos, letters, or even lengthy reports. All these are transmitted via the same system. Sometimes a voice message is 'attached' as a commentary to a document, e.g. "Here's the report you wanted, Sarah. Could you check the figures on page 12 for me, I had to guess at some of the travel costs. Thanks a lot."

Facsimile (Fax), Graphics and Printing

A *facsimile* (or *fax*) of a chart, diagram or even a photograph can be sent between offices on the same network. The course manuals which Euro-training provides for students contain many illustrations. To produce

Fig. 14.5 Eurotraining uses sophisticated graphics and page layout software to design training manuals on the screen ready for laser printing

them as professionally as possible, the company has installed new software, far more sophisticated than their original word processing package. Several different typefaces can be used in a range of sizes, and a graphics program is built in to speed production of drawings and charts. This *desktop publishing* software also has a page layout facility, so that text, headlines and illustrations can be arranged on screen to give the most pleasing page design.

When each page layout is complete, any number of copies can be produced on the laser printer at a rate of about twenty pages per minute. With laser printers now installed in the continental offices too, an entire 200-page manual can be sent to the computer in, say, Bonn in a few minutes, where it will be stored ready for printing.

Benefits of Electronic Mail

Eurotraining staff are now spending *less* time on the telephone. They know that any message they leave will be heard or read as soon as the recipient checks the electronic mailbox; there is no need to rely on a secretary or other colleague to pass the message on. Things seem to get done more rapidly, and nowadays nobody can use the excuse: "Sorry I haven't done such-and-such—I didn't get your note . . .".

Part-time workers find the system especially valuable. Each one has a portable microcomputer with a built-in modem, through which to check the electronic mailbox, day or night, from anywhere in the world.

No other training company can produce such professional up-to-date course manuals. If the European Parliament should approve a change to employment law today, an expert in Eurotraining's Brussels office could revise the relevant course manual overnight and transmit the amended material to the London head office in the morning. New course manuals could be laser printed in time to be used for a course beginning in London tomorrow afternoon.

Eurotraining's customers have certainly noticed the difference. Their queries are rapidly answered, bookings are efficiently processed, and the training course manuals are very well received. Several regular customers use an electronic mail system similar to the one at Eurotraining for rapid communication between the companies.

VIDEOTEX

Eurotraining employees need to gather a great deal of information; they obtain it from a variety of sources.

VIDEOTEX SYSTEMS

Fig. 14.6 Videotex usage is growing in most industrialised countries

Teletext: Ceefax and Oracle

Teletext information is broadcast along with normal TV transmissions, spare lines at the top of the TV picture being used to carry the data. The data is arranged as a few hundred 'pages', each of which fills a whole screen, the pages being broadcast in a continuous cycle.

The signals are decoded by special circuitry built into a teletext television set. The user selects a page by keying its number on a hand-held keypad. The requested page is displayed on the TV screen as soon as its turn in the cycle is reached, usually within a few seconds.

 Q 14.6 *Why is there sometimes a delay in getting the page you want on a teletext TV set?*

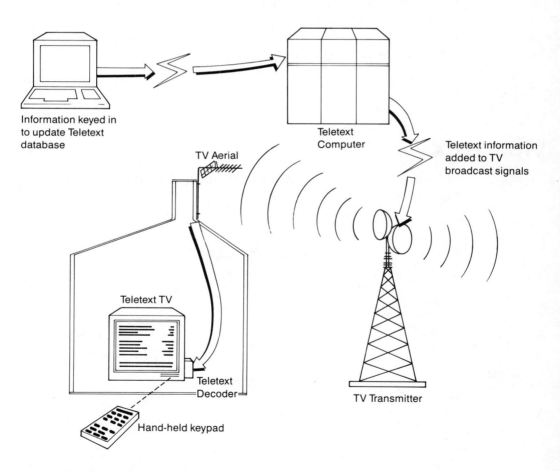

Fig. 14.7 Teletext is a one-way (broadcast) system

Viewdata: Prestel

Viewdata systems such as Prestel work rather differently, involving *two-way communication* (via the telephone network). This enables user input to travel all the way to the viewdata computer and select the data to be transmitted.

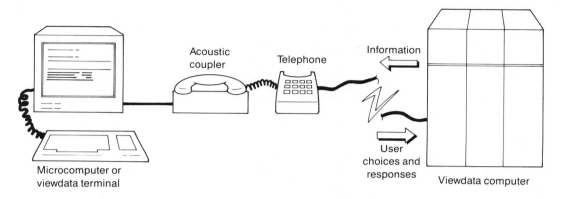

Fig. 14.8 Viewdata systems working through the telephone network allow two-way exchange

> **?**
>
> **Q 14.7** *How far is user input transmitted within a teletext system?*
>
> **Q 14.8** *Why is it so significant that viewdata systems allow two-way communication? What additional services can be provided as a result?*

On-line Databases

The Prestel computers actually hold an *on-line database* (or *data bank*) comprising several hundred thousand pages, supplied by hundreds of *information providers*.

Eurotraining staff often access Prestel from their microcomputers to check, for instance, weather forecasts, travel conditions or business news. Once connection is made, the user keys in his or her account number (for charging purposes) and a password. Information is located by progressing through a series of menus arranged in *tree* structure (Figure 14.9).

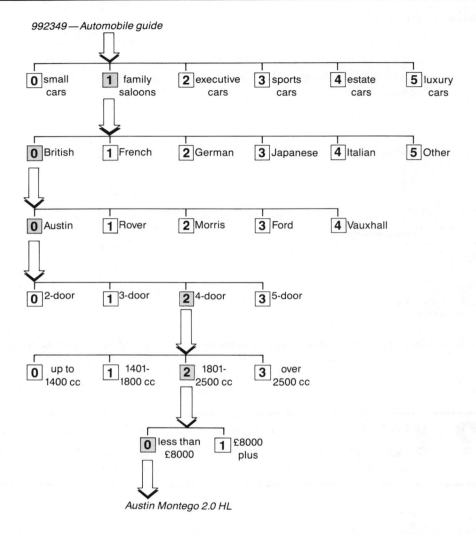

Fig. 14.9 Prestel pages are arranged in a tree structure; here the user has to make six selections by keying 1, 0, 0, 2, 2, 0 on successive pages to reach the information required

Some on-line data bases are enormous, running to millions of pages. Searching through them by successive menu choices (as in Figure 14.9) would be too long and tedious: special software has been developed to allow fast but thorough database searches for given key words.

?
Q 14.9 *Why should passwords (e.g. for Prestel) be changed regularly?*

Fig. 14.10 Typical pages from Prestel. The charge for each page is at the top right-hand corner. (The pages shown here are free.)

Frequently, however, Eurotraining staff require more specialised or detailed information than Prestel provides. The financial director, for example, needs very up-to-date details of currency exchange rates. The legal consultant needs information on the laws in various countries. The lecturers need to look up the latest research findings in their subjects, and so on.

These varied requirements are met by databases stored on computer systems all over the world. They are dialled direct from the Eurotraining microcomputer; the built-in modems can operate at various data transmission speeds or *baud rates* (1 baud—pronounced 'bode'—is usually taken to mean a transmission speed of one bit per second) depending on which computer is being accessed. Thus for Prestel the baud rate automatically switches to 1200/75; i.e. the modem *receives* data at 1200 baud and *transmits* data at 75 baud. Other database systems send and receive at other speeds.

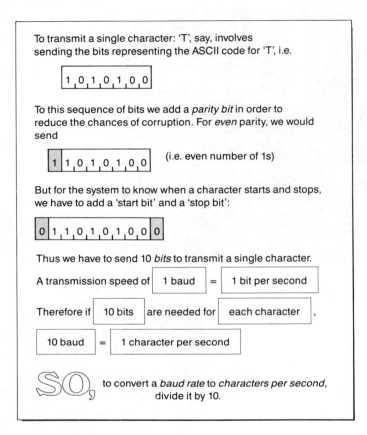

Fig. 14.11 Conversion of a baud rate to characters per second

Q 14.10 *How fast can you type (in words per minute)? If you do not have access to a keyboard, time yourself handwriting—legibly.*

Convert this speed to characters per second (remember to include spaces and punctuation).

Now convert this speed to find out your own 'personal' transmission speed as a baud rate (see Figure 14.11).

The Value of On-line Information

Most information providers charge for their services. The management of Eurotraining watch these costs closely, but believe that it is money well spent. The finance director, for example, claims to have saved the company thousands of pounds by guarding against adverse currency fluctuations. This would have been impossible without up-to-the-minute data.

THE PAPERLESS OFFICE?

The people at Eurotraining were surprised to find that, against all predictions, paper consumption had actually *increased* since computerisation. Of course, the new systems provide much information which was simply unavailable before; consequently Eurotraining is producing an increased number of reports and is updating manuals more frequently.

On the other hand, internal memos have been virtually eliminated. Several bulky filing cabinets have been wheeled out and the master copies (as well as the back-up copies) of all the course manuals are now stored on disk rather than paper.

Eurotraining is about to instal optical disks, giving several gigabytes of storage capacity in a small cabinet. These will enable electronic storage of all internally produced documents. They will not, however, prevent the postman calling every morning with a sack full of non-electronic paper mail. The company is still a long way from the paperless office.

Q 14.11   *Make a list of the different sources of information which you use at school or at home. How many of them are paper-based? Would there be any advantage in switching them to electronic storage media?*

JARGON 14

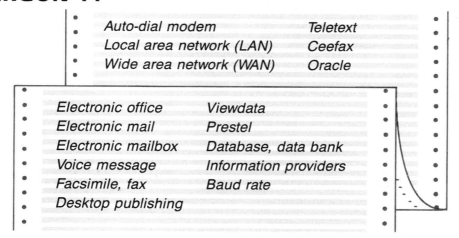

Auto-dial modem   Teletext
Local area network (LAN)   Ceefax
Wide area network (WAN)   Oracle

Electronic office   Viewdata
Electronic mail   Prestel
Electronic mailbox   Database, data bank
Voice message   Information providers
Facsimile, fax   Baud rate
Desktop publishing

EXERCISES 14

1. "The laborious process of moving a letter from one part of the world to another shows the limitations of traditional methods of coding and transmitting." (The Mighty Micro—Dr. C. Evans)

   (*a*) (i) Describe the traditional methods referred to by Dr. Evans.

   (ii) Give four different limitations of these methods.

   (*b*) The traditional methods may be replaced by 'Electronic Mail'.

   (i) Show how this might operate.

   (ii) Explain two advantages and one disadvantage it would have over the traditional methods for a large company.

   (AEB 1982)

2. (*a*) Name the providers of the following services

   (i) Ceefax.

   (ii) Oracle.

   (iii) Prestel.

   (*b*) (i) Which of the three services could be used to book an airline ticket?

   (ii) Why is this service a suitable choice?

   (*c*) State *four* major differences between Prestel and teletext services.

   (*d*) List *three* different costs paid by Prestel users.

   (*e*) Name Prestel's electronic mail service.

   (NWREB)

3. (*a*) Outline the facilities offered by a teletext information system such as Ceefax or Oracle.

   (*b*) Describe the main differences between a viewdata system such as British Telecom's Prestel system and a typical teletext system.

   (*c*) Some people believe that most households will eventually own a Prestel receiver. Describe the effects that this might have on the lives of ordinary people.

   Do you believe that most households will eventually own a Prestel receiver? Give your reasons.

   (CU)

4. Increasingly, microcomputers are no longer the *stand alone* machines of a few years ago, communicating with other computers only occasionally (if at all) via a *modem* and the telephone system at some sluggish *baud rate*. Now, they are part of an *electronic office* linked together in a *local area network*, not only able to share expensive *peripherals* such as *hard*

disks and *laser printers*, but also able to share access to files and to communicate rapidly with each other.

Explain the terms

(*a*) stand alone microcomputer (*b*) modem

(*c*) baud rate (*d*) electronic office

(*e*) local area network (*f*) peripheral

(*g*) hard disk (*h*) laser printer

5. Computers and computerised equipment are increasingly being introduced into business management and office work.

   (*a*) Describe the changes which have occurred, or are likely to occur, because of the introduction of computer-based technology.

   (*b*) State the advantages to management, other workers and the public brought about by the introduction of such technology.

   (*c*) Describe the changing pattern of employment, both in terms of numbers employed and the type of work carried out, as a result of the introduction of such technology.

   (JMB)

6. Once an 'office job' automatically meant a lot of paperwork.

   (*a*) Explain how developments in modern office practice have diminished the importance of paper.

   (*b*) Do you think the 'paperless office' (i.e. an office which does without paper completely) is a likely prospect for the not too distant future?

15 Shops

What do we mean by *stock control*? Huge warehouses humming with fork-lift trucks? Certainly large companies will move raw materials, spare parts and heavy finished goods in this way, but only as *part* of the stock control process.

EVERYDAY STOCK CONTROL

In fact, the principles of stock control are applied at home every day. For example, nearly every household uses (and therefore *keeps a stock of*) milk. Each household knows roughly how much it needs, and so buys *replacement stock* accordingly; perhaps by a standing order with the milkman for three pints a day.

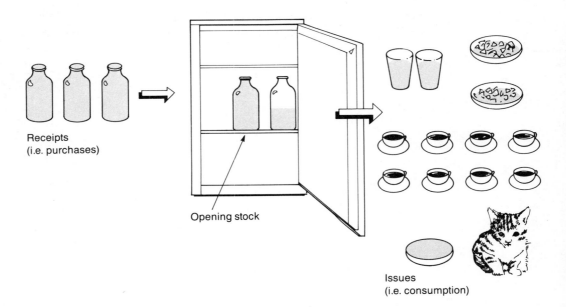

Receipts
(i.e. purchases)

Opening stock

Issues
(i.e. consumption)

Fig. 15.1 Household stock control for milk

If someone drinks more than expected, this miniature stock control system may break down and the household may find itself *out of stock* by the following breakfast time. If this were to happen regularly, it would be sensible to ask the milkman to deliver more. On the other hand if milk stocks build up in the refrigerator, the *order level* is too high and should be reduced.

In this (as all other stock systems) three key questions apply:

- How much do we have now? (i.e. what is the stock level?)
- How much are we likely to use?
- How much is on order?

Obviously, few households would dream of using a computer to control their milk purchases, but most people resort to shopping lists to keep track of the things which have (or soon will have) run out. Even then important items are sometimes forgotten.

 Q 15.1 *Describe some other examples of stock control in everyday life.*

STOCK CONTROL IN SHOPS

If a simple household stock control system can occasionally break down, imagine the problems for even the smallest shop that must stock hundreds of different items. Yet it is vital that the store does not keep running out of things, otherwise its customers will go elsewhere.

 Q 15.2 *A shop could avoid running out of something by keeping two months' supply always in stock. Why is this not practical?*

Obviously, a shopkeeper cannot reorder a can of baked beans every time a customer buys one; if he or she tried, then every basket of groceries sold would generate hours of paperwork. Usually a specific area of shelf space is set aside for baked beans and this is refilled from the storeroom whenever it begins to look empty. (So, in fact, the shopkeeper has to keep track of *two* stock levels: one on the shelf and another in the storeroom.) In principle, however, the shopkeeper's problem is similar to the householder's, and the same basic questions apply:

- What is the stock level? (i.e. how much do we have now?)
- How much are we likely to sell?
- How much is on order?

However, the shopkeeper is dealing with a much greater range of items and the turnover is much faster than the householder's. So the *scale* of the problem is much greater, often large enough to justify using a computer.

Stock records must be kept, for the shopkeeper (unlike the householder looking in the refrigerator) cannot accurately tell all the stock levels at a glance. The records must also be kept up-to-date. It is not very helpful knowing how many tins of baked beans you had in stock last month, if you do not know how many you have now.

But keeping up-to-date records is only half the story. The records must be used to help the shopkeeper to *control* the stocks of everything in the shop.

 Q 15.3 *Can you suggest other information that the shopkeeper needs for efficient stock control?*

BASIC COMPUTER-AIDED STOCK CONTROL

A simple system could work like this. Once a week the shopkeeper does the *stocktaking*, that is physically counts the stocks. It is important that everything is recorded in the right units, i.e. large or small cans of

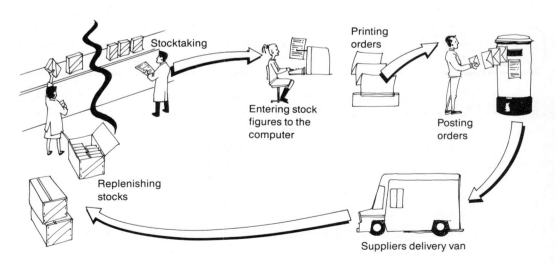

Fig. 15.2 Simple computer-aided stock control in a grocery shop

beans and whether counted singly or in cases. These stock levels are then written down on special *stock record cards* designed for easy input to the computer. The computer then decides for each item whether or not a new order is required. The computer accumulates all necessary orders and, when the information is complete, prints them out so that those various products that come from a single supplier are grouped together. Then all the shopkeeper has to do is send off the orders.

As Figure 15.2 shows, much of the activity is independent of the computer. The machine has no information about the actual movement of goods until someone collects and inputs the data. Equally, the system depends on someone acting on the computer output. Nevertheless, many small stores have invested in microcomputers and have found even this level of automation invaluable.

Stock Master File

Of course the computer does not actually decide anything. It simply acts according to the rules laid down for it. So, for example, the shopkeeper must set the *re-order level* for each item stocked. If stocks fall below this level, then the computer automatically generates an order to the appropriate supplier.

In fact, the re-order level would be only one of a host of details that must be kept for *every* item sold. These details, held as the *stock master file* on magnetic disk, might be:

Data Item	*Example*
(i) item code number	5 00157 004031
(ii) description	Heinz Baked Beans (450 g)
(iii) supply unit	case = 48 cans
(iv) cost price	£16.00
(v) unit selling price	£0.38 (per can)
(vi) number in stock	1.5 (cases)
(vii) re-order level	4 (cases)
(viii) number already on order	4 (cases)
(ix) minimum order quantity	2 (cases)
(x) standard order quantity	4 (cases)
(xi) supplier	Tin Foods Ltd
(xii) supplier number	0017

Q 15.4 *Which order quantity, (ix) or (x), would normally be ordered? Why is the other one held on file?*

Q 15.5 *What factors might determine standard order quantity?*

Q 15.6 *Would an order be printed for this example?*

Q 15.7 *What must the shopkeeper do as soon as the outstanding order (of four cases of beans) is delivered?*

Q 15.8 *What method of file organisation would be best for the stock master file? Why?*

Dialogue Design

Computerisation will save the shopkeeper a lot of time in the routine work of ordering replacement stock. But equally the computer will create extra tasks of its own. The shopkeeper will no longer write out orders, but will key stock data into the computer instead. The net time saving will depend on good *dialogue design* (see Chapter 9); i.e. can the user simply switch on, press a key to select the appropriate program and start entering data with helpful and relevant prompts from the computer?

Q 15.9 *Which of the following must be keyed into the computer after the weekly stocktake?*

item code number   item description   cost price
number in stock

System Flexibility

The system must be able to cope with changing circumstances. For example, unpopular lines may be scrapped and new lines may be introduced, suppliers may change minimum order quantities and prices and so on. All these will necessitate changes to the computer files, which must be quick and easy to update.

Typically, a shop would use a standard software package. The original designers would have tried to cater for a variety of requirements. So, for example, if the package can keep track of outstanding orders it might well go on to record invoices from the suppliers, payments made to them, VAT etc. These parts of the package will require additional files.

Q 15.10 *How many files (apart from the stock master file) are required to monitor outstanding orders, purchase invoices, payments and VAT payments? Design an appropriate record format for each file you suggest.*

SUPERMARKETS

The principles of stock control are no different for a large supermarket, but the *scale* of the problem is much increased. A large store could be selling hundreds of different items per minute through a dozen checkouts. When goods move that fast, even an hourly stocktake may not prevent shelves from becoming empty. Lost sales and the high staff costs suggest a need for an investment in computers.

Avoiding Data Duplication

Even shops that have computerised their re-ordering process nevertheless waste a great deal of staff time by capturing the *same* sales data *three* times.

At the moment the checkout operator rings up a customer's purchase, he or she is aware of the vital details of the transaction, i.e. the item bought and its price. But a moment later, something else is rung up and the data is lost.

A second assistant is checking the shelves, noting which are looking empty and refilling them accordingly. Again, information is collected, acted on and discarded.

The re-ordering process may only begin some time later when the same sales data is collected a *third* time at the next stocktake. If the data could only be captured and *recorded* at the *point of sale*, i.e. when money and goods are exchanged at the checkout, no further stocktaking would be necessary. For then the checkout data could be processed by a computer that automatically issues requests for shelves to be refilled and places orders with the appropriate suppliers to keep the stockroom full.

Point of Sale Terminals

The more sophisticated *electronic point of sale* (EPOS) *terminals* are on-line to the store computer and update stock levels the moment the purchase details have been entered.

So that the machine can rapidly and accurately identify a customer's purchases, nearly everything now carries a unique 13-digit code number, called the *European article number* (EAN), in bar-coded form (see Chapter 5). The bar code can be read by a light pen or laser scanner built into the checkout.

Fig. 15.3   Using a supermarket EPOS terminal with laser scanner

Information Flow

The EPOS terminal directs the machine-read item code to the computer which:

  (i) checks that the item code is valid (the last digit of the EAN is for checking purposes)

 (ii) reads the stock file to identify the item from its code

(iii) sends back to the EPOS terminal a description of the item and its selling price

(iv) reduces by one the number-in-stock figure stored on file

 (v) calls into action replenishment and/or re-order routines if appropriate.

Meanwhile, at the checkout, the EPOS terminal has printed a further line on the customer's receipt showing the item purchased and its price, the running total of the customer's bill has been updated in the terminal's memory and the operator is passing the next item through the laser scanner. The entire process has taken no more than a split second.

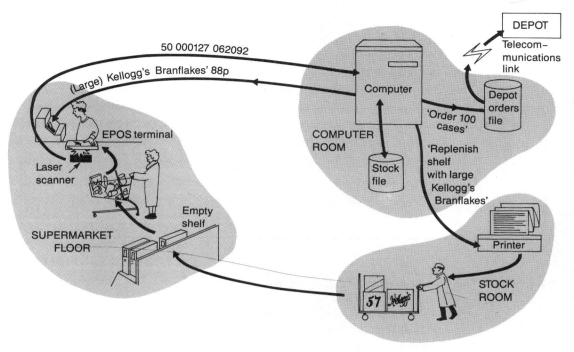

Fig. 15.4 Supermarket EPOS in action

Q 15.11 *A number of possible features of a supermarket EPOS laser checkout system are listed below. For each one, describe how it may come about and whether or not it will be an advantage to: (a) the customer; (b) the management; (c) the shop staff:*

  (i) *itemised receipts*

  (ii) *no individual pricing of goods*

  (iii) *faster checkout procedures*

  (iv) *fewer checkout errors*

  (v) *rapid and detailed sales figures*

  (vi) *fast identification of slow moving items*

  (vii) *high investment in equipment*

  (viii) *faster procedures for price changes*

  (ix) *fewer fresh food stocks*

  (x) *stock-taking almost eliminated*

  (xi) *reduced staff*

  (xii) *number of items sold*

  (xiii) *change owed to customer.*

Of course, the till must always be on-line to the computer which, in turn, must run the correct program all day long. Clearly the hardware and software must be extraordinarily reliable to sustain such constant use without breakdown. But the costs of EPOS installation are still falling, and the reliability of the electronics has been well established so that this has become a cost-effective option even for the smaller retailer.

Q 15.12 *Why are occasional stocktakes necessary even to a supermarket that has fully computerised its POS checkout procedures?*

Q 15.13 *The worst happens: the computer system in a busy supermarket breaks down.*

(a) Is it sensible to allow further customers into the shop?

(b) How should those customers already in the shop be dealt with?

Kimball Tags—Another POS Option

Some shops, particularly clothes shops, use special punched cardboard tags, usually called *Kimball tags*, to capture sales data at the point of sale (see Chapter 5). As the tills are not built to read punched cards, these tags do not offer instant data entry. Instead they are collected together and taken to a special reader for batch entry to the computer system.

This is obviously slower than an on-line laser till but it still has a number of advantages over a manual system: direct measurement of sales. There is no need for frequent stocktaking and no need to key item codes into the computer.

Q 15.14 *What information must be included on a Kimball tag?*

CHAIN STORES

Chain stores offer lower prices than individual shops by combining all their branches' requirements into bulk orders which qualify for suppliers' discounts. To achieve this, sales data from each branch must somehow be gathered together into a central ordering system. Some chains still send batches of tags or checking lists from each of the branches by road. Alternatively, in-store microcomputers can be used to direct the sales information to a central depot. The central computer for one well known clothing store, for example, automatically dials up each of the in-store micros in its branches in the course of the night. Each micro in turn transmits all the day's sales and stock data without any staff supervising the operation.

 Q 15.15 *What information must be included in the data transmitted in this way?*

By combining the requirements of the various branches and automating their procedures chain stores can save on staff time and delivery costs and can offer keen prices and avoid running out of stock. Staff are able to spend more time with the customers and there is less need for them to work after hours.

Q 15.16 *How could a large chain store use its computers to save on delivery costs from the central warehouse to its high-street branches?*

Larger chain stores use computers in many areas: stock control (in stores and depots), distribution planning, training, forecasting sales trends, as well as in the 'office' applications such as accounting, payroll and electronic mail. But the cost of systems has fallen so much that even the corner shop can now afford a computerised till which gives some analysis of sales in addition to helping the shopkeeper to control stock and keep accounts.

JARGON 15

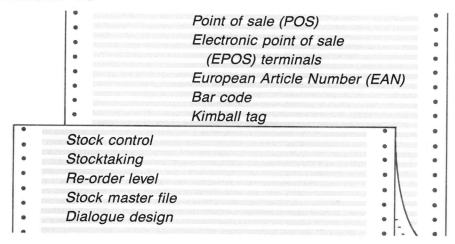

Point of sale (POS)
Electronic point of sale
   (EPOS) terminals
European Article Number (EAN)
Bar code
Kimball tag
Stock control
Stocktaking
Re-order level
Stock master file
Dialogue design

EXERCISES 15

1. In a large supermarket all the checkout tills are linked to a computer. All the items bought by a customer are already marked with a special bar code. This bar code identifies an item and is different for each of the items sold in the supermarket.

    One customer buys a tin of soup and at the checkout the bar code is read by a special sensor and automatically sent to the computer. The computer finds details about the soup and sends them to the checkout till where they are displayed and printed for the customer.

    (*a*) Here is an example of a bar code.

    9 780859 505628

    (i) How is the bar code read by the sensor?
    (ii) Suggest an advantage of using bar codes rather than keying in details of each item on the checkout till.

    (*b*) The computer obtains details about the soup from a file.

    (i) Give two examples of data that must be held for the tin of soup.
    (ii) Suggest a suitable backing store to hold the file and give an explanation for your choice.

    (*c*) Explain one advantage for the customer and one advantage for the supermarket. Give an example to support each explanation.

    (*d*) Suggest one problem the supermarket may have had with the staff who were to operate the new checkout system and give an example to support your answer.

    (SEREB)

2. A large supermarket is closed for a week and the reason given is that the latest computerised checkout facilities are being installed. Describe the changes that you might expect to see when the supermarket re-opens. You should include comments on the type of checkout facilities and the changes in stock management, staffing levels and use of money.

    (SUJB)

3. (a) Where in a supermarket would you find a point-of-sale device, sometimes called a POS device?

 (b) Other than a keyboard, what kind of input device might it use?

 (c) What sort of information is read by this input device?

 (d) How is this information represented?

 (e) List three things that the point-of-sale device prints out for the customer.

 (f) What additional information does the point-of-sale device give specially to help the person who operates it?

 (g) How does the point-of-sale device help to maintain the correct level of stocks?

 (h) Describe briefly how the stock control system would work.

(WMEB)

4. A firm which owns a chain of food stores and a warehouse from which they are supplied, is planning to use a central computer to control the ordering of goods and the delivery of stock between the warehouse and the shops.

 (a) Describe an off-line method of collecting data about current stock levels and say how this data would be sent to the computer.

 (b) Describe an on-line method of collecting data about current stock levels which is suitable for a real time system and say what kind of backing store would be necessary in this case.

 (c) A separate stock file is to be kept for each shop. List three items of data, apart from cost and details of the actual product, which would be kept on this file for each product.

 (d) There is also to be a separate stock file for the warehouse. Name one additional item of information which would be kept on this file.

 (e) What information would be output from the system
  (i) to help to keep supplies in the shops at the right level;
  (ii) to help to keep supplies in the warehouse at the right level?

 (f) What information could be output from the computer to reduce the amount of fuel used by the delivery lorries?

 (g) State one advantage to the customer of using stock control.

 (h) State one advantage to the firm of using stock control.

(WMEB)

5. A small chemist's shop carries, amongst other items, five brands of tooth-paste, labelled TPA, TPB, TPC, TPD, TPE. The manager never allows his total stock to fall below 48 for brands TPA, TPB and TPC; and 24 for TPD and TPE. The maximum stock the manager will ever carry is 72 for brands TPA, TPB and TPC; and 48 for TPD and TPE. Each week, an assistant checks the number of each brand left on the shelves and in the stock-room.

   A simple computerised re-order/stock control program exists to allow the assistant to enter weekly the quantities of each brand in the shop. This program is designed to re-order on pre-printed forms stocks of toothpaste only when necessary, i.e. when they fall below the above quantities. It is also designed to count the number of entries as they are input by the assistant and to prompt the assistant to enter all five entries, including the first.

   (i) Design a simple order form for the system.

   (ii) Draw a flowchart of the stock control/re-order program. Assume all entries are input at the one time and the various quantities stored in the computer's memory.

   (iii) Why would punch cards not be suitable as an input medium for this application?

   (CU)

6. A large chain of shops has point of sale terminals at each of its branches. Data collected throughout the day at each terminal is stored on a cassette tape, then transmitted overnight to a central computer at head office.

   The data may be used

   (a) to organise the delivery of stock from a central warehouse;

   (b) to identify, for each store, particularly busy or slack times of the day.

   Describe how the computer may be used in carrying out these tasks. Pay particular attention to the data that has to be collected, the data files used and the processing that takes place. For each task, describe the output produced and suggest how the output might be used.

   (CU)

7. This systems flowchart shows the stages in the updating section of a stock control system in a wholesale warehouse. Customers take their purchases to point of sale terminals linked directly to a mainframe computer, which uses sequential files.

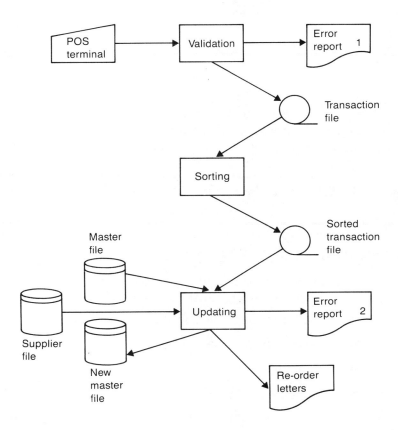

(a) For what purpose is the transaction file used?

(b) What happens to the records during sorting?

(c) Why is sorting necessary?

(d) What happens during updating?

(e) Explain the terms grandfather, father and son in relation to file generation and explain why they are necessary.

(f) Describe three different types of error that might be reported and state at which stage they will be reported.

(g) Explain the output at the "Re-order" stage.

(AEB 1984)

16 Libraries

If they are to avoid losing an unacceptable proportion of their books, libraries must run a highly effective stock control system. Even so, well managed libraries *do* lose a number of books every year, and not just through outright theft.

 Q 16.1 *How else might a library lose books?*

THE WORK OF A LIBRARY

Someone working in a library would do more than check books in and out all day. A library must fulfil a number of tasks:

- keeping track of the routine lending and return of books
- chasing up overdue books
- cataloguing
- introducing new titles to the system and deleting others
- locating specially requested titles held in other libraries
- providing information and research services.

The Traditional Manual System

You probably have experience of the traditional manual system, as it is used by the libraries in most schools and colleges as well as many smaller public libraries.

You choose your book and present it and your ticket to the librarian who transfers the book-card to your ticket and places them both in the file reserved for all loans made that day (and which, of course, will all be due for return by the same date). The book is date-stamped (say, for 8th May) and is yours until then.

Bring the book back and the process is reversed: the book-card is returned to the book, your ticket is returned to you, and the book to the shelf.

Find your library tickets
— one for each book!

Choose your book

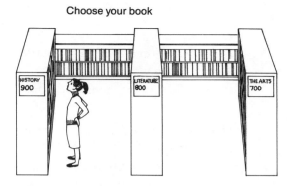

Present chosen
book and ticket
to librarian

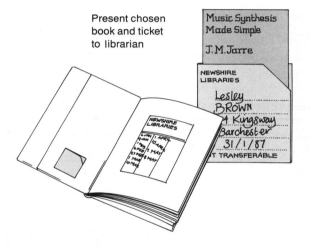

Ticket and book
card filed under
8th May

Fig. 16.1   Manual library system

?   **Q 16.2**   *How should the library arrange the tickets held in one day's file?*

Should you wish to hold the book for longer, you can renew the loan in person. The librarian will simply restamp the book and move your ticket (still with the book-card inside) to the file reserved for books due back on the new return date.

Q 16.3   *You may also renew the loan by telephone or by letter. Why, in this case, would the library not move your ticket to a new return file? What happens instead?*

Q 16.4   *How does a library restrict its members to, say, no more than five books on loan at any one time?*

Q 16.5   *If you borrowed your five books each on a different day, could the library work out the titles you held? Would this be easy for a large library?*

Could the library itemise the books you had borrowed over the last year?

Q 16.6   *How would the library establish how many times a book had been borrowed over the last year?*

How would the library find all the books that had been borrowed (a) more than 30 times, and (b) less than three times over the last year? Any comment?

Overdue Books

If you keep the book beyond the deadline, then your ticket will languish in the '8th May returns' file with the others that are also overdue. After two or three weeks, a librarian will post a reminder to you. Eventually, your ticket will be moved to a special 'long overdue' file, and at some point the library may well terminate your membership.

Q 16.7   *Design a simple postcard size form to remind a reader of an overdue book.*

What information will the librarian need to find (a) on the book-card and (b) on the reader's ticket?

What information should be recorded when the reminder is sent?

Q 16.8   *One very irregular borrower fails to return a book, despite several reminders and even a telephone call. His membership of the library is withdrawn, but he still has four tickets. What is to stop him using them?*

Finding a Book

The books in most libraries are arranged by subject. Most users are happy to check the shelves relevant to their interests and extract a book from whatever happens to be there at the time.

Serious users of the library will want to know what the library holds, rather than restrict themselves to the titles that happen to be available that day. Alternatively a reader may wish to locate a particular author or title he cannot find. And, of course, the library itself must know exactly which books it stocks.

Libraries are therefore obliged to carry some sort of index of their books. In a manual system, this means a cabinet or two full of cards that list the books at least by their authors (in alphabetical order). Many libraries will also carry a second card index, listing the books by subject; and some also have a third, listing the books by their titles. A really good index will include a lot of cross-referencing, which makes it difficult to compile.

It is vital that these catalogues are kept up-to-date (otherwise there would be no point in having them). New books must be indexed before they are put on the shelves, and withdrawn books must be deleted from the catalogue. Occasionally, the catalogues will be checked against actual stock and books on loan (such a stocktake would also show if any books had been lost).

Q 16.9   *Almost all general libraries use the Dewey Decimal System to categorise a book by its subject. Find out what you can about this system. What sort of library might not have a use for it?*

Q 16.10   *Describe how the library staff must prepare a new book before they put it on the shelves ready for borrowing.*

Q 16.11   *A reader requests a particular book listed in the catalogue but which is not to be found on the shelves. How could the library staff find out whether the book is on loan or whether it is lost altogether?*

Assuming the book is on loan, what should the librarian do to ensure the request is met once the current borrower returns it?

Special Requests

If a particular book is not kept at the library a reader may still request it, for the book is almost certainly held somewhere else. To find it, the librarian must contact the County Library Headquarters who will use their master-index (incorporating the catalogues of the many libraries under their jurisdiction) to locate the book.

Q 16.12   *What must the librarian do once the requested book has arrived?*

In the light of this, design an appropriate form for a reader to use when the request is made.

COMPUTERISED CATALOGUES

Not only is cataloguing books a highly appropriate task for a computer, but also many Councils (who are responsible for running the libraries) have ample spare capacity on their mainframes to provide this level of computerisation at very little cost.

The savings are considerable. At branch libraries the librarians are spared the tedious and time-consuming chore of updating their catalogues every time they are sent a batch of new books. And at the library headquarters the problem of locating a specially requested title is reduced to a quick keyboard operation on the computer terminal.

Computerising the catalogue also opens up new possibilities for the library service. For example, the library headquarters could use the computer to extract a county-wide list of titles relevant to a particular subject or, say, of those available on cassette tape. *With* the computer, compiling such a list would be a routine task; *without* it the work involved would be considerable and in many cases the end product (the book list) would probably not justify the effort.

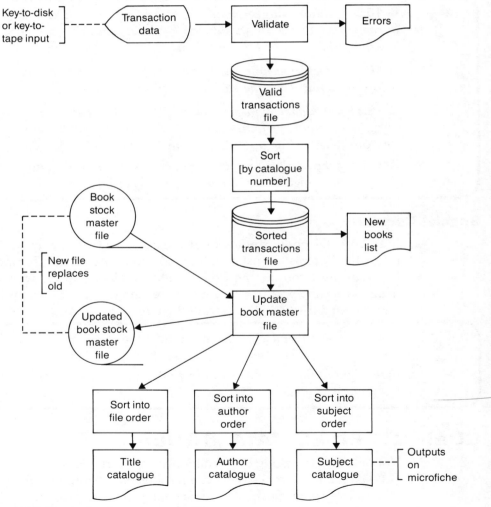

Fig. 16.2 Updating the book stock master file

?

Q 16.13 *What validation checks might be included in the input program?*

Q 16.14 *Why is it necessary to sort the transaction file by catalogue number before updating the master file?*

Q 16.15 *What happens to the transactions file and the old master file once the new, updated master file is ready? Are they destroyed?*

The advantages of computerised catalogues do not end there. For *computer output on microfilm* (COM) techniques (see Chapter 6) allow every library in the county to dispense with its bulky cabinets full of cards and yet to carry a *more extensive* catalogue for its readers. The computer can provide each library with regularly updated microfiche versions of the county catalogue (with author, subject and title entries) so that anyone can locate a book, whichever library holds it.

Fig. 16.3   Using a library microfiche catalogue

This is itself an important improvement in the library service. Since the branch librarians are saved the chore of updating the catalogue, they have more time for other things, and so the service should also improve in other unrelated ways.

Placing several microfiche readers in each library and destroying outdated frames every time a new catalogue is delivered may seem extravagant, but the savings in paper, staff time and floor space considerably offset the costs.

Q 16.16 *Does your school or college library carry separate author, subject and title catalogues? Does your public library? Are they card index or microfiche systems? If microfiche, how old is the system?*

Q 16.17 *In addition to the author, subject and title, the record on each book held on the book-stock master file will include several other items of data. What might they be?*

Design an appropriate record format. Estimate the space required for each field and hence for the whole record.

COMPUTERISING THE LOAN SYSTEM

Computerising the book stock records is a significant step, but automating the loans system is a much greater one. Just as supermarkets have found that their check-out and record-keeping procedures can be considerably improved by using bar codes and laser scanners, so too have libraries. If anything, libraries have adopted these systems more readily than shops, as Councils have recognised the potential for streamlining their libraries' administrative procedures in a way that should simultaneously *improve* the service yet *save* money (primarily on staff costs).

An Off-line System

Each book is identified by a unique code number attached to it in bar code form; there is no need for a book-card. Similarly each reader is identified by a unique membership number held in coded form on a special ticket issued by the library.

Some library services are using OCR systems instead of bar codes (see Chapter 5). However, the majority of computerised library services have preferred bar codes as they are more reliably read by the light pens.

Fig. 16.4 Bar-coded library ticket

Q 16.18 *The library ticket is encased in transparent plastic. Why?*

Q 16.19 *There is no reference on the library ticket to the library branch (Barchester), only to the county (Newshire). Why?*

Obviously the libraries themselves will need a number of items of hardware. Assuming they are off-line, each will need, at the very *minimum*, two light pens, each linked to the microcomputer and to a cassette tape, a keyboard and a small display by which the librarian may see the book codes have been properly read (whether from the light pens or off the keyboard). In fact, as the technology becomes more commonplace, so most computerised libraries are moving away from the cruder and cheaper cassette tape and restricted displays to floppy disks and proper VDUs.

The microcomputer will verify the correct reading of the bar codes (which carry their own check digits, see Chapter 11), and act as an interface between the light pen and the tape. In most systems the microcomputer also has sufficient memory to set a number of *traps*, i.e. it can signal to the librarian that a member has been banned from borrowing books or that a book has been reserved so should not be put back on the shelves.

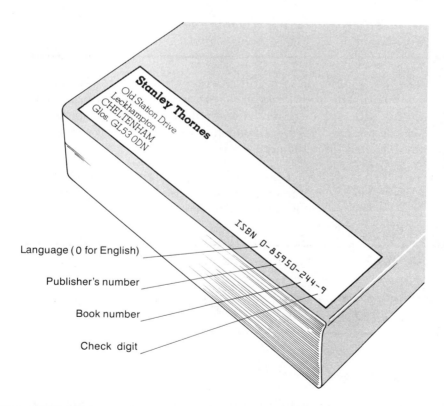

Fig. 16.5 ISBN. The International Standard Book Number or ISBN of this (or any other) book follows the pattern shown. The check digit works as follows: multiply the first digit (0) by 10, the next (8) by 9 and so on; add together the results and fix the check digit so that the final total divides by 11

Borrowing and Returning Books

As in the manual system, you choose a book and present it with your ticket to the librarian. But this time there is no book-card to transfer. Instead the librarian scans the bar code on your membership ticket and on the book until the correct reading of the code is indicated by an audible tone. The book is still date-stamped, partly for your convenience and partly so that when the book comes back the library staff can check whether or not it is overdue and charge fines accordingly.

When you bring the book back there is no need for you to produce your membership ticket, for the scanner will have been pre-coded to receive 'returns' and so it needs only to read the book-number to terminate the loan.

Q 16.20   *If the library is particularly busy, the librarian may just look quickly inside your returned books and put them to one side. Explain.*

Q 16.21   *Why is it not usual for an off-line system to indicate an overdue book with an audible signal, as it might a reserved one?*

Telephone renewals are still possible because the library also has a keyboard. The librarian who takes your call will not need to ask for the author, title or date of return, but will seek instead the book-code which will be punched in on the branch library's keyboard as you read it out, and verified immediately.

The keyboard also acts as a back-up system, in case the light pens should fail. It also allows the input of other information for which a bar code is not available (such as a book currently on issue to be reserved as soon as it is returned).

Q 16.22   *How else might the library guard against failure of the equipment?*

Q 16.23   *What information will the librarians have to note down if suddenly the computerised system does fail?*

The Computer Centre

The details collected during the day at each library and held on tape cassettes or disks must either by physically transported to the computer centre, or down-loaded through the telephone system.

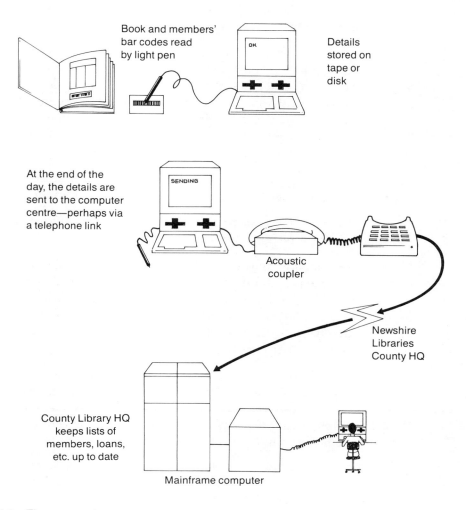

Fig. 16.6 The new system

The information will be transferred to tape or disk to form the *loans* and *reservations transactions files* by which the main files, i.e. the *loans master file* and the *reservations master file*, will be updated.

Since the libraries themselves no longer keep details of their loans, it follows that the computer centre must issue reminders for overdue books. But with a computerised system this is very easy. The computer can automatically identify a loan that is long overdue and, using the member's number recorded when the book was borrowed, extract the relevant name and address from the *borrowers master file*. It will use the book number to extract the relevant title from the *book stock master file* and issue a standard letter to the offending reader. Similarly the computer can remind those who have borrowed more than the allowed number of books that they must return some as soon as possible.

If a record is kept then the computer can automatically identify a reader who regularly borrows more than his entitlement or keeps books well beyond the return date. Every county keeps a 'black list' of banned members whose entitlement to borrow books has been withdrawn. The computer centre updates and circulates this list so that the branch librarians can key it into their microcomputers to ensure that they will be warned if someone on the list tries to borrow a book.

In the same way, the library inputs to its computer the list of specially reserved books so that these may also be trapped automatically.

Updating the *borrowers master file* and the *book stock master file* is also a computer centre responsibility.

When a new member arrives at a branch library he or she completes a form with all the relevant details and is allocated a reader's number and corresponding bar-coded membership ticket. The librarian adds this number to the application form which is then sent to the computer centre or, alternatively, is keyed on to disk or tape at the library together with the new reader's other details.

New books might be treated in the same way, but more usually they are bought, prepared and distributed by the county library headquarters.

Q 16.24   *How would the staff at the library computer centre prepare a new book before sending it to its designated library?*

Q 16.25   *The librarians at branch level have a number of 'warm-up' procedures to go through in order to prepare their equipment for the day's use. What might they be?*

Q 16.26   *If you borrowed a number of books each at different times how easy would it be for the computerised system to establish which books you had? Explain your answer.*

Q 16.27   *Assuming the library restricts its members to no more than five books on loan at any one time, could the computerised system stop you borrowing a sixth on another day?*

Q 16.28   *The system described assumes the library is off-line. This is usually the case, for on-line links are expensive and the off-line system works well. However, some counties are installing on-line systems at their major libraries. How would such an on-line link alter things?*

Q 16.29 *As long as the computer records have been set up with this in mind it is easy for the computerised system to establish a list of the most frequently borrowed books, say those borrowed more than 30 times in a year and those not borrowed very often (say less than three times in a year). Explain.*

Q 16.30 *Again, as long as the computer records have been set up with that intention, it would be possible for the computer to list all the titles you borrowed in the last year. Should library records be this detailed? Can you be sure they are not? If they are, who should have access to that information—you . . . your parents or guardians . . . your principal or headteacher (who is responsible for directing your education and may well have to write about you in a reference for a job or college place) . . . an employer trying to make a fair decision between you and another excellent candidate . . . the police?*

INFORMATION SERVICES

Libraries hold a lot of reference material: extensive encyclopedias, out-of-the-area telephone directories, company directories etc. Many are already supplementing these existing reference facilities with teletext facilities such as Ceefax and Oracle and are experimenting with interactive viewdata services such as Prestel. It may well be that these are setting the pattern for the future and that libraries will become public 'post-boxes' for items of electronic mail.

Libraries are also involving themselves with computers in other ways. Many lend out software tapes (as they do music cassettes and LP records). Some have even established 'computing rooms' in which members of the public may try out their own experimental programs on one of a number of computers kept for that purpose. (Your school or college has no doubt established a similar facility for students' use.)

A lot of local activities are also heavily dependent on the local library for their publicity. Evening classes, clubs, societies, cultural events etc. are advertised in all the libraries of the neighbourhood. Although this aspect of the library service has yet to be computerised to the extent of the lending systems, it is an important and developing area (precisely because the computer is allowing us more leisure). In the near future, it will be possible for the library's computer to print out a list of local events on a particular evening or another list of, say, discos to be held locally in the next month.

Libraries are information centres and they are inevitably deeply involved in many aspects of information technology.

JARGON 16

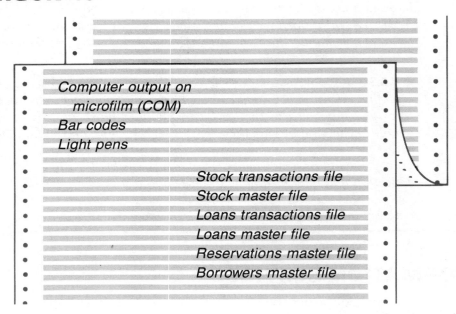

Computer output on
  microfilm (COM)
Bar codes
Light pens

Stock transactions file
Stock master file
Loans transactions file
Loans master file
Reservations master file
Borrowers master file

EXERCISES 16

1. A local County Library Service has decided to install a computer system. It decides on an on-line real-time system with terminals in each of the 15 branch libraries linked to the mainframe at Library Headquarters. The system is designed to control lending and borrowing as well as book re-ordering and receiving.

    (a) State what hardware would be suitable in each branch library and say why.

    (b) Explain suitable methods of collecting data in the following situations.
      (i) when a customer borrows a book
      (ii) when a book is returned
      (iii) when a new book is introduced to a branch library

    (c) State three files that would be needed at headquarters indicating their contents and the purpose they serve.

    (d) Give two advantages of this system over a manual system for:
      (i) customers using the library
      (ii) running the County Library Service.

    (AEB 1982)

2. A large county library is considering the possibility of connecting smaller branch libraries to its main library computer.

   (a) What computing equipment would you expect to find in the branch libraries?

   (b) Give two advantages which might result from such a system.

   (c) Give two possible disadvantages of this system.

   (EMREB)

3. Most library services use the county computer to update their library catalogues.

   (a) Explain with the aid of an appropriate systems flowchart how the computerised cataloguing system works and the procedures necessary for
      (i) the computer staff at library headquarters
      (ii) the local branch librarian
      (iii) the library user.

   (b) Outline the advantages and disadvantages of this computer application over the manual system it replaces.

4. Imagine that you work at the enquiries desk at a library using an off-line computerised loan system as described in this chapter and that a member of the public with no experience of such systems has asked to join the library.

   Outline how the system operates, illustrating your answer with a 'new members joining' form and a membership ticket of your own design.

5. Libraries are no longer just store houses full of books for loan and reference. Increasingly they are becoming 'information centres'. Describe how the latest modern technology is changing the nature of local libraries beyond the simple lending of books.

17 Banks

Most people think that a bank's stock in trade is *cash*. However, the notes and coins that pass over the counters of Britain's high street banks represent only a small part of their total business. The majority of a bank's transactions are made by cheque or automatic payments (such as standing orders and direct debits); no *cash* changes hands at all.

A bank's stock in trade is *information*:

- who is paying out the money?

- how much is involved?

- how much is left in the account?

- who is receiving the money?

- the new total in the recipient's account

- the date of the transaction

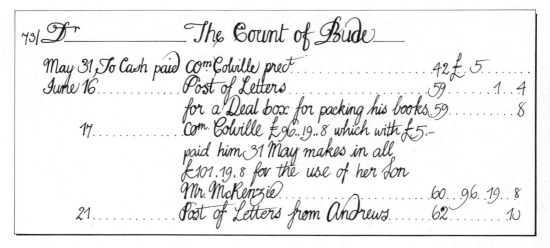

Fig. 17.1 This handwritten account was prepared in 1731. Handwritten ledgers were widely used until the 1950s.

? **Q 17.1** Name the 'big four' banks, i.e. the four largest and best known banks with branches in almost every high street.

How many of the other United Kingdom high street banks can you name?

Q 17.2 For each of the following explain (i) the meaning of the banking term and (ii) the use a customer would have for them.

(a) current account   (b) deposit account

(c) cheque card   (d) cash card

(e) credit card   (f) credit slip

(g) standing order   (h) direct debit

Q 17.3 Is there anyone in your family with a bank account? Ask them to estimate the proportions of their income spent (a) as cash (b) as cheques (c) as automatic payments (i.e. as standing orders, direct debits etc.).

Q 17.4 A large number of bank accounts are held by businesses. Do you think that personal accounts or business accounts will use the higher proportion of (a) cash (b) cheques (c) automatic payments?

Fig. 17.2 Even the technology of the 1960s is hopelessly crude by today's standards. This bank employee is sorting through a card file in order to locate an account that needs updating. She will have used the cash register in front of her (a sort of typewriter cum mechanical calculator) to help her make the necessary amendments. Two or three new entries on one account will have taken a minute or two to complete

BANKING IN THE UK

An Extensive Operation

Around two-thirds of the adult UK population have bank accounts. If business accounts are included, there are some 32 million current accounts throughout the country and *every day* nine million cheques and five million automatic payments have to be processed.

Accounts held at some 14 000 branches have to be brought up-to-date overnight, ready for the following day's business.

Furthermore the banks have to prepare regular printed statements for every customer and keep copies for themselves lest there should be any queries. This too is a mammoth undertaking; for example, in 1986 the National Westminster Bank printed and posted around 100 million statements and answered approximately 150 million account enquiries.

Clearly the banks are faced with a huge and complex administrative problem. Highly sophisticated computing and telecommunications facilities are essential. Imagine tackling such a task with handwritten ledgers, an army of clerks and the ordinary post. It just could not be done.

Fig. 17.3   Modern bank statements are produced on very high speed laser printers such as this

Cheques and Credits

Since 1962 the UK banks have all been using the same cheque processing or 'clearing' system. Each cheque is printed with magnetic ink codes and sorted by machines capable of *magnetic ink character recognition* (MICR), see Chapter 5. Each customer is given a book of cheques that can only be used on his or her account because each cheque has already been printed in special magnetic ink with (i) its own cheque number (ii) the bank and branch code number and (iii) the customer's account number. Look at any cheque and you will see these three codes printed in the highly distinctive MICR typeface along the bottom.

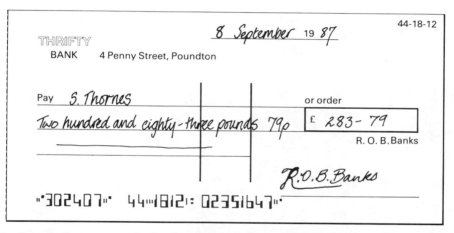

Fig. 17.4 Despite the expense, the banks are impelled to use magnetic ink on cheques for security reasons. Genuine users may write over the codes (perhaps with flowery signatures); fraudsters may try deliberately to alter them. The cheque may be dirtied, possibly through changing hands several times or through other forms of rough treatment. An MICR system should not be upset by any of this, but an OCR (optical) system certainly would be

Of course, the bank cannot know the *amount* to be paid until the person to whom the cheque is made out pays it into *his* or *her* bank. When that happens that bank will print the amount, again in special MICR format, on the bottom right-hand side of the cheque. The cheque is then ready for the computer.

The banks also issue each customer with 'credit slips' (i.e. paying-in forms) which are coded in much the same way as cheques. However, there are nothing like as many of these passing through central clearing (since most customers pay money into their own branch and will use one credit slip to cover several cheques). The banks only began automating this process in 1982, using *optical character recognition* (OCR) as well as MICR.

? **Q 17.5** *Why do the banks continue to use MICR techniques for cheques and not adopt less expensive OCR methods instead?*
Why are OCR methods satisfactory for reading paying-in slips?

Central Clearing

The details of payments made in and out of accounts kept at the same branch that the customer used are down-loaded to the bank's main computer through the branch computer terminal.

Cheques and credits drawn on accounts held elsewhere are transported to the bank's main clearing department which will (i) arrange to swop the cheques and credits of other banks with those of its own (ii) machine read and sort the cheques and credits by branch (iii) prepare the transactions file by which customers' accounts will be adjusted the *following* day.

Fig. 17.5 The cheque reading and sorting machines like those owned by Lloyd's Bank can process 2400 cheques per minute. The UK banks clear some nine million cheques every day but the MICR technology is so efficient that the system is under no pressure; there is still room for considerable expansion of the banking service

The third day's delay is necessary to allow the sorted cheques and credits to be transported back to their respective home branches where they will be checked by local staff to ensure that the handwritten details (i.e. the signatures, the dates and the amounts in words) are all correct. The computer centre will have advised the branch of any customer who has issued cheques that will cause an unauthorised overdraft or if a cancelled ('stopped') cheque has been presented. The branch will then indicate to the central computer those items it does *not* want to go ahead so that all the other payments can be cleared. The whole process will have taken three days.

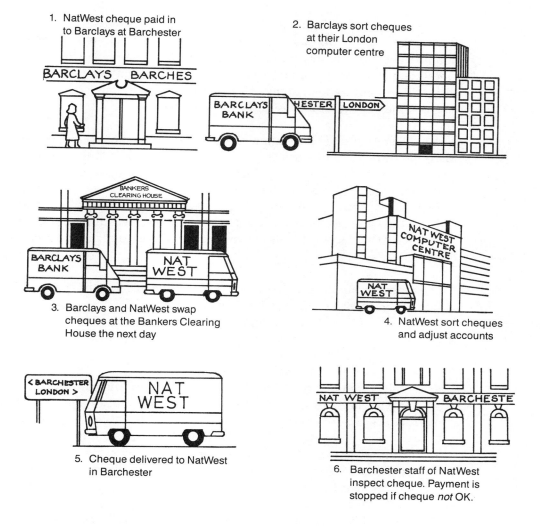

1. NatWest cheque paid in to Barclays at Barchester

2. Barclays sort cheques at their London computer centre

3. Barclays and NatWest swap cheques at the Bankers Clearing House the next day

4. NatWest sort cheques and adjust accounts

5. Cheque delivered to NatWest in Barchester

6. Barchester staff of NatWest inspect cheque. Payment is stopped if cheque *not* OK.

Fig. 17.6 The cheque clearing system

Q 17.6 *What would be the minimum hardware necessary at a branch to operate this clearing system?*

Q 17.7 *What sort of hardware must there be at the computer centre?*

Q 17.8 *What are the dangers of holding all the customers' accounts at the computer centre?*

The Branch Computers

As the available facilities have become increasingly sophisticated so the rôle of the branch computer has grown. Initially the terminals were just 'dumb' links to the central computer, used only for keying in cheque and credit details. Now the branch machines are 'intelligent' processors with disk storage and logic systems of their own and they have become the cornerstones of the branches' local filing system.

The bank staff at one of the main computerised branches no longer have to comb through a profusion of paper files (the older ones probably retrieved from the basement). Instead they can interrogate their own desk-top VDUs. These will have access to all the records kept at the branch, i.e. customers' personal details, credit ratings, shareholdings and the like; they will also have on-line access to the files held at the computer centre, in particular the details of every customer's account as at the close of yesterday's business.

There are many advantages to this, the most obvious being the speed with which comprehensive information is available. Also the data is presented in a single clear form (most manual systems would involve considerable duplication and cross-referencing) and there is an enormous saving of paper and filing-cabinet space.

The branch computers can also handle a number of other routine tasks. For example, the banks, as do other offices, inevitably have to write similar letters to different customers at various times as well as enter into extensive correspondence with others in the business community. The branch computers can readily act as word processing systems and save the secretaries a lot of work (see Chapter 13). Similarly, in advising customers on their financial affairs, the banks are likely to have to calculate rates of return, tax liability and so on that will arise as a consequence of different options. These calculations are involved but, being repetitive and routine, are ideal for the computer.

ELECTRONIC FUNDS TRANSFER (EFT)

The main cheque and credit clearing system is heavily dependent on *paper*. Parcels of cheques and credits are moved around the country every evening as each branch submits its day's business to the bank's central computers, and, once sorted, these same cheques and credits are transported back to their home branches.

The system is also a little slow: three days to clear a cheque may not cause a problem to most household users of the banking system, but for large amounts, three 'dead' days between signing a cheque and the money actually being moved could be a nuisance. For foreign dealings, the delays could be a lot longer and (such is the nature of international business) the amounts involved are likely to be large.

Mindful of the expense of establishing new systems and the considerable advantages that they might all enjoy from full implementation of the new technology, the banks have co-operated on a number of important developments by which funds might be transferred electronically.

Bankers' Automated Clearing Services (BACS)

Organisations with a large number of payments to make (e.g. salaries) and/or a large number of payments to collect (direct debit payments of, say, insurance premiums, HP instalments, TV rental charge etc.) can do so using BACS, the bankers' automated clearing service, jointly owned by the main British banks.

In the past, these organisations would have passed wads of paper vouchers over the counter. Now they simply submit all the necessary details of the payments and collections on computer tape or disk so that the data can then be sorted and processed by the BACS computer directly. No paper vouchers are involved at all.

Both the banking system and the organisations that use BACS save themselves a great deal of clerical work. Furthermore there is no three-day lag; payments are made or collected in a single day.

The system has also proved to be highly reliable—more so than any paper based system—and most major organisations in Britain now use. it. The banks will soon be clearing over 40% of all transactions this way.

Fig. 17.7 Receiving a tape at BACS. The customers' computer output arrives at BACS in a variety of forms: cassette tape, floppy disks and ½ inch tape as well as direct transmissions from a customers' computer centre

?
Q 17.9 *What sort of organisations might use BACS?*

List the names of a number of organisations (taken from different walks of life) who you think probably use this system.

Q 17.10 *The banks do not allow just any company access to BACS. What conditions might the banks set on would-be users of the system?*

Clearing House Automated Payments System (CHAPS)

An *international* system (known as SWIFT) for electronically transmitting payments and other items between the computer centres of the world's leading banks has been operating since 1977.

In 1984 the main clearing banks began using an electronic network (CHAPS) by which the City of London banks could clear large payments (i.e. those in excess of £10 000) between each other within a single day.

In the next few years the service will reach the whole country. It will prove particularly helpful in finalising complicated transactions such as house buying where large sums of money must be transferred up and down a long chain of buyers, sellers and mortgage lenders, all on one day.

Fig. 17.8 Out of a job? Future prospects for the traditional violent bank robber are not good. Electronic Funds Transfer (EFT) will considerably reduce the need for cash. It will also dramatically alter the security problems facing the banks. The bank robber of the future will be a computer wizard clever enough to outsmart the passwords and codes protecting the banks' electronic systems

But electronic funds transfer systems like CHAPS present security problems of their own. As a matter of course every transmission must include internal checks that ensure that the message has been properly received at the other end. Furthermore, the whole system must be protected by elaborate passwords and codes that prevent outsiders breaking into the electronic systems and moving funds illegally into accounts of their own.

Q 17.11 *Look back to Chapter 11 and write a short account detailing how the banks can protect electronic funds transfers from*

(a) transmission error   *(b) outside interference.*

Cash Dispensers

The public at large has had little reason to be aware of the changes that have been taking place in the back offices of the banks, significant though those changes may be. However, one innovation has made considerable impact, namely the 24 hour cash dispensing machines now installed in over half the branches of Britain's banks.

These *automated teller machines* (ATMs) are known by different names. The National Westminter Bank calls them 'Servicetills'; the Midland calls them 'Autobank'; the Royal Bank of Scotland calls them 'Cashline' and so on. They offer slightly different services too.

Fig. 17.9 Using a cash dispenser. The customer must identify herself by inserting her plastic *cashcard* into the machine. The card carries a *magnetic strip code* on the reverse which the machine will read and update. The customer must also prove she is the authorised user by punching in her *personal identification number* (PIN) known only to her and the bank and encoded as part of the magnetic strip

During the day, all these machines are on-line to the banks' mainframe computers, enabling the customers to check the balances on their accounts if they want to, request new cheque books, organise statements (or, on some machines, have a short one printed there and then), make deposits, or, of course, withdraw cash. Most of the banks encode a daily or weekly limit on to the card and the machine will not pay out beyond this limit, even if there are sufficient funds in the account. If the customer is short of funds then he or she will find that the machine will not pay out beyond the account balance, which it will have automatically checked as soon as the customer has been identified from the cash card and PIN. The amount withdrawn is deducted from the account there and then.

Some of the banks do *not* keep their machines on-line to the mainframe computer 24 hours a day, but only while the branch is working (i.e. when the telephone link between the branch and mainframe is already running and the computer centre is collecting details of the day's transactions). From about 6.00 p.m. onwards the central mainframe computer is busy bringing accounts up-to-date. The cash machines go off-line, so can provide only a much restricted service.

Q 17.12 *What minimum information must be encoded on the plastic card for customers of those banks that run permanently on-line machines?*

Q 17.13 *What additional provisions must be made for cash dispensing machines that go off-line at the end of the day?*

What services will the customer be unable to use out of working hours?

How can the banks keep track of who has used the machines and thus prevent people from trying to withdraw large amounts of cash from several different machines (at different branches) on one evening?

Q 17.14 *Some of the banks have arrangements with each other whereby the others' customers can use their machines. At the moment the service is restricted to cash dispensing only.*

How might the banks organise the computing arrangements that make this possible? Would it be possible to offer customers of other banks the full range of services offered to customers of that bank?

It has been possible to shop without cash for some years. Present a credit card such as Access or Visa to the checkout at almost any main store or petrol station and the cashier will fill out an appropriate voucher and record the details on the card by making a copy of the raised letters and code embossed on it. You will be billed for the goods when your monthly statement from the credit card company arrives.

This service would not be possible without extensive computerised account processes within the banks' credit-card divisions.

Fig. 17.10 Buying rail tickets at a PIN point terminal

In the next few years, retailers will be joining an *on-line* system, probably run by the banks, whereby customers will be able to pay for their shopping on production of their plastic cash cards (probably the same cards that already work the automated teller machine at the bank).

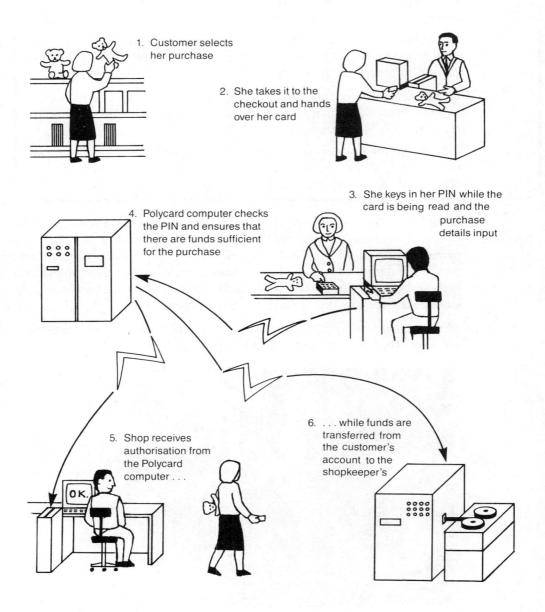

1. Customer selects her purchase

2. She takes it to the checkout and hands over her card

3. She keys in her PIN while the card is being read and the purchase details input

4. Polycard computer checks the PIN and ensures that there are funds sufficient for the purchase

5. Shop receives authorisation from the Polycard computer . . .

6. . . . while funds are transferred from the customer's account to the shopkeeper's

Fig. 17.11 EFTPOS

The cashier will pass the card through an electronic reader while the customer keys in her PIN to verify her identity. No cash will change hands but the bank will move funds from the customer's account to the shop-keeper's at the exact time of the sale.

The banks are calling this *electronic funds transfer* at the *point of sale* (EFTPOS) and are predicting that it will be 'the biggest thing since the cheque book'.

Q 17.15 *What are likely to be the problems in establishing EFTPOS in the next few years?*

Q 17.16 *What will be the main advantages and disadvantages of EFTPOS for (a) the banks? (b) the shops? (c) the customers?*

Home Banking and Teleshopping

As reliable electronic communications networks are woven around Britain, so householders will be able to tap into the same systems and will be able to move funds from their accounts by keying the appropriate codes on a VDU at home.

Indeed, the Nottingham Building Society has been running such a *home banking* scheme based on Prestel and British Telecom links since 1982. The Bank of Scotland launched its home banking scheme in 1985.

Fig. 17.12 Home banking with the Bank of Scotland. The Bank of Scotland was the first bank in the United Kingdom to involve itself heavily with a Prestel-based home-banking service. Customers can pay bills, change standing orders, check their account balances, move money from one account to another (say from a non-interest earning account to one where interest is paid), etc., all from home at any time of day or night, seven days a week

The possibilities for those who use such a home link do not stop at banking however, for retailers will be able to broadcast a catalogue of their wares along the same cable links. The shopper will be able to examine this catalogue on his television set or VDU at home, decide on his purchase and transmit his instructions to the retailer. He can pay in the same way, electronically moving funds from his account to the shop's. He then simply waits for the goods to be delivered. Such *teleshopping* facilities are also part of the Nottingham Building Society's experiment and are no doubt a foretaste of a future lifestyle.

Q 17.17 *Why has it been one of the smaller building societies and one of the smaller banks that have pioneered home banking, rather than the larger organisations?*

The Cashless Society?

Many enthusiasts for the new technology fondly predict a future in which the need for cash will have been completely eliminated by electronic and cable systems. Certainly by the end of the 20th century, which is not so far away, many of the fledgling experiments and pilot schemes of the late 1980s will have become an everyday part of our lives.

Q 17.18 *As electronic funds transfer becomes commonplace will there still be a need for a written cheque system?*

Q 17.19 *Do you think that the technology will ever become so all-embracing that you (or maybe your grandchildren) will ever live in a cashless society?*

JARGON 17

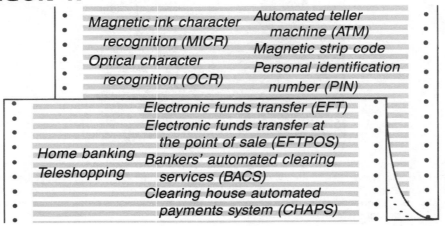

- Magnetic ink character recognition (MICR)
- Optical character recognition (OCR)
- Automated teller machine (ATM)
- Magnetic strip code
- Personal identification number (PIN)
- Home banking
- Teleshopping
- Electronic funds transfer (EFT)
- Electronic funds transfer at the point of sale (EFTPOS)
- Bankers' automated clearing services (BACS)
- Clearing house automated payments system (CHAPS)

EXERCISES 17

1. Processing of customers' cheques is a major part of current account banking.

   (*a*) Why did banks introduce computers into the processing of cheques?

   (*b*) How has the job of a bank clerk changed as a result of computerisation of current accounts?

   (*c*) List the advantages and disadvantages to customers of the computerisation of current accounts.

   (*d*) Bank computer systems use both magnetic tape and magnetic discs as backing storage media. With reference to current account banking what are the main uses of each?

   (*e*) The development of a computerised system would involve, among others, systems analysts and programmers. Give a brief description of the work carried out by each.

   (*f*)

   John Thompson uses the cheque illustrated above to pay £50 to Jean Smith who is a customer of the Thistle Bank.
   - (i) What kind of device is used to read the characters at the bottom of the cheque?
   - (ii) One of these groups of numbers is the customer's account number and includes a check digit. Why are check digits necessary?
   - (iii) List the stages involved in the processing of the cheque, indicating those where computers are used.

   (*g*) The major banks are moving towards 'EFT' (Electronic Funds Transfer). What is meant by this term?

   (Scot)

2. Electronic Funds Transfer is the name given to the computerised transfer of money between different accounts.

   (*a*) Briefly describe one application which makes use of Electronic Funds Transfer.

   (*b*) Electronic Funds Transfer is being used increasingly. Discuss the advantages and disadvantages of Eletronic Funds Transfer for the various groups of people who will be affected by its introduction.

   (Ox)

3. Some computer experts believe that because computer systems are so successful in dealing with money transfers that it would be possible for society to completely do away with cash (i.e. coins and notes).

   (*a*) Name three different ways, other than using cash, of paying for goods or services.

   (*b*) Describe what part the computer system plays in making the money transfer in one of the ways you have named.

   (*c*) It is certainly possible to design computer systems which would enable society to do away with cash but it is very unlikely that a 'cashless society' will occur in the near future. Give two reasons why this is so.

   (SREB)

18 Schools

THE COMPUTER LITERACY PROJECT

By the early 1980s, when the cost of reasonably powerful business machines began to fall, a few microcomputers found their way into schools. In 1981 the Government launched its 'Computer Literacy Project'; every school in the country was to have at least one computer by 1983; the BBC ran a series of television programmes ('The Computer Programme') and began experimenting with *telesoftware* (i.e. transmitted computer programs) so that by hooking a BBC computer and a cassette recorder to a TV set with *Ceefax*, schools were able to build up a bank of suitable software. For those with home computers wanting to know more there was even a postal tuition course.

? **Q 18.1**   *Estimate the total cost of the equipment in the computer room at your school. Do you know where the money came from? Was a parent-teachers association involved, for example?*

Q 18.2   *Was it sensible for the Government to ensure that by 1983 every school had at least one computer? Was one computer likely to be enough? What other problems do you think there would have been?*

COMPUTERS NOT USED FOR COMPUTER STUDIES

It would be wrong to imagine that a school's only use for a computer is as a 'prop' for courses in computer studies. On the contrary computers are beginning to make an important impact in primary schools where computer studies is not taught as a separate subject.

As we have seen, computers are so powerful and so versatile that virtually no organisations can afford to ignore them. Schools are no exception.

Fig. 18.1 No good teacher could fail to notice the fascination many young people have for computer games . . . and wonder how to generate the same enthusiasm in school

As well as being an essential part of computing courses, computers can be of great assistance to schools in five main areas of their activity:

- as a teaching tool in various subjects
- in managing pupils' learning
- as part of an electronic mailing system
- in a school's administration
- in careers advice

Q 18.3 *Before you read on, think how a computer might be used in the classroom for subjects other than computing.*

(a) *Have you had contact with a microcomputer in lessons other than in computing? If so, how was it used?*

(b) *Which subjects might use a computer most readily? Why?*

(c) *Would a computer demonstration (with one computer in the classroom completely under the control of the teacher) be as satisfactory as a session in the computer room with (say) two pupils to a machine?*

(d) *Why do you think that the linguists, historians, social scientists and others have been reluctant to adopt computer-orientated teaching methods?*

For that matter why have some mathematicians and scientists also been reluctant?

(e) *What aspects of a computer make it potentially a good teacher and what aspects make it potentially a bad one?*

COMPUTERS AS TEACHING TOOLS

Fig. 18.2 Increasingly, computers are being used to teach subjects other than computer studies . . . and they are altering significantly the way young people are taught

Ten Strengths

There are ten reasons why, properly used, computers should prove an important learning and teaching tool:

● *Computers are fun*: Above all else, there is a fun aspect to using the computer. Children and adults alike enjoy interacting with a computer and making things happen. Often dull tedious work such as practising multiplication tables and other basic arithmetic, spelling, factual tests in history and geography, and so on, can be presented as a game.

● *Computers are infinitely patient*: Human teachers, being human, can occasionally be moody and irritable. Sometimes they simply get tired and exasperated with someone who cannot understand what is being said even after the 20th explanation (or *will* not understand, for pupils can be moody and irritable too). A computer will keep trying to teach the student tirelessly and without a trace of rancour no matter how slow or mistaken the response. (Of course, a computer can be programmed to deliver raspberries and insults to make the user feel silly when a mistake is made, but that would hardly be good educational programming.)

● *Computer based learning is usually private*: However patient and friendly a teacher—and possibly *because* of that patience and friendliness—there is a 'social pressure' to say 'Yes, I understand' when, in fact, a pupil is not at all sure. The problem is worse in a full class; most people do not want to admit that they have not followed when, it seems, everyone else has. Students can be as stupid, slow, clumsy, or ignorant as they like with the computer, but no one else will know!

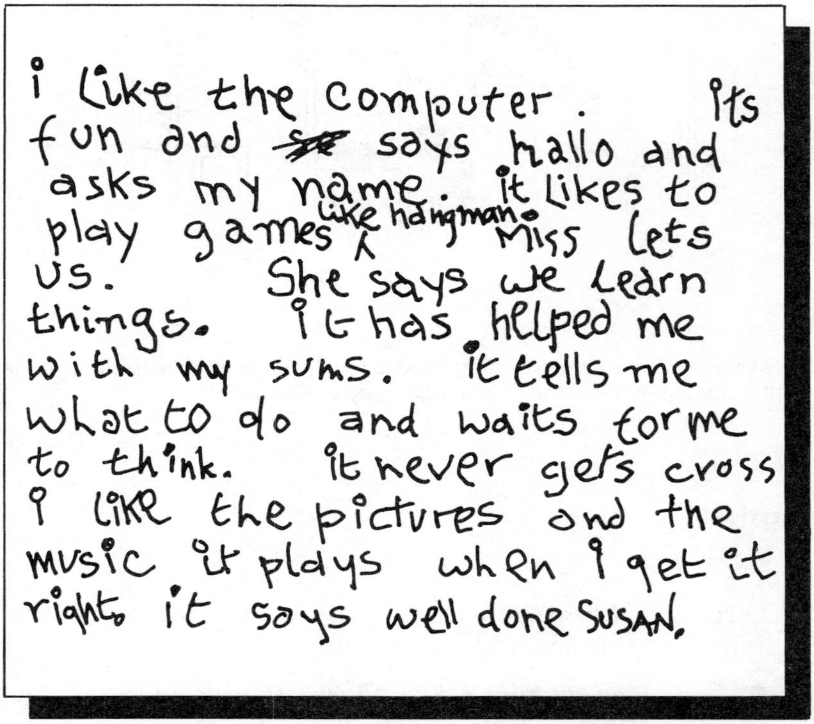

> i like the computer. Its fun and ~~se~~ says hallo and asks my name. it likes to play games like hangman Miss lets us. She says we learn things. it has helped me with my sums. it tells me what to do and waits for me to think. it never gets cross I like the pictures and the music it plays when I get it right it says well done SUSAN.

Fig. 18.3 Susan's reasons for liking the computer. A seven-year-old child, Susan, was asked to write down what she thought of the computer. Her answer makes it plain that she has come to regard the machine as a friend.

● *Computer based learning can also encourage group work*: Many educational programs are designed for two or more people, sometimes to encourage co-operative problem-solving discussion and sometimes to make the children compete in an educational game.

● *Imaginative computer graphics*: Animations can illustrate an idea a lot more clearly than diagrams drawn on a blackboard or displayed by an overhead projector.

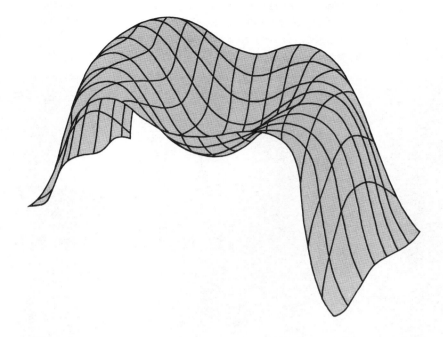

Fig. 18.4 *Supergraph* enables complex mathematical graphs to be drawn on the VDU screen. Many mathematics teachers find such a teaching tool very useful. Although they *could* draw the same graphs on the blackboard, they find that the computer-drawn versions, displayed on a large TV screen in front of the class, are both quicker and more accurate. A computer controlling a single classroom display in this way is often described as an *electronic blackboard*. Of course, the students may well go on to use the program individually to draw graphs of their own

● *Computers can simulate complicated real-life situations*: For example, economic and business games can be played on a computer programmed to react to the student's decisions like a real business would. Airline pilots are trained similarly, in huge simulators that behave like a real aircraft but do not actually crash when the pilot makes an error. In schools, over-costly or dangerous experiments can be simulated on the classroom computer rather than performed in front of the class.

● *Computers can continually generate new problems*: For example, a child's mathematics textbook may contain an exercise of 20 simple additions. When the child has finished, whether or not the questions have been answered correctly, the child has 'done' the exercise. The teacher cannot easily give the pupil further practice at the same level. However, a computer can generate numbers at random and provide the child with as many 'new' sums as are needed.

● *Computers can indicate incorrect answers immediately*: Most people have been in the situation where they thought they understood something only to discover later that a whole piece of work was wrong and needed to be redone. A computer can check an answer immediately it is input, so preventing a student wasting a lot of time in this way.

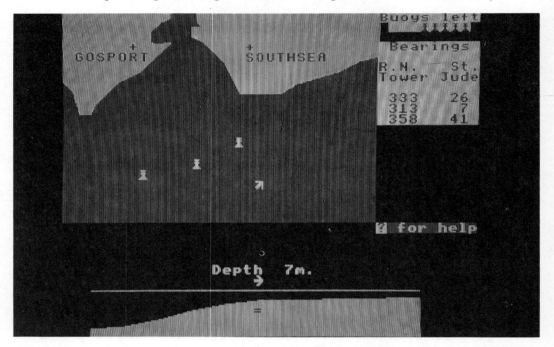

Fig. 18.5 *Mary Rose* is a program intended for primary schools and based on the rediscovery and excavation of King Henry VIII's flagship. The first part simulates the search for the wreck: children navigate a boat around the Solent, looking for anomalies in the seabed using a sonar scan. The second part simulates the underwater excavation of the hull

● *A computer's responses can be tailored to a particular child*: Not only can encouraging messages like 'Well done, Susan' be built into an educational program, but so can different levels of problem difficulty. The computer selects easier or harder questions according to the pupil's skill in answering the opening questions.

Notice that all nine of these reasons apply to any subject and assume nothing about the user's ability to program the computer or his or her background study of computers.

There is also a tenth reason for using computers in schools.

● *Programming a computer is a demanding intellectual problem in itself*: A person's problem-solving skills are likely to be strengthened by solving the problems that arise in trying to make a computer do something.

Fig. 18.6 Computers have begun to make an important impact in primary schools. The program LOGO can be used to control the movement of the Turtle so that it will draw a mathematical shape on a piece of paper. The pupil learns about geometry and maths as well as about computers!

This is true of anyone, whatever their age and whatever computer language they use. But it is especially the case for the very young using an educational language such as LOGO (see Chapter 3) which was devised with this in mind.

The Jargon

The many (and considerable) potential strengths for the computer used as a teaching tool have excited a lot of comment and interest from the theory makers. Inevitably, they have concocted a lot of new phrases.

Teachers talk about *computer assisted learning* (CAL) when the computer is used only to illustrate chosen parts of a course that is taught in the traditional way.

If the computer is used for simple drill and practice (e.g. to teach spelling or 'tables' by a series of simple questions and answers) they talk of *computer assisted instruction* (CAI).

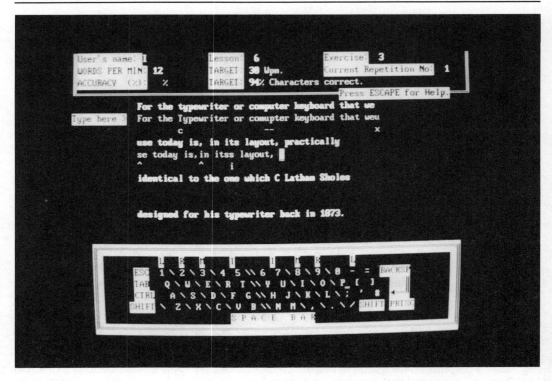

Fig. 18.7 In Iankey, shown here, the user is helped to touch-type by following the directions and exercises indicated by the computer. This is an example of CAI—Computer Aided Instruction

Computer based training (CBT) is used to help people aquire specific practical skills. For example, computer simulation is used to train touch-typists and airline pilots.

As computers play an ever more important and, in the long run, a central role in all aspects of children's schooling, so we shall have *computer based education* (CBE).

Q 18.4 *Touch-sensitive screens, touch tablets and graph pads are likely to be important in educational computing. Explain what they are and why they will be important.*

Q 18.5 *Explain why it may be preferable to train someone by using computer simulations rather than letting them learn the job from real situations.*

Why might a school teacher wish to simulate an experiment?

Q 18.6 *The terms* computer based training *and* computer based education *are not interchangeable. What do you understand to be the difference between 'training' and 'education'?*

Fig. 18.8 (a)   The training of airline pilots is now entirely computer-based. The occupants of the flight simulator appear to be in control of a real aircraft. They see through the cockpit windows exactly what they would see if they were really flying: all the instruments appear to give real readings. Furthermore the aircraft tilts and tips and the jet engines scream just as if they were really flying

Fig. 18.8 (b)   From the outside the simulator is seen for what it is, i.e. a cockpit mounted, on hydraulic pistons that twist and shake the aircraft as if the trainee was actually piloting the real thing. Only a computer could control the sound, visual and movement effects and at the same time co-ordinate the instruments to make the trainee pilot feel as if he was really flying

The Limitations

Although computers are undoubtedly beginning to play an increasingly visible role in schools, there are important limitations on what even the most optimistic of computer-enthusiastic teachers can expect them to do.

For example, young children learn a great deal from each other, not least the vital social skills that enable them to interact successfully with other people. No computer can provide those.

Playing computer games is no substitute for sport and simulated scientific experiments are no substitute for the real thing. Children will still need to learn how to write with their own hands, how to read a book quietly on their own and how to judge what they have read. They will still need to learn how to pull things apart (and how to put them together again), how to debate and act in public, how to play music and how to draw and paint for themselves.

Pre-programmed Responses

Even in those areas where the computer has an obvious role to play there are still very serious objections to the way a computer responds to a pupil's answers.

For the computer can only compare the pupil's answer with a list of possibilities programmed into it. Should the pupil come up with an original, unexpected thought (which happens frequently with any class—whether a group of primary school children or a group of A-level students) the computer will reject it.

However, a good human teacher faced with the same situation would pursue the unexpected idea and extract as much as possible from it.

It may well be that the next generation of computers will be of such increased 'intelligence' that they can be as flexible as a good human teacher (see Chapter 25). But for the moment the problem is a very serious one that cannot be readily overcome.

Practical Problems

There are also serious practical problems obstructing the introduction of computer based learning. For at the moment, and for the foreseeable future, there are simply not enough computer-trained teachers to go round. Of those that there are, almost all are busy teaching computer studies and are not in a position to pioneer new teaching and learning methods in other subjects.

In much the same way there are simply far too few computers.

Fig. 18.9 Computers are a complete mystery to many teachers who have had no training in how to use them. But pupils are only too eager

Using the school's computer is a weekly treat for most primary school children, although ironically it is probably *they* who could gain most from the educational programs that are available at the moment.

But then, of course, the availability of good software is a further problem. There are some good programs for schools but there are rather more very poor ones that fail to offer anything beyond simple drill and practice. There is certainly not a bank of tried and tested programs around which a coherent course could be built.

Even the best software is seriously limited by the processing power of the computers that schools can afford.

Q 18.7 *Do you have a younger brother or sister? If so what are they learning about computers at school? How much 'hands-on' experience are they getting and what sort of programs are they being allowed to run?*

Q 18.8 *When you are next in the computer room have a look at some educational software intended for junior school children. (Your teacher will show you some.) Try to put yourself in the position of a primary school teacher, and comment on the likely success of that program with an eye to*

(a) its likely popularity with the class

(b) what a child might learn from it.

COMPUTER MANAGED LEARNING (CML)

Although computers may not yet be expected to teach a subject, they could well be used to test pupils, monitor the progress they have made, steer them to new areas of appropriate work and, finally, report back, with test scores and recommendations, to the teacher.

The Hertfordshire Computer Managed Mathematics Project

One of the more successful *computer managed learning* (CML) schemes is run in a number of schools in Hertfordshire for mathematics classes for 11 to 13 year olds. There is a series of *modules* each covering a part of the syllabus for that age group. Each module consists of a video tape and other study material, and a series of graded worksheets that the pupils work at individually while the teacher circulates around the class teaching pupils individually.

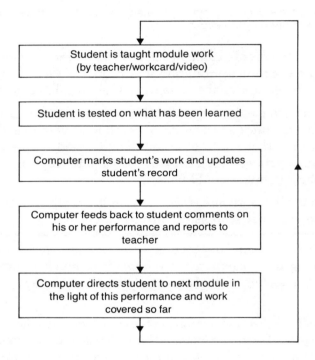

Fig. 18.10 The computer managed learning (CML) cycle

The pupil enters answers on a mark sense card and presents the card to an optical mark reader for input to the computer.

The computer marks the worksheet (by checking the pupil's answers against those held on file), prints out answers and comments (including instructions on which worksheet to do next) and updates the pupil's record. The teacher can obtain a report summarising all the pupil's recent work whenever it is needed.

Q 18.9 *Explain the terms mark sense card and optical mark reader. Why is it sensible for the Hertfordshire Project to use this input method?*

Q 18.10 *Some work in the Hertfordshire scheme is marked by the teacher. Why?*

Q 18.11 *What do you think are the advantages and disadvantages of this scheme (i) to the pupils, and (ii) to the teacher?*

THE TIMES NETWORK SYSTEMS (TTNS)

Sponsored by The Times Newspaper in London, The Times Network Systems or TTNS is a school-oriented database and electronic mailing service, initially based in the United Kingdom but expected to expand worldwide.

Schools can link into the service using a BBC, Research Machines or other microcomputer that will run the appropriate software and a *modem* to convert the computer signals into a form suitable for transmission across the telephone system.

They can then send messages to some or all of the other schools in the network and to County Education offices for the price of one local telephone call. Equally, they can receive messages in their own *mailboxes* and access a wealth of educational information and software help on the mainframe computer in London.

Naturally, access to the system requires knowledge of the school's identity code and access to the school's mailbox is further protected by a password that the teacher responsible for the link can alter if necessary.

Q 18.12 *Re-read the section on electronic mail in Chapter 14. What are the main advantages and disadvantages of electronic mail systems such as TTNS?*

Q 18.13 *Does your school have a TTNS link? If so find out what you can about it. Who uses it? What do they use it for? Why does the ordinary post not suffice?*

COMPUTERS IN SCHOOL ADMINISTRATION

Word Processing

A good deal of school correspondence is routine; for example each year a number of similar circulars are issued to parents and pupils—perhaps the joining instructions for newcomers, perhaps an invitation to a parents' meeting. Only a few details need changing from last year's issue, most obviously the day and the date.

The headteacher may need to write much the same letter to several parents. Or perhaps a reference on a sixth former has to be typed out twice: once for a university application and then again, word for word, for a polytechnic application.

Then there are innumerable lists of pupils and staff that the secretary must periodically retype to keep them up-to-date.

So it goes on. Much of the typing that headteachers' secretaries undertake is repetitive and routine and therefore ideal for word processing. In this, a school secretary is little different from any other secretary in any other office. (In fact, word processing was discussed at some length in Chapter 13, when we saw how a commercial company, Eurotraining Limited, used its office computers.)

?

Q 18.14 *Re-read the section on word processing in Chapter 13. What hardware, other than the word processor itself, would the head-teacher's secretary need?*

Q 18.15 *A letter is sent home to the parents of the fourth form inviting them to a parents' meeting at a given date and time; a list of teachers who teach the fourth year is included.*

(a) *What changes would be necessary before the same letter could be sent to the parents of the fifth form?*

(b) *Explain how the word processor could be used to produce*
  (i) *the fifth year's letter*
  (ii) *the list of fifth year teachers.*

(c) *What benefits would the headteacher expect to gain from having a word processor in the administrative office?*

(d) *What benefits would there be to the secretaries?*

Q 18.16 *Although most schools now own more than one computer many schools have yet to provide word processing facilities to the administrative secretaries. Why?*

Q 18.17 *What use would the teaching staff have for a word processor? What other benefits might there be if a computer were permanently based in the school staff room?*

Q 18.18 *How might a simple and easy-to-use word processor be of help to school students?*

Subject Options

Organising students' choices of optional subjects is not as simple a task as you may think.

Fig. 18.11 In most schools today pupils are offered a very wide range of subjects to choose from

There are a surprisingly large number of possible combinations of subjects. The school must ensure not only that each pupil is choosing the correct number of subjects but also that the choices are sensible. Subsequently the school must ensure that each class will be of reasonable size and will have appropriate teaching staff.

Schools can buy a number of software packages to help them. The teachers responsible will input available subject choices and the number of subjects each pupil must choose. There may also be other special requirements (e.g. Spanish may not be chosen without French) to input.

Once students' details (their names, forms, subject choices etc.) have been input and verified, the computer can produce various lists of pupils by form (showing the choices made), by subject and by teaching group. It would also produce a 'rethink' list of those pupils whose choices could not be met.

SUBJECT CODE (3)	SUBJECT NAME (20)	TEACHERS (24)		NUMBER OF PUPILS (3)	NUMBER OF LESSONS PER WEEK (1)	NUMBER OF DOUBLES (2)	TIMETABLE BLOCKS AVAILABLE (6)
MAT	MATHEMATICS	JCB DEC JSF BMH	SEH SAL SAZ	234	5	0	C

Fig. 18.12   An extract from school's fourth form subjects file

The computer will also ease the problem of planning classes for the coming year, for it will show how many pupils have chosen each subject and where classes are likely to be too small or too large.

It is likely that there will need to be some changes in the light of these figures. The computer can help by indicating how many students have opted for various combinations, so that the headteacher can see how many might be affected by any changes proposed and list the names of the pupils who need to be told of the decision once it is made.

?

Q 18.19   *What files would be necessary for this computing application? Draw a suitable record format for each and estimate its likely size. (An extract from the subjects file is shown in Figure 18.12.)*

How would the information stored in these files be input to the computer?

Q 18.20   *Design a form suitable for a pupil to complete indicating his or her option choices.*

Bear in mind how this information might be input to the computer.

What validation checks would be necessary as soon as the pupil's options choice form is input to the computer?

Timetabling

The school's planning problems do not end there. Timetabling classes (once the available combination of options is agreed and teachers are allocated) is probably the most difficult annual administrative task that faces any school or college.

Every class must be given the right number of lessons for each subject at a time that the appropriate subject teacher is available. There must never be more classes than there are rooms in the school buildings, and some subjects (such as computing) have to be taught in specialist rooms.

Each teacher must be given the agreed share of classes of the right age group and ability and the right number of lessons to teach per week.

Each student must have the right number of subjects to take, the right number of lessons in each and be able to take the options that he or she has previously chosen.

Clearly this is a complex business. Most schools in most years find that it is simply not possible to solve all the problems and compromises have to be made. Some teachers or students then find themselves having to take subjects that were not their first choice.

Fig. 18.13 Most schools in most years find they have to make compromises. Some teachers and students find themselves taking subjects that were not their first choice

A computer could explore the many thousands of possible combinations very much faster than a human timetabler and possibly find solutions to the various timetabling problems that would otherwise have been missed.

However, the software required to make an efficient timetabling program is itself hugely complex. Schools have no option but to buy such programs 'off the peg'. Many have then found that their problems are peculiar to their individual schools and are not catered for by the general purpose program.

Nevertheless, as computers continue to increase in power and school administrators become more adept at using them, this important aspect of a school's organisation will inevitably be given over to them.

?

Q 18.21 *Itemise the data that would need to be input to a computer for it to complete a school timetable successfully.*

What sort of data might be peculiar to one particular school?

Q 18.22 *What must happen if the computer indicates that it cannot find a solution to the special requirements of the timetable as input?*

Students' Records

A computer's capacity for rapid sorting and updating of large files makes it ideally suited to managing students' records.

Some of the records will be purely administrative, containing each student's name and address, subjects studied and previous qualifications gained. Some will be more obviously educational, e.g. showing marks gained in a recent set of examinations.

It is sensible to keep these records on a computer, for schools are continually having to produce sorted lists of various kinds. When the school year begins the teachers need a list of students expected to join each new class. During the year the progress of each pupil will be monitored and the students in the class will often be ranked from top to bottom (usually according to some recent examination mark) so that they and their parents, as well as the teacher, can see how well they are doing. The students from a whole year group will have to be listed alphabetically when the school sends candidate lists to the examination boards (such as the one that runs your GCSEs).

Schools also have to keep a careful check of their numbers and regularly inform the county education authorities of the numbers of students they have: how many boys, how many girls, their exact ages, class sizes etc.

All this routine record keeping can be managed a lot more quickly and accurately on the computer; alphabetically sorted lists of students can be produced in little more than the time it takes to print them out.

Computerised record keeping can also make possible more sophisticated analysis of students' achievements (by teacher, by age, by previous school etc.) and of the trends that might affect the school (e.g. the changes in the popularity of different subjects or in examination results).

?

Q 18.23 *Itemise the data that it would be appropriate to keep on a computerised students' record file.*

Q 18.24 *Design an appropriate record format. Estimate the size of the record and hence the size of a file on 1000 students.*

Q 18.25 *Would you object to any of this data being held on you in your school? What data items might a headteacher want to keep on file that would be of a sensitive kind? Who should have access to the school files and how could access be restricted?*

Q 18.26 *Imagine your headteacher comes to you for advice on how to handle a computerised file. Write a short report outlining good file handling procedures; your report should include explanations of the following terms:*

(a) back-up   *(c) transactions file*

(b) master file   *(d) grandfather, father, son files*

Q 18.27 *Should a school or college's administrative computers be the same make and model as those used in the classroom?*

Should they at least be compatible with the classroom computers?

CAREERS GUIDANCE

There are several successful computer-assisted careers guidance programs at work in careers offices and schools. Essentially they match students' interests and abilities with a large data bank in which is stored all the qualifications and aptitudes necessary for different jobs.

Having helped the student to select possible appropriate careers, the computer can also inform him or her of possible routes to them, examination requirements, working conditions, pay, prospects etc.

Of course such programs are only as good as the data bank they access. The information stored is not necessarily wider or more up to date just for having been input to a computer!

Storing so much information is also a problem. However, there are already careers information services available on Prestel and on TTNS,

JIIG-CAL Answer Sheet
Job Ideas & Information

Form P2

Use an HB PENCIL
Mark like this
NOT this
Rub out mistakes thoroughly

Centre Group Student

0 0 0 0 0 0 0 0
1 1 1 1 1 1 1 1
2 2 2 2 2 2 2 2
3 3 3 3 3 3
4 4 4 4 4 4
5 5 5 5 5 5
6 6 6 6 6
7 7 7 7 7
8 8 8 8 8 8
9 9 9 9 9

Name_____ Date_____

Address

DO NOT MARK this section unless asked to do so

Mini-print

MODE 0 1 2 3 4 5 6 7 8 9

Interest Profile

Type 1 / Type 2 / Type 3 / Type 4 / Type 5 / Type 6

Sections A / B / C / D / E / F

Would you like or dislike a job where you?

CONDITIONS — had to put up with
Heat
Cold
Damp
Dust
Dirt

PANT PANT

PLACE — worked mainly
in the Same place
Different places
Travelling
on a Boat/Ship
Driving about

OBSTACLES — had to cope with
Rough ground
Ladders
Heights

EXERTION — worked mainly
Being active
Lifting weights

CONDITIONS — had to put up with
Oil & Grease
Blood
Noise
Smells
Fumes

CLOTHES — had to wear
Protective clothes

CLOTHES — had to wear
Uniform

EXERTION — worked mainly
Sitting
Standing

PRIORITIES — Low Med High
Place
Conditions
Exertion
People
Live
Study

Would you like a job which used these

MAIN SUBJECTS
Arithmetic
Maths
Computing
Engineering Science
Physics
Chemistry
Biology
Physiology
Agric. or Hortic. Science
Geography
History
Modern Studies
English
Greek
Latin
French
German
Spanish
Woodwork
Metalwork
Tech Drawing
Art
Cookery
Dress & Design
Economics
Accounting/Bookkeeping
Secretarial Studies
Physical Educ.
Music
Drama

Do you have any Serious/Slight Disability affecting your?
Ser Slt None
Fingers
Arms
Legs
Feet
Chest
Back

Ser Slt None
Heart
Head
Eyesight
Colour Vision
Hearing
Smell/Taste

Fig. 18.14 JIIG-CAL

and as more and more schools link into these services it is likely that, in the not too distant future, extensive and interactive computerised careers services will become available to every school.

JARGON 18

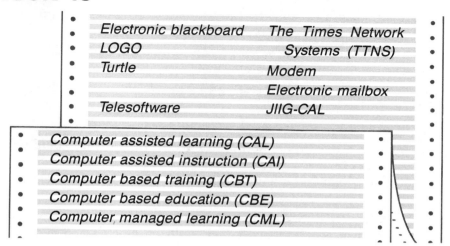

Electronic blackboard   The Times Network
LOGO   Systems (TTNS)
Turtle   Modem
                         Electronic mailbox
Telesoftware   JIIG-CAL

Computer assisted learning (CAL)
Computer assisted instruction (CAI)
Computer based training (CBT)
Computer based education (CBE)
Computer managed learning (CML)

EXERCISES 18

1. The majority of secondary schools have a microcomputer system. The backing storage used may be either cassette tapes or floppy disks. Most microcomputers can be programmed in BASIC. Many of them can be programmed to display pictures and diagrams; this feature is known as *graphics*.

   (*a*) Describe a floppy disk and give one advantage of using a floppy disk rather than a cassette tape to store programs.

   (*b*) Explain two features of BASIC that, in your opinion, have made it the most popular programming language for microcomputers.
   Give an example of each feature to support your explanation.

   (*c*) Write a paragraph describing an application where pupils could use the microcomputer and at least part of the output would be in the form of a graphic display. You should:
   - (i)   state two or three data items that are input,
   - (ii) write three or four sentences describing the use of the input data and processing involved,
   - (iii) sketch, and explain, the graphic display.

   (*d*) Suggest a difficulty that pupils might have when first using the microcomputer.

   (SEREB)

2. A school microcomputer has a number of useful applications packages. It is mostly used by the maths and science departments, but the games and PE staff use it as well.

(a) What is a microcomputer?

(b) Suggest a reason why the school microcomputer is mostly used by the maths and science departments.

The PE staff use the word processing and database enquiry packages. They write some software of their own.

(c) What is a word processing package? What could a PE teacher use it for?

(d) What is a database? How could it help a PE teacher?

(e) (i) Give an application for which the PE staff could write their own software.

  (ii) Name a suitable programming language for them to use and give a reason for your choice.

(f) Describe how a computer, linked to a video system, could be used to help people improve their skills in athletics and gymnastics.

(SEREB)

3. How might a computer be used in the classroom by

(a) a primary school teacher

(b) a secondary school teacher of science

(c) a secondary school remedial english teacher

(d) a teacher of sixth form advanced mathematics?

4. A school has a microcomputer which is used:
 (i) in the teaching of computing studies;
 (ii) in the teaching of other subjects, e.g. simulating and displaying events in science or geography, or information retrieval in history;
 (iii) for school administration by the school secretary, e.g. keeping a record of all the pupils in the school.

Below is a list of features of the computer system. For each one, explain which of the three uses above will be affected favourably or adversely by the feature.

(a) The system has a maximum of 32K 8 bit byte of usable RAM.

(b) The system uses cassette storage and has no disks.

(c) The system has an assembler.

(d) The high level language interpreter produces poor error messages.

(e) The visual display unit is a 12 inch black and white television.

(f) The printer produces a poor quality dot matrix output rather than typewriter quality printing.

(LU)

5. Glendale School has its own microcomputer consisting of a 32K processor, keyboard, television set and twin mini-floppy disk drives. Recently a teacher has written some programs, in BASIC, to allow a file of pupil records to be set up and processed. The record for each pupil contains data that includes date of birth and home address.

   (a) List two advantages of writing the programs in a high level language rather than a low level language.

   (b) The date of birth is held in the form: day/month/year e.g. 11th March, 1977 is held as: 11/03/77

      (i) List four checks that a program could make, to detect errors on the date of birth of any pupil.

      (ii) Give an example of an error in the date of birth which could not have been found by checks built into a program.

   (c) The school wishes to use its microcomputer to produce address labels for sending letters to parents.

      (i) What extra piece of equipment is needed?

      (ii) Suggest one advantage for the school of using a computer to produce address labels.

   (d) Suggest one reason why some parents were worried when the school decided to computerise pupil records.
   Give one advantage of using a microcomputer at the school rather than a large computer at a local college.

   (SEREB)

6. The headteacher of a school wishes to use the school's own microcomputer to help in the running of the school. In particular, the headteacher is considering storing some current information about pupils on the computer.

   (a) What details about each pupil would probably be held on the computer?

   (b) What benefits would the headteacher expect to gain from this use of the computer?

   (c) What possible dangers could there be in storing pupil records on a computer, rather than keeping them in a filing cabinet?

   (d) What precautions and rules would be needed to reduce these dangers?

   (JMB)

7. A school has a computer file of pupils' names and addresses. Explain why each of the following can be used to process the file:

    (*a*) sorting   (*b*) searching   (*c*) amending   (*d*) deleting
    (*e*) inserting.

    (NWREB)

8. The head teacher of a secondary school wishes to create a data file relating to all the pupils in the school, by collecting the following items of data for each pupil:

    —name;
    —date of birth;
    —sex of pupil;
    —class (each class is given a number between 1 and 5, followed by the initials of the class teacher, e.g. 3JLH);
    —address;
    —telephone number;
    —name of parent or guardian.

    (*a*) Design a form which, without further explanation or assistance, could be completed by a pupil to provide the required data.

    (*b*) If the data were input to a computer, describe tests which the computer could perform to check the accuracy of the data.

    (*c*) For any data item which is found to be in error, it will be necessary to produce an appropriate error report. Design a suitable format for error reports, giving examples of three types of error which might be detected.

    (CU)

19 What If . . .?

BUILDING MODELS

We build models for many reasons. Human dummies undergo head-on car crashes (to test the strength of a passenger compartment) or artificial respiration (to teach life-saving skills). Models of aeroplanes and cars are tested in wind tunnels (to determine lift, drag etc.).

Models come in all shapes and sizes; architects proudly display scaled-*down* buildings (to give a 3-dimensional impression unobtainable from drawings alone), science teachers show students vastly scaled-*up* representations of molecules, and Jumbo Jet pilots train in a *life-sized* model of a cockpit.

All the above examples of models are used because *using the real thing would be impractical*. It would be too dangerous, too expensive or simply impossible.

Many models are built in an attempt to predict how something might behave *in the future*. Would an aeroplane shaped like *this* take off? Would all the rooms in *this* planned hotel enjoy a sea view? Would a driver of *this* car be likely to survive a 30 mph crash into a brick wall?

Q 19.1 *Think of more examples of models. What is the purpose of each one?*

Q 19.2 *Why might predictions made with models go completely wrong?*

Computer Models

Frequently models must be tested under a *range* of conditions: answers are needed to a number of different *'what if . . .?'* questions. What if the wings pointed further forward? What if two more storeys were built on the hotel? What if the head-on crash took place at 40 mph? . . . and so on.

Although it may sometimes be the only choice, it is obviously expensive and time-consuming to build a new (physical) model for every possible case. Computer models can often provide information in minutes which could take days or weeks to obtain by other methods. They are not merely graphical representations of the real world, but can incorporate many characteristics: strength, stress, chemical or physical composition, density, elasticity, resistance (to wind, electricity, corrosion, deformation and disease), growth, movement, decay, or any other properties the model-builder wants to examine. Complex calculations are carried out on the model in the computer in order to predict the behaviour of its real-world equivalent.

Sometimes a computer model is the *only* type possible; it is impossible to build a *physical* model of, say, a nuclear reaction or next week's weather.

COMPUTER-AIDED DESIGN (CAD)

Computer *drafting* software, one type of *computer-aided design* (CAD), is helping many organisations to speed up the laborious process of producing plans, scale drawings, maps and designs.

These can all be thought of as 2-dimensional models of the real world. But even 3-dimensional modelling by computer is becoming widespread, providing perspective line drawings (Figure 19.1), or full-colour, realistically shaded 'solid models' (Figure 19.2).

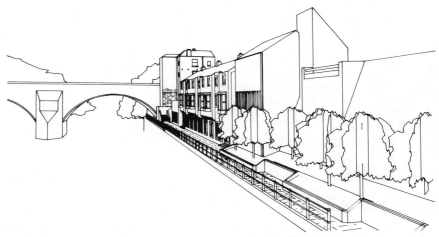

Fig. 19.1 A realistic impression of a planned riverside development is given by this computer-modelled perspective view

?   **Q 19.3**   *Are the above examples truly 3-dimensional models?*

Fig. 19.2 Computer-generated 'solid models'

Designing Drugs

Drug manufacturers have gained enormously from CAD. Researchers can now 'synthesise' compounds on their computer screens and investigate many of their properties before attempting to make the real stuff in their laboratories. The *shape* of a molecule is a major factor determining its other properties and so 3-dimensional modelling (Figure 19.3) can provide real insights into the behaviour of molecules involved in diseases, and guide scientists as to the shape and nature of drugs that might be of value. Much time and expense is saved, since only the most promising substances are actually made for 'real' testing.

Fig. 19.3 Modelling molecules on screen saves drug companies years of research effort

Designing Cars

Car makers use CAD in many ways, not only to evaluate the visual appeal of alternative designs. For example, before a car design is finalised it is vital to ensure that such a car would be safe and comfortable to drive with sensible positioning of instruments, controls, mirrors etc. A special CAD system enables the designer to 'build' a 3-dimensional computer model of the vehicle complete with a model driver (Figure 19.4). By moving the human model to reach all the controls, any layout can be tested rapidly. Changes can be made and evaluated in minutes, and designs can be viewed from any angle: a job which previously involved as much as two days' work redrawing the design by hand.

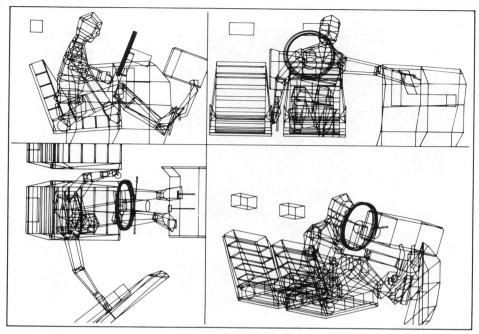

Fig. 19.4 SAMMIE (System for Aiding Man-Machine Interaction Evaluation) making sure that 'he' could comfortably reach the door handle on this car design

 Q 19.4 *Could such a model as SAMMIE cater for all sizes of male and female drivers?*

From Design to Manufacture

Computer assistance often goes beyond design to the manufacturing stage. *Computer-aided manufacturing* (CAM) and CAD are often combined to form an integrated CAD/CAM system. The system that helped to design the Ford Sierra, for example (Figure 19.5), provides:

- 3-dimensional design
- ability to view models or components from any angle
- calculation of weight and other properties
- detailed analysis of structure (hence of strength)
- output of numerical data for control of machine tools that will actually produce the component.

The input/output and processing requirements of CAD/CAM systems are huge. Specialised terminals connected to minicomputers or mainframes are usually needed (Figure 19.6). As microcomputers have increased in power, some micro-based CAD/CAM systems have been developed, but they cannot provide all the features described above.

Fig. 19.5   Using a light pen to modify a car body design

Equally, CAD/CAM *software* is so complex that only specialist companies (or giant manufacturers like Ford) can afford to develop their own; most companies buy 'off-the-shelf' packages.

Fig. 19.6   These specialised CAD/CAM terminals are being used to plot a life-sized drawing of passengers in a car

FINANCIAL MODELLING

Although CAD/CAM is only of use to manufacturing companies, *financial modelling* is used by nearly *all* organisations. Business managers, civil servants, head teachers . . . in fact *anyone* managing resources (people, materials, money and time) needs to make plans and to ask *'what if . . . ?'* questions.

Budgets

Those plans and questions always have financial implications. A financial plan (whether it is one family's plan for household spending or a national plan for the whole country) is called a *budget*. The simplest financial modelling involves creating a budget for say, the next year, and then seeing how different assumptions might affect the outcome.

Imagine *you* are the manager of Barchester United, a second division football club. Your job is not only to win games but also to manage the business side, making sure that the club does not run out of money. How could a financial model help you to plan your next season?

```
BARCHESTER UNITED — ANNUAL BUDGET
                                          £
Ticket Sales (mostly home games)      450,000
Supporters' Club   Fundraising         58,000
Sponsorships and Advertising           65,000
     TOTAL  INCOME  estimated —       573,000

Wages/Salaries (including players)    324,000
Office costs                           30,000
Electricity                             9,850
Repairs and maintenance                72,000
Rent and Rates                         86,400
Printing and Publicity                 24,900
Security and Police                    70,500
Interest on Bank Loans                 13,200
   TOTAL EXPENDITURE estimated        625,850

Estimated Loss for next year
    = 625,850 − 573,000 = £52,850!!
```

Fig. 19.7 As a football club manager planning your next season, you might begin with a simple budget like this. It looks as though your club is heading for financial trouble next year!

You might start with a simple budget (Figure 19.7), showing your estimates of where all the money should come from next year (income), and how you intend to spend it (expenditure). The budget is more useful broken down into months and so you expand it on a sheet of paper ruled with rows and columns (Figure 19.8). You add up all the rows and columns as shown and the total of all the columns (months) should equal the total of all the rows (this is a useful check for accuracy). Total income minus total expenditure gives your profit (or loss).

BARCHESTER UNITED FOOTBALL CLUB — ANNUAL BUDGET

INCOME £	JULY	AUG	SEP	OCT	NOV	DEC	JAN	FEB	MAR	APR	MAY	JUNE	TOTALS
TICKET SALES	0	36000	36000	54000	54000	54000	54000	36000	54000	36000	36000	0	450 000
SUPP'T'RS CLUB FUNDR'G	2000	2000	3000	4000	4000	22000	4000	4000	4000	4000	3000	2000	58 000
SPONSORS/ADVERTISING	0	0	15000	0	0	15000	5000	0	15000	0	0	15000	65 000
TOTAL INCOME	2000	38000	54000	58000	58000	91000	63000	40000	73000	40000	39000	17000	573 000

EXPENSES £													
WAGES / SALARIES	27000	27000	27000	27000	27000	27000	27000	27000	27000	27000	27000	27000	324 000
OFFICE COSTS	2500	2500	2500	2500	2500	2500	2500	2500	2500	2500	2500	2500	30 000
ELECTRICITY	0	900	0	0	1250	0	0	1650	0	0	1050	0	4 850
REPAIRS / MAINT'CE	6000	6000	6000	6000	6000	6000	6000	6000	6000	6000	6000	6000	72 000
RENT & RATES	7200	7200	7200	7200	7200	7200	7200	7200	7200	7200	7200	7200	86 400
PRINTING / PUBLICITY	200	2000	2000	2900	2900	2900	2900	2000	2900	2000	2000	200	24 900
SECURITY / POLICE	250	5650	5650	8350	8350	8350	8350	5650	8350	5650	5650	250	70 500
INTEREST ON LOANS	1100	1100	1100	1100	1100	1100	1100	1100	1100	1100	1100	1100	13 200
TOTAL EXPENSES	44250	52350	51450	55050	56300	55050	55050	53100	55050	51450	52400	44250	625 850
PROFIT (loss if minus)	-42250	-14350	2550	2950	1700	35950	7950	-13100	17950	-11450	-13400	-27250	−52 850

Fig. 19.8 Breaking the budget down by month takes some time, but now you can see the month-to-month fluctuations in your profit (or loss). The totals column is the same as Figure 19.7

? Q 19.5 *(a) Why is it more useful to split the budget into 12 months?*
(b) Why not break it into 52 weeks?
(c) Why does there seem to be no electricity expenditure in July?

As you can see from Figure 19.8, your club is likely to make a small loss next season unless you can work out how to improve the prospects. But what if ticket sales are, say, 10 per cent down on your initial estimate? You recalculate your plan with this more pessimistic assumption (Figure 19.9); despite small savings you would be heading for a loss of £88 850. You (and your bank manager!) would be very worried.

BARCHESTER UNITED FOOTBALL CLUB – ANNUAL BUDGET Assuming 10% lower ticket sales

INCOME £	JULY	AUG	SEP	OCT	NOV	DEC	JAN	FEB	MAR	APR	MAY	JUNE	TOTALS
TICKET SALES	0	~~36000~~	~~36000~~	~~54000~~	~~54000~~	~~54000~~	~~54000~~	~~36000~~	~~54000~~	~~36000~~	~~36000~~	0	~~450 000~~
		32400	32400	48600	48600	48600	48600	32400	48600	32400	32400		405 000 (Down 10%)
SUPR'S CLUB FUNDR'S'G	2000	2000	3000	4000	4000	22400	4000	4000	4000	4000	3000	2000	58000
SPONSORS / ADVT'S'G	0	0	15000	0	0	15000	500	0	15000	0	0	15000	65 000
TOTAL INCOME	2000	~~38000~~	~~54000~~	~~58000~~	~~58000~~	~~91400~~	~~63000~~	~~40000~~	~~73000~~	~~40000~~	~~39000~~	17000	~~573 000~~
		34400	50400	52600	52600	85600	57600	36400	67600	36400	35400		528 000
EXPENSES £													
WAGES / SALARIES	27000	27000	27000	27000	27000	27000	27000	27000	27000	27000	27000	27000	324 000
OFFICE COSTS	2500	2500	2500	2500	2500	2500	2500	2500	2500	2500	2500	2500	30 000
ELECTRICITY	0	900	0	0	1250	0	0	1650	0	0	1050	0	4850
REPAIRS / MAINT'CE	6000	6000	6000	6000	6000	6000	6000	6000	6000	6000	6000	6000	72 000
RENT / RATES	7200	7200	7200	7200	7200	7200	7200	7200	7200	7200	7200	7200	86 400
PRINTING / PUBLICITY	200	~~2000~~	~~2000~~	~~2900~~	~~2900~~	~~2900~~	~~2900~~	~~2000~~	~~2900~~	~~2000~~	~~2000~~	200	~~24 900~~
		1820	1820	2630	2630	2630	2630	1820	2630	1820	1820		22 650
SECURITY / POLICE	250	~~5650~~	~~5650~~	~~8350~~	~~8350~~	~~8350~~	~~8350~~	~~5650~~	~~8350~~	~~5650~~	~~5650~~	250	~~70 500~~
		5110	5110	7540	7540	7540	7540	5110	7540	5110	5110		63 750
INTEREST ON LOANS	1100	1100	1100	1100	1100	1100	1100	1100	1100	1100	1100	1100	13200
TOTAL EXPENSES	44250	~~52350~~	~~51450~~	~~55050~~	~~56300~~	~~55050~~	~~55050~~	~~53100~~	~~55050~~	~~51450~~	~~52400~~	44250	~~625 850~~
		51630	50730	53970	55220	53970	53970	52380	53970	50730	51780		616 850
PROFIT (loss if minus)	-12250	~~-14850~~	~~2550~~	~~2950~~	~~1700~~	~~35950~~	~~7950~~	~~-13100~~	~~17950~~	~~-11450~~	~~-13400~~	-27250	~~-52850~~
		-17230	-330	-1370	-2620	31630	3630	-15980	13630	-14330	-16380		-88850

(margin note: some savings — print fewer programmes & need fewer police)

Fig. 19.9 Changing just one assumption in your plan, (e.g. 'what if' we sold 10% fewer tickets?) involves recalculating dozens of figures before you can see the result—your club's losses would jump to nearly £90,000! Your plan soon looks very untidy!

SPREADSHEET SOFTWARE

You might want to test many other possibilities to see how they might affect the future profit or loss. But each time you change a single assumption in your model, you have to do much tedious re-calculation, and, as you can see from Figure 19.9, your sheet of paper soon becomes illegible. This is where your computer comes to the rescue with a *spreadsheet program*. This enables you to enter your figures on a 'computerised sheet of paper' with rows and columns. The rows are numbered from 1 upwards and the columns lettered from A to Z. So each position (which is called a *cell*) on the spreadsheet can be identified by a grid reference: cell A1 is the top left hand corner and cell L15, for example, contains the figure for May's wages.

The spreadsheet is often too big to fit on a normal computer screen; the cursor (arrow) keys are used to move around the spreadsheet so that the required position is displayed. Figure 19.10 represents the actual screen display, showing part of the Barchester United plan.

```
HELP          F1            Enter Data and Formulae Directly...
COMMANDS      F2            To Enter Text, First Type "...
CANCEL        ESC                      ...Then Press ENTER

    .         K     .     L     .     M     .     N
13.
14.
15.         27000       27000       27000      324000
16.          2500        2500        2500       30000
17.             0        1050           0        4850
18.          6000        6000        6000       72000
19.          7200        7200        7200       86400
20.          2000        2000         200       24900
21.          5650        5650         250       70500
22.          1100        1100        1100       13200
23. ------------------------------------------------------
24.         51450       52500       44250      625950
25. ------------------------------------------------------
26.        -11450      -13500      -27250      -52850
27. ======================================================
?
CELL    L19        CELLS USED   A1:N27        MEMORY    114K
CONTENTS  7200
```

Fig. 19.10 Only a small part of your spreadsheet can be displayed at once on your computer screen. Here the program is waiting for input; your cursor position (cell L19) is highlighted

Q 19.6 *(a) What part of the Barchester United budget is shown on screen in Figure 19.10?*

(b) What does the figure highlighted by the cursor represent?

A single cell can contain two types of data: text (such as the descriptions in column A or the month headings in row 3) or numbers (values such as those in cell C9 or cell M22). A number could be typed into a cell directly but a cell can also store a *formula*, which enables *automatic* calculation and recalculation of values. Figure 19.11 shows the formulae which you might enter into different cells. In cell D24, for example, the formula SUM(D15:D22) means 'add up all the figures in column D from cell D15 to cell D22 and put the total here in cell D24'.

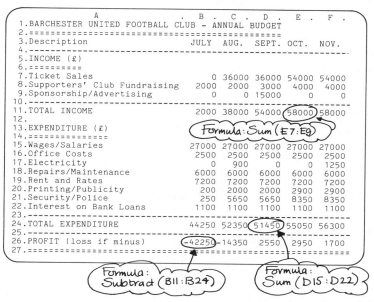

```
        A          .  B  .  C  .  D  .  E  .  F  .
 1.BARCHESTER UNITED FOOTBALL CLUB - ANNUAL BUDGET
 2.================================================
 3.Description                JULY  AUG.  SEPT. OCT.  NOV.
 4.------------------------------------------------
 5.INCOME (£)
 6.==========
 7.Ticket Sales                  0 36000 36000 54000 54000
 8.Supporters' Club Fundraising 2000  2000  3000  4000  4000
 9.Sponsorship/Advertising       0     0 15000     0     0
10.----------------------------------------------
11.TOTAL INCOME               2000 38000 54000 58000 58000
12.
13.EXPENDITURE (£)          Formula: Sum (E7:E9)
14.===============
15.Wages/Salaries            27000 27000 27000 27000 27000
16.Office Costs               2500  2500  2500  2500  2500
17.Electricity                   0   900     0     0  1250
18.Repairs/Maintenance        6000  6000  6000  6000  6000
19.Rent and Rates             7200  7200  7200  7200  7200
20.Printing/Publicity          200  2000  2000  2900  2900
21.Security/Police             250  5650  5650  8350  8350
22.Interest on Bank Loans     1100  1100  1100  1100  1100
23.----------------------------------------------
24.TOTAL EXPENDITURE         44250 52350 51450 55050 56300
25.----------------------------------------------
26.PROFIT (loss if minus)   -42250 -14350 2550 2950 1700
27.================================================
```

Formula: Subtract (B11:B24)

Formula: Sum (D15:D22)

Fig. 19.11 By placing *formulae* in particular cells, you can get your spreadsheet to calculate your totals *automatically*, and now, when you *change* any of your figures, all the totals are automatically (and immediately) adjusted

Cell B26 contains the formula B11-B24, which means 'subtract the figure in cell B24 (total expenditure for July) from the figure in cell B11 (total income for July) and put the answer here in cell B26'. Similar formulae are placed in each cell along row 26 to give, automatically, the profit (or loss) for each month. Other, more complex, calculations are easily achieved with the appropriate formulae.

Using these formulae, the program not only instantly calculates all the results, but, if any of the numbers in the spreadsheet is changed, the results are automatically recalculated throughout. Note that formulae are expressed differently in different spreadsheet packages.

? **Q 19.7** *What formulae would you expect to find in cells B24, B11, D9, E26?*

Now you can quickly check out the probable results of different actions you might take next year as manager. One of the possibilities is shown in Figure 19.12; there are many other options which you might consider as manager *before* you finally decide. It is easy to see how the spreadsheet model could help you to take better-informed decisions. In fact the best-selling software package *ever* is a spreadsheet program. It even outsells the most popular word processing programs.

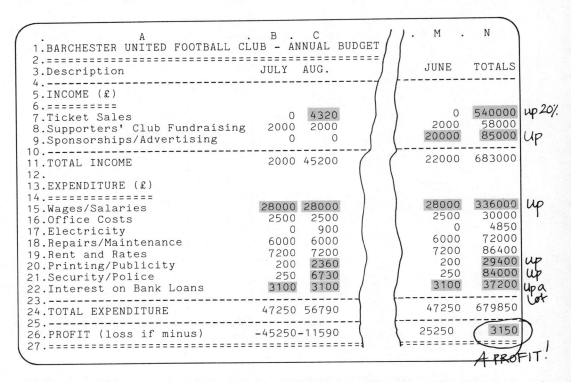

```
       .          A          .   B  .  C            .   M   .  N
 1.BARCHESTER UNITED FOOTBALL CLUB - ANNUAL BUDGET
 2.================================================        ===========
 3.Description                     JULY  AUG.            JUNE   TOTALS
 4.                                ----------            -----------
 5.INCOME (£)
 6.==========
 7.Ticket Sales                       0  4320               0  540000   up 20%
 8.Supporters' Club Fundraising    2000  2000            2000   58000
 9.Sponsorships/Advertising           0     0           20000   85000   up
10.                                ----------            -----------
11.TOTAL INCOME                    2000 45200           22000  683000
12.
13.EXPENDITURE (£)
14.===============
15.Wages/Salaries                 28000 28000           28000  336000   up
16.Office Costs                    2500  2500            2500   30000
17.Electricity                        0   900               0    4850
18.Repairs/Maintenance             6000  6000            6000   72000
19.Rent and Rates                  7200  7200            7200   86400
20.Printing/Publicity               200  2360             200   29400   up
21.Security/Police                  250  6730             250   84000   up
22.Interest on Bank Loans          3100  3100            3100   37200   up a lot
23.                                ----------            -----------
24.TOTAL EXPENDITURE              47250 56790           47250  679850
25.                                ----------            -----------
26.PROFIT (loss if minus)        -45250-11590           25250    3150   A PROFIT!
27.================================================        ===========
```

Fig. 19.12 Try again ... *What if* the bank lent us a quarter of a million to buy that Brazilian player? He would definitely pull the crowds! Let us say ticket sales up 20 per cent ... sponsorship deals up ... cost a fortune in interest, risky but ... we would make a PROFIT!

Q 19.8 *(a) Produce a budget for your own personal finances covering, say, the next six weeks. One student's version is shown in Figure 19.13 as a guide, but you probably receive and spend money quite differently. Work out your headings on paper first and then use any spreadsheet software that may be available. If this is not possible use a calculator.*

(b) Now calculate the impact of (i) a 20 per cent cut in your income, and (ii) general price increases of 8 per cent.

(c) What happens if you make a 'loss' or 'profit' one week?

PERSONAL INCOME AND EXPENDITURE

INCOME £	Week 1	Week 2	Week 3	Week 4	Week 5	Week 6	Total
Pocket money	2.50	2.50	2.50	2.50	2.50	2.50	15.00
Saturday Job	13.80	13.80	13.80	13.80	13.80	13.80	82.80
Car Washing	1.00	1.00	1.00	1.00	1.00	1.00	6.00
Birthday Presents	–	–	–	35.00	–	–	35.00
TOTAL INCOME	17.30	17.30	17.30	52.30	17.30	17.30	138.80
EXPENDITURE £							
Clothes	13.00	–	–	28.99	10.50	–	52.49
Records/tapes	–	4.50	–	8.98	–	–	13.48
Cinema	–	6.00	–	–	6.00	–	12.00
Sweets/Drinks/Snacks	2.30	8.25	1.90	3.30	9.80	2.20	27.75
Magazines	1.20	1.20	1.20	1.20	1.20	1.20	7.20
Fares	.70	1.60	.55	2.90	1.50	.90	7.65
TOTAL EXPENDITURE	17.20	21.55	3.65	44.87	29.00	4.30	120.57
PROFIT/LOSS	.10	– 4.25	13.65	7.43	–11.70	13.00	18.23

Fig. 19.13 Spreadsheet of a student's income and expenditure over six weeks

SIMULATIONS

The manager of Barchester United, when considering the option in Figure 19.12, made specific assumptions about the probable future behaviour of the Club's supporters (e.g. 20 per cent more fans would be likely to come to home games if £250 000 were spent on a star player). More sophisticated models take this process further, attempting to predict the future by actually *simulating* behaviour.

Financial simulations are run with detailed assumptions built into their computer programs about the behaviour of, say, customers and competitors. Various statistical methods are used to analyse trends, forecast events and assess their probabilities. The Government (and some independent forecasters) use simulations to try to predict (with varying success) the behaviour of the whole economy.

Industrial Simulations

We have seen how computer modelling can improve the *design* of a car; simulation can ensure that its *production* will be feasible and cost-effective. Using a package called See-Why, a complete simulation of the

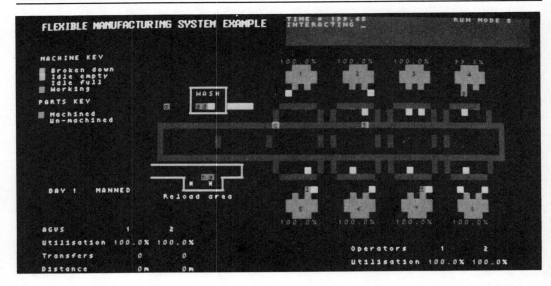

Fig. 19.14 The See-Why package simulating a proposed production line to reveal bottlenecks, underused machinery etc.

production line for the Austin Metro was run *before a single car was built*. The effects of breakdowns of machines, late deliveries, excesses or shortages of parts were all possible mishaps that were tested in the model. Thus many potential problems and bottlenecks were avoided *in advance*, long before production commenced. The package can even be asked: 'What happens if half of this department's staff catch the 'flu?'.

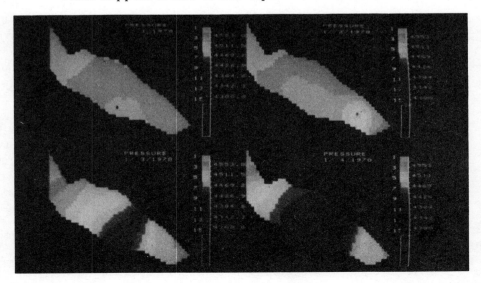

Fig. 19.15 Simulation is invaluable for oil and gas exploration; here a gas reservoir is being modelled to assess its capacity in advance

Simulation for Education and Training

SAMMIE (Figure 19.4) was one example of simulating a human being to improve vehicle design. MacPuff (Figure 19.16) simulates humans in order to save lives. This program models the way we breathe, simulating the role of the lungs and the blood in carrying oxygen around the body. A medical student is given charge of the simulated patient and is supplied with vital information (level of carbon dioxide in the blood, temperature etc.).

The 'patient' may suffer from various ailments, and may stop breathing completely. The student must decide on the appropriate course of action (drugs, artificial ventilation etc.). The situation is not, of course, as realistic as treating a human patient but the need to act quickly and decisively does place the student under very real stress. By giving the wrong drug or inadequate ventilation, or just by taking too long to decide what to do, the student may allow the 'patient' to die.

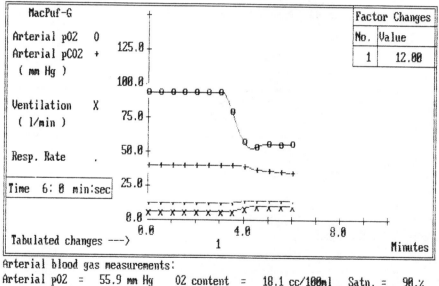

Fig. 19.16 A simulated patient's condition is displayed to a medical student by MacPuff; the 'patient's' life depends on speedy, appropriate treatment

 Q 19.9 *Can you think of any possible dangers of such medical training simulations?*

Full-size flight simulators (as opposed to the ever popular home-computer versions) are also used for instruction in matters of life and death. We saw a passenger aircraft simulator earlier (Figure 18.8). Simulation is an essential part of pilot training. The latest simulators provide all-round vision and accurately model all the known capabilities such as speed and manoeuvrability of the pilot's own aircraft as well as the layout and approach to the world's major airports.

Operators of systems or equipment ranging from North Sea drilling rigs to fire engines to word processors have benefited from lifelike computer simulations in their training courses.

Readers may have seen educational software simulating the operation of a nuclear reactor. Full-size models of reactor control rooms are built to simulate the operators' complex task. By exhaustive simulation of hundreds of events that might occur it is hoped to reduce the likelihood of human error, the major cause of radiation leaks. Simulation *after* the event (e.g. the Chernobyl disaster in 1986) can help to establish the causes of accidents.

?   **Q 19.10**   *Can you think of other training or educational tasks for which a computer simulation could be effective?*

Simulation in Research

Researchers in all fields rely increasingly on computer models to support their work. Physicists model hypothetical particles to predict how they *might* behave if they *did* exist, while historians model population movements in the Middle Ages to examine the effects of past epidemics or famines.

One team of researchers is exploring the evolution of plant life by 'growing' plants which obey various rules and hypotheses (Figure 19.17). By comparing the trends exhibited by these simulated plants with the actual trends found in fossil plants, the accuracy of the evolutionary hypotheses can be tested.

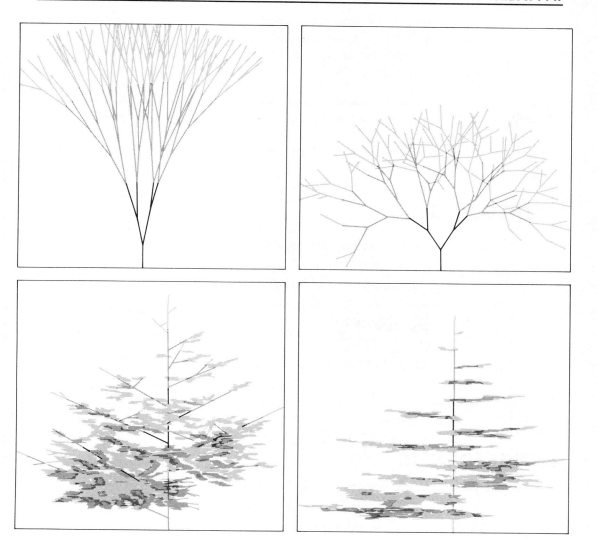

Fig. 19.17 Different 'evolutionary strategies' result in dramatically different growth habits in these simulated plants

Predicting the Unpredictable

The major improvements in weather forecasting (see Chapter 21) are due to simulations that model local or worldwide atmospheric changes. Another global simulation, predicting more sinister results than any weatherman, was conducted by a team of scientists in 1983. Their three-dimensional model of the world's weather system showed how a nuclear war would cause smoke clouds which, rising to the stratosphere, would spread until they covered the entire planet, completely blotting out the sun. The result, according to the model, would be the so-called 'nuclear winter' which could last for several years, threatening all life on the planet.

 Q 19.11 *How far should such a simulation be relied upon?*

JARGON 19

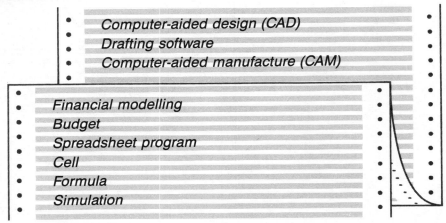

- Computer-aided design (CAD)
- Drafting software
- Computer-aided manufacture (CAM)

- Financial modelling
- Budget
- Spreadsheet program
- Cell
- Formula
- Simulation

EXERCISES 19

1. (a) Explain the term 'spreadsheet package'.
   (b) Describe one such package known to you.
   (c) What use would a businessperson have for it?

2. (a) Simulations are often used in applications where direct experimentation would be expensive, dangerous or impossible. Describe briefly three simulations, one from each of these three categories.
   (b) A bus company uses an applications package to simulate the effects of changes in fares and services.
      (i) Suggest the advantages of using the simulation rather than implementing the changes and observing their effects directly. Are there any disadvantages of using the simulation?
      (ii) What reasons might the company have had for buying an applications package rather than developing their own software?

(CU)

3. Computer simulations are used to help people learn to fly large aircraft. A small room is fitted out like the cockpit of the plane and the view through the windscreen is created by a computer. The aircraft's instruments and controls are connected to the computer which, as the 'pilot' steers the plane, alters the view through the windows. The layout of most of the world's airports is stored in the computer's memory so that a trainee can learn to land and take off without risking lives.

   (a) The simulator uses a real-time computer system.
      (i) What is a real-time system and why is it essential in this application?
      (ii) Suggest a suitable backing store device for the simulator and give a reason for your choice.

   (b) Describe the ways in which the simulator computer outputs information to the trainee pilot.

   (c) What improvements have made it possible to carry computers in the cockpits of real aircraft?

   (d) Describe how computer simulation is used in the training for one other profession and explain why it has been such an important development.

   (e) Describe a simple simulation program which could be run on a school microcomputer, to help in a particular topic in a school subject. You should mention briefly how the simulation could work, how it could be used and why it might be of benefit in the classroom.

   (SEREB)

4. On a certain road there is a bridge which carries the road over a river. The bridge has been found to be in need of repair and, until the repairs can be carried out, it has been decided to allow only one-way traffic on the bridge. Traffic lights are to be placed at each side of the bridge to control the flow of traffic in each direction. The periods of time for which the lights show red and show green (the 'timing' of the lights) can be altered. It is important that the timing is adjusted so that traffic is delayed as little as possible.

   (a) Describe the advantages of modelling this situation before the traffic lights are installed.

   (b) If the situation is to be modelled, describe the data which should be collected to enable the model to be as realistic as possible.

   (c) Describe how a computer-based model of this situation could be implemented.

   (CU)

20 In Control

CONTROL SYSTEMS

An electric fire is a useful but stupid device. When it is working it will deliver heat constantly, day and night, no matter how hot the room becomes and whether or not anyone is there.

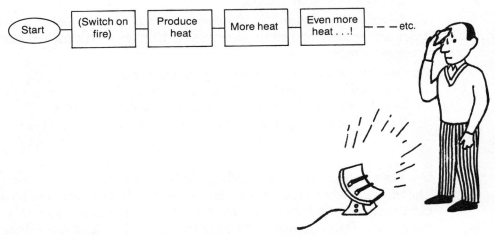

Fig. 20.1 A 'blind' control system carries on the process regardless

 Q 20.1 *Draw a flowchart to show the decisions involved in controlling an ordinary electric fire.*

The Importance of Feedback

This additional ingredient of *feedback* turns a *'blind' control system* (Figure 20.1) into a *closed loop control system* (Figure 20.2). An *activity* or *process* (e.g. passing electricity through a fire) gives a *result* (e.g. heating a room and its occupants). *Information* about the result (e.g. 'It is too hot in here') is *fed back*, resulting in a *change in the process* (e.g. the fire is switched off) and the control loop is thus closed.

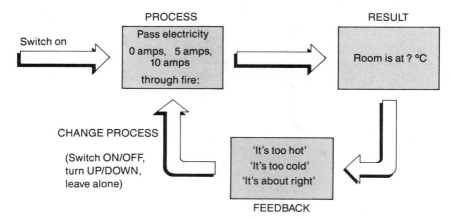

Fig. 20.2 Feeding back information which is used to alter a process creates a 'closed loop' control system. This diagram could be redrawn as a program flowchart

> **?**
>
> **Q 20.2** *Can you think of other simple examples from daily life of:*
>
> *(a) 'blind' processes*
>
> *(b) closed loop control systems using feedback?*

We all use sensory feedback all day long without ever thinking about it; e.g. when walking, picking up a pen, reading or communicating with other people.

> **?**
>
> **Q 20.3** *What type of information is fed back in order to help us control each of the above four processes?*
>
> **Q 20.4** *(a) How easy is it to exercise control over someone by communicating without any feedback? Try getting a friend to draw a geometric pattern from your verbal instructions alone. You must not watch the drawing and your friend must not ask questions.*
>
> *(b) Now repeat the exercise with visual and verbal feedback. Use a different pattern this time.*

AUTOMATIC CONTROL

Manual control systems can be a nuisance because they require more or less constant supervision. A home central heating system, unlike an electric fire, relies on a thermostat for *automatic control.*

The thermostat takes over the job of sensing the temperature from the person, who merely sets the device (once only) to the required temperature. When the temperature falls slightly below the target, the thermostat switches on the heating until the temperature hits the target again.

Q 20.5   *In fact, the thermostat allows the temperature to go as much as two or three degrees below (or above) the target before switching the heating on (or off). Why?*

Q 20.6   *What other advantages, besides convenience, are gained with automatic control systems?*

Computer Control

The features that computers bring to *any* system—programmability, flexibility, reliability, processing speed—are particularly valuable for automatic control.

Computerised control systems (which are necessarily *real-time* systems) usually require *analog-to-digital* (A-to-D) and *digital-to-analog* (D-to-A) *converters* in order to convert continuously varying quantities (e.g. temperature, pressure, speed, voltage, weight or distance) into digital form for processing and vice versa.

Q 20.7   *Most microcomputers provide several input/output connectors (called ports) some of which can be used for control applications. On the BBC (Model B and Master 128), for example, there is the analog port, the user port and the cassette port. Find out, for each port,*

(a) can it be used for input, output or both?

(b) does it transmit or receive digital or analog signals or both?

Q 20.8   *What is meant by real-time? Why must computerised control systems be real-time systems?*

Q 20.9   *Can you think of examples of analog-to-digital or digital-to-analog conversion in the home?*

Q 20.10   *Two examples of computers controlling processes were seen in Figure 8.9 (page 147) and Figure 8.14 (page 154). For each of these:*

(a) What data is gathered to find out how the process is going? Is it analog data?

(b) What data is transmitted to correct or control the process? Would it have to be converted, and which way (D-to-A or A-to-D)?

CONTROLLING ENERGY

Saving Energy

Computer control, widely used in manufacturing, communications and military applications, is also starting to take over in our homes.

A central heating system can be enhanced by a microcomputer controller (Figure 20.3). This can be programmed to vary heating and hot water requirements for each day of the week: you might know that you will be home late on Friday and want a lie-in on Saturday; the microcomputer will save fuel by turning the heat on only when it is required.

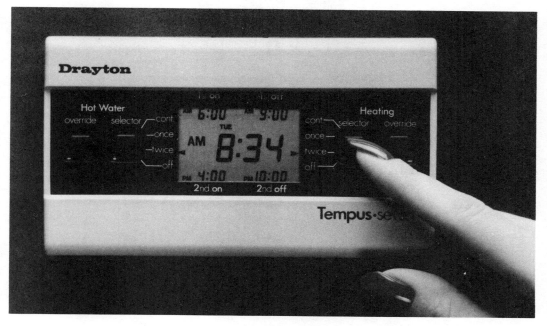

Fig. 20.3   This programmable controller can vary the heating supplied on each day of the week

Even more energy is saved by computer-controlled heat pumps, which can actually deliver more energy than they consume! They do not break the laws of physics, but extract the extra heat from the immediate environment. These devices can cool in summer or heat in winter.

The latest building control systems monitor security and safety as well as temperature and energy use. The building's 'senses' are thermostats, smoke detectors, humidity sensors, telephone systems and access-control card readers. In the event of fire, for example, the control system will activate sprinklers, call the fire brigade, adjust the ventilation, open fire doors and send all the lifts to the ground floor.

Fig. 20.4 The 'intelligent' building monitors energy use while controlling access, telecommunications and the working environment

Another common energy saving device is a computerised ignition system which saves fuel on a modern car.

Fig. 20.5 This electronic ignition system in the Jaguar Sovereign adjusts the fuel mixture hundreds of times per second to ensure optimum performance

Producing Energy

Controlling energy *consumption* is clearly important for ordinary families and organisations of all sizes; controlling energy *production* is vital, even for countries rich in oil, gas or coal. As problems such as 'acid rain' and nuclear safety cast doubt on some energy sources, interest in alternative energy sources increases. Low-cost microprocessor controllers are making solar power more attractive, even for cooler climates. Controlling *wind* power is not a new problem. The traditional windmill (Figure 20.6), of which many are still standing, some of them in working order, relied on the miller's skill and judgment. He had to make the most of the wind available to grind corn for local farmers, but he also had to watch the weather carefully, making sure he could stop the sails before a storm blew up. If the wind became too strong the mill could run out of control and sparks flying from the hurtling millstones could set it alight. Many wooden mills were burnt to the ground.

Fig. 20.6 The traditional windmill, used for grinding corn or drainage, required skilful *manual* control (But see Q 20.11)

  Q 20.11 *Traditional mills such as that shown used an automatic control system to turn the sails to face the wind. See if you can find out how it adjusted to changes in wind direction.*

Computer technology has come to the aid of the modern 'miller', who makes electricity rather than flour. Vertical axis wind turbines (Figure 20.7) capable of generating several megawatts have sophisticated computerised control and monitoring systems. As many as 200 sensors are fitted to the rotor, tower, masts, transmission gear, brakes and generating equipment. Data is transmitted by optical fibres to no less than three minicomputers.

One computer automatically controls the angle of the blades in order to maintain a constant rotation speed and hence constant power output. The other computers 'tune' performance, to achieve even greater efficiency.

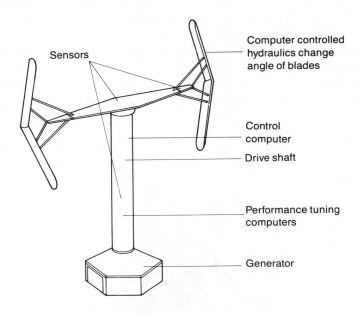

Computer controlled
hydraulics change
angle of blades

Sensors

Control
computer

Drive shaft

Performance tuning
computers

Generator

Fig. 20.7 Modern windmills, like this vertical axis wind turbine, are automatically adjusted and controlled by computer. Feedback is provided by numerous sensors which send data along optical fibres to the minicomputers

Q 20.12 *The computer does* not *turn the windmill in Figure 20.7 to face the wind. Why not?*

GUIDANCE CONTROL

Many *guidance control* systems require processes of staggering speed and complexity; human beings simply could not do the job.

Weapons

The guidance accuracy of modern weapons is chilling. A cruise missile, flying near the ground to dodge enemy radar, continually corrects its course by comparing its *own* radar sightings with maps stored in its computer memory. It is capable of travelling thousands of kilometres and delivering its deadly payload within thirty metres of a target.

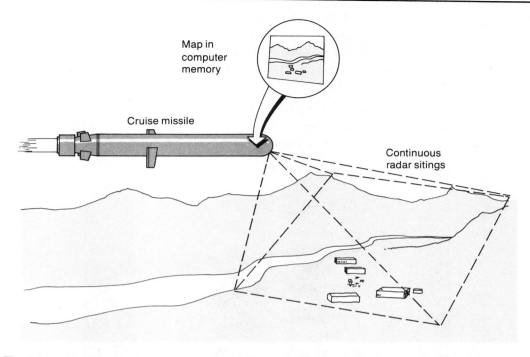

Map in
computer
memory

Cruise missile

Continuous
radar sitings

Fig. 20.8 A cruise missile keeps on course by comparing the terrain below with maps stored in its computer's memory

The British Sting Ray torpedo, on the other hand, listens while it works. The computer in its nose finds the spare time to compare the noises it picks up with stored sound patterns, so that it can tell submarines from whales and friend from foe—and ignore decoys.

Navigation

Ocean-going yachtsmen and tanker skippers can navigate with pinpoint accuracy thanks to signals from satellites. They can also carry a small 'black box' which automatically transmits their position to the satellite; rapid processing of this data has saved the lives of shipwrecked sailors.

Transport

Microcomputers control a fleet of buses in California, monitoring passenger numbers, delays and congestion and at the same time checking the oil and water. The information is relayed by radio to a control centre for management to correct problems.

London Regional Transport are using minicomputers to monitor and control underground train movements. As cables can easily be laid along the tunnels, tracking movements by taking a 'snapshot' of train positions every thirty seconds is relatively easy. Positions are displayed on a 9 m (30 ft) screen in the control room.

Local computers store the timetables and control the signals at each junction. Should a train break down or be cancelled, an updated timetable can be sent from central control to any affected junction within seconds.

Fig. 20.9   This display helps to reschedule underground trains when breakdowns or delays occur

MANUFACTURING CONTROL

A simple view of the complex business of manufacturing could be:

1 Make sure you have all the parts and materials you need.

2 Get them to the right place at the right time.

3 Put them all together.

4 Sell the product at a profit.

Controlling Parts and Materials

Much of the cost of manufacturing is incurred before assembly even begins; automated systems can help to minimise this expense. Savings can be made in at least three areas:

● cost of keeping too many parts (money 'tied up', storage space)

● cost of shortages of parts (delays, workers and machines idle)

● cost of handling materials (storing, moving parts to the point of manufacture).

To avoid having too many or too few components, a manufacturer must know exactly which products are to be made and the combination of components needed. If that sounds too obvious bear in mind that an airliner is made up of *millions* of parts, and even a domestic oven may require hundreds!

The manufacturer's computer system will perform a *parts explosion* for the items that the company intends to make. This process is less exciting than it sounds; the system merely produces an exact list, to the last tiny nut and bolt, of all the parts needed to make a product.

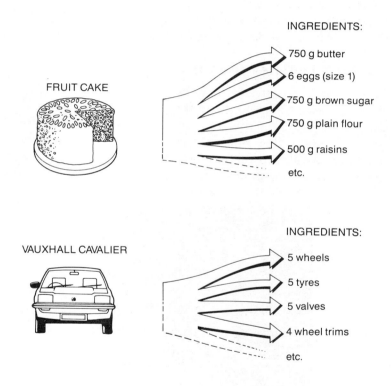

INGREDIENTS:

750 g butter

6 eggs (size 1)

750 g brown sugar

750 g plain flour

500 g raisins

etc.

FRUIT CAKE

VAUXHALL CAVALIER

INGREDIENTS:

5 wheels

5 tyres

5 valves

4 wheel trims

etc.

Fig. 20.10 A 'parts explosion' can be compared with the list of ingredients in a recipe

This information is usually produced after receiving a customer's order, at least a few days before assembly is to take place, so that stock levels can be checked and parts that are in short supply can be obtained. If the current stock levels, outstanding orders *and* all forthcoming requirements are stored in the computer system, this restocking process can itself be fully automated.

> **?**
>
> **Q 20.13** *Why is it often preferable to make products to order, rather than making them first and selling them later?*
>
> **Q 20.14** *Why must not-yet-delivered supplies and forthcoming requirements for parts be stored in the system?*

Materials Handling

Components being delivered to the factory must be unloaded and carefully stored in the right place (*bin location*). When the parts are actually required for assembly, the correct number of items must be retrieved from that location and delivered to the correct point of assembly at the proper time (it is no good having wheels ready if the chassis is not available).

Automatic Guided Vehicles (AGVs)

This storage and retrieval may be under automatic control, with *automatic guided vehicles* to do all the fetching and carrying. Some of these depend on wires in the floor to guide them around the shop floor; 'smarter' AGVs (Figure 20.11) can find their own way around. The machine has a map of the warehouse (or factory) floor stored in its memory, and navigates by calculating how far it has gone—forward, left or right—from the rotations of its wheels.

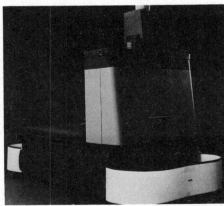

Fig. 20.11 This automatic guided vehicle (AGV) can 'roam' freely (under program control) around a warehouse or factory floor

But this is a case of blind control; inaccuracies can creep in (e.g. owing to worn tyres or uneven floors) and the AGV needs sensory feedback to stay *exactly* on course. So the AGV periodically checks its position by reading bar code position markers (with a built-in laser scanner). In addition, it checks for obstacles (such as fellow AGVs) by infra-red or sonar sensors.

Bar codes are also used to make sure the right parts are delivered to the production line; each bin location has a unique bar code, which the automatically controlled crane will check before stacking components onto the AGV.

 Q 20.15 *What other input method could be used by the AGV to check its position?*

Automated Assembly

With the correct parts delivered to the *assembly line* (Figure 20.12), the product being assembled, a van, for instance, moves along from one *workstation* to another. At each station the same operations are carried out on each vehicle, e.g. welding two body panels together or attaching further parts.

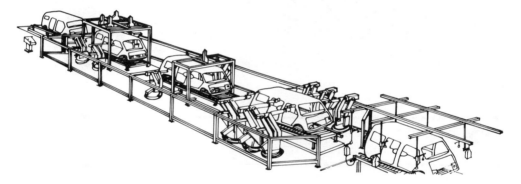

Fig. 20.12   There are over one hundred robots on the Ford Transit assembly line in Southampton

This system can accelerate production enormously but there are drawbacks:

- Every operation must be completed within a set time.
- Any problem may stop the entire assembly line.
- It is very difficult to make more than one model at once.

For human workers, an assembly line creates boredom and stress, making these problems worse. People under pressure all too easily lose concentration and make mistakes or start arguing. You may have heard car owners complaining that theirs is a 'Friday afternoon' car.

 Q 20.16 *Volvo does not use the assembly line method, preferring to use a team of workers to assemble a complete car. What are the benefits and drawbacks of this approach?*

Robots for Assembly

Using *robots* can reduce these problems. They have no difficulty in accurately performing, say, a precision weld (Figure 20.13), over and over again, every 12 seconds. Once purchased they do not demand pay (or rises) and will not strike. They fall 'ill' much less often than humans and can operate round the clock. In short they greatly improve *productivity*.

Fig. 20.13 Robot welding a car door

  Q 20.17 *Despite the advantages, by the mid-1980s fewer than 1 per cent of British factories had installed robots. Why?*

Robot Perception

Robots have been welding and spraying paint for years (e.g. on the Austin Metro) but with enhanced *sensory* ability they are acquiring even more remarkable skills. Increased *perception* and flexibility helps them to overcome some of the other drawbacks of the assembly line.

One specialised robot in a canning factory can 'see' any misshapen can coming along the high-speed line and reject it before another machine attempts to fill it. Human workers might have to stop the line in such circumstances.

More elaborate visual skills are demonstrated on the Ford Transit line in Southampton (Figure 20.12). Robots here check each partly assembled body to see which model it is; there are 36 options. They then make sure that the correct parts are fitted to each shell. In this way, a single assembly line can cope with many models without the odd one ending up short of a door!

Computer Integrated Manufacturing (CIM)

Manufacturers are increasingly attempting to link all their systems, i.e. business, CAD/CAM, materials planning, purchasing, stock control, production and distribution, to form an integrated whole.

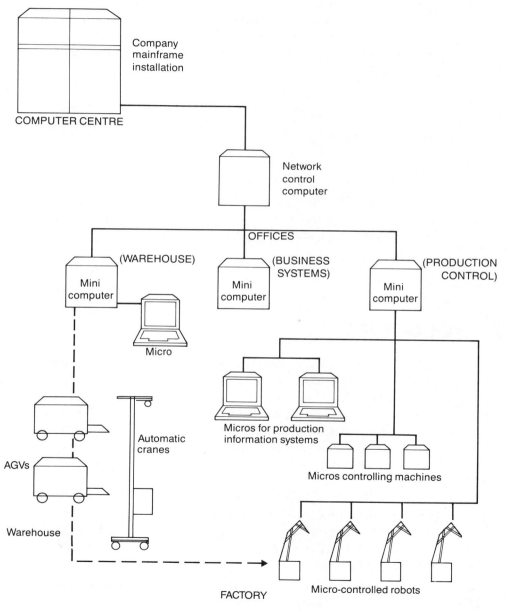

Fig. 20.14 A typical computer network for a manufacturing company with highly automated production

This is an ambitious and complex task, especially as different suppliers and manufacturers often use completely different types of system. Just transferring data from one system to another can present huge problems.

The rewards are great for companies that solve these problems. Before computer systems came along to help, achieving 70% of *planned* production was considered good going: now the figure can be 95% or even 100%. Even after allowing for the heavy investment in machinery, systems and software, automation can cut manufacturing costs dramatically.

The Rest of the Robots

Most robots so far have been designed for factory work; perhaps the ultimate examples are the computer-controlled robots that build computers. However, the robot population *outside* the factory gates is beginning to grow. Robot miners are already extracting coal in the most modern pits and there are even robot sheepshearers.

'TO BOLDLY GO . . .'

Mankind increasingly needs to control activities in places where it is too difficult or too dangerous for human beings to work. Robots do not complain when they are sent to do dirty work. Six special robots were developed to clean up a contaminated nuclear reactor building after the accident at Three Mile Island in Pennsylvania. Robots are frequently called upon in various trouble spots to examine suspicious cars for terrorist bombs and to defuse, where possible, any they may find.

Much of the Russian space effort has been concentrated on unmanned flight. Many successful missions owe their scientific achievements to spacefaring robots. Serious studies have been made into the possibility of sending 'self-replicating robots' on voyages to build mines and factories on remote planets.

 Q 20.18 *Do you think this is mere science fiction? If not, do you think it is a good idea?*

JARGON 20

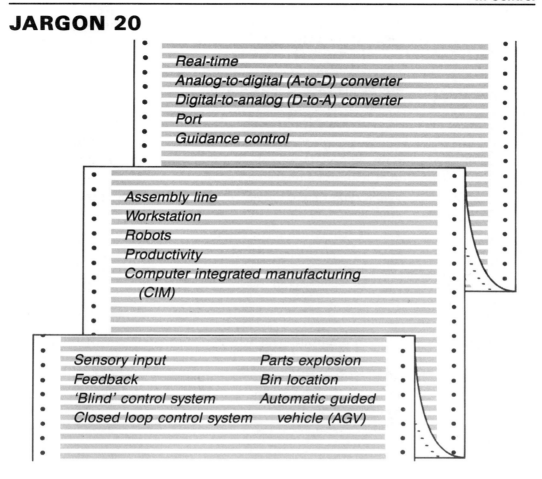

Real-time
Analog-to-digital (A-to-D) converter
Digital-to-analog (D-to-A) converter
Port
Guidance control

Assembly line
Workstation
Robots
Productivity
Computer integrated manufacturing
(CIM)

Sensory input   Parts explosion
Feedback   Bin location
'Blind' control system   Automatic guided
Closed loop control system   vehicle (AGV)

EXERCISES 20

1. The process of steel rolling consists of compressing a hot bar of steel between rollers to produce a longer, but thinner, bar. A computer-controlled steel rolling mill automatically takes steel bars from a furnace, once they are sufficiently hot, and rolls them until they are of a required length. If the temperature falls below a pre-defined level before the rolling is complete, the bar is returned to the furnace for reheating.

    Give two possible analog inputs to the computer, saying briefly why each is an analog quantity.

    Give one possible output from the computer, stating whether it is analog or digital.

    Why must this computer system operate in real time?

    (JMB)

2. A car-park has a capacity for 50 cars. As a car arrives at the entrance, a sensing-pad adds one to a count. If the count is less than 50, a ticket is issued with the date and time, and a barrier is raised to allow entrance to the car-park. When the car-park is full, a notice is displayed saying 'CAR-PARK FULL'. Each time a car approaches the exit to leave the car-park, a second sensing-pad reduces the count by one. If the 'FULL' sign is on and the count of cars is less than 50, the display sign is switched off.

   (a) Draw a flowchart to solve this problem, assuming that the car-park is initially empty. (Hint: note that there are two sensing-pads, either of which may operate at any instant.)

   (b) (i) What type of computer would best suit this process-control application? Explain your answer.

   (ii) Why is it important for the program to be able to distinguish which sensing-pad is being activated?

   (iii) Under what conditions could a car leave the car-park yet still leave the 'FULL' sign on?

   (Ox)

3. (a) Describe an application in which a computer is used for process control. Include a description of the data input to, and output from, the computer and the processing which is carried out.

   (b) Explain why the system you have described is an example of a real time system.

   (c) Why is the computer an essential part of the system that you have described?

   (CU)

21 Serving the Public

The Government uses computers extensively; for all sorts of administrative and accounting tasks at national and local levels, for tax and social security records, for processing national statistics, for aiding scientific research in the universities and other establishments, for developing new military equipment and controlling that already in use and so on.

It would be impossible to explore all the ways in which computers are used to serve the public and so in this Chapter we shall look at just three important examples:

- computers at work forecasting the weather
- computers at work in the police service
- computers at work in the health service.

FORECASTING THE WEATHER

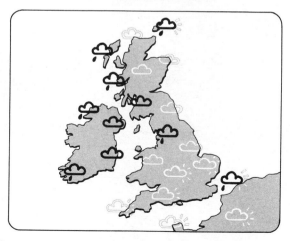

Fig. 21.1 Predicting the weather. Today's TV weather forecasts make extensive use of computer graphics

A Complex Task

Many of us watch our favourite weather forecasters on television each night without giving a second's thought to how the predictions are made (and yet we scorn them unforgivingly the following day if they get them wrong).

Forecasting the weather is a hugely complex task. Firstly, the weather depends on many complicated and interacting factors. The earth's atmosphere moves and swirls about in many different ways, not all of which are predictable.

Secondly, the weather can vary considerably over relatively small distances. So although the general pattern can be accurately forecast, local effects may cause the weather to behave differently in one particular area; for exampled correctly predicted 'light showers for the north-west' may turn out, for Manchester, to be a two-hour rain storm.

The Met Office makes regular use of weather balloons to indicate the air temperature, pressure and humidity high above the ground.

The balloons are usually filled with helium and carry a number of electronic instruments that broadcast their findings back to the weather station that launched them.

The wind could carry the balloons anywhere and so they are tracked by radar. When the balloon finally bursts a parachute carries the instruments back to earth.

If you should find one of these balloons, send it back to the Met Office who will reward you with a small 'finder's fee'.

Fig. 21.2 Launching a weather balloon

Thirdly, modern weather forecasts require the collection and rapid processing of massive quantities of data from a network of weather stations throughout the country, from weather balloons, from weather reports from merchant ships at sea, lighthouse stations and the coastguard, from reports of wind speed and direction from aircraft in flight, from foreign weather stations and from satellites in space.

In fact, the Meteorological Office (the 'Met Office') responsible for monitoring and forecasting the weather in the UK, receives over 20 million items of weather data every day. Without computers, such a vast quantity of data from many different sources could not be processed in time for the resulting weather forecasts to be of any use.

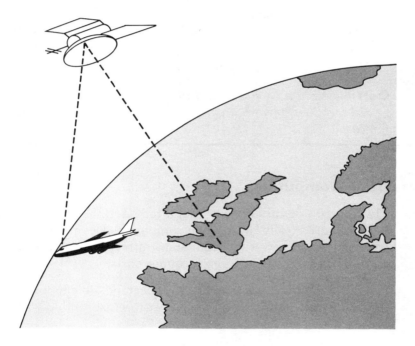

Fig. 21.3 A satellite directing a weather report from an aircraft in mid-flight. Satellites orbiting the earth at very high altitudes are not the best instruments for checking the weather near the earth's surface. But they provide valuable photographs of cloud formations and relay data from all over the world

The Importance of Forecasts

Completely accurate weather forecasting is simply not possible. Nevertheless weather prediction is an important service of which the TV and radio weather forecasts are only a small part.

Air and shipping lines depend heavily on weather forecasts for planning their safest routes, farmers can better plan their sowing and harvesting, and trawlers can travel to more promising fishing grounds with advance knowledge of the weather. The building and tourist trades plan many of their activities in the light of weather forecasts, as do the armed forces and the oil companies operating in the North Sea.

Because weather forecasting is so important, successive governments have invested heavily to keep the Meteorological Office well up to date with some of the best computer equipment in the world.

Q 21.1 *List as many users of weather forecasts as you can. For each explain why the forecasts are important to them.*

Q 21.2 *List as many sources of weather reports as you can. Why is it essential that all this information is processed very quickly?*

Q 21.3 *Why is forecasting the weather so difficult? Is it more difficult in Britain than in some other parts of the world?*

Q 21.4 *Keep a careful record of both the weather forecast and the actual weather for your area for several days. How accurate were the forecasts?*

The Met Office Computers

The Meteorological Office headquarters, in Bracknell, Berkshire, are at the hub of a fully integrated computer/telecommunications system collecting and processing data, transmitting information to customers and exchanging it with foreign counterparts.

With this computer equipment it has been possible to improve both the reliability and accuracy of the weather forecasts and to widen the range of forecasting services on offer.

Predicting the Weather

Much of the enormous volume of information received by the Met Office is transmitted electronically through the telecommunications network and is fed directly into a fleet of minicomputers that organise the data for input into two IBM mainframes called the *front-end processors*.

Some of the information received by the Met Office, however, is still on paper and this is either keyed into the computer system or is read using OCR techniques.

The front-end processors select data relevant to a particular region and time and then check that all the data items input are consistent with each other and with data input earlier. (Data which is markedly different from the rest is displayed on a VDU and subsequently input only if a human meteorologist decides it is acceptable.)

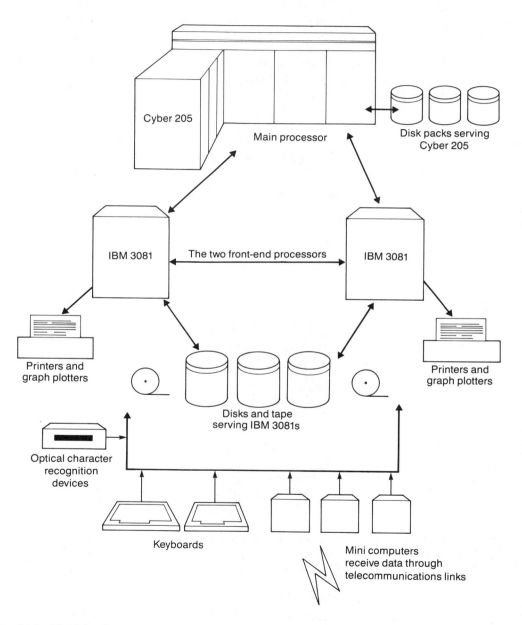

Fig. 21.4 The Met Office system

? **Q 21.5** *Are the front-end processors* verifying *or* validating *this data? Explain.*

Q 21.6 *What are OCR techniques?*

The sorted data is then fed to the *main processor*—the Cyber 205 super-computer—which runs a complex program *simulating* the earth's atmosphere using a complex mathematical *model* (see Chapter 19).

The atmosphere is treated as a three-dimensional grid, divided into squares of 150 km layered 15 deep. (A finer grid of 75 km is used for the Northern Atlantic model.)

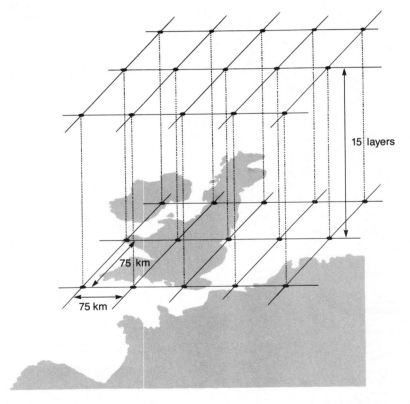

Fig. 21.5 The Met Office model of the atmosphere is entirely mathematical, you cannot feel or touch it. Literally millions of imaginary points represent the atmosphere at known geographical positions. At each point various weather variables are calculated and then recalculated for a short interval later

From the data fed to it the main processor calculates the likely temperature, humidity, wind direction and wind speed for each corner of every square at every level.

Changes in any one of these *weather variables* will have a 'knock-on' effect on all four variables in all of the neighbouring points; above and below, to the left and to the right, in front and behind.

Fig. 21.6 The Cyber 205 is one of the world's most powerful 'number crunchers', performing *millions* of complex mathematical calculations per second

It takes the Cyber 205 just $1\frac{1}{4}$ seconds to follow a set of hugely complicated mathematical formulae and calculate the likely new values for every one of these several million weather variables $7\frac{1}{2}$ minutes later. In $1\frac{1}{4}$ seconds more (i.e. in $2\frac{1}{2}$ seconds altogether) the calculations have been done again, suggesting the likely values in 15 minutes time, and so on.

In about six minutes the computer is predicting the likely development of the weather over the North Atlantic and Europe in 36 hours' time.

A less detailed global model, suggesting world-wide weather developments for the following six days, is produced in much the same way.

This forecasting program is run twice daily, once in the early hours of the morning and again in the early afternoon, based on observations made the world over at midnight and mid-day GMT.

The predictions that are made are continually checked with the actual weather. The Met Office's forecasts are accurate about 85 per cent of the time.

Any major errors in the forecast are studied in detail. More often than not the errors are due to insufficient initial information. As the data from satellites increases in quantity and improves in quality, so the number of errors should be reduced still further.

Output of the Results

The front-end processors are linked to a number of graph plotters and six 6-hourly staged predictions are produced in the form of weather maps such as that shown in Figure 21.7. Such a map would take hours to draw by hand.

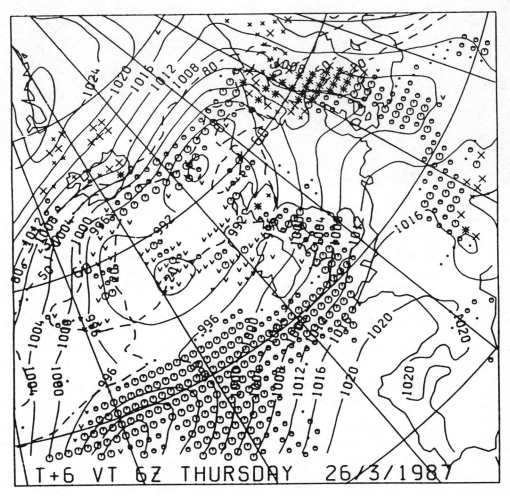

Fig. 21.7 The weather map for 26/3/87 predicted the day before. Computer controlled pen-plotters can produce these maps—in colour—in a matter of minutes

The forecasts broadcast on radio and TV are made by the human meteorologists using these computer-generated maps. For some purposes, such as airline flight planning, the computers themselves prepare and transmit the actual forecasts.

The computer output, with forecast added, is also transmitted to various regional offices of the UK Meteorological Service (such as the London Weather Centre), to important users such as the BBC and British Airways, and to other weather forecasting agencies around the world.

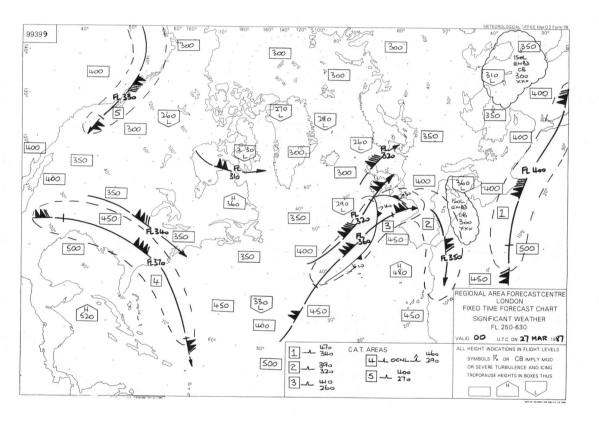

Fig. 21.8 The Met Office predicts the weather for all parts of the world—not just for the United Kingdom

The maps and forecasts are also transmitted in other forms; e.g. the Met Office is an *information provider* for Prestel. Similarly, the Met Office provides TTNS (the schools' electronic mail service) with extracts from the predicted weather maps so that schools can try to forecast tomorrow's weather from the information used by the professionals!

Data Storage

Weather information is stored on-line in the Met Office's extensive data bank for some 60 hours before it is transferred to disk in off-line files. Maps and other charts and satellite photographs are stored on microfilm or microfiche. This information is available not only to scientists in the Met Office but also to others, e.g. university researchers wanting a detailed analysis of weather patterns in the past.

?

Q 21.7 *Why is it essential to maintain accurate records of the weather?*

Q 21.8 *What would happen if the main processor at Bracknell should fail completely? What steps do you think the management of the Met Office have already taken to minimise the consequences of this?*

Q 21.9 *Will it ever be possible to predict the weather with complete accuracy?*

Q 21.10 *The Met Office has stopped broadcasting general 'long-range' weather forecasts. Why do you think this is?*

Q 21.11 *The Cyber 205 cost several million pounds to install in the early 1980s. Do you think the improved reliability in weather forecasts justifies the expense?*

Q 21.12 *The Met Office is a sizeable organisation employing a large number of people. How else might it use computers?*

COMPUTERS IN THE POLICE SERVICE

Since the police began extensive application of computers to their work in the early 1980s there has been a dramatic increase in the number and the sophistication of police computer systems. The police are now using computers to support virtually all aspects of their work.

The advantages are considerable: easy access to detailed information held nationally; rapid, accurate search and manipulation of local information; better detection rates but a reduction in paperwork and administration.

The computer is now probably the most important single tool in the fight against crime . . . and there are many new plans (such as a national fingerprint recognition system) 'in the pipeline'.

The Police National Computer (PNC)

There is no national police force in Britain; broadly speaking each county has its own and so there are 51 independent police forces in the United Kingdom. However, all the local police forces have access to the *police national computer* (PNC) in London, where large computerised databases (criminal records, lists of stolen vehicles etc.) are held.

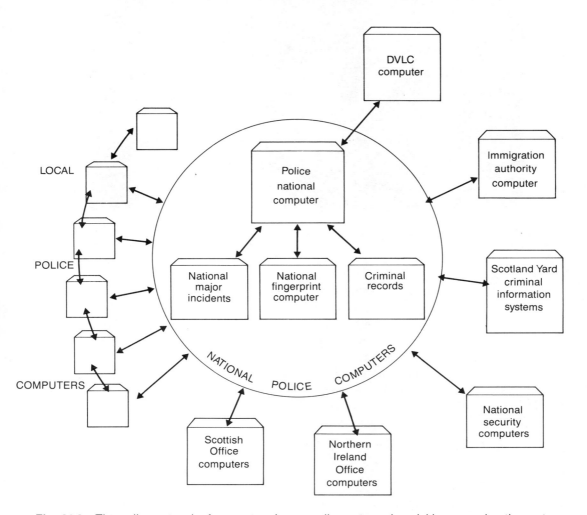

Fig. 21.9 The police network of computers is expanding extremely quickly, accessing the system of many national authorities, such as the DVLC and immigration, as well as linking the local police computers together

Nationwide computer networks have also been established, linking the PNC with the local police computers. These are being extended to include input from other major computers (such as the Driver and Vehicle Licence

Centre in Swansea which sends details of all car registrations and drivers' licences on tape for input to the PNC). And the Home Office (the Government department responsible for the police) is encouraging local police forces to standardise their computer systems and procedures to allow easier transfer of data and of personnel from county to county.

Fig. 21.10   The Information Room at New Scotland Yard houses the Metropolitan Police command and control network. At the time it was installed (in 1982) it was the biggest police computer in the world

All the police computers are on-line so that answers to queries are available within a few seconds. All their systems are duplicated so that, if any part should fail, there is a back-up system ready to take over immediately; society cannot afford its police service to grind to a halt because of a computer breakdown. And all of their systems are carefully secured against unauthorised use or alteration.

Q 21.13   *What is meant by the term 'real-time'? Does police computer software need to be real-time?*

Q 21.14   *Why is it essential that police computer systems are backed up by expensive duplicates?*

Q 21.15   *How might the police ensure that unauthorised persons cannot tamper with their computer systems?*

Q 21.16   *Why is it important for the 51 local police forces to standardise their computer systems? Would it be better if Britain had one national police force?*

Q 21.17   *What aspects of local police computer systems need to conform to national standards?*

Emergency! Dial 999!

All of Britain's local police forces are faced with a daunting number of emergency 999 telephone calls. For example New Scotland Yard, where emergency calls in Greater London are processed, regularly receives *five or six hundred* such calls *in a single hour.*

Obviously not all of those calls will be matters of life or death, but some of them will. If the police are to respond effectively, they must get to the scene extremely quickly.

Before the police can respond to any 999 call, the officer taking it must be absolutely sure of the precise location of the problem. Even when the person reporting the emergency is calm and clear there can still be problems. *'Come quickly! There is a big fight in the pub. "The Dogs" on Albert Road',* may seem a clear enough cry for help. But Albert Road is one of Britain's most common road names (for example there are over 30 Albert Roads in the Greater London area;) and, without a computer, it would take a police officer several minutes to check which one the caller meant.

But often the caller is in a state of panic and gets precise details wrong. 'The Dogs' may in fact be a local nickname for a pub called 'The Fox and Hounds'.

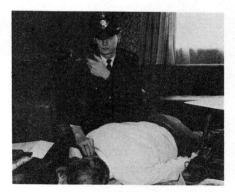

Fig. 21.11   This policeman's emergency radio message is relayed by computer

To ensure that each 999 call is rapidly and accurately 'put on the map', the police use large and powerful mainframe computers to enable them to locate a call extremely quickly. (New Scotland Yard can pin-point a call in an average time of $1\frac{1}{4}$ seconds.) For this the computer holds hundreds of facts and figures about every street, every phone box, public building, school, park, pub (real name and nickname) and all the details of an area that might be of use in locating an emergency call.

A second problem, every bit as important as locating the call, is finding the nearest available police 'panda' car and directing it to the scene of the emergency. The computer will not only tell the radio operator which panda cars are in the vicinity of the emergency, and which is the nearest—it can even put an area map onto the VDU screen so that, should the driver not be sure of the quickest route, the radio operator can direct him.

?

Q 21.18 *How do the police keep their local information, such as pub nicknames, up to date?*

Q 21.19 *The computer does not hold lists of private telephone numbers and addresses. Why do you think this is?*

Q 21.20 *How could a computer double check that a call was made from, say, Albert Road SE20 not from Albert Road SE25?*

Fig. 21.12 Police computer systems automatically keep track of crime statistics. This helps the police to identify quickly any local trouble spots and to deploy police patrols appropriately

Controlling Traffic

The traffic lights in Britain's major cities are now controlled by computers operated by the local police.

The computer allows the lights to respond to different levels of traffic flow. In the morning, for example, the traffic coming into the city would be given priority (so that lights would stay green for longer on inward routes). In the evening, priority would be given to traffic leaving town.

Using sensors in the road, the computer is able to detect any unusual hold-ups in the traffic (e.g. an accident). It will alert the operators who can direct a police motorcyclist to the area if necessary. Further, by altering the traffic light timings, the computer can encourage traffic to take alternative routes that will miss the jam altogether.

Stolen Cars

All police forces in Britain have access to the Stolen and Suspect Vehicles and to the Vehicle Owners Indexes held on the Police National Computer.

1. A police 'panda' car spots someone driving fast and erratically through the town centre. They decide to follow him.

2. As they follow the car, they contact the local operations room to report 'Am following a blue Metro WPM 547Y. Please check. Over.'

3. The radio operator uses his terminal to check with the Police National Computer in London and reports back to the panda car. 'Car has not been reported stolen. The registered owner is Francis Brown, of New Road, Barchester. Over.'

4. Even though the car is now *not* thought to be stolen, the police stop it for speeding. Once the driver's identity has been established a further check with the PNC shows him to be a disqualified driver. Further questions reveal that he has no idea who owns the car and when pressed admits that he stole it from a Barchester car park about an hour ago. The police make an arrest and impound the car. It will be returned to Francis Brown later that day.

Fig. 21.13

A policeman suspicious of a car can find out within a few seconds, *before* he stops the vehicle, whether or not a car has been reported stolen. He can also establish who is its rightful owner—something a car thief is unlikely to know.

?

Q 21.21 *Why is the list of stolen cars held nationally on the Police National Computer in London rather than on the computers of the local police?*

Q 21.22 *Why do the police place such importance on tracking stolen vehicles as quickly as possible?*

Q 21.23 *Quite frequently the police find a stolen car before its owner is aware of its loss! Explain how computerised checking of the Vehicle Owners Index makes this possible.*

Why does the computer make this more likely than if the system were a manual one?

Q 21.24 *The police have experimented with computerised cameras that can automatically read the number plate of every vehicle that passes by and then check that number against the Stolen and Suspect Vehicles Index.*

What use would such a machine be to the police? Why do you think some people object to the police using computers in this way?

Criminal Records

As well as details of vehicles, the Police National Computer also holds a number of other files on missing persons, stolen property, fingerprints, disqualified drivers etc.

Fig. 21.14 Checking fingerprints manually is a tedious and time consuming activity. Since 1984 New Scotland Yard has been using a computerised fingerprint recognition system which has proven extremely fast and effective. A National Fingerprint Computer will come on-line in the near future

In particular the PNC was extended in 1986 to include a full criminal records index. Not only will the names and aliases of all those individuals convicted of offences in the United Kingdom be held on the computer, but so will a mass of other personal information such as physical descriptions and details of the crimes committed.

The PNC is to be further extended to include a sophisticated fingerprint recognition system which will store some three million fingerprints and be able to establish quickly the likely identity of fingerprints machine read by computer terminals in every major police station in the country.

Major Enquiry Systems: Computers as Detectives?

Stories of Sherlock Holmes and other fictional detectives give a false idea of how detectives work. Generally a major crime is solved not by the inspired genius of one man but by a team of both ordinary police and detectives interviewing hundreds, sometimes thousands, of members of the public and using the information given to build up huge files of data. In the past these files were indexed manually, usually by a full-time 'collator' at each police station. This was an extremely laborious task. The investigators then search through these files to find the connections they need to identify the individuals responsible for the crime.

Fig. 21.15 A police officer scanning through computerised files of criminals' photographs. The optical disks used in this system store tens of thousands of 'mugshots', saving hours of manual searching

Too Much Information

The problem, however, is that the sheer volume of information collected in the course of major enquiry (reports from individual policemen, statements from witnesses, descriptions of cars and other items used in the course of the crime, forensic evidence etc.) quickly becomes unmanageable. The files become so large that it is simply not possible for human beings to search through them quickly, flexibly and accurately.

Computerised record keeping throughout any major enquiry is an obvious and important advance for the police.

Fig. 21.16 Any major investigation into a serious crime generates a lot of police activity; almost all of it collecting and processing *information*

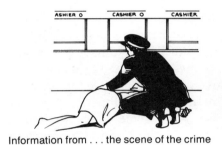

Information from . . . the scene of the crime

From known informants

Forensic evidence

Statements from witnesses

From individual policemen and women

. . . and from the suspects themselves

Information from existing police
records on computers and on
paper files

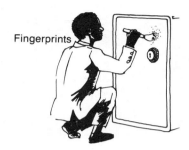

Fingerprints

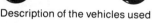

Description of the vehicles used

... and descriptions of the faces
seen

Because the files are so very extensive, highly sophisticated software is necessary to make rapid searching possible. On many of the police systems almost every word of the file is indexed, so that the records can be searched for any word or phrase (such as 'red Ford Escort') that might be important in linking together statements from different people.

To make sure that detectives working on any major enquiry are familiar with forms, screen displays and procedures, the Home Office has laid down standard formats for the various computer records. If the volume of information collected becomes very large, processing can take place on the Police National Computer as well as on the local police mini-computer systems. This *Home Office Large Major Enquiry System* (HOLMES) allows the police to set up a fully computerised enquiry into any major crime anywhere in the UK.

Police Computers versus Civil Liberties

Few people would suggest that the police should not use computers at all. On the contrary, when it took the police well over a year to catch the 'Yorkshire Ripper' who murdered nearly a dozen more girls during that time, the police were severely criticised for *not* using them. The killer had been questioned several times in the course of the investigation but by different policemen and the interviews were not linked. The enquiry had grown too large for the manual filing systems to cope.

But many people are disturbed by the rapid growth of police computer systems and the higher levels of surveillance that become possible with the new technology.

Firstly, concern has been expressed about the size of the police records; already the Police National Computer contains nearly 5 million names and over 3.5 million fingerprints.

Secondly, easy, speedy access to these records has meant a considerable increase in the number of enquiries that police officers make. For example, the Merseyside Police check their manual criminal records 635 times a day on average, and yet they were planning (until prevented by the Merseyside Council) to install a computerised system that could handle 11 000 enquiries a day—nearly a two-hundred fold increase.

A policeman who receives someone's criminal record in the course of the first 'stop and search' may be more likely to make an arrest than if he did not have that information to hand. In the past, the policeman would have needed sufficiently strong suspicions to make an arrest *before* he went through the laborious process of having a copy of the paper files sent to him. So a man's criminal record may now *lead* to his arrest rather than, as in the past, confirm the good sense of it.

Thirdly, wholly new methods of monitoring the public become possible. The automatic car number-plate reading and checking machine is one example; another system, still under development, can read and check faces in a crowd.

Fourthly, the police records are not subject to the same regulations that govern other computer files (see Chapter 22 for details of the Data Protection Act). If ever the police should hold some information about you on their computers (perhaps one day you might be the innocent witness to a major crime) you have no right to check it. Yet it could be completely incorrect, possibly even given to the police maliciously by someone trying to connect you with the crime.

The police, however, argue that they are not collecting much in the way of new information because of the computers; they are simply using what they have very much more efficiently. The computers may help them find the connections between a suspect and a crime, but the case against someone still has to be proven in court. And undeniably, the computer systems are a major help in combating crime. Fast and efficient detection of criminals is to *everyone's* advantage, except, of course, the criminals.

> **?**
>
> **Q 21.25** *Why are members of the public not allowed to check and contest the records the police hold on them? Should they be able to?*
>
> **Q 21.26** *In Britain a defendant's criminal record may not be used against him or her in court. The prosecution must prove he or she committed the new crime using new evidence. Should the police only be allowed access to criminal records after they have made an arrest? Should criminal records be read out in court?*
>
> **Q 21.27** *Soon it will be possible for every panda car to carry a small flat-screen computer terminal allowing the crew immediate 'on-the-road' access to almost all police records. Would you welcome this?*
>
> **Q 21.28** *A National Fingerprint computer with facilities to store and recognise millions of fingerprints would make it feasible to keep on police files the fingerprints of every man, woman and child in the country. This is not planned but do you think it a good idea?*
>
> **Q 21.29** *(a) Imagine that you are a county councillor and that you and your party intend to refuse your county police permission to install a new extensive computer system. Write a brief draft of a speech justifying that decision.*
>
> *(b) Now imagine that you are a senior police officer. Draft your reply to the councillors.*
>
> *(c) Who do you think is right?*

COMPUTERS IN THE NATIONAL HEALTH SERVICE

Hospital Administration

Like many other large organisations, a hospital requires a large database carrying the details of the patients it serves. A typical city hospital with 1000 beds could have several hundred thousand patients registered with it, for large numbers of patients will be visiting the hospital as out-patients undergoing tests and consultations before (possibly) being called into the hospital to stay, perhaps for a single week.

The administration involved in organising so many people is extensive. Appointments have to be made with the right consultants in the right place at the right times.

It is necessary to know which patient occupies which bed at any one time and when the bed will be available for the next person on the waiting list. Meals and other non-medical services need to be organised for each day's 'in-patients'. And, as patients leave, their regular doctor, i.e. their *general practitioner* (GP), and any clinic to which they may have been referred must be informed.

Such a huge administrative problem can be considerably eased by using computers, to the general benefit of the public who will be treated more quickly if the hospital is well run and beds are rarely empty.

Patients' Records

For purely administrative purposes, a computer record for any patient registered with the hospital would include details such as the patient's National Health Service number (a code of seven characters which the NHS used to identify patients long before it began using computers); the patient's name, address, date of birth and sex; the name of his or her GP; whether the patient is an in-patient or an out-patient; which doctor is overseeing the treatment and, if appropriate, the date of admission to the hospital; which bed the patient occupies and the expected date of discharge.

Q 21.30 *Explain the terms*

(a) NHS number

(b) General practitioner

Q 21.31 *Do you know your National Health Service number? If not look for your NHS medical card and find out!*

Q 21.32 *What hardware would a hospital need to run a basic registration and appointments system to keep track of patients and beds?*

Q 21.33 *Is it important for hospitals' administrative systems to be standardised with other computer systems in the NHS?*

Medical Records

Most large hospitals now run a computerised administrative system; these are increasingly being extended to include *medical* records as well.

Your main medical record, showing a complete history of all the medical treatment you have been given since you were born, is kept by your GP, usually on paper. Hospitals are obliged to tell your doctor of any treatment they administer to you so that this record is always kept up to date.

Whether or not the system includes provision for medical notes it can be used as a reminder system, and so, for example, a patient told to return every year for a chest X-ray after a successful lung operation some time ago can be reminded automatically with little effort.

It can also be used to identify and call in all those people treated by the hospital between certain dates or times who might have had contact with another patient subsequently found to be carrying a highly infectious disease. This sort of emergency does happen in hospitals; if the hospital record system is a manual one then tracing the right patients is a major undertaking. With a well-designed computer system it would be relatively simple and routine.

Fig. 21.17 Hospital administrative systems are well established. Many hospitals are now computerising their patients' medical records as well. Here a nurse is updating a patient's record as the two doctors discuss the case

Q 21.34 *What extra hardware would be necessary if a hospital's administrative system was to be extended to include medical notes?*

Q 21.35 *Doctors place great stress on keeping a patient's medical notes confidential. They will not only keep them from other people but also from the patients themselves. Why?*

How could the hospital ensure that the medical notes added to an extended administrative system remained confidential?

Q 21.36 *Your regular doctor, i.e. your GP, asks you for advice on the possibility of computerising patients' records. (Suppose there are three doctors working in the surgery serving some 8500 patients.)*

(a) Why would a computer system be preferable to a manual one?

(b) What hardware would be necessary? Draw a systems flowchart to illustrate your answer.

(c) Where and how should the surgery acquire the software it will need?

(d) What information would need to be recorded on each patient's file?

(e) How might the system be used to issue repeat prescriptions?

(f) How might the system improve the quality of the service the doctors offer their patients?

Hospital Meals

Hospital food may not be luxurious but the meals are served regularly, and are carefully checked for nutritional value. (Irregular and/or inedible meals will undermine patients' morale and hinder their recovery.) Furthermore, since a hospital is serving a large number of people with various restrictions to their diet and in various states of sickness, it must also offer a choice of food at each meal.

In these circumstances it would be very easy for the hospital caterers to misjudge the numbers required for each dish, wasting unacceptably large quantities of food as a consequence. So that this does not happen, the nurses check the patients' choices for each meal before anything is cooked. But it takes many hours to collect and process this information manually.

Here too the hospital computer can help. Patients select their choices for each course on mark sense cards (Figure 21.18) which the nurses distribute once they have written in the ward names and bed numbers.

The cards from the different wards are processed in batches using an optical mark reader; this might take all of ten minutes depending on the machine and the number of menu choices.

```
                    BARCHESTER GENERAL HOSPITAL
                           MEALS SERVICE

   YOUR CHOICE FOR:       DINNER [ TUES. ]    WARD: [ PRINCE HAL ]
                                              BED:  [ 112 ]

   Chicken Soup                    ⊂⊃
   Grapefruit Cocktail             ⊂⊃
   Melon                           ⬤

   Steak and Kidney Pie            ⊂⊃    Boiled Potatoes     ⊂⊃
   Lamb Chops                      ⊂⊃    Green Beans         ⊂⊃
   Cold Honeydew Ham               ⊂⊃    Carrots             ⊂⊃
   Plain Omelette                  ⬤    Side Salad          ⊂⊃

   Hot Rhubarb Crumble             ⊂⊃    Tea                 ⊂⊃
   Hot Rhubarb Crumble and Custard ⊂⊃    Coffee (white)      ⊂⊃
   Chocolate Crisp Cake            ⊂⊃    Coffee (black)      ⊂⊃
   Piece of Fruit                  ⬤    Milk (glass)        ⬤
   Cheese and Biscuits             ⊂⊃
```

Fig. 21.18 Barchester General Hospital has computerised its meal service. This patient has chosen to have a melon, a plain omelette and a piece of fruit for dinner, together with a glass of milk

The computer can summarise how many helpings of each dish have been ordered for the whole hospital, and indicate the overall quantities of the various ingredients the catering staff will need. The computer will also keep a running total of the food in stock and indicate those items that need reordering. And if that were not enough, the computer can also print a list of meals for each ward, so easing the problem of distributing the meals once they are ready.

?

Q 21.37 *Explain the terms*

(a) *mark sense card*

(b) *optical mark reader*

(c) *batch processing.*

Why is OMR the most sensible method of data capture for the hospital meals service to use?

How does the computer know which meals have been ordered by different wards if the nurses write the ward names and bed numbers on the card by hand?

Other Administrative Tasks

The hospital computer will be involved in the other administrative tasks of the hospital, e.g. keeping the accounts, monitoring drug stock levels, keeping a rota of staff (a hospital must run for 24 hours a day and so elaborate shift systems are necessary) and keeping track of the hours each person works for pay purposes.

? Q 21.38 *How could the hospital pharmacist use the computer to help control the stocks of the drugs that it keeps?*

(You might like to read the section on stock control in Chapter 15.)

How might a computerised system help the pharmacists establish that someone in the hospital is misusing a drug (morphine, say, which is related to heroin)?

Patient Care

One of the reasons that the National Health Service is for ever short of money is that as medical knowledge advances the treatment offered to patients becomes more dependent on very expensive technology.

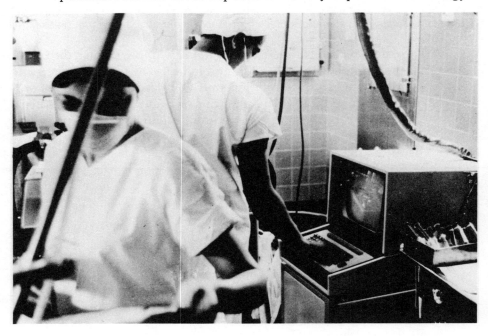

Fig. 21.19 Doctors are now using computers to assist them in treating patients. Here the surgeon is consulting the computer in the course of an operation

Many techniques that are now well established were simply not possible a few years ago, and they depend very much on computers.

Some of the applications of computers to clinical medicine are relatively routine, e.g. blood sampling is now computerised in a number of hospitals. Others are rather special, e.g. the body scanner.

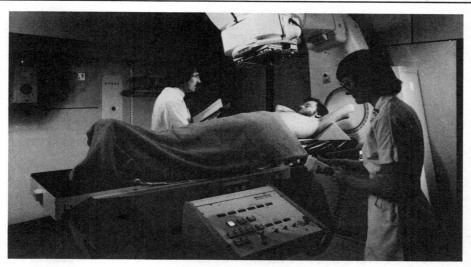

Fig. 21.20 Many of the latest treatments would be impossible without new technology; this computer is calculating a precise radiation dose

Medical Research

Computers are also used extensively to aid medical research, not only in monitoring the progress of various scientific experiments but also in processing a large number of statistics. Often the best way of discovering which is the most effective of several possible drugs that might be used to treat a particular ailment is to prescribe them to different groups of patients and compare the different recovery rates statistically.

Expert Systems

When a patient first describes his or her complaint, the doctor must decide the most likely cause of the trouble, i.e. must *diagnose* the illness. This can be a tricky business for there may be several possible causes for the patient's problem, and there is always the possibility that a patient has a serious disease that the doctor has not met before.

The doctor will set about deciding the possible cause of the illness rather like a detective. He or she will look for as many 'clues' as possible, by discussing the patients' problem with the patient and undertaking any necessary medical tests. As the information builds up the doctor will eliminate some of the possibilities considered originally until the evidence points to a single conclusion.

Often the doctor will not be able to come to a firm decision and so will refer the patient to a specialist who, in turn, may require the patient to stay in hospital for 'observation' or 'exploratory surgery'.

Much of this diagnostic process can be automated. Highly experienced specialist doctors record their knowledge in a carefully designed computer system. Less experienced doctors can then input all the patient's known symptoms so that the computer can (i) select the most likely causes of the patient's problems and (ii) indicate to the doctor those medical tests that should be undertaken next.

A computer used this way is, in effect, acting as an adviser and consultant to the doctor, giving the less experienced doctor the benefit of expert specialist knowledge.

Such *expert systems* are already used in a number of surgeries in the USA. Their success rate in diagnosing illness has already rivalled human doctors, so they will become widespread.

Of course the ability of the computerised expert depends very much on the medical skills of the doctors used to establish the medical database. But the possibilities are almost endless and one day perhaps we shall be able to obtain expert medical advice from our home computers, and only visit the doctor's surgery when the computer recommends a medical test that we could not carry out at home.

Q 21.39 *Initial experiments have shown that patients tend to tell a computer expert system more details of their problem than they would a human doctor. Why do you think this is?*

Q 21.40 *Do you think local GPs will welcome computerised medical expert systems?*

Q 21.41 *What other professional advisers might be replaced by computerised expert systems?*

JARGON 21

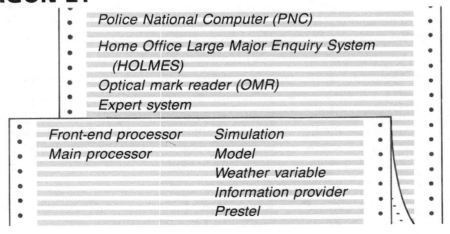

Police National Computer (PNC)

Home Office Large Major Enquiry System (HOLMES)

Optical mark reader (OMR)

Expert system

Front-end processor	Simulation
Main processor	Model
	Weather variable
	Information provider
	Prestel

EXERCISES 21

1. Explain how the UK Meteorological Office uses computers to fulfil its role as one of the prime weather forecasting agencies of the world.

2. The Police National Computer is in London. Many local police stations are linked to this central computer. The Police use a computer to help them to trace stolen cars.
   (a) What piece of information is most likely to be input and used by the computer to find the record for a car?
   (b) Suggest a suitable device which may be used to input this data.
   (c) Why might the use of this computerised system lead to a stolen car being found sooner than if the system was not used?

   (SREB)

3. It has been reported that the Cleveland police authority intends to purchase a large computer system which could be connected to the Police National Computer, giving access to the records of a large number of people and car registrations.
   (a) (i) State two disadvantages to the police authority of installing the computer system.
       (ii) For what other reason are individual members of the public likely to object?
   (b) What type of backing store would be used if it is required to obtain details of any car owner within 30 seconds?
   (c) Carefully describe, including the names of any computer peripherals, how the system would be used if a police officer on patrol came across a suspect vehicle.
   (d) The Cleveland police authority intends to purchase two identical computers. Suggest a reason for this.
   (e) Name one additional task for which the computer could be used.
   (f) List two steps which could be taken to ensure that only authorised people have access to the computer.
   (g) What could be done to make sure that the information held about individuals on the computer is correct?
   (h) Give two reasons for supporting the use of computer systems similar to the one described above.

   (YHREB 1983)

4. How might a team of detectives use computers to help them solve a major crime?

5. Computers are used in hospitals in a variety of different ways; ward meals ordering and control, assisting scientific investigation in a pathology laboratory, monitoring patients in intensive care units, patient records and appointments.

   (*a*) (i) State one application that uses batch processing.

   (ii) State one application that uses a real time system.

   (*b*) For *each* of your stated applications in part (*a*):

   (i) Explain how the data is captured.

   (ii) Describe the output and its format.

   (iii) Describe the items of hardware.

   (iv) Explain the choice of backing store.

   (v) Explain why the processing method was chosen for this application.

   (vi) Give one advantage for the patient which the computerised system may have over the previous manual one.   (AEB 1984)

6. A hospital is to use its own computer to maintain and process a file of medical data. The file will contain one record for each patient. Doctors and nurses must be able to obtain medical data from this file when they are in the wards.

   (*a*) What is a record and a file?

   (*b*) (i) Suggest a suitable backing store to hold this medical file and give an explanation for your choice.

   (ii) Name a suitable device that doctors could use to get data from the file. Why is it a disadvantage to use only a patient's name to search for his medical record?

   (*c*) Explain one benefit and one disadvantage of computerising medical records. Give examples.   (SEREB)

7. A city's health authority decides upon an immunisation campaign that will involve every child in its area. Each child is to be vaccinated against six possible illnesses; three of these illnesses require three injections, two require two injections and one requires one injection. Every child's parents will need reminding when to take their child to the doctor, for some of the injections need to be applied at certain ages and separated from others by a certain length of time.

   (*a*) What would be the advantages of using computers for this application?

   (*b*) What information should the health authority's system hold on each child? Design an appropriate record format.

   (*c*) Describe the computer system the authority might use for this application, illustrating your answer with a systems flowchart.

22 Changing Society

A TECHNOLOGICAL REVOLUTION?

Technology is advancing so rapidly and changing so many aspects of our lives that many people talk of a 'revolution', as important to us in the 20th century as the Industrial Revolution was in the 18th and 19th centuries.

A Backward Glance

What *was* revolutionary about that period which began, in England, over 200 years ago? The country underwent the most astonishing and profound upheaval: a largely primitive, poor, farming society was transformed into the first ever industrial one. Industrialisation involved the application of new technology to manufacturing processes, enabling many goods to be made more cheaply and efficiently—and leading to the invention of many more. The nation's wealth was greatly increased, and the economy was vastly more productive.

By our standards, conditions for the working poor were still appalling in the first half of the 19th century. But by the 1850s the economy was supporting, i.e. feeding, clothing, housing and employing, a much larger population than before. No *pre*-industrial society has ever sustained such dramatic population growth without suffering terrible famine, disease or both. The Industrial Revolution 'delivered the goods' to meet the needs of the time.

? **Q 22.1** *(a) What do you know of the Industrial Revolution? When and where did it start? What were its consequences for Britain and the world?*

(b) Find out who or what were:

> *(i) James Hargreaves*   *(ii) Spinning Jenny*
> *(iii) Joseph-Marie Jacquard*   *(iv) Luddites.*

(c) Do you think the changes taking place today are or will be as important?

THE INFORMATION REVOLUTION

We are witnessing the coming together, or *convergence*, of several technologies, namely computing, microelectronics and communications; it is becoming impossible to separate them. Take, for example, a typical microcomputer. It is obviously a computing device which could not sit on a desk top without the miniaturisation afforded by microelectronics. It uses communications technology to link with other machines, whether in the same building or thousands of miles away.

This combined power of *information technology* is causing chain reactions of innovation and enterprise in many fields, both traditional and new. For a good example of this 'technology breeding' process we need look no further than our living rooms. The 'old' technology of television has been invigorated by video recording to the benefit of viewers and producers alike. Laser disks are already common in hi-fi systems and arcade games, and they are spreading rapidly through the training and computer industries. Satellite TV (relatively new to Europe) has for years been beaming education programmes to millions of people in developing countries. Other powerful tools such as viewdata and teleconferencing have resulted from marrying information technology with the humble TV screen.

A Quiet Invasion

As we have seen, few organisations now exist without harnessing new technology in some form. It is also steadily invading our homes, meeting very little resistance on the way. There are two major reasons for this.

Firstly, as we remarked at the beginning of this book, we do not always notice the technology; it has slipped unobtrusively into our lives. People just do not think about microprocessors or computers when cruising along the motorway, or doing the shopping, or switching on the washing machine.

Secondly, it is, quite simply, *useful*. It is useful to have a telephone that remembers the numbers of your closest friends, to have a tumble drier that senses when clothes are dry, to be able to alter a report without typing it all over again, to drive a car which tunes itself every second and which will automatically prevent a skid. These are not mere gadgets; they save time, money and even lives.

 Q 22.2 *How is information technology affecting your life?*

HOW WORK IS CHANGING

The Information Worker

More and more people in industrialised countries work with information: managers, administrators, secretaries, clerks, librarians, reporters, journalists, authors, workers in television, radio, post and telecommunications, teachers, lecturers, scientists, mathematicians, doctors, lawyers, bankers, accountants, sales and marketing people—the list is almost endless. All these people are involved in creating, storing, analysing, manipulating, retrieving or sending information.

As we have seen, just about all of them use computers in their work. While these 'information workers' continue to increase in number, manual workers become fewer and fewer. Producing goods continues to be vitally important but modern farms and factories can produce a greater output with a fraction of yesterday's workforce.

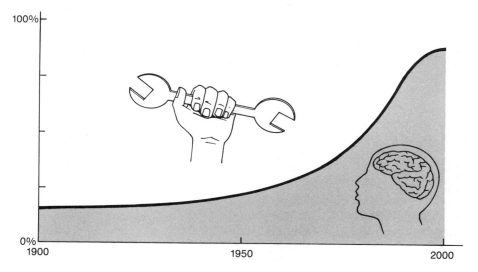

Fig. 22.1 By the year 2000 manual workers will be greatly outnumbered by information workers

Information has always been one of the keys to prosperity; only now is its real value beginning to be recognised. It is information, or know-how if you prefer, which turns a pile of iron ore into a steel girder. It is information, gleaned from years of education, research, experiment, computer modelling, and trial and error, which enables a genetic engineer to gain a five-fold increase in the yield from a grain of wheat. It is information which turns wind or waves or sunshine into power.

NEW JOBS FOR OLD?

While it is true that computers have destroyed a number of jobs, many completely new ones have been created. Any large company has a *data processing* (DP) *department* which may employ hundreds of people.

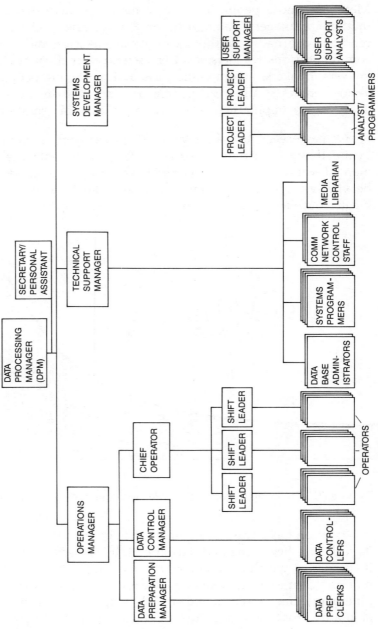

Fig. 22.2 The data processing department of a large company

Organisation of a DP Department

There are many ways of organising such a department; the structure we have shown is fairly typical. The *data processing manager* (DPM) is responsible for all the company's computing activity; a DPM may have two or three senior managers reporting to him or her.

Computer Operations

The *operations manager* takes care of the day-to-day running of the main computer facilities and systems and will oversee the work of a large proportion of the data processing employees, including the following:

Data controllers receive and check data from user departments, ensuring for example that all source documents are received on time, and that nothing is missing as the batches of forms are passed on to the *data preparation* staff. These people (sometimes called *keypunch operators*) key in the data which is stored on disk or tape (even punched cards are still used) prior to processing, so naturally they require excellent keyboard skills. The demand for data preparation staff is diminishing as more users key in their own data.

A large installation will normally keep its mainframes processing round the clock, so the *computer operators* who actually run the machines normally work shifts. Each shift has a *shift leader* in charge of a number of operators.

Large computers, as we have seen, often run a number of applications simultaneously and may have hundreds of users on-line via remote terminals at any time. Anybody concerned with computer operations— controlling input, output, batch processing and telecommunications links—requires considerable skill, technical knowledge and the ability to work well under pressure.

Technical Specialists

There may also be several specialist groups working for a *technical support manager*. Some of these are described below:

Systems programmers have to get the best possible performance from the available software and hardware. To this end they instal and maintain the systems software, especially operating systems, checking and ensuring that all programs (including applications software) remain compatible with each other.

Most large installations involve telecommunications. A network of users at remote locations may have access to the mainframe, while many companies have several computer sites which need to exchange data rapidly. *Communications* and *network control* staff are employed to look after the special software and hardware needed.

A DP department uses hundreds, even thousands of disks and tapes. Misplacing just one of them could be disastrous, so a *media librarian* organises and controls their storage and issue. This individual will be heavily involved in maintaining security and back-up procedures.

There may also be one or more *database administrators*, in organisations which use database management systems. They look after DBMS software and control the methods by which the database itself is accessed.

Systems Development

The *systems development manager* is responsible for building new applications systems for user departments as well as maintaining existing systems. Sometimes this maintenance of old systems takes up the lion's share of the time.

Working for the systems development manager may be several *project leaders* each in charge of a team of *analyst/programmers*. Project leaders may tackle a single development project or may have to manage the development of several systems in parallel.

The roles of *systems analysts* and *programmers* were examined in Chapter 9. Some companies still have separate teams of analysts and programmers, but many prefer to combine the functions; most of their development staff are analyst/programmers. They need a wide range of skills: dealing with people, interviewing, analytical skills, writing and presentation skills, design skills, logical ability, attention to detail etc. No wonder they are in short supply and rather well paid.

User Support Centres

A company's major 'bread-and-butter' systems (accounting, payroll, stock control etc.) are still developed and maintained by its DP department. But now that many managers have powerful microcomputers on their desks, they are handling more and more information, and even creating systems, by themselves.

As they are not 'computer people', users often need help with technical problems. *User support centres* provide a pool of computer expertise on which users can draw. User support staff must combine ample technical knowledge with interpersonal skills, as well as understanding the user's own work and particular problems.

Computer Bureaux

This support need not always come from within the organisation. Independent *computer service bureaux,* which were introduced on page 153, employ support staff to help other companies make effective use of their systems.

Other Computer-Related Jobs

Many other jobs have been created by the rise of the computer. For example:

- Computer manufacturing
- Peripheral manufacturing
- Sales and customer support
- Engineering and maintenance
- Software and systems houses
- Computer consultancies
- Training companies

plus a substantial number of self-employed contract staff. Overall, millions of new jobs have been created in the industrialised countries.

Q22.3 *(a) Have you thought about a job in computing?*

What aspect of the computer industry most attracts you?

(b) If you do not want to work in the computer industry directly, what do you want to do? How do you think that job will have been affected by computers?

(c) Can you think of any jobs which might be completely unaffected by new technology?

UNEMPLOYMENT

On the other hand, a great many jobs have been destroyed by computers and automation. Huge numbers of clerical workers have been directly replaced by office systems (although many have of course been retrained to use computers). This major shift is more or less complete, but hidden job losses continue; the office worker can be so much more *productive* with automated systems that there may be no need to replace people who leave or to hire extra staff to cope with growing workloads.

The decline in manufacturing employment has been accelerated by new technology. Unskilled and semiskilled jobs are being replaced by improved materials handling and automated assembly. Designers, buyers, draughtsmen, engineers and others are still in demand, but they too are much more productive with automated tools. This obviously affects employment. Even jobs as skilled as welding, paint spraying and component inspection are increasingly carried out by robots (see Chapter 20).

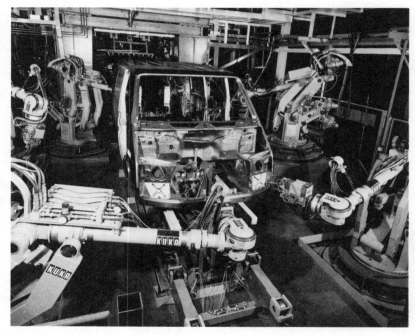

Fig. 22.3   Robots working on a Ford Transit body

It is extremely difficult to *quantify* the job gains and losses caused by new technology because so many other factors affect the numbers of employed and unemployed, for example:

● Annual growth of the total workforce
● Foreign competition
● Levels of taxation, especially employment taxes
● Government spending and borrowing
● Economic cycles: booms and recessions

Threat or Opportunity?

Despite this complexity, the authors believe that the long-term effect of the whole-hearted application of information technology will be a substantial increase in unemployment.

If this belief is correct, the dangers are obvious. Society could easily split into 'two nations'. Those in work, more than comfortably off, would become ever more productive with technological aids and new skills. Those out of work, surviving 'on the dole' or on other welfare payments, would be less and less able to change their circumstances as their knowledge and skills became increasingly irrelevant.

This is a daunting problem, faced not just by the UK but by all the industrialised countries. Readers should be well aware of the distress suffered, especially by the long-term unemployed. It would be foolish to present simplistic solutions. Yet the problem could, with imagination and effort, be turned into an unprecedented opportunity, if only we could challenge some deep-rooted assumptions.

Some Assumptions

The first assumption we can challenge is our attitude to work itself. It is regarded as normal, proper and desirable to work full-time from leaving school until at least the age of 60. Other activities such as spending time with families and friends, entertainment, artistic and sporting interests, voluntary work, travel, reading or education are all crammed into 'spare time'. This might have been necessary when labour-intensive industries, whether agricultural or industrial, were in their heyday, but is it appropriate now?

Q 22.4 *'Full-time' work now means about seven and a half hours per day. How long was the working day in (a) 1800 (b) 1900? How long do you think it will be in the year 2000?*

Another assumption we challenge is the prejudice against those we have called the information workers. There is a feeling that abstract stuff like knowledge cannot generate *real* wealth, like producing cars or cattle. But it is precisely because of the information worker that *production* work continues to become more efficient. It should surely be regarded as a healthy trend if a smaller proportion of a workforce can physically produce the goods which a whole country needs. Or do we always want large numbers of people working long hours in noisy and dangerous environments like mines and factories?

There is also a general belief that education is a once-and-for-all business completed at some age between 16 and 21 in time for working life to begin. A *continuous* life-long education process is needed to maximise the opportunities which technology provides. People will need to be continually updating their skills and to be prepared to retrain for new or different jobs in the course of their lives. All employees of a successful South Korean company, for example, benefit from a wide-ranging education programme, including a daily English lesson.

Q 22.5 *(a) Your teacher probably did* not *study computing at school. Ask him or her how and when they learned about computers.*

(b) Find out from other adults you know how their working lives have been affected by computers, and what retraining, if any, they have received.

NEW WAYS OF WORKING

New ways of organising work are emerging. The new computer skills have become *almost* as important as the 'three Rs' (Reading, wRiting and aRithmetic').

Q 22.6 *Do you think being able to use a computer is more important than, say, letter-writing or mental arithmetic skills? Why?*

As manufacturing has given way to service industries, so part-time work and self-employment have expanded enormously (more than one worker in ten is now self-employed). Many organisations have adopted flexible working hours while others have reduced the working week. The retirement age is slowly creeping down. The UK has dabbled at job-sharing schemes; other countries have gone much further.

More radical change is beginning. Telecommunications and portable computers are starting to reduce the number of time- and money-wasting commuter journeys. Not everyone could work this way, but some are very effective at home, armed with a telephone, a computer and clearly agreed work objectives. They may go to the office once a week for meetings and social contact with colleagues. Such *homeworking* is proving popular for both employees and the organisations that have introduced it. It enables work to be fitted into people's lives, rather than to dominate them.

Several computer services companies are using homeworking to harness the talent of women with young families who need (or prefer) to be at home.

Thriving in a Competitive World

The changes outlined above are surely for the better; they encourage a flexible productive approach to work which can only help us to survive and prosper against tough competition from all over the world. Industrialised countries especially must go for maximum productivity gains and exploit every advantage new technology has to offer.

Economies all over the world have survived the displacement of agricultural labour by manufacturing labour. There were of course casualties, whose livelihoods were swept away by the tide of change. But most people eventually prospered because productivity was so much increased.

Similarly, the rise of information and service industries, displacing much manual labour, is nothing to fear, as long as people are equipped to cope. Young people, fortunate enough to learn about computers at school, will *not* be the helpless victims of change. The casualties this time will be those who (through stubbornness, age or ignorance) cannot or will not adapt.

Managing Change

The plight of the casualties of change cannot be ignored. If the social tensions caused by new technology are to be minimised, then ways must be found to share work and its rewards among the whole population without undermining the ambition of the most gifted and industrious. Innovations such as job-sharing, homeworking, job rotation, community work programmes, extended study or research leave should be welcomed and extended. The increased leisure time which many will enjoy should be seen as a gift, not a curse.

Q 22.7 *Are the rewards of work purely financial?*

Q 22.8 *Could the UK insulate itself from the economic and social problems associated with new technology by not using it?*

THE QUALITY OF LIFE

Buying Time

If computer systems are well designed, well chosen and well implemented, they can save their users a considerable amount of time.

A travelling salesman can now reorder goods for customers while sitting in his car. After visiting each customer he stores the orders in his portable microcomputer; to dispatch them, he dials up the depot on his carphone, plugs in the acoustic coupler and his day's orders are submitted in 30 seconds—without paperwork.

An office worker no longer has to wait until late in the evening to get a message to a colleague in Los Angeles. She types it herself (no need to bother her secretary) and sends it immediately to an 'electronic mailbox' which her colleague examines on screen when *his* office opens.

In the home, too, technology is starting to give people back some time. If your neighbours ask you round at a time when you wanted to watch your favourite programme, you can touch a few buttons and the microprocessor in your video recorder solves the problem by 'shifting' the programme time.

'Armchair shopping' is on the increase. People are buying (and selling) more and more goods and services by telephone and through viewdata services such as Prestel. Householders in some trial *teleshopping* schemes have stopped trekking round the shops for the weekly groceries. They now order them remotely for the supermarket staff to pack. Bicycle deliveries could make a comeback.

Leisure Activities

These developments are giving people more leisure time, some of which is filled by such 'new technology' developments as home computers, video and satellite TV. The continuing pressure for places at the Open University gives some idea of the huge demand for education, not just as a pre-work interlude—students from 18 to 80 are gaining degrees. Local classes in arts, crafts, sport and computing are often oversubscribed.

Diversity in Products and Services

Computers and automation, it is widely feared, must result in total standardisation of products and services. The reverse is often the case. As more creative and 'intelligent' software is developed, systems are starting to achieve the best of both worlds: the economies of automation and mass production plus a degree of 'custom design'.

For example, individual designs of furniture, kitchens, and even clothes, can be offered with the aid of automated design tools. The prices are far lower than custom design ever was before. Even traditional craft skills are being revived with boosts from technological innovations.

Many small publishing houses have sprung up, often catering for minority interests. New production methods have drastically lowered the costs of producing magazines and books, so that these ventures can be viable with much smaller sales.

HELPING TO MEET SPECIAL NEEDS

Surprisingly, one in every six people has a 'special need', as a result of physical or mental handicap, or other deprivation. Their needs are really no different from anyone else's: all of us need to be able to communicate with each other, to learn, to work, to play and to be independent. The difference is that some people are cut off from some or all of these activities, which the rest of us take for granted. For them, special provision must be made to restore opportunities, so that their needs can be met.

The most severely handicapped may need constant support and care by experts in specialist institutions, but most people with 'special needs' nowadays live and work in ordinary homes and communities and are educated in ordinary schools. Computers are helping to make this possible, although much more could be done if the money was available.

Communication

Computers can assist in overcoming obstacles to speech, hearing, reading and writing.

Among the aids to speech are systems that produce a unique pattern on screen for each different sound uttered. Speech therapists can use this visual feedback to help people to pronounce words correctly.

Voice recognition systems can 'translate' speech which is unintelligible to us—either into commands to control machinery (e.g. a motorised wheelchair) or, via a *speech synthesiser*, into recognisable speech.

Q 22.9 *Why do deaf people often have speech difficulties?*

Microtechnology has allowed some exciting developments in hearing aids. A special processor linked to an electrode placed in the inner ear can help some partially deaf people distinguish between, say, 'b' and 'p', or 'd' and 't'.

Many people with impaired hearing benefit from Ceefax or Oracle subtitles on television programmes.

Deaf people can even make telephone calls by having them switched through a special exchange run by the Royal National Institute for the Deaf. The hearing person speaks to someone at the exchange, who types the words into the exchange computer, which transmits them to the deaf person's special terminal. The terminal then displays the words on their screen.

There are even devices to help blind people to read. To operate one kind of reading machine, the blind person places a printed book face down on a glass plate (rather like a photocopier). An OCR scanner then reads the text and the machine's *speech synthesis* circuits speak the words aloud. As yet these machines are extremely expensive, but cheaper models are sure to follow.

Q 22.10 *(a) What are the technical terms for the input and output methods used by this machine?*

(b) What problems are associated with each method?

(c) Describe the computer processing which you think would be necessary between input and output.

Word processors can help people with learning difficulties and those with limited hand-coordination to learn to write.

Two young, physically handicapped boys were asked by their teacher to co-operate to write an adventure story. Their microcomputer was able to accept input from either of them. One boy could spell words in full on the ordinary keyboard, while the other (unable to hit individual keys) selected words from his more limited vocabulary by pressing them on his 'concept' keyboard—a touch-pad similar to that in Figure 5.6. They worked together superbly. Their finished story was imaginative and detailed: there was not the slightest clue that its authors were handicapped.

Q 22.11 *How could electronic mail systems be used by*
(a) deaf, and
(b) blind people? What equipment would be needed by each?

Independence

Even those with severe disabilities can be remarkably independent if they can at least operate a single switch. This can be worked in many ways: by sucking and blowing, by making noises, body or head movements; even eye movements can be effective.

With only side-to-side head movement, a paralysed user can work a remarkable variety of devices (Figure 22.4).

Fig. 22.4 This user, Patrick Bates, is severely paralysed and cannot speak, but with two head-switches and an Elfin keyboard emulator he can operate a microcomputer and many other devices. He took his computer studies examination with the aid of this equipment, which was paid for by finance raised by the pupils of Llantwit Major comprehensive school

Voice *input* to control cars may soon be viable for disabled drivers, while voice *output* is already helping blind pedestrians to use public transport more easily with such innovations as 'talking timetables'.

Computers have also enabled disabled people to carry out ordinary jobs, sometimes with adapted equipment, perhaps with individually designed controls or switches.

Leisure

Computers have opened up enormous possibilities for the use of leisure time. Computer games, placed against the machine or against another player (perhaps over the telephone) can be especially valuable for disabled players: they are enjoyable and can often improve skills such as hand-eye co-ordination, manipulation and reasoning power. At least one computer game was actually designed by doctors to treat a form of defective vision in children.

Other programs are enabling music, art and design to be enjoyed by disabled people for the first time.

Fig. 22.5 The talking bus stop can provide the blind with timetable information on approaching buses

Q 22.12 *Explain how computers have helped (or might help in the near future)*

(a) someone suffering from a significant speech defect

(b) a blind person

(c) a deaf person

(d) someone paralysed from the waist down

(e) a limbless person

(f) an educationally subnormal person

(g) an educationally gifted person.

FREEDOM AND CONTROL

So far we have portrayed information as a beneficial and powerful tool, enhancing people's lives by generating wealth, free time and diversity. But the power conferred by possessing information will not necessarily be used wisely or fairly.

Personal Data

An inevitable consequence of computerised billing and payroll systems, mail order, teleshopping, home banking etc. is that a growing number of companies have computer records about individual people. In itself that is not harmful, but it may be if the data is used for *other purposes*. You or your family may have been plagued by 'junk mail', i.e. 'personalised' letters inviting you to buy goods or subscribe to magazines or take out insurance. This results from the sale of your name and address by one company (with whom you have had dealings) to another.

Privacy

That may be no worse than irritating until you consider that some of the data might be confidential. A mail-order company might keep in its computer files, for example, a record of how promptly you paid your bills. If that data were sold to a finance company, who refused you a loan as a result, you would have good cause to feel aggrieved, especially if the data was inaccurate. You might have *always* paid promptly, but if the mail order company had themselves lost one of your cheques, you might be branded as a 'bad risk'.

Government and Other Public Organisations

If private companies store a worrying volume of personal data, the amount in official hands is truly alarming. Figure 22.6 shows *some* of the public bodies who store computer records about individuals. Many of these computer systems are linked by manual or automatic means.

There is clearly cause for concern when *thousands* of officials may have the right of access to private and personal details. The likelihood of error increases with the volume of data stored, while the likelihood of abuse increases with the ease with which telecommunications can whisk data from one system to another, between companies or government departments.

The Data Protection Act

A bill was passed in Parliament in 1985 to address some of these concerns. The law now requires any organisation in the UK storing personal data (i.e. data about living individuals) which could be processed by computer, to register under the *Data Protection Act*.

The organisation must say what data it is storing, for what purpose, and where the data was obtained. If the data is subsequently used for another purpose, the organisation is breaking the law, unless it notifies the Registrar of the new use.

Any person about whom data is stored has the right of access to the data, so that he or she can check it and correct it if inaccurate.

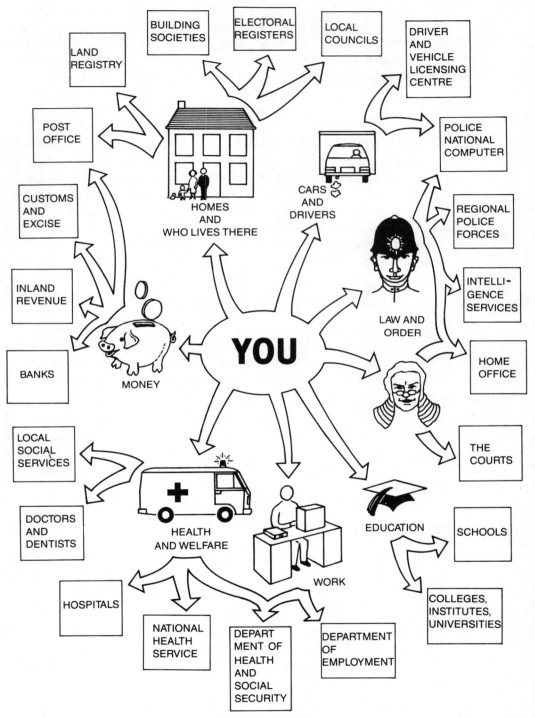

Fig. 22.6   Some of the many governmental and official holders of information about people in the UK

Q 22.13 *(a) Do you think the Act is likely to reduce misuse of personal data? Why?*

(b) Manual *records are exempt from the Act.*

Do you think they should be included? Explain.

Crime and Policing

While many people feel uneasy about personal data being stored in unknown computers, they are generally far more alarmed at the rising tide of crime in recent years. The police are increasingly turning, as we saw in Chapter 21, to new technology in order to catch terrorists and other criminals.

If police forces store data which is inaccurate, or based on hearsay, wrongful arrests and other miscarriages of justice could result. On the other hand, it can be argued, the more comprehensive and detailed their personal databases, the more success they will achieve in the fight against crime. It is not easy to judge when 'too much information' is being gathered or stored in order to defeat criminals and preserve law and order.

Q 22.14 *Police systems are partially exempt from the Data Protection Act. Do you think this is justified?*

Q 22.15 *(a) If football hooliganism could be reduced by compelling fans to wear identity badges which could be checked by computer, should this be done?*

(b) If terrorist movements could be restricted (with possible saving of innocent lives) by compelling all citizens to carry machine-readable identity documents, would this be justified?

The Dilemma of the Information Age

The demands of individuals for freedom and privacy sometimes conflict with the demands of society for order. The powerful tools of information technology can help to spread the news, views and ideas which are associated with a free society. On the other hand, they can be used as the tools of monitor and control. Any democratic society must strive to find a balance acceptable to the majority of its citizens.

How that balance is struck will depend on the readers of this book.

JARGON 22

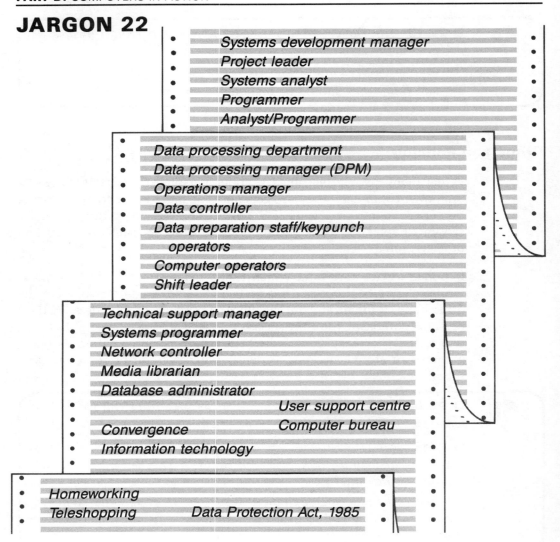

Systems development manager
Project leader
Systems analyst
Programmer
Analyst/Programmer

Data processing department
Data processing manager (DPM)
Operations manager
Data controller
Data preparation staff/keypunch
    operators
Computer operators
Shift leader

Technical support manager
Systems programmer
Network controller
Media librarian
Database administrator
                                    User support centre
Convergence   Computer bureau
Information technology

Homeworking
Teleshopping   Data Protection Act, 1985

EXERCISES 22

1. Either (a) 'The large scale use of computers represents another industrial revolution.' Discuss.

   Or (b) What do you think will be the economic and social effects of the latest advances in micro-electronics?

   (O & C)

2. (a) Describe how future developments in microtechnology may affect our shopping, banking and use of money.

(*b*) Describe two common household items where a microprocessor might be found in the latest models. What is the reason for the use of the microprocessor and what advantages does it bring?

(SUJB)

3. The 'Computer Revolution' is frequently referred to as a problem which is imminent. Well-meaning and authoritative articles are to be found warning of the social problems that will occur. The reality is that the revolution has been successful. Many businesses could not now function without their computers. Microcomputer automation in engineering has been found to be essential if firms are to remain competitive. Computer based information systems are available on everybody's television.

(*a*) Name a business that is committed to the extent suggested in the above passage and explain why it would not be able to manage without computers.

(*b*) Give an example of microcomputer automation and explain why it is more efficient than the system it replaced.

(*c*) Name a system that provides computer based information via home television. State two advantages for people obtaining information in this way.

(ALSEB)

4. (*a*) Draw a diagram to show how the jobs of the following are linked.

    (i) The data processing manager.

    (ii) The programmers.

    (iii) The computer operators.

    (iv) The data preparation staff.

(*b*) Describe briefly two tasks of any two of the above people.

(*c*) List two other jobs you would expect to find at a large computer installation.

(EMREB)

5. Alongside each of the following job titles, describe a particular task which the person will perform as part of his or her duties.

(*a*) Systems analyst

(*b*) Computer programmer

(*c*) Operations manager

(*d*) Data preparation clerk

(*e*) Computer operator

(*f*) Computer engineer

(YHREB 1985)

6. The increasing use of computers has led to loss of jobs in some industries. However, other opportunities have been created.

   With this in mind,

   (a) Give an example of an occupation which is at risk and explain why.

   (b) Give an example of a specific occupation in which opportunities for employment have been improved, giving a reason for your choice.

   (c) Why will it be important for workers in the future to adapt to technological advances?

   (SEREB)

7. 'Microelectronics has led to the increased use of devices which can retrieve data from files held in a central computer, perhaps hundreds of miles away. The implications of having rapid access to large files of personal data have gone unnoticed by many people, and yet we should all be concerned at this potential invasion of our privacy.'

   (a) Describe two computer systems which allow remote access to files of personal data.

   (b) The writer above is concerned about the implications of having rapid access to personal data. Explain why the writer might be concerned.

   (c) What would you say if you had to try to persuade the writer that there was no need to be concerned?

   (CU)

8. Read the article below before answering the questions.

   > Files of personal information have always been held by many people such as government departments, doctors, hospitals, finance companies and the police. Some people believe that storing this information in a computer data bank increases the threat to an individual's privacy.

   (a) Suggest one reason why using a *computer* to store and retrieve personal information is considered a threat to privacy. Give an example to support your reason.

   (b) One view is that people should have right of access to data about themselves.

(i) Give one reason to support this view.

(ii) Explain in two or three sentences how a person might obtain this information.

(c) In certain cases it might be better if a person was prevented from seeing some information held in his record.
Give an example of such information and an explanation for your choice.

(d) Suggest **one** way in which personal data held on a computer could be misused and give an example, to illustrate your answer.

Explain briefly how this misuse could be prevented.

(SEREB)

9. (a) Describe two methods of ensuring that information coded into a computerised data bank is only available to those people authorised to use it.

(b) Outline one method of ensuring that the data held in a data bank is relevant and correct.

(c) When data is processed by computer it can become corrupted as a result of hardware and software faults. Describe one method of guarding against the loss of data as a result of such corruption.

(d) Recently a Data Privacy bill became law. Amongst its provisions it insists that the users of computerised personal data banks are 'registered' users and that individuals are generally able to receive a copy of the data relating to themselves which is held in a computerised data bank.

(i) Why was this legislation introduced?

(ii) What is the purpose of two sections of the legislation mentioned above?

(iii) Some computerised personal data banks are excluded from the legislation. Give one example of such a data bank and explain why it is excluded.

(JMB)

10. Briefly outline four items of concern to the general public with regard to computer usage on a national scale.

(EMREB)

11. 'Computers are a part of everyday life'.

(a) Describe how an average family might use a computer in everyday life.

(b) What computer developments do you think may be made that will benefit 'everyday life' during the next five years?

(c) List three devices that might be found in the home and that use some form of computer.

(EMREB)

12. Computers have become cheaper and more widely used in recent years. Discuss the effect that this has had on the lives of ordinary people and the implications of this development for society at large. Your answer should cover privacy, employment, leisure and other relevant aspects.

(CU)

23 Data Representation

REPRESENTING CHARACTERS

Three Types of Data Character

Any computer must be able to represent three types of character

- alphanumeric characters
- graphic characters
- control characters.

The letters of the alphabet, A–Z, and the numericals, 0–9, form the set of *alphanumeric characters*. Often the other printed symbols and punctuation marks that are found on an ordinary typewriter are also included.

A	B	C	D	E	F	G	H	I	J	K	L	M
a	b	c	d	e	f	g	h	i	j	k	l	m

N	O	P	Q	R	S	T	U	V	W	X	Y	Z
n	o	p	q	r	s	t	u	v	w	x	y	z

1	2	3	4	5	6	7	8	9	Ø	+	–	*	/	=
<	>	!	"	£	$	%	&	'	(	)	=	,	.	?

Alphanumeric characters including punctuation marks, can be found on an ordinary typewriter.

Graphics characters vary from one computer to another. They would not be found on an ordinary typewriter.

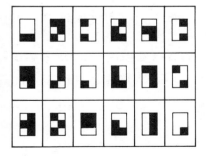

Fig. 23.1 Alphanumeric and graphics characters

Many microcomputers also allow the programmer to build up pictures and shapes using a special set of shapes or *graphics characters*. These tend to differ from computer to computer and would certainly not be found on an ordinary typewriter.

Control characters cannot be printed out or made to appear on the screen, but when typed on the computer cause something to happen. For example, pushing the RETURN key to indicate a new line sends a particular code to the computer's central processor causing it to respond appropriately. Control codes are also necessary to govern the operation of the peripherals; for example on BBC computers 'Control B' activates the printer and 'Control C' turns it off.

Q 23.1 *What graphics characters are possible on the computer you use? How do you access them?*

Q 23.2 *Make a list of as many control characters as you know. Some, like RETURN, should be obvious; they are part of the computer keyboard and you use them frequently.*

Bits and Bytes

All modern computers are *digital*, representing data of any kind as a series of 1s and 0s (*binary digits* or *bits*) grouped together into codes. As there must be a unique code for every character the computer uses, these codes need to be fairly lengthy. A *byte* is the smallest number of bits required to encode a single character and is usually eight bits long.

Binary codes tend to be very long. This is an obvious disadvantage, making it difficult for a human programmer to instruct the computer at its own level. Hence the need for 'high-level' languages with associated interpreters and compilers (see Chapter 3) that translate them into the binary codes that the computer uses. However, the ease of representing numbers as a series of electrical pulses that are either 'on' or 'off' and the relative simplicity of designing electrical circuits that perform arithmetic and logic operations in binary numbers are indispensible advantages.

What Determines Byte Length?

It should be clear that one bit offers two possible unique codes: 0 or 1.

2 bits offer 4 possible codes: 00 10
                                01 11

3 bits offer 8 possible codes: 000 100   001 110
                                001 101   011 111

4 bits offer 16 possible codes:

0000	1000	0100	1100
0001	1001	0101	1101
0010	1010	0110	1110
0011	1011	0111	1111

5 bits offer 32 possible codes . . . and so on; the number of possible binary codes doubles with each extra bit.

Mathematically a byte that is n bits long allows 2^n possible different codes.

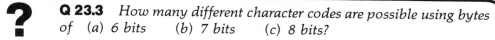

Q 23.3 *How many different character codes are possible using bytes of (a) 6 bits (b) 7 bits (c) 8 bits?*

Q 23.4 *How many different alphanumeric characters are there if only the capital letters A–Z and the digits 0–9 are included?*

Would it be possible to assign a unique code to all members of this set using a 5 bit byte? Why not?

Why do you think some early digital computers used a 6 bit byte?

Q 23.5 *How many different alphanumeric characters are there if we not only include the numerals 0–9 and the capital letters A–Z, but also the lower-case letters a–z, a basic set of 16 important punctuation marks, perhaps space ! ? , . ; : " £ $ % & ' ( ) @ and seven essential mathematical symbols, namely*

$$* \quad + \quad - \quad / \quad = \quad < \quad >$$

Would it be possible to assign a unique code to all the members of this set using a 6 bit byte? Why not?

What is the smallest number of bits that could be used?

THE ASCII CHARACTER CODE

Almost all modern computers now use an 8 bit byte. This allows room for a 7 digit character code, with the 8th bit reserved for a parity check (see Chapter 11).

The *American Standard Code for Information Interchange,* usually referred to as ASCII (pronounced 'ass-key'), is easily the most important of such codes and is used in most computers. It uses a 7 bit code (so there is room for 128 different character codes) and an even parity check in the 8th bit (on the left-hand side).

The 7 bit code for 'J' is | 1 | 0 | 0 | 1 | 0 | 1 | 0 |

As this number contains an odd number of 1s, the 8th bit, on the left-hand side, is set to '1' so ensuring that the byte contains an even number of 1s.

The complete code for 'J' is thus | 1 | 1 | 0 | 0 | 1 | 0 | 1 | 0 |

The 7 bit code for 'S' is | 1 | 0 | 1 | 0 | 0 | 1 | 1 |

This already contains an even number of 1s and so the left-hand bit is '0'. The complete code for 'S' is thus | 0 | 1 | 0 | 1 | 0 | 0 | 1 | 1 |

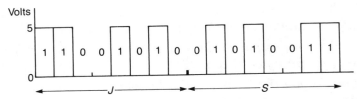

Fig. 23.2 The character string 'JS' would be represented by a stream of 5V electronic pulses as shown

Q 23.6 *Copy and complete the 8 bit ASCII codes (i.e. including the even parity bit) for the letters F and t.*

F: | 1 | 0 | 0 | 0 | 1 | 1 | 0 | t: | 1 | 1 | 1 | 0 | 1 | 0 | 0 |

What is the purpose of the parity bits?

Draw the electronic pulse stream for the character string Ft.

WORDS

Many mainframes and some microcomputers have processors powerful enough to handle more than one byte at a time. Such machines string several bytes together to form a *word*, which can then be treated as a single unit by the central processor.

The *word length* is usually measured in bits (rather than bytes) and varies considerably from one machine to another. Thus, for example, 16 bit microcomputers are common, and there are 32 and 64 bit machines capable of processing 2, 4 and 8 characters at once, respectively.

Note that a byte is almost universally regarded as eight bits but the length of a word varies from machine to machine.

The microprocessors inside the smaller home computers use 8 bit words; those inside most desk top business computers use 16 bit words and the most powerful mainframes use 64 bit words.

REPRESENTING WHOLE NUMBERS

Whole numbers, or *integers*, may well be treated as text characters using the appropriate ASCII code.

For example, if you instruct the computer as follows:

PRINT "3 + 1 equals" 3 + 1

The computer will display on the screen

3 + 1 equals 4

i.e. the computer does not work out the sum 3 + 1 when it first appears because the quotation marks indicate a *string* of text characters so the computer simply prints 3 + 1 and equals as instructed.

But 3 + 1 appears a second time and *outside* the quotation marks. This time the computer treats them as numbers and *does* calculate the results which it displays on the screen as the number 4.

Obviously the computer must be told when a particular code is to represent a character and when it represents a number.

To understand how numbers are represented inside the computer we need to understand the number base the computer uses, i.e. base two or *binary*.

BINARY CODE

As we have ten fingers, we naturally work in base ten—or *denary* arithmetic.

The number 8381 means 'eight thousand three hundred and eighty-one'. Each digit has *place value*; i.e. it is recognised to mean thousands or hundreds or tens or units according to its place in the number. Thus in the number 8381 the digit 8 means eight thousands in the first position and eight tens in the third.

Place value (base 10)	Thousands 1000	Hundreds 100	Tens 10	Units 1
Digit	8	3	8	1

In base two, or *binary*, the place value of each digit doubles for each place we move left. For example the number 1 1 0 0 1 written in base two represents a value considerably less than 'eleven thousand and one'. It is usually written 11001_2 and means:

Place value (base 2)	Sixteens 16	Eights 8	Fours 4	Twos 2	Units 1
Digit	1	1	0	0	1

The base ten value of the number is

$$(1 \times 16) + (1 \times 8) + (0 \times 4) + (0 \times 2) + (1 \times 1) = 25$$

In base two the number 10_2 means two (i.e. one lot of twos and no units); it follows that we shall never need the digit 2 while working in binary. Nor shall we need 3 (represented by 11_2) or anything other than 0 and 1, which, of course, is the reason binary is a suitable base for electronic computers.

Converting From Binary to Base Ten

An eight digit binary number can be converted to base ten by simply considering the place value of each of the bits. The right-hand bit has the lowest place value (i.e. 1) and is called the *least significant bit*. The left-hand bit has the highest place value (i.e. 128) and is called the *most significant bit*. For example, consider $1011 0111_2$:

	most significant bit ↓						least significant bit ↓
Place value (base 2)	128	64	32	16	8	4	2	1
Digit	1	0	1	1	0	1	1	1

The base ten value of $1011 0111_2$ is

$$
\begin{aligned}
128 \times 1 &= 128 \\
64 \times 0 &= 0 \\
32 \times 1 &= 32 \\
16 \times 1 &= 16 \\
8 \times 0 &= 0 \\
4 \times 1 &= 4 \\
2 \times 1 &= 2 \\
1 \times 1 &= 1 \\
\hline
\text{Total} &= 183
\end{aligned}
$$

Q 23.7 *What is the base ten value of the following 8 bit binary numbers?*

(a) | 0 | 0 | 0 | 0 | 1 | 0 | 1 | 1 |

(b) | 0 | 0 | 0 | 1 | 1 | 1 | 0 | 1 |

(c) | 0 | 0 | 1 | 0 | 1 | 0 | 0 | 1 |

(d) | 1 | 1 | 1 | 0 | 1 | 1 | 1 | 0 |

(e) | 1 | 1 | 0 | 0 | 0 | 1 | 1 | 1 |

(f) | 0 | 1 | 1 | 1 | 0 | 1 | 0 | 1 |

(g) | 1 | 0 | 1 | 0 | 0 | 1 | 1 | 0 |

(h) | 1 | 1 | 1 | 1 | 1 | 1 | 1 | 1 |

Converting From Base Ten to Binary

A number in base ten could be converted to binary by repeatedly subtracting, if possible, successive powers of 2 as shown.

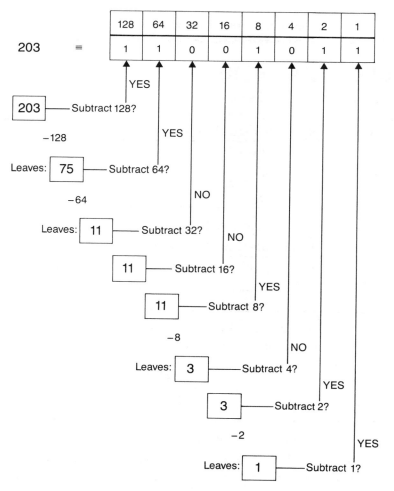

Fig. 23.3   Converting to binary

Q 23.8 *Convert the following numbers into binary and show how they might be represented in an 8 bit byte:*

(*a*) 9   (*b*) 13   (*c*) 28   (*d*) 89

(*e*) 105   (*f*) 155   (*g*) 232   (*h*) 255

Q 23.9 *Convert 387 into binary; why can this number not be simply represented by an 8 bit byte?*

Numbers larger than 255 can be represented as binary numbers if two (or more) bytes are linked together. What is the largest number that can be represented using two bytes (i.e. 16 bits)?

Q 23.10 *Write a program that will*

(*a*) *Take eight inputs of 1 or 0 and convert the 8 bit binary number into base ten*

(*b*) *(Much harder) Convert a base ten number into binary.*

HEXADECIMAL (HEX)

In base 16, or hexadecimal, the place value of each digit increases 16 times with each move from right to left. Thus the number 36_{16} represents considerably more than thirty-six.

Place value (base 16)	16×16 = 256	Sixteens 16	Units 1
Digit	—	3	6

$$36_{16} = (3 \times 16) + (6 \times 1) = 54$$

The binary equivalent of this number is

Place value (base 2)	128	64	32	16	8	4	2	1
Digit	0	0	1	1	0	1	1	0

If we divide this byte into two blocks of four bits, we find the first block, 0 0 1 1, is the binary code for 3 and the second block, 0 1 1 0, is the binary code for 6.

$$3\,6_{16} = \overbrace{0011}^{3}\ \overbrace{0110}^{6}{}_2$$

It is always possible to write an 8 bit binary code as a two digit hex number in this way, for each 4 bit section necessarily codes one of 16 numbers (from 0 to 15 inclusive).

But (there is always a snag) in base 16 the number 10 would mean sixteen (*not* ten), 11_{16} means seventeen (*not* eleven), 12_{16} means eighteen (*not* twelve), 13_{16} means nineteen etc.

It follows that the number we ordinarily know as ten *cannot* be written as '10' if we are writing numbers in hexadecimal. '10_{16}' means sixteen.

So we use A for ten instead. For eleven we use B, for twelve we use C, for thirteen D, for fourteen E and for fifteen F. In hex, sixteen is written 10 and so we need no further special characters.

Note that just as in base *two* we use *two* digits (0 and 1) and in base *ten* we use *ten* digits (0, 1, 2, 3, . . ., 9) so in base *sixteen* we use *sixteen* different digits: 0, 1, 2, 3, 4, 5, 6, 7, 8, 9, A, B, C, D, E, F.

The set of hexadecimal digits with their binary and denary equivalents is shown in the following table:

Hex (base 16)	Binary (base 2)	Denary (base 10)
0	0000	0
1	0001	1
2	0010	2
3	0011	3
4	0100	4
5	0101	5
6	0110	6
7	0111	7
8	1000	8
9	1001	9
A	1010	10
B	1011	11
C	1100	12
D	1101	13
E	1110	14
F	1111	15

Hexadecimal and Binary

Hexadecimal can be of considerable help when converting from binary to base ten. For example, consider the number 0 1 0 0 1 1 1 0 in binary.

In hex this would be   4   E

which, converted into denary, gives: $(4 \times 16) + 14 = 78$

We can convert hex numbers into binary with equal simplicity. For example, all we need to do in order to convert 7D from hex to binary is replace 7 with its four digit binary equivalent, i.e. 0 1 1 1, and D with its four digit binary equivalent, i.e. 7D $\equiv$ 0 1 1 1 1 1 0 1

The denary value is $(7 \times 16) + 13 = 125$

With a little practice you will find hex *does* save you time and you may well use it to help you convert from denary to binary. For example, you could convert 147 to binary as follows: 147 ÷ 16 = 9 remainder 3.

Hence 147 ≡ 93 (hex) ≡ 1001 0011 (base 2)

?   **Q 23.11**   *Convert the following hexadecimal numbers to denary:*
(*a*) 14   (*b*) 51   (*c*) 1A   (*d*) 2C   (*e*) C9   (*f*) BE

Q 23.12   *Convert the following binary numbers into hexadecimal and hence to denary:*
(*a*) 0001 0001   (*b*) 0011 0110
(*c*) 1000 1100   (*d*) 0100 0110
(*e*) 1001 1011   (*f*) 1010 1111

Q 23.13   *Convert these denary numbers into hexadecimal and hence to an 8 bit binary code:*
(*a*) 22   (*b*) 38   (*c*) 51   (*d*) 62   (*e*) 172   (*f*) 249

NEGATIVE NUMBERS

Sign and Magnitude Method

A simple way of representing negatives is to use the most significant bit (i.e. the bit on the left-hand side) as a *sign bit*. Usually 0 indicates a positive number and 1 indicates a negative number. The remaining seven bits are then used for the *magnitude* of the number. In this way, it is possible to code numbers from −127 to +127.

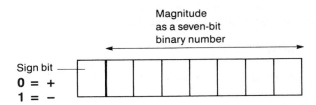

Fig. 23.4   Sign and magnitude

The main advantage of the sign and magnitude form is its simplicity. It is the method that human beings use; −3, for example, denotes a negative number with a sign (−) and a magnitude of 3.

However, there are two important drawbacks. Firstly there are two possible codes for zero: a 'positive' and a 'negative' zero. The computer may arrive at either in the course of a calculation and so extra programming is necessary to deal with both possible codes.

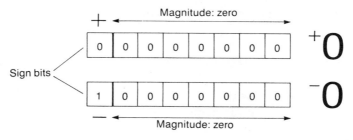

Fig. 23.5 'Positive' and 'negative' zero

Secondly numbers represented this way do not follow the normal rules of binary arithmetic. Again extensive extra programming is necessary to deal with even simple calculations.

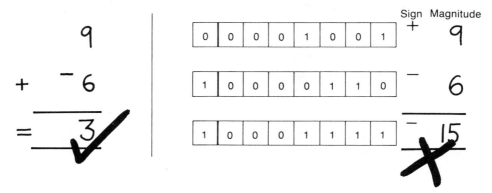

Fig. 23.6 Positive and negative numbers written in sign-and-magnitude form do not follow the ordinary rules of binary arithmetic

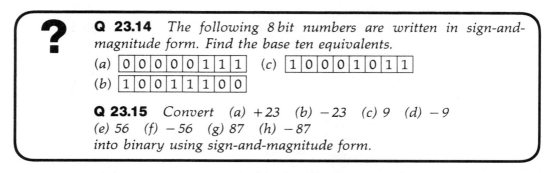

Q 23.14 *The following 8 bit numbers are written in sign-and-magnitude form. Find the base ten equivalents.*
(a) 0 0 0 0 0 1 1 1   (c) 1 0 0 0 1 0 1 1
(b) 1 0 0 1 1 1 0 0

Q 23.15 *Convert* (a) +23 (b) −23 (c) 9 (d) −9
(e) 56 (f) −56 (g) 87 (h) −87
into binary using sign-and-magnitude form.

One's and Two's Complements

The *one's complement* of a binary number is formed simply by changing all the 1s of the original to 0s and all the 0s to 1s.

For example, the one's complement of 0 1 0 1 0 0 1 1
                                                              is   1 0 1 0 1 1 0 0

Adding the original number to its one's complement gives all 1s:

Original number	0 1 0 1 0 0 1 1
+ one's complement	1 0 1 0 1 1 0 0
gives all ones	1 1 1 1 1 1 1 1

Adding one to the one's complement gives the *two's complement*:

Original number	0 1 0 1 0 0 1 1
One's complement:	1 0 1 0 1 1 0 0
Add one to get the two's complement:	1 0 1 0 1 1 0 1

Adding the two's complement and the original number together gives a power of two—hence the name:

Original number	0 1 0 1 0 0 1 1
+ two's complement	+1 0 1 0 1 1 0 1
gives a power of two	1 0 0 0 0 0 0 0

(Remember that powers of two are represented in binary by 10, 100, 1000, 10000 … etc.)

Representing Negatives in Two's Complement Form

In two's complement form, all positive numbers begin with 0 and are stored in conventional binary; all negatives begin with 1 and are stored as two's complements.

Thus the number 0 1 0 1 1 1 0 1 is positive (since it begins with 0) and can be converted to base ten in the ordinary way; it represents +93.

Its two's complement, 1 0 1 0 0 0 1 1, represents −93. The 1 at the beginning indicates a negative number that should *not* be converted directly to base ten.

Finding the Value of a Negative Number

We can find the value of a negative number by treating the most significant bit as negative, i.e. -128 and the others as positive as shown in Figure 23.7

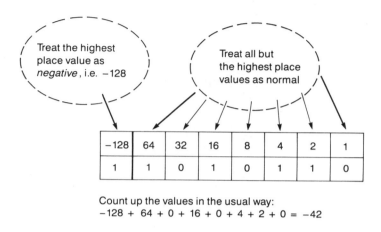

Count up the values in the usual way:
$-128 + 64 + 0 + 16 + 0 + 4 + 2 + 0 = -42$

Fig. 23.7   Converting a two's complement to base ten

Advantages of Two's Complements

The most important advantage of the two's complement is that negative numbers stored this way can be used in ordinary binary calculations with one additional rule:

Lose the extra (ninth) digit that arises on the left-hand side in the course of the calculation

$$
\begin{array}{rcl}
-7 \text{ is represented by:} & 1111\,1001 & -7 \\
\text{and } -5 \text{ is represented by:} & 1111\,1011 & +\;-5 \\
\end{array}
$$

Adding these gives -12 (in two's complement form) after the extra bit is lost: $1\,1111\,0100$ -12

↑
lose the extra bit

Moreover, there is only one code for zero (the two's complement of zero is zero).

Subtraction by Complementary Addition

A third advantage is that a computer can subtract two binary numbers by adding the two's complement, a process known as *complementary addition*.

For example, to calculate $99 - 42$, first convert to binary:

$$99 = 0110\ 0011_2$$
$$42 = 0010\ 1010_2$$

Find -42 as the two's complement of $+42$, i.e. $1101\ 0110$ (as above), and add 99 and -42:

$$
\begin{array}{rl}
99 & 0110\ 0011 \\
-\ 42 & +\ 1101\ 0110 \\
\hline
57 & \mathit{1}001\ 1001
\end{array}
$$

↑
lose the
extra bit

'Losing' the leftmost bit gives the answer $0011\ 1001$ (in binary) equivalent to 57 (which checks with the base ten calculation).

Q 23.16 *Find the 8 bit two's complements of*

(a) | 0 | 0 | 0 | 0 | 0 | 0 | 1 | 1 | (b) | 0 | 0 | 0 | 0 | 1 | 0 | 1 | 1 |

(c) | 0 | 0 | 0 | 0 | 1 | 1 | 0 | 0 | (d) | 0 | 0 | 0 | 0 | 1 | 1 | 1 | 1 |

Q 23.17 *Show that the two's complement of*

| 0 | 0 | 0 | 0 | 1 | 0 | 0 | 1 | *is* | 1 | 1 | 1 | 1 | 0 | 1 | 1 | 1 |

and that the two's complement of

| 1 | 1 | 1 | 1 | 0 | 1 | 1 | 1 | *is* | 0 | 0 | 0 | 0 | 1 | 0 | 0 | 1 |

Q 23.18 *Find the (8 bit) two's complement of the following:*

(a) | 0 | 1 | 1 | 0 | 0 | 0 | 1 | 1 | (b) | 0 | 0 | 1 | 1 | 0 | 0 | 1 | 1 | (c) | 0 | 1 | 1 | 1 | 1 | 1 | 1 | 1 |

Q 23.19 *What negative numbers are represented by these 8 bit two's complements?*

(a) | 1 | 0 | 1 | 0 | 0 | 0 | 0 | 1 | (b) | 1 | 0 | 1 | 1 | 1 | 0 | 1 | 0 | (c) | 1 | 1 | 0 | 1 | 1 | 0 | 1 | 0 |

Q 23.20 *Show that the two's complement of zero is zero.*

Q 23.21   *What base ten values do these 8 bit bytes represent (assume two's complements represent negatives)?*

(a) | 0 | 1 | 1 | 1 | 1 | 1 | 1 | 1 |

(b) | 1 | 1 | 1 | 1 | 1 | 1 | 1 | 1 |

(c) | 0 | 0 | 0 | 0 | 0 | 0 | 0 | 0 |

(d) | 1 | 0 | 0 | 0 | 0 | 0 | 0 | 0 |

What is the range of values that can be represented by an 8 bit byte using two's complement notation?

Q 23.22   *What base ten number is represented in binary by*

| 0 | 0 | 0 | 0 | 1 | 0 | 0 | 1 | ?

Find the two's complement. What number does this represent?

Q 23.23   *Copy and complete the following complementary addition:*

$$13 \qquad \boxed{0\,|\,0\,|\,0\,|\,0\,|\,1\,|\,1\,|\,0\,|\,1}$$
$$-\ \underline{\ 9} \quad + \boxed{\,.\,|\,.\,|\,.\,|\,.\,|\,.\,|\,.\,|\,.\,|\,.\,}$$
$$\underline{\ 4} \quad \not{1} \boxed{\,.\,|\,.\,|\,.\,|\,.\,|\,.\,|\,.\,|\,.\,|\,.\,}$$

↑
lose the
extra bit

Q 23.24   *Use complementary addition to subtract the following 8 bit binary numbers. Convert the numbers to base ten to check your results.*

(a) 0011 0110   (b) 0110 1101   (c) 0101 0101
   − 0010 1101   − 0101 0110   − 0010 1011
   ───────────   ───────────   ───────────

   ───────────   ───────────   ───────────

(d) 0110 1101   (e) 0011 1010   (f) 1010 0001
   − 0110 0110   − 0101 1111   − 0001 0001
   ───────────   ───────────   ───────────

   ───────────   ───────────   ───────────

REAL NUMBERS

So far, we have considered only *integers*, i.e. whole numbers. Computers must also be able to calculate with *real numbers*, i.e. those that can also take fractional values.

In base ten we indicate the beginning of the fractional part of a real number with a decimal point. Thus

$$1.75 = 1 \text{ unit} + 7 \text{ tenths} + 5 \text{ hundredths}$$

In base two, we can do much the same, but rather than tenths, hundredths thousandths ..., the fractions are halves, quarters, eighths .... For example

$1.11 = 1$ unit $+ 1$ half $+ 1$ quarter $= 1\frac{3}{4}$

Fixed Point Representation

The simplest way of representing fractions is to fix the point in a preset position. In a byte of eight bits this might be, say, two bits from the right-hand end so that the two least significant bits represent fractions (i.e. halves and quarters).

Thus $1\frac{3}{4} = 1.11$ would be represented by

0	0	0	0	0	1	1	1

Similarly $5\frac{1}{2} = 101.1$ would be represented by

0	0	0	1	0	1	1	0

Note that the point is not actually stored in the byte and so it does not use up valuable storage space. Instead, it is assumed to be placed at a predetermined position between two bits.

Q 23.25 *Given that the point is fixed two bits from the right-hand end of the byte, work out the decimal value of the following:*

(a)
0	0	0	0	1	1	0	1

(b)
0	1	1	0	1	0	1	0

(c)
0	1	1	1	1	1	1	1

What is the largest number that can be represented this way?

Q 23.26 *Represent these numbers in an 8 bit byte fixing the point two bits from the right-hand end*

(a) $1\frac{1}{4}$ (b) $2\frac{1}{2}$ (c) $9\frac{1}{4}$ (d) $12\frac{3}{4}$ (e) $\frac{1}{4}$

Floating Point Representation

Fixed point representation may be used when all the data is of much the same size, but for most other applications an alternative, *floating point representation*, is preferred since a much greater range of numbers can be represented.

For example, the base ten number 2 000 000 000 could be written as 2×10^9 in standard form. Moving the point in this way means the point can no longer be said to be 'fixed'; instead it is said to 'float'.

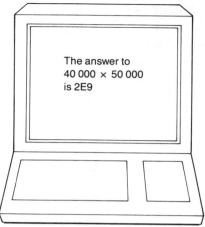

Fig. 23.8 The computer will use standard form to display large numbers. Here 2E9 means 2×10^9. (E stands for 'exponent'). Your calculator probably does something similar.

Computers use *normalised form*, similar to standard form used in science and mathematics, but in which the numbers always start with the decimal point, followed by the number.

Thus 2 000 000 000 would be written as $.2 \times 10^{10}$.

Numbers written in normalised form have two parts: a fractional value (called the *mantissa*) and a power of ten (called the *exponent*).

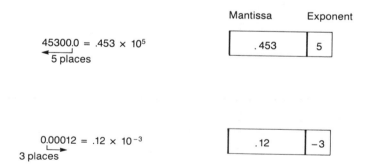

Fig. 23.9 Mantissa and exponent

Q 23.27 *Write the following numbers in normalised form:*
(a) 134.2   (b) 43.24   (c) 16.302   (d) 221.03
(e) 0.012   (f) 0.000 21   (g) 0.00031   (h) 0.000 023

Binary Floating Point Numbers

The principles of floating point representation in binary are identical, except that all numbers—including the exponent—are represented in base two. Furthermore, the exponent represents a power of two and not ten. For example, given the following byte structure:

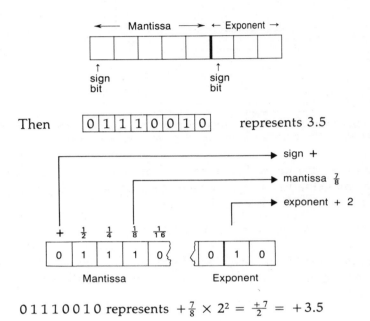

Then ⟨ 0 1 1 1 0 0 1 0 ⟩ represents 3.5

$$0\,1\,1\,1\,0\,0\,1\,0 \text{ represents } +\tfrac{7}{8} \times 2^2 = \tfrac{+7}{2} = +3.5$$

Q 23.28 *Find the base ten value represented by the following given that the bytes have structure identical to the example given above:*

(a) 0 1 0 1 1 0 0 1   (b) 0 1 0 1 0 0 1 0

(c) 0 1 1 0 1 0 1 1   (d) 1 1 0 1 1 0 1 0

(e) 0 1 1 1 0 1 1 1   (f) 0 1 1 0 0 1 0 1

In practice, because binary numbers are so long, many microcomputers use two bytes to represent an integer and four for a real number (treating the two parts of the real number—the mantissa and the exponent—as separate numbers).

ACCURACY OF COMPUTER ARITHMETIC

Overflow

We have seen that the integers that might be represented in binary using an 8 bit byte and two's complements range from -128 to $+127$. What happens if the answer to a calculation goes outside of this range?

The simple answer is that the extra, most significant, bits on the left are lost, just as in complementary addition. Some computers will deliver the wrong answers when this happens; others are better designed so that the program stops and the *overflow* (so called because the extra bits 'spill out' of the space provided for them) is drawn to the user's attention.

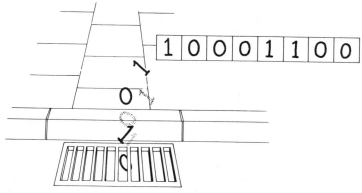

Fig. 23.10 Overflow happens to the most significant bits and so it causes serious errors in the computer's arithmetic

Truncation

Real numbers come in two parts: the mantissa and the exponent. Overflow occurs when the possible range for the positive exponent is exceeded.

If the mantissa is longer than the space allowed for it, the computer will ignore the extra digits on the right, i.e. the least significant bits. This *truncation* or 'chopping off' of the number means that there is some loss of precision, i.e. there is some *truncation error*, but the arithmetic will still be correct to a given number of decimal places.

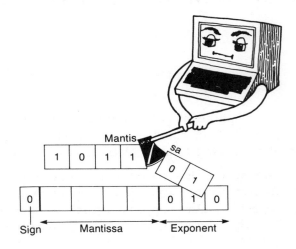

Fig. 23.11 An overlong mantissa is chopped off (or *truncated*) at the least significant end so that it fits the space allowed for it. Some precision is lost but the computer's answers will still be about right.

Inexact Binary Representation

Another separate limitation upon binary arithmetic is the impossibility of representing many fractions exactly using base 2.

For example it is not possible to represent 0.4 exactly using binary (although it is a very simple fraction in base 10). With eight bits, the nearest to it is 0 . 0 1 0 0 1 1 0 which works out to be 51/128 or 0.3984375.

If we use a 16 bit or 32 bit word to represent this fraction we can get very much closer to but *never exactly* equal to 0.4.

It follows that even the arithmetic of a supercomputer can only be correct to a finite number of decimal places.

> **?**
>
> **Q 23.29** *A certain computer uses* two *bytes to represent an integer in sign and magnitude form (the most significant bit acting as a sign bit). What is the magnitude of the largest positive integer that can be represented without overflow?*
>
> *What would be the largest positive integer if two's complements were used to represent negatives instead?*
>
> **Q 23.30** *Try to find the nearest 8 bit binary fraction to*
> (a) 0.1   (b) 0.3   (c) 0.7.

JARGON 23

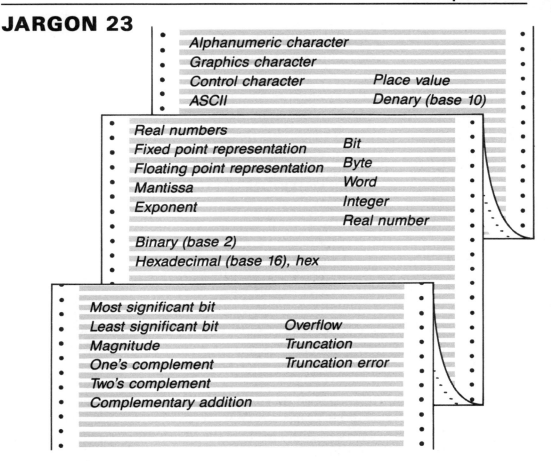

Alphanumeric character
Graphics character
Control character   Place value
ASCII   Denary (base 10)

Real numbers
Fixed point representation   Bit
Floating point representation Byte
Mantissa   Word
Exponent   Integer
                               Real number

Binary (base 2)
Hexadecimal (base 16), hex

Most significant bit
Least significant bit   Overflow
Magnitude   Truncation
One's complement   Truncation error
Two's complement
Complementary addition

EXERCISES 23

1. (*a*) What is a binary number?

   (*b*) Why do computers use binary numbers?

   (*c*) Why is it that people do not need to know about binary numbers to use computers?

   (SEREB)

2. Which of the following statements about the byte | 1 | 0 | 1 | 0 | 1 | 1 | 1 | 0 | could be true?

   A   It has exactly five bits

   B   Its hexadecimal equivalent is AE

   C   It represents an even number

   D   Its binary value is equivalent to 172

   E   It has odd parity

3. A character set uses a seven bit binary code. An additional bit may be added to give the codes an odd parity.

   (a) How many different characters can be represented by a seven bit code?

   (b) What is the meaning of 'odd parity'?

   (c) What purpose is served by the parity bit and when is it used?

   (SEREB)

4. Below is the listing of some of the ASCII codes as used in a computer.

CHARACTER	DECIMAL	HEXADECIMAL
<	60	3C
=	61	3D
>	62	3E
?	63	3F
'	64	40
A	65	41
B	66	42

   (a) Why do characters need to be represented by numeric codes?

   (b) Why do we use both Decimal and Hexadecimal codes?

   (AEB 1982)

5. In the ASCII code used on computers A has a code value of 65, B has a code value of 66, C has a code value of 67 and so on. The codes for lower-case letters are 32 higher than the code for upper-case; for example 'a' has a code value of 97.

   (a) What is the code value for T?

   (b) What letter has the code value 110?

   (c) Why are two code values needed for each letter?

   (d) Decode the following message:

   67,   79,   77,   80,   73,   76,   69,   82

   (e) There are 128 possible values in the ASCII code. Apart from letters and figures give two other types of character which can be represented.

   (EAEB)

6. (a) Convert the binary number given into its two's complement showing your working:

   01100101

   (b) For what purpose is two's complement used by computers?

   (SEREB)

7. A computer uses an 8 bit location to hold positive or negative integers.
   (a) What is a bit?
   (b) Name one other type of data which may be held in this location.
   (c) (i) Show how the number − 9 would be represented in this location using 2's complement. You must show your working.
       (ii) Draw a ring round the bit in your answer that represents the sign of the number.
   (d) Write down the sign bit for a positive number.

   (SEREB)

8. (a) A number can be represented in denary (base ten) or in binary. Copy and complete the following table showing equivalent numbers:

Binary	Denary (base ten)
10011	19
....	35
110110	....
....	46
111001	....

   (b) When a number is written in binary how can you tell if it represents an even number?
   (c) Work out the answers to the following binary calculations:

   (i) 11101
        1101   +
        ‾‾‾‾‾‾‾

        ‾‾‾‾‾‾‾

   (ii) 101101
        10100   −
        ‾‾‾‾‾‾‾

        ‾‾‾‾‾‾‾

   (d) (i) What is − 13 (base ten) in 5 bit two's complement form?
       (ii) What denary number is represented by this two's complement number?

       1 1 1 1 1

   (EREB)

9. (a) Convert the decimal integer 23 to binary. Show all your working.
   (b) A computer uses 8 bit storage cells like the one shown here.

   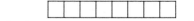

   (i) Show how the binary representation of the decimal integer 23 would be stored in these cells.
   (ii) Show how its 1s complement would be stored.
   (iii) Show how its 2s complement would be stored.
   (c) Why are complements of numbers used in computers?

(d) Noticing that $46 = 23 \times 2$, use your answer to (b)(i) to write down the binary representation of the decimal integer 46 in an 8 bit cell.

(e)   (i) Show how to do the sum $46 - 23$ in 8 bit cells using 2s complement binary arithmetic.

     (ii) Why could you not do the same sum in 6 bit cells?

(WMEB)

10. A computer uses an 8 bit byte in which negative numbers are held in two's complement form. Convert the denary numbers $+35$ and -121 to binary and then add the two binary numbers together.

(YHREB 1983)

11. (a) With an example explain what are binary and hexadecimal numbers.

(b) Using a decimal number as an example, explain the meaning of these two terms

     Fixed-point notation,
     Floating-point notation.

(c) Give one benefit and one limitation of using floating point notation.

(AEB 1984)

24 The CPU

THE CPU

The CPU or *central processing unit* is the heart of the computer system. The CPU is responsible for all the computer's calculations, all the receiving, sorting and editing of data, the arrangement of the screen display, the control of the printer and disk drives etc.

Other parts of the computer system, whether input, output or storage devices, are known as *peripherals* (since they are connected to the outside—or 'periphery'—of the CPU) and are not responsible for the processing of data.

Although the CPUs of different computers operate quite differently from each other (and in ways that are extremely complex), the CPU of any computer consists of three basic components:

- the *control unit*
- the *main memory*
- the *arithmetic and logic unit* (ALU)

The Control Unit

The control unit co-ordinates all the operations of the computer including the peripherals.

The control unit must be able to decode and carry out instructions input by the programmer; it must also be able to output signals that trigger the peripheral devices and activate the memory and calculator circuits; it must also synchronise everything.

It must also be able to respond to signals it receives from input and output devices and modify the speed or path through the program as necessary.

For example printers generally work very much slower than the computer and so the CPU will interrupt or delay the running of a program in order to accommodate the printer.

Q 24.1 *Next time you print out a program listing, results or graphics note that the screen display is never more than a line or two ahead of the printer. Explain, in your own words, exactly what is happening.*

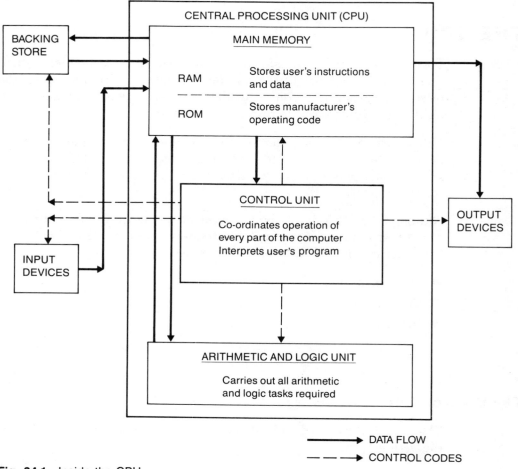

Fig. 24.1 Inside the CPU

The Main Memory

The main memory, also called *central memory, main store* or *immediate access store* (IAS), is that part of the CPU in which the current program instructions and data are held ready for immediate use as the program runs.

ROM and RAM

As we have seen, some of main memory is *read-only memory* (ROM). This is storage space not available to the user, for here the computer holds the operating instructions built in by the manufacturer (see Chapter 2). These instructions are permanent and cannot be erased. ROM is also *non-volatile*, i.e. its contents are not lost when the computer is switched off.

The user's program and data are stored in *random access memory* (RAM) either until new information is written over it or if the memory is volatile (which is usually the case) until the machine is switched off.

?   **Q 24.2**   *What forms of non-volatile RAM do you know?*

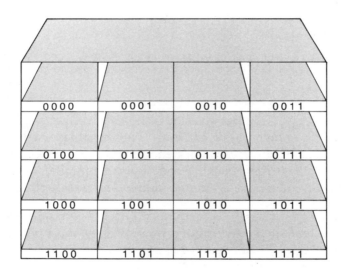

Fig. 24.2   Central memory can be thought of as a set of pigeonholes

Memory addressing

You might think of main memory as a set of pigeon holes. Each pigeon hole is known as a *memory location*, and is identified by an *address*.

The memory locations may contain any information relevant to the computer's operation: the manufacturer's software, the user's program instructions, character codes relevant to the screen display or text written by the user, values of variables input in the course of the program etc.

A good programmer using a high level language such as BASIC will identify the memory locations that he or she uses by labelling them with some meaningful variable names such as *total*.

Fig. 24.3 Each memory location must have its own unique address. If address codes are duplicated then the computer cannot tell to which location data should be 'posted' (or from which location to collect it)

However, the computer will identify each memory location by a binary number known as its *address*. (The variables used in the high level language program are allocated numerical addresses when the program is translated into machine code by the compiler or interpreter.) Each location must have a unique address and not duplicate another's code.

Since each memory location must have its own address, it follows that the extent of main memory is limited by the number of bits in the numerical address code. For example, a computer using a 16 bit address code can identify 2^{16} i.e. 64 K memory locations.

Extending a computer's memory beyond its address limit is possible but special, complex software is required.

The Arithmetic and Logic unit (ALU)

The arithmetic and logic unit (ALU) carries out all the arithmetical calculations that the computer requires (in binary of course). Its circuits also perform simple comparisons (i.e. is this number greater than, less than, or equal to that?) and logical operations (such as OR in the command: 'IF this is true OR that is true THEN do something').

The Accumulator

Both the ALU and the control unit include a small number of memory locations (known as *registers*). However, these are not regarded as part of the main memory for they are reserved solely for special purposes specific to ALU or control functions.

For example an important component of the ALU is the *accumulator*, a special register which stores temporarily the result from each individual step in a calculation.

When you use a calculator to solve a problem it effectively acts as your ALU, performing each calculation—adding, subtracting, multiplying and so on—according to your instructions one step at a time. It temporarily stores on its display (the equivalent of the accumulator) the data relevant to the next step of the calculation (which you input from the key pad) and each subtotal as it is reached.

Fig. 24.4 Your calculator acts as your ALU; it performs the necessary arithmetic and stores, temporarily, the subtotals arrived at in the course of the calculations

Simple Logic in the ALU

The internal workings of the ALU are extremely complicated.

Basic arithmetic (such as adding two binary digits together) and simple decision making or *logic* (such as deciding whether one thing OR another thing is true) can be carried out using two reasonable simple electrical circuits (called the OR gate and the AND gate) and a third (called the NOT gate) which changes 0s to 1s and 1s to 0s. By combining these gates together into increasingly elaborate *logic circuits*, unintelligent and unthinking electronic machines can be made to perform complicated arithmetic and to take involved logical decisions.

The AND Gate

A very basic operation in logic requires a decision to be made on whether or not two conditions A AND B are both true.

Anyone possessing an elementary knowledge of electrical circuits (namely that a circuit must be complete before current will flow) and able to wire together a few bits and pieces could build an electric circuit that simulates this decision:

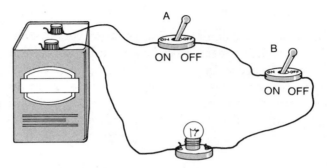

Fig. 24.5 Build a simple electrical circuit like this and the light will shine only if both switch A AND switch B are turned on

Current will only flow in this circuit (and so cause the light to shine) if both switches A AND B are on.

This electrical *switching circuit* is capable of a simple 'logical' operation, deciding whether both A AND B are 'true' (i.e. switched on).

The electronic equivalent is known as a *gate*, for there are no moving switches but, instead, minute transistors that can either block an electrical current (i.e. switch it off) or let it pass through.

The possible on/off (or true/false) combinations for A and B (the inputs to this gate) and A AND B (the output) can be shown diagramatically using binary digits 1 for 'on' and 0 for 'off'.

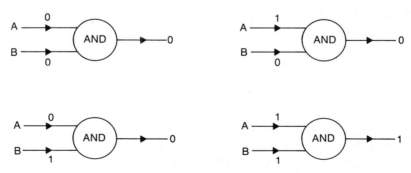

Fig. 24.6 AND gate

Often the possible combinations are summarised in a *truth table*:

| Inputs | | Output |
A	B	A AND B
0	0	0
0	1	0
1	0	0
1	1	1

Q 24.3 *A washing machine is microprocessor controlled. It will only start the wash cycle when the switch W is set to 'wash' AND its front door D is properly closed AND the hot water tap H is on.*

A simple logic circuit and part of a truth table illustrate the possible combinations:

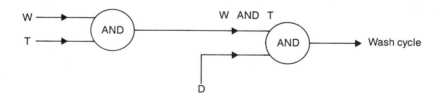

W	D	H	Wash cycle
0	0	1	0
0	1	1	0
1	1	1	1
1	0	.	.
1	.	.	.
.	.	.	.

Explain the first three completed lines. Has the wash cycle begun? If not, why not?

Copy and complete the table. (There are eight lines altogether.)

The OR Gate

A second basic operation in logic requires a decision to be made on whether at least one of two conditions A OR B are true.

Imagine (or build for yourself) a simple electrical circuit consisting of two switches A and B connected to a power source and light bulb as shown in Figure 24.7.

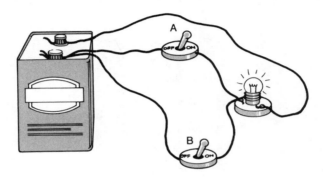

Fig. 24.7 Build a simple electrical circuit like this and the light will shine if either switch A OR switch B is turned on (or both)

Current will flow through the completed circuit causing the light to shine if either A or B (or both) is switched on.

The corresponding truth table is

Inputs		Output
A	B	A OR B
0	0	0
0	1	1
1	0	1
1	1	1

The NOT Gate

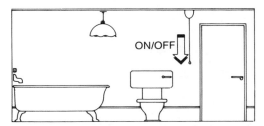

Fig. 24.8 A NOT switch: the string-pull switch in your bathroom at home is akin to a NOT gate: pulling the switch turns the light off if it is on and on if it is off

A third basic circuit is called a NOT gate. It will reverse the binary digit input i.e. turn a 0 to 1 and turn a 1 to 0.

Input A	Output NOT A
0	1
1	0

Building Up a Circuit: an XOR Gate

Suppose we wish to build up a circuit with the following truth table:

Inputs A	B	Output A XOR B
0	0	0
0	1	1
1	0	1
1	1	0

The circuit is to be completed (output 1) if just one of switches A or B is on. A OR B *but not both* is known as *exclusive* OR, often written XOR.

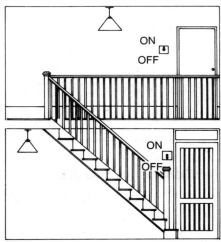

Fig. 24.9 Your hall and landing lights at home are probably controlled by 'two-way' switches that act together as an XOR switch. If either the switch in the hall downstairs or the switch on the landing is 'on' the light will shine. But if both are 'on' then the light goes off

This circuit is of considerable importance and is usually shown as a single gate.

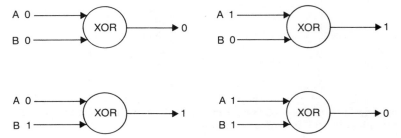

Fig. 24.10 XOR gate

In fact the XOR gate is built up from AND, OR, and NOT gates as shown in Figure 24.11.

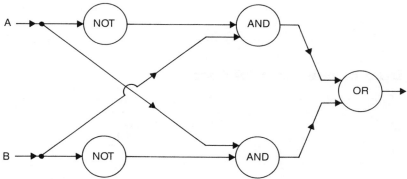

Fig. 24.11 An XOR logic circuit

Q 24.4 (a) Make a copy of Figure 24.11 and show what happens given 1 for input A and 1 for input B.

Show in red those wires that are conducting an electric pulse (so indicating the binary digit 1) and in blue those which are not (so indicating the binary digit 0).

Repeat the exercise for the three other possible input patterns:

(b) A = 1; B = 0
(c) A = 0; B = 1
(d) A = 0; B = 0

Arithmetic in the ALU

With OR, AND and NOT gates it is possible to build up the complex circuits of the ALU by which all the calculations are completed. However, the processes are complicated and beyond the scope of GCSE.

FOLLOWING INSTRUCTIONS

Storing the Program

When a program is input to the computer it is simply stored in main memory. The first instruction of any program is stored in one particular memory location and subsequent instructions are stored in consecutive locations, one after another in sequence. (So if the first instruction is stored in location 0000 the second will be stored in 0001, the third in 0010 and so on.)

Until the command RUN is given, nothing else happens.

Control Unit Registers

The control unit is responsible for reading the program statements in the proper sequence, decoding each instruction and translating it into action.

Inside the control unit there are two registers of particular importance.

(i) The *instruction register* which stores the current instruction, i.e. what the computer is doing at the moment.

(ii) The *program counter* (also known as the *sequence control register*) which stores the address of the next program instruction, i.e. where the computer can find out what it should do next.

Fig. 24.12 An instruction code comes in two parts: an operation code (e.g. 'add', 'move data to ALU' etc.) and a data address

Instructions are held in the instruction register in two parts. Firstly an operation code indicates what has to be done (perhaps, for example, a simple arithmetic operation such as adding or subtracting) and secondly an address where the necessary data can be found.

The control unit circuitry will decode each part of the instruction and signal appropriate control codes to the ALU and the central memory.

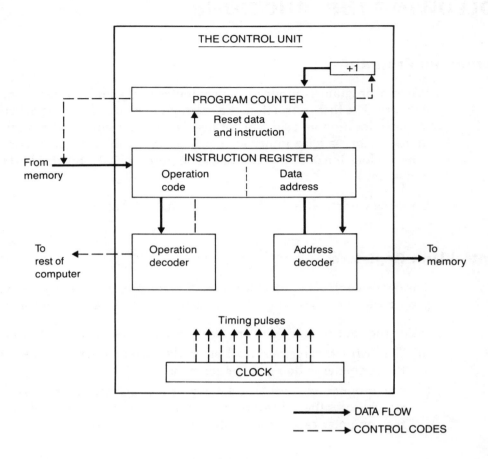

Fig. 24.13 Basic components of the control unit

The Fetch—Execute Cycle

When the program is running, the control unit will inspect the memory location (indicated by the program counter) that stores the next program statement and copy the contents into the instruction register; this is the *fetch* phase of the cycle. The program counter is automatically increased by one (so that the computer will know where the next instruction can be found) while the control unit carries out, i.e. *executes*, the instruction.

Sometimes, of course, this instruction will require the program to loop back to an earlier part of the program or jump to a subroutine; in this case the execution of that instruction resets the program counter to a completely new value.

> **Q 24.5** *How does the control unit know where to find the first program instruction?*
>
> **Q 24.6** *How does the control unit know where to find the next program instruction?*
>
> **Q 24.7** *What BASIC command words would cause the program counter to be reset to a completely new value (rather than be automatically increased by one)?*

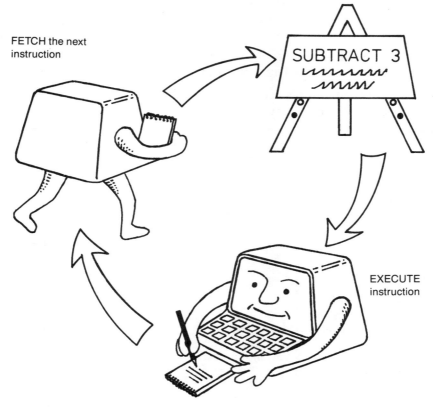

FETCH the next instruction

SUBTRACT 3

EXECUTE instruction

Fig. 24.14 The fetch–execute cycle

Once an instruction is finished with, the process is repeated: copy the next instruction from central memory and carry it out . . . copy the next instruction from memory and carry it out . . . copy the next instructon from memory and carry it out . . .

This *fetch–execute cycle* continues until either all the instructions that make up the program have been carried out or some *interrupt* (perhaps someone hits the ESCAPE key) occurs.

Suppose the next instruction in a program reads

LET score = points − penalties

This means that data stored in two separate locations (labelled 'points' and 'penalties') have to be found, one subtracted from the other and the result placed into a third location (to be labelled 'score').

STEP 1: The control unit copies the instruction into its instruction register.

STEP 2: The data held in the memory location labelled 'points' is copied from the central memory into the accumulator.

STEP 3: The data held in the memory location labelled 'penalties' is subtracted from the data held in the accumulator.

STEP 4: The result of the subtraction is copied from the accumulator to a third memory location labelled 'score'.

The control unit is actively involved at every stage, supervising both the ALU and the central memory (see Figure 24.15).

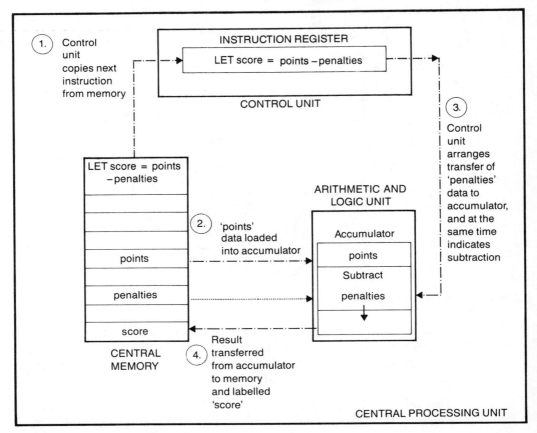

Fig. 24.15 Following an instruction

MACHINE CODE

In fact carrying out one instruction written in a high-level language such as BASIC is considerably more involved than this because the machine can only operate at a very simple level taking very small steps at a time and using codes written entirely in binary.

High-level languages are *human orientated* (i.e. they are designed to be relatively easy for people to use) and *problem orientated* (i.e. they are all designed for solving particular types of problem).

Low-level languages are *machine orientated* (i.e. they are designed for a particular machine and cannot be easily transferred to another).

Before a BASIC program (or one written in another high-level language) can be run by the control unit it needs to be translated from its original form, called the *source code*, by a *compiler* or *interpreter* into a form that the control unit can understand. It is this *object code*, i.e. the same program written in machine code, that the computer will follow in the step-by-step manner described above.

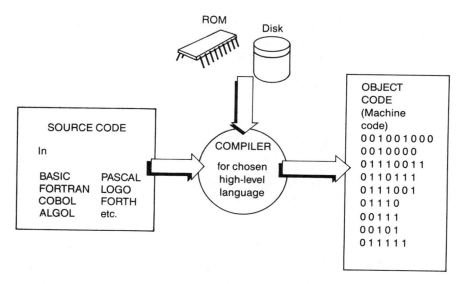

Fig. 24.16 Source code written in a high-level language is usually translated by a compiler into the computer's machine code (the object code). Each high-level language instruction is translated into several machine code instructions. The compiler program may be part of ROM or loaded from disk

Generally, a single instruction written in a high-level language will translate into many lines of machine code, for the machine must be guided through the instruction one tiny step at a time.

A Simple Machine Code.

Consider the following simple machine code consisting of nine simple operations:

01	Add to contents of accumulator
02	Subtract from contents of accumulator
03	Multiply contents of accumulator
04	Divide contents of accumulator
05	Load data from memory location into accumulator
06	Transfer data from accumulator into memory location
07	Input from keyboard to accumulator
08	Output contents of memory location (to screen)
00	End

The simple BASIC program:

```
10 INPUT points, penalties
20 LET score = points − penalties
30 PRINT score
40 END
```

would translate into the following nine lines of machine code program:

Operation code	Data address	Comment
07	—	Input 'points' data to accumulator
06	201	Transfer 'points' data from accumulator to memory location 201
07	—	Input 'penalties' data to accumulator
06	202	Transfer 'penalties' data from accumulator to memory location 202
05	202	Load contents of location 202 into accumulator
02	201	Subtract contents of location 201 from contents of accumulator
06	203	Transfer data (representing 'score') from accumulator into memory location 203
08	203	Output contents of location 203 on screen
00	—	End

Without line by line explanation the machine code program would look like this.

Clearly, machine code programs are not easy for human beings to follow!

07	—
06	201
07	—
06	202
05	202
02	201
06	203
08	203
00	—

Q 24.8 *What high-level languages have you heard of and/or used? What type of problems are they designed to solve?*

(Reread pages 44 to 51 if you cannot answer this question!)

Q 24.9 *The program shown is written in the same machine code as that shown on page 458. Copy out the program and explain what is happening at each step.*

```
07 —
06 101
07 —
03 101
06 102
08 102
00 —
```

In fact, working in machine code is considerably more difficult than this suggests. In the first place, we have used base ten codes. The computer uses binary, making our nine line program even more difficult to decipher:

```
0111 —
0110 11001001
0111 —
0110 11001010
0101 11001010
0010 11001001
0110 11001011
1000 11001011
0000 —
```

And secondly we have used a very restricted set of instructions. Some machine codes use as many as 200 or more different operation codes!

Q 24.10 *How many different operation codes are possible using a 4 bit code as above?*

Q 24.11 *How many different operation codes are possible using an 8 bit code?*

Advantages of Machine Code

Writing machine code directly into binary is an awkward and tedious task. Even experienced programmers need to keep looking up the numeric codes they are using for they are unlikely to remember many of the codes with any certainty. And working with long strings of 1s and 0s (or even the hexadecimal equivalents) is unlikely to be accurate.

Yet there are advantages to writing programs in machine code, rather than in a high-level language. Firstly, machine code programs run extremely rapidly; interpreting high-level language programs is very slow in comparison. Secondly, the machine code produced by a compiler from a high-level language source program takes up more memory space and runs more slowly than a machine code program written by an expert machine code programmer. These are vitally important considerations in some applications of computers, e.g. for computer games (when speed is essential) on microcomputers (where memory is limited).

ASSEMBLY LANGUAGE

In practice, rather than trying to program directly into binary, machine code programmers use *assembly language*, a code closely related to machine code but using parts of words instead of numerical codes for the different operations. Thus the code for 'subtract' is SUB rather than 0010; the code for 'load the accumulator' is LDA rather than 0101 and so on. These *mnemonic codes* are much easier for a programmer to use and remember.

The mnemonic codes equivalent to the simple machine code used on page 458 might be:

Numeric operation code	Mnemonic code	Operation carried out
01	ADD	Add to contents of accumulator
02	SUB	Subtract from contents of accumulator
03	MUL	Multiply contents of accumulator
04	DIV	Divide contents of accumulator
05	LDA	Load data from memory into accumulator
06	STO	Transfer data from accumulator into memory
07	IN	Input from keyboard to accumulator
08	OUT	Output from memory location to screen
00	END	End

Even more importantly, the memory locations can also be given symbolic names rather than numerical addresses. The variable 'points' in our BASIC program became 'location 201' in machine code; in assembly language we could use a simple abbreviation such as 'PTS'. Similarly, we might use 'PNLT' for penalties and 'SCOR' for 'score'.

The assembly language equivalent to our first machine code program is shown on page 461.

Note that each of the nine steps in the original machine code program has an exact equivalent in assembly language. Assembly language programs always correspond to their machine code equivalents on this one-to-one basis; the steps are the same but the operation and address codes have been described in short words rather than numerical codes.

Operation code	Data address	Comment
IN	—	Input 'points' data to accumulator
STO	PTS	Transfer 'points' data from accumulator to memory location PTS
IN	—	Input 'penalties' data to accumulator
STO	PNLT	Transfer 'penalties' data from accumulator to memory location PNLT
LDA	PNLT	Load contents of location PNLT into accumulator
SUB	PTS	Subtract contents of location PTS from content of accumulator
STO	SCOR	Transfer data (representing 'score' from accumulator into memory location SCOR)
OUT	SCOR	Output contents of location SCOR to screen
END		End

Note, too, how much more readable the assembly language program looks, even without the line by line commentary you might well be able to decipher each step.

When the assembly language program is complete, the computer will translate it, i.e. *assemble* it, into its machine code equivalent.

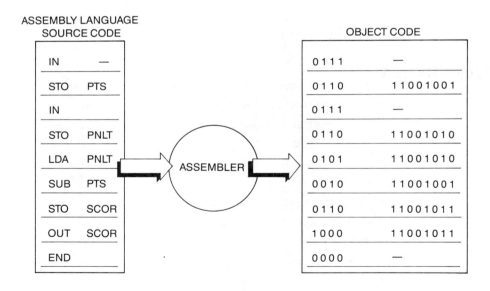

Fig. 24.17 The assembly language source program is translated line for line by the *assembler* (provided by the computer manufacturer) into the equivalent machine code object code

Q 24.12 *The two programs below are written in the same assembly language as the one on page 461.*

PROGRAM I			PROGRAM II		
1	IN		1	IN	
2	STO	PRICE	2	STO	PAY
3	IN		3	IN	
4	STO	QUANT	4	STO	ALLOW
5	LDA	PRICE	5	IN	
6	MULT	QUANT	6	STO	RATE
7	STO	VALUE	7	LDA	PAY
8	OUT	VALUE	8	SUB	ALLOW
9	END		9	MULT	RATE
			10	STO	TAX
			11	OUT	TAX
			12	END	

(a) *Work through program I given that the inputs are PRICE = £2 and QUANT = 20. Explain in your own words the purpose of each line and of the program as a whole.*

(b) *Work through program II given that the inputs are PAY = £200, ALLOW = £60 and RATE = 25%. Explain in your own words the purpose of each line, and of the program as a whole.*

JARGON 24

- Arithmetic and logic unit (ALU)
- Central processing unit (CPU)
- Peripheral Device
- Control unit
- Main memory

- Logic gate
- Logic circuit
- AND gate
- NOT gate
- Switching circuit

- Read-only memory (ROM)
- Random access memory (RAM)
- Volatile RAM
- Memory location
- Address
- Register
- Accumulator

- OR gate
- XOR gate
- Truth table
- Instruction register
- Program counter
- Sequence control register
- Fetch-execute cycle
- Interrupt

- High-level language
- Low-level language   Machine code
- Source Code   Assembly language
- Compiler   Mnemonic code
- Object code   Assembler

EXERCISES 24

1. The figure below represents schematically the layout of a typical computer system, and shows the flow of data and control signals between the various parts.

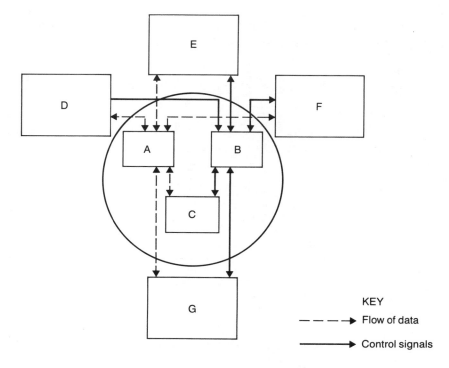

KEY

---- ▶ Flow of data

——————▶ Control signals

(a) Give a name for that part of the computer within the circle.

(b) Give names for the boxes marked A, B, and C, making clear which is which.

(c) State the functions of each of A, B, and C when a program is being run.

(d) Name an actual device which could be represented by each of the boxes marked D, E, F and G, making clear which is which.

(Ox)

2. Explain the function of the following components of the CPU:

   (a) control unit

   (b) central memory

   (c) arithmetic and logic unit

   (d) accumulator.

3. What is a memory location and how is it identified within the computer? Why cannot the owner keep plugging extra memory 'chips' into the circuit boards inside a computer in order to extend the memory space available?

4. What is a register? Give three examples of registers inside the CPU and explain the function of each one.

5. What is the fetch–execute cycle? What are interrupts?

6. Which column A, B, C or D of the truth table describes the output of the logic gate shown in the diagram?

X	Y	A	B	C	D
0	0	0	0	0	1
0	1	0	1	1	0
1	0	0	1	1	0
1	1	1	0	1	0

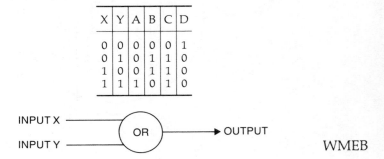

WMEB

7. From the following truth table write down the type of gate shown by

   (a) the output P.

   (b) the output Q.

INPUTS		OUTPUTS	
A	B	P	Q
0	0	0	0
1	0	0	1
0	1	0	1
1	1	1	1

(EMREB)

8. (a) Complete the truth tables for each of the logic gates.

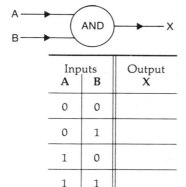

| Inputs | | Output |
A	B	X
0	0	
0	1	
1	0	
1	1	

| Inputs | | Output |
A	B	X
0	0	
0	1	
1	0	
1	1	

(b) Use your answers to part (a) to complete the truth table for the following logic network.

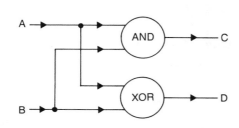

| Inputs | | Outputs | |
A	B	C	D
0	0		
0	1		
1	0		
1	1		

(c) What use could be made of this network in the logical processing unit of a CPU?

(WREB)

9. A computer uses a binary number to show which peripherals are on (1) or off (0). The number is made up in the following way:

Hard disk	Floppy disk	Tape unit	VDU	Printer

(a) (i) Copy and fill in the above boxes to show the binary number formed when all the peripherals except the tape unit are switched on.

(ii) What is the value of this number in base ten?

(b) What would it mean if the value of the number was:

(i) less than 16?   (ii) even?

(SEREB)

10. The logic network of a burglar alarm for a room has four inputs:

D = 1 if the room door is closed.
    0 if the room door is open.

W = 1 if the window is closed.
    0 if the window is open or broken.

M = 1 if there is any movement in the room.
    (otherwise **M** = 0)

S = 1 if the alarm system is switched on.
    (otherwise **S** = 0)

The output from the logic network is **A**.

A = 1 when the alarm bell should ring.
    (otherwise **A** = 0)

(a) State in words the conditions which should cause the alarm bell to ring if it is to give the best possible protection.

(b) Complete the truth table for this logic network.

(c) Draw a logic network suitable for the burglar alarm.

Inputs				Output
D	W	M	S	A
0	0	0	0	
0	0	0	1	
0	0	1	0	
0	0	1	1	
0	1	0	0	
0	1	0	1	
0	1	1	0	
0	1	1	1	
1	0	0	0	
1	0	0	1	
1	0	1	0	
1	0	1	1	
1	1	0	0	
1	1	0	1	
1	1	1	0	
1	1	1	1	

(NREB)

11. (a) Explain what you understand by a *machine code instruction.*

(b) A certain computer uses 16 bit words. One word in main store contains the following string of bits:

$$0\,0\,0\,0\,0\,0\,1\,1\,0\,0\,0\,1\,0\,1\,0\,1$$

Stating any assumptions that you make, describe how the contents of the above word might be interpreted as either

   (i) an integer, or

   (ii) a machine code instruction, or

   (iii) two characters.

(c) Describe the cycle of operations which is necessary for the execution of a sequence of machine code instructions.

12. Each of the 'programs' P, Q, R below adds two numbers together. The programs are written in different languages. One is in machine code, another is in an assembly (mnemonic) language, and one is in hexadecimal code. Programs *P* and *Q* are equivalent.

hexadecimal address	P	Q	R
0100	00111010	3A	LD A, (61H)
0101	01100001	61	
0102	00000000	00	
0103	01000111	47	LD B, A
0104	00111010	3A	LD A, (54H)
0105	?	54	
0106	00000000	00	
0107	10000000	80	ADD A, B
0108	00110010	32	LD (60H), A
0109	01100000	?	
?	00000000	00	

(*a*) State which program is in which language.

(*b*) Give the eight missing bits in *P*?

(*c*) Give the missing number in *Q*?

(*d*) Which is the fastest program to execute and why?

(*f*) Which part of the central processing unit carries out the instruction located at address 0107?

(*f*) What kind of software converts program *R* into program *P*?

(*g*) Give the missing hexadecimal address in full.

(*h*) Given that there are five steps in each program, which is the address of step 2? (NWREB)

13. (*a*) (i) What is an assembly language?
    (ii) What is an assembler?
    (iii) State two tasks of an assembler.

(*b*) In one assembly language the following instructions have the meanings given.

LOAD   42   means copy the contents of store 42 into the accumulator.

LOAD N 42   means place the number 42 into the accumulator.

ADD   42   means add the contents of store 42 into the accumulator.

ADD   N 42   means add the number 42 into the accumulator.

(i) If store location 20 contains the value 4, what value will be left in the accumulator after the following instructions have been obeyed?

> LOAD N 20
> ADD   20

(ii) If store location 30 contains the number 3 and has the symbolic address TOTAL what value will be left in the accumulator after the following instructions have been obeyed?

> LOAD   TOTAL
> ADD   TOTAL

(iii) What mistake do you think that the programmer has made in the following sequence of instructions?

> LOAD   42
> ADD N 42
> LOAD N 42

(iv) Why would the instruction LOAD N 42 take less time to obey than the instruction LOAD 42?

(WMEB)

25 The Future

THE PERILS OF PREDICTION

One prediction can be made with certainty: some of the following predictions will be false. Computer technology will be harnessed in totally unexpected ways, whereas some of the developments confidently expected may never materialise. Without a crystal ball, the best that we can hope to do is to make some informed guesses about the future. Do not be afraid to question the following; you may well make better guesses.

FUTURE POWER

Staggering increases in computing power will continue. We have *already* seen the processors in desktop machines leap from 8-bit to 16-bit and then to 32-bit capacity. The one megabit chip, and processing speeds of one billion (a thousand million, or 10^9) instructions per second are already history.

It is hard to imagine how fast that is. Suppose *you* tried processing a billion instructions—additions, say. If you were fast enough at mental arithmetic to carry out one per second, it would take you nearly *32 years!* Computers already in use can perform this task in less than one second; and each year will bring increased speeds.

Peripheral storage growth will be equally dramatic. With laser disks and other devices, storage capacities of several gigabytes will soon be the norm on *home* computers; commercial systems will store far more.

The Limits to Growth?

The space between adjacent transistors, on chips storing several megabits, is approaching the size of molecules. We seem to be nearing the ultimate physical limit to miniaturisation.

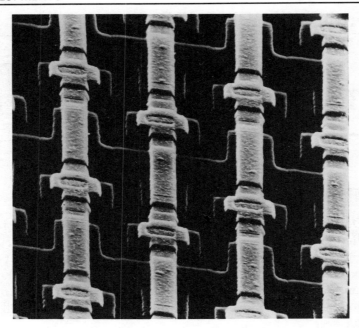

Fig. 25.1   One of the densest circuits yet produced magnified 23 000 times. On this scale, a human hair would be over four feet thick

Yet chips of even greater power will *still* be developed. Some researchers have already succeeded in using larger areas of silicon, others are adding more layers to chips. There are even teams working on *biochips*, which might one day replace silicon with organic materials.

Another limit to processing power is the *speed* at which electric current travels through the chip. Even using alternative materials to silicon, electrons travel at well below the speed of light (300 000 km/s—the fastest speed at which *anything* can move).

Researchers have demonstrated processing devices which use *light itself* to represent data. These optical equivalents of transistors are called *transphasors*. Massive sums of money will be poured into developing viable, light-based computers, an order of magnitude faster than any previous machine.

Parallel Processing

Even the fastest conventional computers can process only *one instruction at a time*. This further speed limit is now being overcome by *parallel processing*. The new computer designs will incorporate multiple processors, so that many instructions can be executed simultaneously.

Storage capacity and processing power will therefore continue to advance. How will they be used?

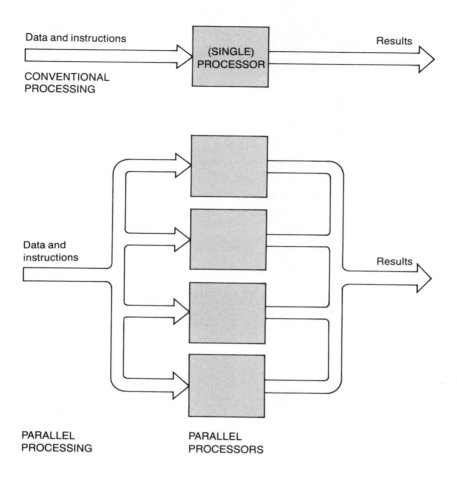

Data and instructions

(SINGLE) PROCESSOR

Results

CONVENTIONAL PROCESSING

Data and instructions

Results

PARALLEL PROCESSING

PARALLEL PROCESSORS

Fig. 25.2 The new computer designs allow a number of instructions to be executed simultaneously

Applying the Power

Barring nuclear war or other global catastrophe, the trends outlined in Chapter 22 will accelerate. Work with information will dominate employment, the length of the working day or week and the length of a person's working life will continue to decline, while leisure time will increase. Yet despite working less, people will produce more, and prosperity will keep on growing. If this seems over-optimistic, remember that we are merely extending the patterns already firmly established.

THE FUTURE OFFICE

Voice-activated word processing will invade most offices within the next decade, with dramatic consequences for secretarial work and already shrinking typing pools. Audio typing and shorthand will be obsolete skills by the end of the 20th century.

The Office Workstation

The advanced word processing ability will be one of the many functions built into the *office workstation*. It will also give access to local office networks and systems, as well as to geographically remote locations within the same organisation. On-line databases, holding financial, technical, legal, scientific, historical, news, weather or other information, will be available in seconds, even though their host computers may be on different continents.

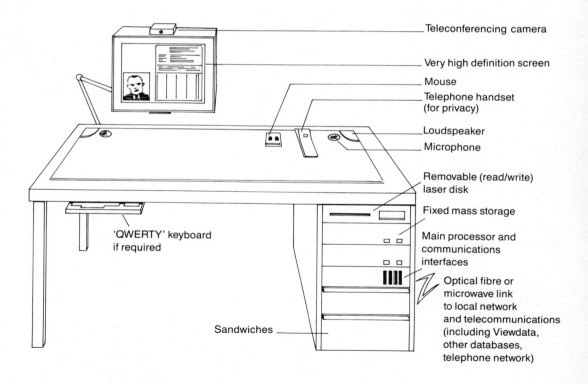

Fig. 25.3 A possible version of the future office workstation

Although keyboards will remain part of the hardware setup for some time, voice will control most of the workstation functions. *Voice messages* will be one of the major forms of *electronic mail* sent and received by the workstation, along with letters, other documents, figures, drawings and photographs (probably in colour).

The telephone will be an integral part of the workstation, although the dial will not survive. Most 'dialling' will be automatic, using *stored directories*; e.g. 'Get me Jenny Parker at Universal Records, please . . .'. The workstation will hear, interpret, look up the number and dial. Numbers not stored will be input vocally (probably updating the directory in the process). A handset will not be necessary, but may be retained for privacy.

The use of paper will dwindle. Some drawings and photographs may be kept in paper form, although the superb, *very high definition* (VHD) *screen* will reduce the need for hard copy. The law will insist on printed contracts for some time, but it will eventually succumb, accepting electronic versions as legally binding, provided that copies are transmitted to an archive where they cannot be altered.

Home or Office?

The increase in *homeworking* will blur the boundaries between the office and the home, which will feature a computer with many functions in common with its office cousin.

THE FUTURE HOME

'Home computing' will take on a very different meaning from our present understanding of the phrase. The home computer, many thousands of times more powerful than its fiddly, game-playing ancestors, will play a central role in the household.

The Home Controller

First of all the computer will control the home environment, maintaining heat and light at desired levels, with the minimum energy consumption. This may involve, for example, sensing that everyone has left a room and turning off the light, or turning the heating up when an automatic telecommunication from the owner's car indicates that it is within ten miles. Many devices will be monitored by the computer. It will call the fire brigade and sound the alarm if smoke is detected, or reduce the oven temperature when the chicken is 'done'.

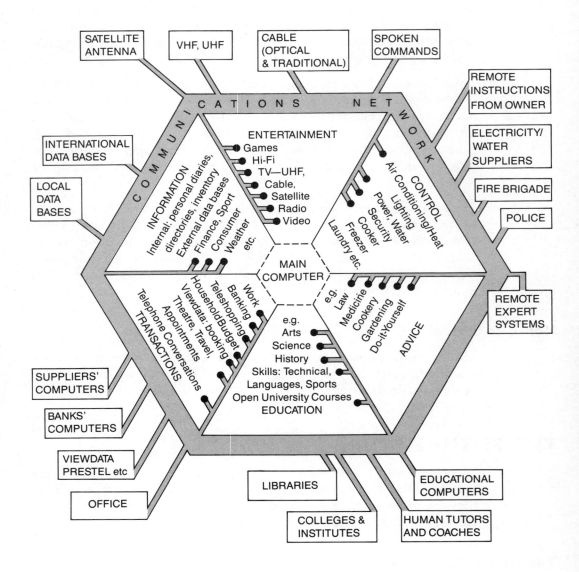

Fig. 25.4 The communications network will be vital to the future home computer system

The Home Entertainer

The home computer will still play games, but they will be incredibly sophisticated. Simulations will be unnervingly real, while the machine's prowess at games of skill will be staggering. A computerised opponent will be available for any game, from novice to world champion standard.

The very high definition flat wallscreens on which these games will be played will also receive television broadcasts, including satellite and cable channels. Video rental will not involve a visit to the local video store; video films will be chosen at home and 'downloaded' whenever required.

Hi-fi systems of amazing quality will also be controlled by the central computer. Analog recording and reproduction devices will be collectors' curios (your favourite record may be an antique!), while classical as well as popular music will be accompanied by video on laser disc.

The Home Manager

All the mundane detail necessary in 'running' a household will be effortlessly handled by our inanimate servant. Bank accounts will be monitored, expenditure will be planned and controlled, household bills will be paid, supplies will be ordered, mostly without wasting the time of the householders. Extensive viewdata facilities will be available for teleshopping, booking concert or theatre tickets, travel, holidays, appointments with hairdressers, doctors, dentists etc.

Like the office workstation, the home computer will maintain telephone directories, dial automatically (under voice command) and send and receive messages in any form, day and night.

The Home Adviser

The home computer system will also display extraordinary expertise in a wide range of areas. It will advise on financial affairs, first aid, legal matters, gardening, cookery, do-it-yourself, medicine; in fact on just about every topic which may be of interest. Such advice will not be superficial, but will comprise detailed, accurate information based on the specific problems which are encountered by its owner.

Furthermore, the system will be capable of effective delivery of an extraordinary range of educational material. The impact of this is hard to exaggerate; we shall return to it shortly.

THE FUTURE FACTORY

There are already automated warehouses, operating successfully, devoid of people. Depopulation of factories will follow, with robots of ever-increasing sophistication producing the goods which society requires. The robots' sensory powers will advance greatly; enhanced vision will be particularly crucial to their ability to produce and sustain the high quality which consumers will demand. The human factory worker will cease to be involved in manual labour, taking on a purely supervisory, troubleshooting role.

Robot Servants

Robots will not be confined to factories. Toy robot 'butlers' have already been sold as expensive but ludicrous drink dispensers. Real household robots will not look like their masters, nor like the machines they replace. The robot lawnmower may be a small device, taking all day to chomp its way quietly around the lawn, more like a rabbit than the noisy, sometimes smelly, machines that people are using in the 1980s.

ARTIFICIAL INTELLIGENCE

Many of the developments outlined above will be impossible unless systems acquire considerably greater *intelligence*. Even an adequate definition of intelligence would be beyond the scope of this book, but the subject is too vital to be ignored. *Artificial intelligence* (AI) is the key which will truly unlock and set free the power of computers in the next generation.

Can a Machine Think?

Some people insist that intelligence is a property of humans alone. Confronted with a chimpanzee devising a tool or even a rat finding its way out of a maze, they will shift their ground; intelligence is a property possessed solely by biological systems. Program a 'robot rat' to get out of the maze faster, using better strategies than its furry cousin and the doubters retort: 'But it is only doing what it has been programmed to do.' But *so is the real rat*. Some observers would argue that, we are programmed too. But *our* programs are wonderfully adaptable, enabling us to respond flexibly and imaginatively to situations and problems which we have never encountered before.

Computer programs can also show great flexibility and what appears to be (if you did not know it was a program) imagination. They are also just beginning to outperform people in complex intellectual tasks. The classic example is chess. Computers can *already* beat 99% of human chess players and their standard is approaching grandmaster level. We may not like describing it as such, but this would certainly appear to be intelligent behaviour.

The Turing Test

Alan Turing, a central figure in the history of computing, devised a test for the thinking machine, which works as follows. The machine to be tested is placed in one room, a human being in another. Each is connected to a computer terminal in a third room, operated by the human judge. The judge must decide, solely by conversations on the two terminals, which is connected to a human and which to a machine. If the judge cannot tell which is which, the machine has passed the test.

At present, machines are nowhere near passing the Turing test. The best chess programs sometimes play so 'brilliantly' that their human opponents cannot believe that they are up against a machine. But ask the same program what is the capital of France, or to add two and two, and it will be way out of its depth.

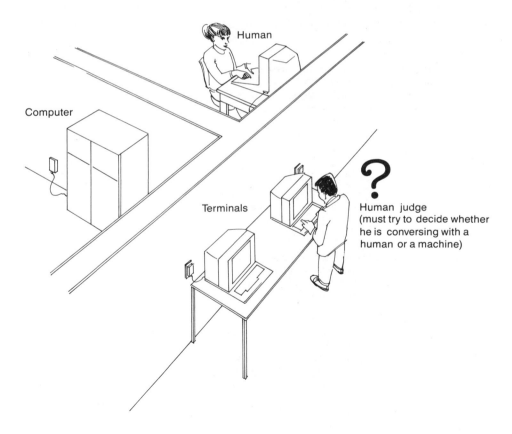

Fig. 25.5   The Turing test for thinking machines

Expert Systems

General-purpose thinking machines are some way off, but there are already programs clever enough to be very useful to humans, often out-performing them. One system successfully diagnoses diseases (within a specialised range) with consistently more accuracy than any individual human doctor. Such *expert systems*, thinking or not, are being developed and applied in dozens of fields. They are in use, for example, searching for oil and mineral deposits, managing foreign exchange dealings, servicing engines, running mainframe computer installations and advising on employment law.

The designers of such systems have managed to extract the knowledge from human experts and build it into the software as sets of rules, e.g. a rule built into a car maintenance system might be: IF the engine is turning over AND the distributor is delivering sparks correctly THEN check the fuel supply. The 'home adviser' systems already described will be similar in principle, but will be more skilled, flexible and subtle.

The *first generation* of computers were developed in the Second World War and depended on electronic valves, like the one shown here. These were unreliable and readily over-heated.

The *second generation* of computers were developed in the 1950s and used smaller and more reliable transistors instead of valves.

Then in the 1960s, ways were found to build many transistors into a single *integrated circuit* held on a microchip. Computers were moving into a *third generation*.

In the 1970s and 1980s a *fourth generation* of interactive, compact but powerful microcomputers (like the ones you use at home or at school) became commonplace.

Perhaps in the 1990s we shall have a *fifth generation* of voice activated intelligent computers.

Fig. 25.6 The computer generations

Natural Language

We have seen examples of computers *appearing* to communicate in natural languages such as English (Figure 9.7). Useful though it was, that system did not, of course, *speak* English in the sense that we human beings do. Even with a speech synthesiser, it could only have repeated preprogrammed phrases, like a parrot. Much research is directed at building machines with which we can genuinely converse.

The potential benefits of such a development are incalculable but the problems are huge. We do not yet even understand how *humans* acquire language. Trying to teach machines language is giving insights into how *we* ourselves learn the language we take for granted.

Despite the difficulties, more and more sophisticated 'natural language processors' will emerge in the next couple of decades. Eventually, we believe, machines with real linguistic ability will emerge.

FUTURE EDUCATION

As computer software continues to become more flexible, adaptable and easy to communicate with, it will acquire extraordinary power changing our lives in many ways. The most profound transformation will be in the way we learn.

Learning Machines

The first generation of *intelligent* teaching tools is already in use. Many of them are based on interactive videodisk. Building society staff are learning complex procedures, soldiers are learning how to operate sophisticated equipment and programmers are learning new computer languages, all with a speed, economy, consistency and success rate that no human teacher could dream of achieving.

The second generation will make learning even more compelling. They will be far more powerful, yet only pocket-sized. Their range of knowledge, their communication skill and their ability to 'understand' students' problems or confusions will make them indispensible. Their patient and subtle selection of ideal material to maximise the opportunity for successful learning, will enable them to rival all but the very best teachers.

But learning machines will certainly not be confined to the classroom. All organisations will use them. Above all, millions of people will use them at home to gain knowledge and skills throughout their lives.

THE ULTRA-INTELLIGENT MACHINE

If intelligent machines can be built then there would seem to be no reason why their intelligence level should not continue to advance. This raises the amazing prospect of machines rivalling and even exceeding the human intellect.

Many people believe that to predict such a machine is no more than science fiction and therefore can be utterly discounted. Yet it must be observed that computers' intellectual achievements so far (although in strictly limited areas) are impressive.

A Prediction

Let us go out on a limb and predict that by the year 2000 the world chess champion, if he or she agrees to play, will be defeated by a computer. If that would not be a supreme intellectual achievement, then it is hard to see what would be.

If that happens, and *if* the ability can be extended across the myriad facets of the human intellect, then we shall, perhaps within a hundred years, be sharing our planet with machines more intelligent than ourselves. To explore the implications of *that* would need another book.

Index